Youth
in
Politics

Youth in Politics

EXPECTATIONS and REALITIES

Sidney Hyman

Basic Books, Inc.

Publishers / New York / London

© 1972 by Twentieth Century Fund
Library of Congress Catalog Card Number: 72–84104
SBN 465–09374–4
Manufactured in the United States of America
DESIGNED BY THE INKWELL STUDIO

TO
Shayne, My Sister

Preface

DURING one of the Lincoln-Douglas debates, two Illinois farmers in the audience jointly observed that Stephen A. Douglas' legs were as unusually short as Abraham Lincoln's legs were unusually long. Afterward, in discussing the difference, they became embroiled in a hot argument about how long a man's legs should be in relation to the upper part of his body. Angry words passed between them, but they finally agreed to drive to nearby Springfield and put the question directly to Lincoln.

"That is a difficult question," said Lincoln solemnly when the two farmers called at his law office. "It has been a source of controversy for untold ages. It has led to bloodshed in the past and there is no reason to doubt that it will in the future. After much thought and consideration, not to say worry and mental effort, it is my opinion, all side issues being swept away, that a man's lower limbs, in order to preserve harmony of proportion, should be at least long enough to reach from his body to the ground."

The story, in its own way, bears on the proportions and the arrangement of the material I have used in constructing a view of present-day American youth in electoral politics. In this work of construction, I have been aware of two realities. First, people who have been direct parties to the events I've drawn on in developing my thesis seldom agree with each other on any aspects of those events—their constituent facts, force and form, cause and effect. Secondly, the same material I have used in my own treatment of the subject could in other hands not only receive a wholly different treatment and application, but could also lead to essentially different conclusions.

Things standing so, it would be vainglorious to imagine that readers of this book will uniformly assent to the views it contains. It is to be expected, rather, that competent judges of the material I have drawn on, will dissent at many points, whether in connection with issues of fact, perspective, proportion, emphasis, interpretation. It is my hope, however, that the same judges will be disposed, after reading the text through, to agree that the "legs" upholding this book are long enough to reach from the body of my analysis to the ground for a rational line of argument.

In any case, it remains for me here to acknowledge the debts I owe to the many individuals who aided me in the preparation of this study—and at the same time, to absolve them of any responsibility for my own sins of omission or commission.

First, funding approved by the trustees of the Twentieth Century Fund, under the chairmanship of James Rowe, covered most of the costs incurred in the preparation of the text. At the point where the costs outstripped the reach of the grant, I was helped by a timely loan from the Hyde Park Bank and Trust Company of Chicago—a nonphilanthropic institution whose growing prosperity is due in no small measure to the fact that its literate officers understand that people are the only economic reality.

Over and above the financial assistance I received from the Twentieth Century Fund, I benefited at every turn from the generous editorial help that was forthcoming from the directors and staff members of the Fund. Richard P. Rust, a staff member, provided me with a steady flow of documents and data I would otherwise have missed, besides being an unfailing source of good counsel on the structural form and exposition of my text. He was, to a pronounced degree, my de facto collaborator.

To M. J. Rossant, the director of the Fund, I owe a special thanks for the initiative he took in cleansing the final text of its blemishes, in spotting and filling gaps in the narrative, and in providing the extra margin of energy that made possible the publication of the text in a race against the absolute of time itself. Richard W. Richardson and John E. Booth, who are associate directors of the Fund, and Judith Jacobson, a staff member, have a claim on my gratitude for the help each gave me during an hour when it seemed that this study could be completed only if I had God's power to make a crab walk straight.

Lawrence Henderson who has worked in Washington with many senators and Senate committees, joined me in the spring of 1970 when the work plan for this study was initially designed. But our mutual hope for close collaboration in executing the plan, foundered on the many intervening demands on his attention. Thanks are due him, however, for his early role in helping to recruit field reporters who monitored the 1970 congressional contests that were chosen for study in connection with this book. The field reporters, listed by name and general area, were Mrs. Steven Roberts, Tom Dove, and Donald MacDonald for California; Stephen Schlesinger for New York, supplemented by Professors Leon S. Cohen and Roy Speckhard of State University of New York at Albany; Professor Richard Warner of the University of Vermont for Vermont; Kenneth Bode for Virginia; Professor Mike Downs of Indiana University for Indiana; Professor Arthur Naftalin of the University of Minnesota for Minnesota; and Tom Bevier for Tennessee.

Limitations of space prevented a full use of the raw material assembled by Professor Naftalin. He was, however, a source of valuable insights on the occasion in December 1970 when all the field reporters for this study were brought to New York by the Twentieth Century Fund for an appraisal and overview of the campaign as a whole. Other helpful participants at this meeting were Oliver Quayle of the polling organization which bears his name; John O'Sullivan, the director of Grassroots

Preface

Inc.; James Johnson, the midwest director of the 1972 Muskie for president drive; and Professors Henry Bienen of Princeton University; and William Murphy of Brown University who conducted a postelection survey of voter responses to student campaigners for this study. I am indebted to them for their work. I am also indebted to Professors Jack Dennis and Austin Ranney of the University of Wisconsin whose own survey, conducted for this study, focused on a comparison between the electoral performance in the 1970 congressional campaign of students who attended "Princeton Plan" institutions where a bloc of time was released for students to spend on campaigning (if they so desired), and of students at "non-Princeton Plan" institutions.

Finally, I am indebted to my students at the University of Chicago. A number of them who worked in different parts of the country for the election of candidates of their choice in 1970, later provided me with candid accounts of their personal experiences. They included Philip Hess of New York who campaigned in Vermont; Evelyn Hutt of Colorado who campaigned in Indiana; Robert Keonig who campaigned in his native Pennsylvania; Mike Mahern who campaigned in his native Indiana; Wendy Mink who campaigned in her native Hawaii; Peter Pitsch of Wisconsin who campaigned in Illinois; Frank Prochan who campaigned in his native Virginia; Don Quander of Montana who campaigned in South Dakota; James Scheurmann of Pennsylvania who campaigned in Illinois; and Barbara Yandorf of Washington, D. C., who campaigned in Indiana. These students differed widely in their political affiliations, yet the common sense they brought to their political experiences recalled to my mind Bacon's remark that "virtue is like a rich stone—best plain set."

S. H.

X

Contents

Contents

PART III

Conclusions

PART I

Setting the Scene

1
Focus

I

When the Spartans sacrificed to their deities on the eve of battle, the honor of the first offering went to the God of Poetry; the second to the God of War. The sequence may seem odd, but the thought behind it was not. The Spartans, a people who valued things according to their power had hit upon a great truth; namely, regardless of the outcome of a battle, the poets have the last word, for they can change a real victory into defeat, a real defeat into victory, and establish their interpretation of an event as a "self-evident truth" for later generations. Accepting this as a fact of power, the Spartans squared their religious rituals accordingly. The future would run in their favor, so they reasoned, only if they first won to their side the divine source of poetic inspiration.

On the eve of a national election in the United States, no offering, not even a frog's leg, is made to the God of Poetry. Nor is any made during two stages of actual battle—the first being the clash within the parties for their nominations; the second, the clash between the parties for the prizes of office. Ever since the age of Jackson, however, there has been a third stage to the American national election battle, and it is at this point that something like the Spartan ritual appears. The third stage starts the moment after the votes are counted, and takes the form of a clash among opinion makers over what the election "really meant." Each opinion maker, stimulated by his own vision, proclaims the meaning he has discovered in the sign of the national vote, and then strives to imprint that meaning on the psyche of a particular audience. Each in this way seeks to win the assent of that audience to the "causistic legitimacy" of the decisions he wants to see made in the realm of practical political action.

All this, in its own way, prefigured the text of this study. The study was first conceived while the 1970 congressional election was still in its springtime nominating stage. Yet the sight and sound of things in motion at the time pointed to a clear prospect on the far horizon. After the national vote had been cast in November and the usual clash over the meaning of the election was underway, an unusual question arose as central to the general dispute: to what extent had the actions of American youth and the attitudes of other people toward those actions affected the election results?

The saliency of the question could be foreseen, since the two political code words which sounded on all sides in the spring of 1970—"frontlash," and "backlash,"—jointly seemed to suggest that the congressional election was shaping up as a national referendum on the place and value of American youth in the national polity. Each of the terms, when decoded, covered a set of perceptions about the nature of youth-related events that had dominated much of the news in the last half of the 1960's. Each stood for a theory about how the 1970 congressional election would be decided—whether by the frontlash intervention of American youth in the electoral contests, or by the public's backlash hostility to that intervention. The respective theories, in turn, were vivified in the way various congressional candidates at the outset of their campaigns positioned themselves with respect to American youth.

Since the first law of politics is the law of surprise, it remained to be seen whether the springtime electoral picture

4

would appear the same by November, or whether it would be modified in the interval and become something other than what it first seemed to be. Still, in advance of what the passing weeks and months revealed about the realities the days hid, the mere appearance of the 1970 congressional election as a referendum on American youth had no precedent in the history of American electoral politics. It was a new phenomenon under the political sun and, as such, warranted the springtime start on a study of the role of youth in the 1970 congressional election.

The case for such a study, however, did not by any means stand only on the ground of an eye-catching "gee whiz" novelty. The larger ground involved two critical factors, of which more will be said in a moment. It is enough to say here—without stressing the implications—that the first of the two was the demographic projections, available in the spring of 1970, bearing on the size of the 18 to 26-year-old age group in the coming decade in proportion to the total electorate. The second factor, closely linked to the first, appeared only as a possibility in the spring of 1970. The possibility later materialized in the form of assorted legal changes which lowered the voting age from 21 to 18, set a 30-day limit on the residency requirements for voting in federal elections, liberalized absentee voting provisions, and abolished literacy tests which bore hard on ethnic groups such as Spanish-speaking Americans.

II

In the structure of the study, "youth" was defined as young men and women between the ages of 18 and 26. However, this definition was not meant to exclude from consideration young people whose age fell within a few years outside of either limit. The ages 18 to 26, corresponding to the years when a young American male was subject to the military draft, merely identified the gravitational center of the working definition.

Moreover, it was the conscious purpose of the study to transcend the culture-bound tendency to think of youth as being only college students and nothing more, or just "liberals and doves" and nothing more. It is banal but necessary to observe that youth is not just one thing cut to a uniform size like slabs of two by fours stockpiled in a lumber yard. It has many components apart from college students, and there are as many differences within each cadre as among them. Right now, for example, of the 11.5 million individuals under 21 who will be eligible to vote for the first time in 1972, 4 million are presently in college; 4.1 million are working full time in the labor force; 900 thousand are in high school; 800 thousand are in the armed forces; 1 million are housewives; and the remainder are found in odd-lot places ranging from the open road to prisons, from hospitals to the spots favored by beachcombers.[1]

Yet the intention to examine the role of youth as a whole, and not just college youth, encountered the constraints of data that could not be secured with the resources at hand. In the end, the study tended to focus mainly on three cadres of youth: those in high school; those in college; and those in business and the professions. The sketchiness of the references to youth in the labor force, and the total absence of reference to those in the armed services, seriously limit the study. The only honest thing to do is to admit the limitation, although I find a measure of spiritual comfort in the outlook of the preacher who said, "And now, brethren, let us boldly face our difficulties, and boldly pass them over."

The same applies to the scope of the election contests that were studied. Leaving out of account the cases where incumbents were re-elected without opposition, there were more than 460 specific congressional election contests in 1970. Each differed in some degree from the others, and each ran concurrently with neighboring contests for a great array of state and local offices affecting and affected by those for the Congress. Each congressional contest had its own local issues, its own tensions, its own activists, its own strategies, emergencies, expedients, limits, and opportunities. Each in some degree and to its own nature depended for its outcome on the interaction among many variables.

It was impossible to cover a major portion of all the contests, or even to trace all the nuances within a single one of them. Within the limits of the resources at hand, therefore, it seemed best to confine the study to a group of representative contests, chosen by general type and geographical location after consultation with candidates, party leaders, experienced political reporters, and full-time academic students of American electoral politics. It was hoped that the sample of election contests chosen for study, supplemented by across-the-board survey material, might yield a body of organized knowledge whose suggested truths regarding the role of youth in the 1970 congressional elections might apply to contests that were not at the focus of attention in the study.

III

Although the present study focuses expressly on the role of youth in the 1970 congressional election and also examines a set of auxiliary questions which came into view in that context, its aim goes beyond a self-limiting reconstruction of who did what, why, and with what result. The larger aim is to look at the 1970 congressional election for what it indicates about the "metabolic rate" of the body politic—the circulation of individuals, groups of people, interests, and opinions which feed and purge all parts of the political process, which tear down old power relationships, which maintain the kinetic equilibrium of things in being, and which build up new political forces, alliances, demands, and priorities.

The value of understanding this "metabolic rate," at least to some degree, is underlined by the two critical factors mentioned earlier: the demographic changes in store for the nation in the 1970's, and the recent legal changes affecting the status of young people as voters.

In the Eisenhower years of 1953–1960, because of a low birth rate during the Great Depression of the 1930's, the youth vote—or eligible voters who were 26 years old or under—was only 12 percent of the national total of eligible voters. This relatively low figure, may have contributed to the seeming political quiescence of American youth during the 1950's. All the while, however, a dramatic demographic quantum jump was in the making. The seven years after World War II marked the high peak of family formation followed by a baby boom. In due course, a human tidal wave of children born during the boom successively hit the kindergartens, the grammar schools, the high schools, and finally the colleges.

By the early 1960's—before American politics was Vietnamized—that same human wave had begun to encroach on the structure of American political life, until at last the demographic impulses generated by the post–World War II baby boom have intersected with the legal changes that lowered the voting age to 18. At present, young people are reaching voting age at the rate of almost 2.5 million a year. The 1970's will be the first time since the early 1900's when more than one-fifth of the eligible voters (between 22 and 23 percent) will be 26 years old or under. The figure is expected to hold on through the 1980's, dip slightly in the 1990's (due to the current sharp decline in the birth rate) and come back to nearly 23 percent by the year 2000.

Census projections also point up a number of potentially important political spin-offs from the cultural traits and trends of the 18 to 26 age group. In the 1970's, individual members of the group, for example, are four times as likely to have had some form of higher education as their parents' generation. Racially, they will be 50 percent more likely to be black than two decades ago, although blacks will comprise only 15 percent of the total age group. Viewed from the standpoint of geographical location, more than 85 percent of the group as a whole will live in urban areas. Further, because of the growing popularity of sun-belt areas as places of residence, the 26 and under group will have its greatest increase in proportionate potential strength in California, Oregon, Utah, Nevada, Arizona, New Mexico, Colorado, Louisiana, Florida, Maryland, and Nevada. Its smallest proportionate increase will be in states like Maine, Rhode Island, West Virginia, and Kentucky. Restated in regional terms, the 26-and-under age group will be proportionately more significant in the Southwest, the Florida Gulf Coast, the Pacific Coast, the Mid-Atlantic states and the Cleveland-Chicago-Milwaukee "Golden Triangle," in roughly that order of descending importance. It will be weakest as a bloc in northern New England, Appalachia and in the prairie states.

More immediately, an estimated 32 million people comprising the age group of 26 and under will be eligible to vote for the first time in the 1972 presidential election. The figure includes not only the 11.5 million potential new voters under 21 who have been recently enfranchised, but the 13.5 million first-time voters between 21 and 24 who were too young to vote in 1968, plus 7 million potential voters now between 24 and 26. Even if all these 32 million potential voters between the ages of 18 and 26 voted and voted exactly alike they would still be a minority in a national total of 144 million people who are potentially eligible to vote in 1972. Yet, without overtly trying to draw analogies—the fall of man began with a false analogy— one comment is worth at least a stage whisper. In the early

1900's, the last time the 26-and-under age group comprised between 22 and 23 percent of the national vote—as it will again
in the 1970's—the Progressive movement was at the flood stage
of its reformist work.

In advance of election day 1972, current speculation about
how many of the newly enfranchised voters will actually vote,
and how they will vote, finds opinion divided between two main
camps.

Adherents to what can be called the "minimalist" camp
argue that the newly enfranchised voters will not turn out in
overwhelming numbers, and in any case, will have a relatively
slight impact on the election result. Part of the evidence cited
in support of this view comes from Great Britain's last general
election, in which 18 to 20-year-old voters voted for the first
time. In that case, the turnout was not as great as had been anticipated, and since those who did vote were divided along
traditional—i.e., parental—lines, their participation did not
materially affect the election results. Further evidence is drawn
from American experience. It was observed that in the few
states where 18 to 21 year olds previously were eligible to vote,
only a third actually did—in contrast to a 72 percent voting
participation by the 30 to 64 age group. It was also observed
that in major American national elections held over the past 10
years, an average of 51 percent of the potentially eligible age
group below 26 actually voted, in contrast to 70 percent voter
participation in the eligible group over 26.[2]

Adherents to the "maximalist" camp, in their rejoinder,
tartly observe that politics in England and in the United States
are noncommutative. To assume that what is true of youth in
one place is equally true of youth in the other is to invent un-
realistic symmetries. Although young American voters at one
time tended to vote along parental lines, from a variety of
causes relevant to the present hour, a substantial number of
young people have cut the umbilical cord binding them to the

10

political outlook of their parents. Furthermore, past evidence showing that a relatively low proportion of the 26-and-under age group actually voted was obtained under legal conditions that no longer prevail. The high physical mobility of this age group once made them more vulnerable than any other population segment to the nullifying legal effects of either lengthy residence requirements before they could even register to vote (two years in some places), or the complex legal barriers they had to surmount in order to vote by absentee ballot. The 26-and-under age group is still the most mobile human part of the nation—42 percent of its members currently change their place of residence annually, as against only 15 percent for the age group over 26. Yet the change in the residence requirements to 30 days, the liberalization of absentee voting provisions, and the abolition of literacy tests will enable many more of them to vote than ever before. Consider a national survey taken in December 1971 by the Youth Citizenship Fund. It found that approximately 35 percent of eligible 18- to 20-year olds had, at that point, registered to vote. Based on these figures, the sponsors of the survey anticipated at least a 60 percent turnout of young voters in 1972.[3]

The foregoing will be true, so the "maximalists" assert in conclusion, regardless of how the courts decide pending cases involving the definition of the term "residence" as it applies to the college component of new young voters, or how local election boards interpret and enforce residence requirements. Whether the ruling permits students to vote on campus, or requires them to apply for an absentee ballot or go home in order to vote, college students are not always "out of town" students. Hundreds of thousands of college students live under parental roofs while they attend local private or public colleges. These could not readily be denied the right to a local voter registration—not even by registrars like those, for example, in Champaign-Urbana, Illinois, who, in determining residency in-

11

tent, have asked prospective young voters if they meant to be buried in the localities where they attend school.

This study, drawing on what the 1970 congressional election reveals about the "metabolic rate" of youth in electoral politics, will deal with the "minimalist" and "maximalist" lines of argument. This is not to say that the 1970 congressional election provides the basis for a flat prediction about the actual number of newly enfranchised voters who will vote, and how they will vote in 1972. If some people ended on a mourner's bench because in anticipating the 1970 congressional election they confused it with the 1968 presidential election, the same bench awaits anyone who assumes that the 1972 presidential election will conform in every respect to the 1970 congressional election. What these pages will suggest—hopefully in a coherent way—are the variable terms of youth electoral behavior that could affect the course of the 1972 presidential election, and beyond that, those which could conceivably affect the course of electoral politics in the first half of the 1970's.

Youth electoral behavior means more than just voting behavior. It means the leadership of youth by youth in electoral contexts. It means work performed inside campaign structures in direct support of policies and candidates. These matters, which are important in an inquiry as to how youth influences elections will be examined in this study of youth's role in the context of the 1970 congressional elections. The same context also provides an excellent object lesson analogous to a feature in the study of medicine. In medicine, the conditions which promote health are surmised by an examination of unhealthy bodies. So too, the conditions which stimulate a vigorous electoral participation by youth, appear in a study of the elements that created their 1970 apathy.

This being said, something may be gained in long distance understanding by focusing, in the next chapter, on a close-in view of the electioneering theories which dominated the political air in the spring of 1970, and studying, in the following chapters, the roots of the illusions which became entwined in the texture of the theories.

NOTES

1. U. S. Department of Commerce, Bureau of the Census, *Statistical Abstract of the United States,* 1970.
2. *Statistical Abstract of the United States,* 1960–1970.
3. *Youth Citizenship Fund Newsletter* (January 1972).

2
The Illusion of
Central Position

I

When a cyclone is bearing down on Kansas, a global meteorologist in the Weather Bureau in Washington can puff on his pipe and note that at that very moment, elsewhere calm air blankets vast regions of the world. In Kansas itself, a farmer huddled with his family in a storm cellar is not likely to be that scientifically objective about the twist of the fierce wind over his head. The cyclone on top of him *is* his world.

So too, in the case of the storms whirled by different groups of American youth in the last half of the 1960's. Few people caught in the eye of any one storm—whether they were white radical students or black militants, parents or teachers, school administrators or reporters, businessmen in the ghettos or political officials, policemen or National Guardsmen—were inclined to see their personal experiences objectively. Each of these, in his illusion of central position, naturally assumed that the United States, from coast to coast, was just one vast tornado with no stretches of calm in between. This was true regardless of how they viewed other aspects of the matter; whether they traced the origin of the tornado to permissiveness or to repression, whether they denounced or welcomed its effects, whether

14

they wished to hurl it back by coercive force, to accelerate it by confrontations and violent politics, or to have its tensions discharged by an appeal to the polls.

The illusions of central position were verbalized in the spring of 1970 in the theories of political action embedded in the code words of "frontlash," and "backlash." Each of the theories corresponding to these words was based on assumptions that were seldom closely examined, and, perhaps because many adherents to the respective theories seemed to suffer the deformations of perception that mark the disease of self-centered advocacy, each implicitly raised questions that were seldom asked. The disease in their case, to be sure, was not as extreme as in the case of Heinrich Himmler, the Nazi exschoolmaster who planned on founding an academy of astrophysics to prove his preset conclusion: that stars were made of ice. Yet even in a milder form, many true believers in the "frontlash," and "backlash" theories respectively were led by their self-centered advocacy to seek in the political picture around them only what they wanted to find, to find only what they were looking for, and thus not to see or inquire into the shape of the critical questions which stared them in the face.

Taken in order, the assumptions that needed examining and the questions that needed asking in connection with each of the theories follow.

Frontlash

In the spring of 1970, the invasion of Cambodia by American forces, followed by the killing of students at Kent State and Jackson State, led to a seeming nationwide "strike" of American college students, and then to a seeming genetic urge on their part to work exclusively for "peace" candidates in the 1970 congressional elections.

In this connection, it was vaguely but earnestly predicted that "countless" American colleges and universities would adopt what came to be known at the time as the Princeton Plan, and would close for two weeks before the November election so that students could electioneer full time for their favored congressional candidates. The word "countless" is of course open-ended, and no one could say exactly how many colleges would actually adhere to the Princeton Plan. Nor was anyone certain how many students would actually take part in electioneering work. Estimates ranged from a low of 100,000 to a high of two million. Either figure, however, could mean that a young army of doorbell-ringing "frontlash soldiers for peace," would troop into the precincts with voter lists, fresh faces, cogent arguments and starkly compelling opening lines like, "Hello, I'd like to talk to you for a few minutes before I die in Vietnam."

In advance of the actual mobilization of the young army, the more vocal adherents of the frontlash vision tended to assume that youth meant only college students; that college students were of one mind; and that all college students had gone out on strike in reaction to Cambodia and Kent State. They also appeared to assume that all college students—and all college graduates as well—were then, and had always been, against the Vietnam War; that nothing in the Vietnamese picture itself had changed between 1968 and 1970; that nothing about it was likely to change between the spring of 1970 and election day; and that the seemingly intense springtime commitment among students to work for peace candidates in the congressional elections would remain in full force on election day.

The vision of a young army mounting an electioneering frontlash on behalf of "peace candidates" drew part of its buoyancy from publicized episodes in the last half of the 1960's in which American youth had organized itself on an impressive scale for varied purposes. Students, for example, in some places had staged large scale protests against university authorities. Young people had come together for oceanic "happenings" like Woodstock and its variants. Resistance to the Vietnam War, starting with the first teach-ins in March 1965, and extending to Moratorium-Mobilization days in the fall of 1969, had been marked by massive demonstrations young people organized in Washington, D.C., San Francisco, New York, and other cities across the nation. All such episodes were cited as evidence that young people could—and would—mobilize themselves in massive numbers in support of peace candidates in the 1970 congressional election.

The most favored analogy drawn from the last half of the 1960's, and perhaps the one central to the whole frontlash theory, was the role of young people in the 1968 bids of Senators Eugene McCarthy and Robert F. Kennedy for the Democratic presidential nomination; yet the true nature of that role —its scope, form, aim, duration and effect—was obscured by incrustations of golden legend. Still, even if the truth of the matter conformed to the legends, it was worth asking whether the 1968 contest for the presidency was in all respects analogous to the 1970 congressional contests for mere House and Senate seats, and whether young workers who could be mobilized on a national basis for a presidential contest without regard to their place of residence, could be similarly mobilized for congressional contests. It was also worth asking if young people who could be self-starting volunteers in a presidential contest—where the main national and international issue in their own eyes was the Vietnam War—could be equally stirred to volunteer for congressional contests where national and international issues are often superseded by the issues of "personality," by local bread and butter matters, or by questions of who had done or could do the most for the specific interests of a local community.

The usefulness of other highly trumpeted episodes of the 1960's, as indications of what frontlash-minded youth would do in the 1970 congressional election, depended on the convertibility between *event* politics and *process* politics, and between *po-*

litical participation generally, and *electoral* participation specifically.

The greater part of student activism in the last half of the 1960's was in the form of *event* politics where students used particular events to personify their political message and to introduce their ideas quickly and forcefully into public discourse. Event politics, as Jerome Edmund Lord has cogently observed, was ideally suited to students.[1] By choosing a dramatic event students could control the time and place, and the issue and the demands to ensure public attention to their rhetoric. They could even frequently devise an event in which institutional, and other responses, would be perfectly predictable. No national leadership, or organization, or ideology, or political program could impose its constraints on the protest or demonstration. Event politics was discontinuous, self-contained, visible, a one-shot explosion, and instantly gratifying.

Process politics, on the other hand, as in the case of a drive to secure the enactment of a law, or the election of a candidate, or the administration of a program, involves "gratifications deferred." It is slow, often tedious, expensive, bureaucratic, and usually invisible. It demands sustained attention to detail, and the very hard work it requires will be borne only by people who act either under the incentives of a profound commitment, or of good pay. There are many responsibilities and many diversions—books, brew, sex, and frisbees—facing students who think in terms of process politics.

It is true that a traumatic experience in event politics can lead a person into process politics, but so can it lead a person to migrate out of politics altogether and to live isolated within himself. In any case, it did not automatically follow, as many frontlash theorists seemed to assume, that student involvements in the event politics of the last half of the 1960's and the spring of 1970 would be automatically convertible into a roughly equal degree of involvement in the process politics required in the 1970 congressional campaign. Nor did it follow, as some frontlash theorists also seemed to assume, that political participation by youth was automatically convertible into electoral participation.

Political participation, divorced from electoral participation, can take many forms. It can take the form of a demonstration or protest, writing a letter to a newspaper or congressman, circulating or signing a petition urging the adoption of a stated policy, testifying at a governmental hearing about an issue of public policy, or membership in a civic organization which works to promote certain aspects of community life. All these can have important spin-off effects on electoral politics, but the word "electoral" denotes a distinct mode of political participation. Electoral participation can be the simple act of voting. In its more complex form it is performed directly on behalf of a candidate to promote his prospects for victory. This work can involve leafleting, canvassing, manning telephone banks and sound trucks, stuffing envelopes, fundraising, and doing research. It can include scheduling the appearances of a candidate, or drafting press releases or the texts for possible speeches. It also can include identifying eligible voters and getting them registered to vote, baby-sitting on election day so that voters who might otherwise be forced to stay at home can go to the polls, driving voters to the polls, poll watching on behalf of a candidate, and so on.

Masses of Americans are uninterested in even the voting aspect of electoral participation. In the 1968 presidential election, for example, an estimated 47 million of 120 million eligible voters failed to vote; the proportion of nonvoters is even higher in the average congressional election. In view of the drudgery that is often involved in the more complex forms of electoral participation, it by no means followed that a young person who had been the first to volunteer for a highly visible or dramatic form of political participation, like a demonstra-

19

tion, would spring forward with equal zest to volunteer for the necessary yet often uninspiring and bone-fatiguing chores of electoral participation.

Meanwhile, some frontlash theorists appeared to assume that the phrase "the New Politics," which had come into vogue among some young people during the closing years of the 1960's, stood for something organically new in the world of American politics—like a new Adam on the first day of a second creation. The Old Politics was said to embody all the things that led to a fall during the first creation. It was marked by an indifference to issues, a preoccupation with careerist ambitions, and a lust for pork barrels or naked political power. But the New Politics, looking to the future instead of the past, contained undefiled energies and a self-reliant, issue-oriented idealism. It was considered inevitable that it would find forceful expression in the 1970 congressional elections and would sweep all things before it.

In point of fact, however, how new was the New Politics? Was it just a rhetorical flourish, or was it grounded in objective reality? It was easy enough to maintain that the New Politics meant that "the issues" gave young people their main propulsion into electoral politics, but to maintain this view did not allay all doubts. It was still fair to ask if an issue-oriented New Politics could really be divorced from all the mechanistic electioneering aspects of the Old Politics. It was also fair to ask if the notion that it could, was as mindless as the hope that one could build a mountain range without valleys.

One more matter comprised the heart within the heart of everything worth asking about all the things that came under the cover of the code word frontlash remains. Since only an estimated three percent of the American people in recent decades took part in electoral politics beyond the act of voting, what would be the impact on the 1970 campaign if in fact young volunteers did turn out in huge numbers for electoral work? [2]

20

The Illusion of Central Position

There is, in reality, a limit on the number of volunteers of any age who can be effectively used in the electoral aspects of a House or Senate contest. What would happen to the young people who came forward as volunteers, only to be turned away because no effective use could be made of them? Would they become soured on the electoral process? On the other hand, suppose that the number of youthful volunteers who actually came forward for electoral work fell far short of the springtime predictions, but still remained considerably higher than the past average of 3 percent. What then? Wouldn't the shortfall between what was expected and what materialized tend to detract from the value placed on the work actually done by the young people who volunteered for electioneering projects? Alerts should have sounded to warn would-be critics against rendering a final verdict on the basis of a false standard for judgment. If such alerts were indeed sounded by a few frontlash theorists, cellos instead of trombones and drums were used.

Backlash

The lead-off assumption of the backlash theory went to the effect that the public, enraged by the actions of students and other young people during the last half of the 1960's and the spring of 1970, was coiled to strike down congressional candidates who were conspicuously supported by the forces of youth. To bolster this assumption, opinion polls were cited showing that 83 percent of the American public was hostile to student demonstrations and that a very high percentage also placed the blame for deaths at Kent State on the students themselves.[3] It was noted that in the first party primaries held right after the Cambodian invasion and the student strike, student-backed candidates—like Peter Eikenberry who opposed Representative John J. Rooney, the Brooklyn Democrat, and Lew Kaden who opposed Representative Edward Patten, a New Jersey Democrat —were defeated.

Then there was the evidence drawn from a popular (and distorted) version of the thesis set forth in *The Real Majority* by Richard M. Scammon and Ben J. Wattenberg.[4] In their profile of American voters, the typical voter was neither young, nor a student, nor black, nor poor. She was a middle-aged white Dayton housewife whose husband was a mechanic, whose cousin was a policeman, and who was more concerned about "the social issue" than about anything else. Since "the social issue" alluded to a cluster of things with which youth had been negatively identified—campus violence, drug addiction, riots in the ghettos, crime in the streets, and attacks on the structure of American institutions—it was assumed that any candidate linked in the public mind with youth would immediately suffer from the reflex hostility of the Dayton housewife, her husband, and her cousin.

All this in turn seemed to be massively confirmed by graphic signs of a backlash visible to the naked eye. In New York, for example, a group of construction workers clubbed a group of protesting students in a matter involving the American flag, while the New York City police looked on. The clubbing in turn was followed by a piece of White House theater where President Nixon semaphored his liking for the construction workers, and thus helped convert their "hard hats" into a synonym for the word "patriot." The nation was swept by a pantomime resembling the totems and taboos used in tribal purification rites. To assert their own cleanliness as loyal Americans in opposition to the desecrations of people like students who protested against the Vietnam War, many Americans pasted decals of American flags onto windshields, pinned American flags to their lapels, sewed American flag shoulder patches to their sleeves and covered their automobile bumpers with stickers reading:

AMERICA,
LOVE IT OR LEAVE IT.

The Illusion of Central Position

At the same time, it was clear that political operatives working for the Nixon administration would adhere to an order of battle for the 1970 congressional election calling for an exacerbating attack on American youth, garnished over by law and order polemics, and topped by a regional drill in the form of the Southern Strategy. To this end, the administration's operatives, along with like-minded Republican candidates for congressional seats, would do little to comfort the afflicted in the nation, much less do anything to afflict the comfortable. The main object of their 1970 electoral battle would be, in James Reston's phrase, "to comfort the comfortable" by appearing to be their best shield and striking arm against all the things comfortable people feared and detested most. Hence, protesting students and dissident young people of any description would be lumped together and rendered indistinguishable from violent campus revolutionaries, urban guerillas, hoodlums, drug addicts, rapists, arsonists, muggers, gun-flourishing black militants, and the bosses of organized crime.

To the backlash theorists, the Nixon administration's order of battle somehow proved that their backlash theories were correct. They reasoned that President Nixon would not be president if he lacked the ability to read the signs of the times, and to skillfully turn them to his own account. He was president because of his political gifts, hence, if the president assumed the presence of a massive backlash in the making, and premised his administration's 1970 order of battle on it, then the basis for their hope in the backlash potentiality was affirmed. It seldom occurred to those who thought this way that the American Constitution provides for every accidental contingency in the executive except for episodic vacancies or confusion in the mind of a president.

In challenge to the backlash theory, for example, it was worth asking whether the defeat of student-backed candidates for party nominations for House and Senate seats in several contests held immediately after the springtime student strikes proved conclusively that a backlash existed. In the case of Representative Rooney, a long entrenched Democrat, the margin of his victory over a student-backed rival was less than his margin over other rivals for the party nomination on earlier occasions in his career. Anyway, could one enlarge the dry facts of his victory into a generalization that candidates who were multi-term incumbents, or who had the backing of a regular party organization, must invariably triumph over insurgent candidates backed by students or by other young people? It would be difficult to reconcile any assumptions to this effect with later primary results pointing to an opposite effect. In Connecticut, for example, Joseph Duffy, backed by the young, won the Democratic nomination for the Senate over the opposition of the regular Democratic state organization. In New York, Bella Abzug, backed by students, won the Democratic nomination to a House seat in a contest where her opponent, a veteran congressman with a liberal voting record, was backed by the regular organization. In California, Ronald Dellums, a black man and a radical, backed by militant young blacks and by white students from Berkeley, won the Democratic nomination to a House seat in a contest where his rival, a white man, was not only a multiterm incumbent with the support of labor and the regular party organization, but a congressman whose voting record in the House was long viewed as a model of liberalism.

In these cases, was the backing of students and of other young people the decisive factor in the victories won? Or was it but a single factor in a fishline tangle of things that produced the ultimate result, just as another fishline tangle of things led to the earlier defeats of student-backed candidates seeking party nominations?

Whatever could be said directly about these contests it was conceivable that a significant part of the public which reacted with hostility to student demonstrations would draw a distinction between those who demonstrated and those who participated in electoral politics—assuming they even knew that the campaign workers who contacted them were students. In some local contexts, for example, the voting public might react favorably to a student-supported candidate precisely because he appeared to be the vehicle that carried young people into electoral politics and away from demonstrations. Parents, haunted by the fear that their children—out of boredom—would succumb to the temptations of the drug culture might be grateful to any candidate—even of a party opposed to the one they ordinarily favored—who made a place for young people in his campaign structure, and thus kept them safely busy.

Meanwhile, though it was fair to assume that a candidate could lose his bid for office if he publicly took a vocal stand on the wrong side of "the social issue," it was hard to imagine that many candidates would be so addled as to speak in favor of violence, drug addiction, and crime in the streets. Candidates were more likely to pin a gleaming sheriff's badge on their chests before they opened their mouths even to say hello. It was also worth asking whether a candidate could win simply by being on the right side of "the social issue," unsustained by anything else, after the manner of a Hollywood stage set: all front and no back. Further, what if the social issue encountered a strong rival in the economic issue of rising unemployment and unchecked inflation? Which of the two would prevail?

Behind that question was the ancient enigma of voter motivation which challenged the simplistic aspects of the frontlash and backlash theories and, as will be seen in a moment, a third theory as well. The voter is not a man chained in perpetuity to running an elevator in a two-story building. He has diverse interests and responds in various ways to different impulses that impinge on his senses. He can reshuffle the combination and the order of priorities he assigns to his interests. He can make now one, and now another, an expendable or standpat factor in his politics of net gain. But what is decisive with him at any one moment? His religious, or ethnic, or economic interest? His worries about the issues of war and peace? His hates, his nostalgia, his apathy, his confusion? Statistics may tell us *how* he will vote, but the reasons *why* he votes as he does are not readily determined. In a metaphor used by James Bryce in a different connection, when the *why* of the matter is at issue, statistics are like "a candle which floods with light the small side chapel of a cathedral, only to sink to a spark when brought into the soaring vault of the nave." [5]

Questions of a different order were worth asking specifically about the backlash assumptions underlying the commitment of the Nixon administration to a "law and order" plan of battle in the 1970 congressional election. It could be said that the object of a law and order campaign was to stabilize an imperiled social frame. But what would happen to the stability of a society whose young people were cast in the role of enemy aliens in their own homeland, and said to be the cause for everything that was out of joint? What would be the reaction of the young people who had tried to "work within the system" in order to bring about social change, yet on that very account were reviled as though they were ambassadors of evil? Would the young people be lost for good to the ways of democratic electoral politics? Would they be driven in the direction of violent politics, or conversely, into an alienated, brooding, and no less dangerous subcultural isolation?

A final point. One could agree with the Scammon and Wattenberg thesis that from an historical standpoint, American politics is centrist in nature. Or, using a football metaphor, one could agree that the main game for American politics is played between the two forty yard lines on the gridiron. But American political history also shows that the field is not set in reinforced concrete. It is laid out on movable ground so that with each shift in the field as a whole the location of its center also tends to shift.

The Illusion of Central Position

American political history has something else to add in this connection. For one thing, under a two party system, significant third party movements—like the Free Soil party on the eve of the Civil War, the Populists at the end of the nineteenth century, the Progressive and Socialists before World War I and the La Follette Progressives of the mid-1920's—were often the source of the impact that forced the two major parties either to shift the gravitational center for their arena of politics, or at least to shift the ball from the 40 yard line on the right side of the field to the one on the left side. Further, from the eve of the American Revolution onward, a distinctive human line has tended to divide the agitators who prepare the grounds for a coming shift and the executives who manage the handling of actual events during the shift. It is the line personalized by the difference between Sam Adams and John Adams, between Patrick Henry and George Washington.

If so, it was worth considering whether the predictions about a backlash took into account the possibility that the election ahead could show not the revolutionary radicalism of American youth, but rather its traditionalism. It might turn out, for example, that in place of the impression given during the 1960's that the main body of American youth was bent on overthrowing all things together, youth accepted the centrist rules for the political game. It might turn out that in the absence of any third party such as those known in the past, a segment of the main body of American youth during the last half of the 1960's had been a kind of *ad hoc* third party or at least a third force in politics; that its paramount object had been to advance the ball to the leftward 40 yard line; that though its demonstrations had been decried, its views and values had been accepted unawares by increasing numbers of mature adults; that the gap between generations was closing instead of growing wider. It might also turn out that in the context of the 1970 election, the agitators among the most advanced segment of politically active youth

27

would put themselves, or be put, on the sidelines reserved for spectators, while the executives would be the human strain that would carry on the function of youth participation in electoral politics. Whether or not any of these possibilities would actually materialize remained to be seen, but even if only some were actualized, their effect would be to impose some sort of check on a predicted backlash.

Sidelash

A sidelash theory of political action which became operative in 1970 developed later in the year as answers to the questions posed by frontlash and backlash theorists became more difficult to find because of contradictory primary results and confusing public opinion soundings. Student-backed candidates won in twenty-four out of thirty primary contests,[6] yet Gallup and Harris surveys revealed a continuing public hostility to student demonstrators over the summer months. Apparently, those candidates who sidestepped student support were more willing to ignore the primary results than the surveys which carry the stamp of immutable scientific truths.

In some ways, the sidelash theory and its underlying assumptions were more interesting than those associated with the two preceding theories. Perhaps it is more precise to say that what made it more interesting was the people who subscribed to it, since they included a number of political figures who had long been associated with the liberal wing of the Democratic party.

Some of these people, largely because of their opposition to the Vietnam War, had previously been the heroes of left-of-center students. After the 1968 presidential election, however, the conclusions they reached about the meaning of that contest were reflected in their ambivalent attitude about students and other young people. They could not and would not change themselves from avowed friends of the young to overt enemies. The one course of action open to them as they assessed the meaning of the 1968 presidential election and the confusing primary and opinion poll results was a sideways movement designed, or so it seemed, to avoid the dangerous consequences they saw in being aligned with the young on the wrong side of the social issue. In this special sense, they accepted the reality of an impending strong backlash against any candidate who was conspicuously associated in his campaign with those issues championed by young people.

The line of reasoning underlying the sidelash movement went something like this. The Democratic party lost the 1968 presidential election because millions of white blue-collar workers —and those in ethnic groups—who ordinarily voted for Democratic presidential nominees, had gone over to the third party candidacy of Wallace because of the racial, the social, or the law and order issue. Hence the key to victory in 1970 turned on the extent to which Democratic defectors to Wallace could be won back. But how could they be won back without traveling the route of appeals to racism? The answer lay in the hypothesis that if Wallace himself were purged of his racism, he would appear as a populist on economic issues. The pursuit of success for liberal Democrats, then involved a positive and negative line of action.

The positive side included a straightforward populist appeal to blue-collar workers and to ethnics. The programmatic content of the appeal in the year 1970 was not entirely clear, but it seemed to imply an updated version of the New Deal and the Fair Deal. On the negative side, care was taken not to stir up the racial issue, the social issue, or the law and order issue. That meant that students and other young people could not appear in the front rank of campaign workers. It also meant that no heavy stress could be placed on a stand against the Vietnam War, or on any other theme distinctively identified with youth, because these themes would arouse the reflex hostility of the white blue-collar workers and the ethnics in the Wallace vote, and thus distract them from paying close attention to the populist economic pitch.

The foregoing argument here had the flavor of a maxim. But what about its underlying assumptions? Questions about the reality of Wallace's populism could be waved aside as being of secondary importance. One could wave aside the overt or covert assertions that the ethnics were racists, and, along with the white blue-collar workers, strongly favored the American war effort in Vietnam. The ethnics as a whole were far less addicted to racism than were the white Anglo-Saxon Protestants. And, in fact, the most steadfast supporters of the Vietnam War were not the white blue-collar workers with a grammar or high school education, but people who had graduated from college. (More about this later on.) Still, all this could be waved aside, along with the question whether a populist strategy designed to win back the Wallace vote for liberal Democrats actually differed from or was only a dressed-up version of the Nixon administration's naked Southern Strategy. Questions that could not be waved aside were whether an economic appeal alone could win back the Wallace vote, and whether a concealed price might be paid if students and other young people were given up as hostages to it. Least of all could one afford to ignore the tactical dilemmas posed by the populist strategy.

Cases could be foreseen, for example, where liberal Democrats bent on pursuing a populist strategy could not count on the support of a regular Democratic organization, because that organization had no interest in populism, was hostile to it or, more to the point, did not exist. Where could a candidate in that situation find the campaign workers he needed? Suppose it turned out that virtually the only potential source upon which he could draw were students and other young people? Would he be forced to modify his populist strategy to bring students and other young people into visible positions in his campaign structure? Could he get the students he wanted if, in the course of his economic appeal to the Wallace vote, he presented himself over and over again as a "Democrat in the tradition of those great leaders of the Democratic party, Thomas Jefferson, Andrew Jackson, Woodrow Wilson, Franklin D. Roosevelt, Harry S. Truman and John F. Kennedy"? Would the students he wanted have any interest in the tradition of the Democratic party? Or would the invocation of that tradition strike them as being an invocation of what they called the Old Politics and hence something to their distaste?

Above all, if the populist appeal to white blue-collar workers and ethnics implied that the liberal Democratic candidate must avoid the themes that could stir up the racial issue, what would be its effect on black people—and on young blacks in particular—for whom those themes were of special interest? Would young blacks have any incentive to come forward as volunteers in the campaign of that liberal Democratic candidate? The question took on a cutting edge in the middle border states and in those of the upper South. To win an election in any of these states, a liberal Democrat must have as one of the important ingredients of his victory maximum support from eligible black voters. That, in turn, meant getting them registered to vote and bringing them to the polls on election day. But would young blacks volunteer for the organizational legwork involved in this two-stage operation if they suspected that the liberal Democratic candidate was bargaining for the Wallace vote at the expense of black people? If young blacks were turned off, who could be looked to for help in getting the black vote registered and to the polls? On the other hand, if the black vote was left inchoate and unexpressed in electoral terms, would the gains made in the white populist element of the Wallace vote be sufficient to insure an election day victory to the liberal Democrat? Was populism itself outstripped by the march of American history? If it was not, was there something to be learned about how to make it viable in a future election?

II

The more one examined the assumptions underlying the front-lash, backlash and sidelash theories, and the more one was confronted by the questions they raised, the more it became clear that the theories, to a marked degree, were shaped by a number of illusions about youth-related events extending from the 1960's through 1970. It was therefore necessary to examine the events of the period in detail, to see how the illusions sprang into being, and how they influenced the different lines of approach to the 1970 congressional election. When this was done, one could come to see how a failure to distinguish between event politics and process politics, and again between political participation and electoral participation, was common to most of the assumptions underlying various 1970 congressional campaign efforts.

To set the stage for the electoral drama of 1970, therefore, the following chapters will reconstruct the salient episodes in the history of youth political activism in the 1960's.

NOTES

1. Jerome Edmund Lord, paper prepared for the Academy for Educational Development, p. 8.

2. This estimate was made by Oliver Quayle of the polling organization which bears his name.

3. "Student Unrest Seen As the Nation's Top Problem," *The Gallup Poll Index* no. 61(July 1970).

4. Richard M. Scammon and Ben J. Wattenberg, *The Real Majority* (New York: Coward-McCann, Inc., 1970).

5. James Bryce, *The American Commonwealth* (New York: Macmillan, 1944), p. 475.

6. "Antiwar Congressional Candidates—1970," *The New Republic* (May 1970).

3
The Politics
of Hope

I

The geological term "posthumous faulting" refers to a condition in which a tear in the earth's crust, due to some sort of internal explosion, continues to widen in a seemingly autonomous way long after the initial explosion has spent its force. The term also lends itself to use in connection with human affairs when the crust of a belief, a practice, or a pattern of power, is breached at some point by the impact of an event. The event itself can come on with a hush or with the roar of Niagara, yet long after it occurs, the breach it made in the social frame seems to extend itself by the force of its own being into ever widening areas of the same frame.

Few American examples of "posthumous faulting" at work in human affairs are as striking as the one following the 1957 personal decision of Mrs. Rosa Parks, a black woman working as a domestic in Montgomery, Alabama, not to stand up in the crowded rear of the bus on her way home. She was tired from her day's work, her feet hurt, and she sat down on an empty seat in the front of the bus reserved under a Montgomery ordinance for white people. Her arrest for violating the ordinance, and the response to it, were destined to open up a new, and for a while hopeful, era in the black student phase of the civil rights movement.

In reaction to the arrest of Mrs. Rosa Parks, Dr. Martin Luther King, Jr., a black clergyman then serving a black congregation in Montgomery, led the black community in an economic boycott that successfully broke the city's bus segregation pattern. The mass protest remained within the law. But aside from its success, an eye-catching feature of the boycott was the people who made it effective. They were the church-going members of the black working class who depended for their daily bread on traditional Southern relationships between whites and blacks. They showed a cohesiveness, determination, and fearlessness that had not been generally conceded to blacks by southern whites. Their example helped set the stage for a larger turn of events.

Up until that time, and for a while afterward, civil rights organizations like the National Association for the Advancement of Colored People (NAACP) had relied on the federal courts and Congress to overturn southern segregation patterns built into local law. A breakthrough judicial victory appeared to have been won on May 17, 1954, when the Supreme Court declared that race could not be used in determining admission to public schools. A breakthrough legislative victory appeared to have been won three years later, when Congress, in the summer of 1957, approved a civil rights bill—the first since Reconstruction days—designed mainly to secure for blacks the right to vote.

Southern resistance to the Supreme Court decision, however, slowed public school integration to a snail's pace, while physical intimidation at southern polling booths kept new Negro voting registration to token levels. Frustration from both sources drew the thoughts of black activists away from the arena of the courtroom and legislature and toward the use of more direct methods, like the Montgomery bus boycott, to gain their objectives. As part of this swing, the national center for black leadership shifted away from the NAACP, and settled on the Southern Christian Leadership Conference (SCLC), a loose coalition of Southern black clergymen that had formed around Dr. King during and immediately after the successful Montgomery boycott.

King's direct-action approach and assimilationist objectives had historical roots in the pre-Civil War abolitionists, in youth-led left-wing ghetto groups in the 1930's, in the youth-led Congress of Racial Equality (CORE) in the early 1940's, and in A. Phillip Randolph's proposed March on Washington in March 1941—a march that was called off when President Franklin D. Roosevelt agreed to create what became the Federal Fair Employment Practices Commission. The new ingredient King injected into the evolutionary line of descent was a doctrine of nonviolent civil disobedience combining Christian tenets with those of Thoreau and Gandhi. As applied to concrete situations in the South and preached from many church pulpits, the doctrine meant something more than massive, legal protests like the Montgomery bus boycott. It entailed the deliberate but nonviolent breach of local segregation ordinances either to force a legal test of their constitutionality, or to force the enactment of federal legislation that would make them void.

At the same time that King and the SCLC were first gaining national prominence, a different organization with a different kind of leadership was sinking deep roots in soil of its own in the northern ghettoes. It was little noticed at the time or, if noticed, was generally the subject of ridicule. It was the organization by Elijah Muhammed of the Nation of Islam, a vehicle for those segments of the black community that no one else at the moment was representing: the urban blacks, jam-packed in northern ghettoes. Elijah Muhammed's movement, with its bent toward separatism and black nationalism, also had historical roots which ran backwards from Marcus Garvey to Martin Delaney to the American Colonization Society in the eighteenth century. His movement was destined to produce its own off-shoots in new forms of black militancy whose watchwords were black power, black liberation, black independence, and black self-defence.

But it was King's doctrine of civil disobedience, with its direct action tactics and its assimilationist objectives, that appealed to groups of black students of southern middle-class background. They agreed that social and political conflicts were best handled if the civil disobedient respected the moral worth of his adversary, distinguished between measures and persons, and abstained from crude forms of coercion. They agreed that civil disobedience must be a public instead of a private act, that its object must be to disarm and persuade the adversary, that the civil disobedient must prepare for the act of civil disobedience not in a burst of emotional enthusiasm, but by a cool cross-examination of his own motives in order to reinforce his fearlessness, his moral strength and the authenticity of his character as a civil resister. They also agreed that the civil disobedient must be prepared to suffer the legal punishment of his law-breaking act, and that in all the things he did he must preserve his bonds with society. Further, he must take care not to fall into the habit of breaking all laws simply because they are laws, but his pin-pointed law-breaking must be animated by an intent to bring to birth the terms of a new law that would remove the grounds for the injustice which aroused his protest.

In February 1960—almost a year before President Kennedy's inauguration—these tenets of civil disobedience as taught by King became the foundation of the direct action program launched by groups of black students mostly of southern middle-class background. Beginning with their direct challenges to specific segregation ordinances in Greensboro and Nashville, there ensued in the months immediately following, a wave of black student sit-ins, stand-ins, kneel-ins, and read-ins as part of an intensified drive to end racial segregation in such nongovernmental areas of southern public life as lunch counters, theatres, churches, and libraries.

In Columbia, Georgia, for example, a peaceful sit-in of black students at a dime-store lunch counter was disrupted when a white man stabbed one of them. The students returned to the scene the next day and resumed the sit-in. In Nashville, Tennessee, when black students were staging a stand-in at theatres and some of them were stoned by white hoodlums, a student leader told his followers: "Let every stone thrown at you be an opportunity to know yourself, your moral strength, your moral conviction in the justness of your cause." [1] In Jackson, Mississippi, white police used tear gas, clubs, and dogs to break up a peaceful march of Negro students protesting the arrest of other students who had attempted to break the segregation barrier in the public library. The students later regrouped and resumed the march.

All such efforts stemmed from the individual initiatives of local black student leaders. But in October 1960, Ella Baker of the Southern Christian Leadership Conference brought the student heads of the various sit-ins together in Atlanta, Georgia. The result was the formation of the Student Nonviolent Coordinating Committee (SNCC), with John Lewis, then a student, as its first president. In a time of retrospect, the authors of a staff study prepared for the National Commission on the Causes and Prevention of Violence in America,* underlined a major point bearing on the genesis of SNCC. It was that most of the original members of the organization—and their white counterparts in the North who tried to support the southern sit-ins by pick-

---

* Whether or not the difference between plagiarism and scholarship is the difference between kidnapping material from one book as against kidnapping it from many books, I must here gratefully acknowledge the immense debt I owe to the authors of the various staff studies prepared for this Commission. I have often gone to their well of information and judgment and snatched much from it.

eting and boycotting the northern branches of Woolworth's and Kresge's—trusted both the protective power of the federal government and the moral sensibility of white America, in both North and South. They viewed the political and social order as being relatively healthy, and assumed that racism—despite the warning flares of Harlem uprisings in 1935 and 1953—was a localized southern malignancy, that could and would be rooted out by American morality and American institutions once "a sense of shame had been awakened" in the general American conscience and in the conscience of the immediate white southern adversary. It was implicitly assumed that the adversary *had* a sense of "moral shame" to awaken, and that "this awakening would lead to the peaceful dismantling of all segregation barriers." [2]

II

That assumption, which existed before President Kennedy came to power, seemed to be justified on January 20, 1961—his Inauguration day. At that time, the television cameras playing on the contrasting figures of the outgoing president, Dwight D. Eisenhower, and the incoming president, John F. Kennedy, seemed to convey a meaning that went beyond a change of presidents and parties in control of the White House. The larger meaning seemed to be that a sweeping but peaceful revolution had occurred in the generational center of power in the United States, and with it, a hopeful revolution in the nation's governing outlook, values and purposes.

In the aging figure of Eisenhower—Supreme Commander of the Allied invasion of Europe on D-Day, hero of V-E Day, Chief of Staff, Supreme Commander of NATO—one could see the eclipse of the old generation that had managed World War

II and brought it to a successful conclusion. In the figure of Kennedy—commander of a PT boat crew in the Pacific War, a hero survivor of the loss of the boat, a young congressman, a young senator, and the youngest man ever to win the White House in a direct election—one could see the ascendancy of the new generation that had made none of the great strategic decisions during the war, but rather bore the brunt of the front-line fighting. As a man still in his early forties, President Kennedy seemed to write large the national fact that the war had accelerated by a half a generation the age at which men normally come to places of great power in the structure of American politics.

Kennedy made these feelings explicit in his Inaugural address. "Let the word go forth from this time and place, to friend and foe alike," he said, "that the torch has passed to a new generation of Americans, tempered by war, disciplined by a hard and bitter peace, proud of our ancient heritage, and unwilling to witness or permit the slow undoing of those human rights to which this nation has always been committed, and to which we are committed today at home and around the world."

This sense of things was not limited to the heady atmosphere of Inauguration day. It was extended in the weeks that followed, when troops of bright New Frontiersmen gained their clarity of line either as White House staff aides to President Kennedy or as his personal lieutenants strategically placed throughout the government. In their group profile—leaving a handful of exceptions out of account—they appeared cerebral, yet young (ranging in age from their late 20's to their early 40's), physically vigorous, cool, crisp, assured, and stripped for battle.

The press had reported that the poet Robert Frost advised President Kennedy: "Poetry and power is the formula for an Augustan age. But be more Irish than Harvard. Don't be afraid of power." [3] The advice, though apt, was superfluous when re-

peated to the New Frontiersmen. Their own consuming preoccupation had been with the realities of power—"how to get it,
how to keep it, how to use it." They had seen the Soviet Union
skillfully organize power out of scarce resources and become a
threat to the United States. They had seen Senator Joseph Mc-
Carthy organize the power of a politics of revenge and endanger
civil liberties within the United States. They had seen many
things deteriorate in the structure of American life because of
the deliberate nonuse of presidential power in the Eisenhower
years. Moreover, the innermost circle of Kennedy intimates had
proven their own capacity to organize the components of electoral power and to win against great odds, first, the Democratic
nomination for the presidency, and then, against greater odds,
the presidency itself. Now that the management of the government was in their hands, they meant, by a sharp sensitivity to
the factors of national power, to manipulate men and things toward their own vision of the public good. On these and other
counts they considered themselves political realists, with no patience for the "woolly-headed liberalism of the past."

The young men of the New Frontier were part and parcel of
an American tradition, dating back to colonial times. Most
of the early colonials and many of those who fought in the
Revolution, pioneered in settling the wilderness, and took on
the burden of government were youthful in age as well as in
spirit.

Perhaps because of the nation's colonial past, its revolutionary and civil wars, its settlement of the West and its openness to
immigrants, there has been a premium on youth in the United
States. While this development—so different from European
tradition—never led to a youth culture, young men were often
at the forefront of politics. The second Continental Congress,
for example, contained James Madison, 24, James Monroe, 25,
and Alexander Hamilton, 26, among its elected delegates. Andrew Jackson reached the Senate at age 30, while Henry Clay,

41

like Edward Kennedy a hundred years later, was elected to the senior house of congress at 29. And, as American party politics took form, the young always had a role and a place that kept them from opposition to the established way of doing things.

Even in the 1930's, when the great depression brought about a radicalization of American youth—as well as of many older Americans—there was no serious attempt to abandon the system. Most young Americans supported Franklin D. Roosevelt and the New Deal, which itself was staffed in large measure by the same type of cool, bright, and forceful younger men who were in the vanguard of the New Frontier. Even those who were more radical, the Communists, Trotskyists and other splinter groups favoring revolution, made a point of pursuing their objectives within the existing framework of political action. Moreover, the radical young knew their place. They were "Young" Socialists or "Young" Communists—the shock troops rather than the leaders of the political avant-garde.

Leaving aside the many differences between what the New Frontier seemed to be and what it actually was, it presented at the start of the 1960's a glowing contrast with the familiar European versions of the youth and power. In modern European history, as Walter Laqueur has written, the leaders of both right-wing and left-wing student movements or revolts were often alike in their cultural pessimism, in their anticapitalist and antibourgeois policies, and in their addiction to viewing events in an apocalyptic light.[4] As they stood outside the citadels of power looking in, or as they laid siege to those citadels, they hurled anathemas at the older generation of men in command.

European youth movements had always claimed that the older generation had made a mess of everything. It had established and backed an order that was corrupt to the bone, and beyond redemption by any means of regular reform, be it "more democracy," or "more liberalism." The institutions of democracy and liberalism were bogus. To be sure, the men in command of them made much of the freedom of choice they offered voters on election day. Yet they saw to it that the actual range of choice was confined to convertible sets of cowards, blockheads, poltroons and traitors who lived off the rest of the country. There was no choice to be made between them. All belonged to the same rotten system whose very existence cut the connection between talk and the possibility of being heard, between real pain experienced and a saving remedy, between mankind and world, between idea and reality. Meanwhile, mass culture, crass materialism, spiritual bankruptcy, and a consuming obsession to grab and get had planed all things down to a dead level of mediocrity and to a cloying, suffocating boredom.

The remedy proposed by youth was the same, whether in Czarist Russia, pre-Fascist Italy, or pre-Nazi Germany. The remedy was a national rebirth—a radical overturn of the old in favor of a new beginning, a great national purge to be led by youth. The high cause in view permitted no concessions to moralistic notions like tolerance. It demanded suspension of all moral restraint on action so that youth could realize its full potential as an agent of moral regeneration.

In contrast to the European picture, the case of American youth as embodied in the New Frontiersmen glistened with health and promise. These young Americans were not consumed by cultural pessimism, and paranoia, nor did they view events in an apocalyptic light, full of sudden ends and beginnings. They did not maintain that all the institutions of democracy and liberalism were rotten to the core, or that the nation was so far gone in degeneration as to justify the suspension of moral restraints on action so that youth could realize its full potential as the agent of moral regeneration. True, they noted and decried the contradictions between the precepts and the practices of democracy and liberalism. But they also assumed that

43

the roots and trunk of the national tree were healthy and that the rotten branches could be removed in an orderly way by the pruning forks of democracy and liberalism.

Above all, these young Americans did not stand outside the supreme citadels of power looking in, while old men inside used violent or nonviolent means of coercion to protect their monopoly of power. By their own use of the electoral process, after a campaign in which their banner read: "Let's get America moving again," they had won the White House itself. They were in a position where they could presumably make good on the call sounded by President Kennedy in his Inaugural address: "Ask not what your country can do for you—ask what you can do for your country." They would, presumably, live at every pore the great sounding words, excellence, and quality, which ceaselessly rang out from their lips. They were in a position to use the social power of the presidency to invest the arts and sciences with a fresh dignity and to make the White House a teacher to the nation of high cultural tastes.

The atmosphere in the neighborhood of the White House seemed vibrant with possibilities for all other young Americans. Simply to be young and an American was to live in an effulgent moral condition and to have a full-time career in making events become what they ought to be. The same sense of things buoyed the spirits of the black students who founded SNCC before the coming to power of the New Frontier, and was to buoy the spirits of the white students who were to found the SDS a year after the advent of the New Frontier.

More will be said later about the founding and the announced aims of SDS. Yet with future developments in mind, it is worth noting that neither the founding members of SNCC nor those of SDS saw the university as a microcosm of the great society around it, or as an enemy fortress to be taken by storm and changed from within to their own liking. They initially viewed the university as a special kind of small society—a

44

sanctuary city governed by special values and laws which set it apart from the nonsanctuary cities surrounding it. It was considered a privileged place, not to be invaded by the feuding forces of the larger society in hot pursuit of an adversary. It was a place where black and white students could be prepared for the tasks awaiting them when they left to reenter the great society around it.

It is true that the founding and early members of SNCC and SDS set in train two lines of force that would eventually be transfigured and fused with some of the more violent episodes of American youth in the 1960's. Yet they began as American meliorists or incrementalists, in the tradition of most American political reform movements. Like the other reformers, the founding members of SNCC and SDS decried what they asserted were assaults on the ethic of citizenship. Each demanded an end to the manner in which the American experiment was being corrupted by an exploiting class who would have Americans take the shadow of liberty for the substance, the name for the reality, the promise for the possession. Each warned that the American dream would become the American nightmare if specified wrongs were not set right. In all this, however, it was the rare young critic who called for a frontal assault on all existing institutions. In a sportive mood, they were more likely to suggest, when asked what heaven was like, that it was governed under the American Constitution.

III

The Kennedy administration's symbolic gestures of executive support for the cause of civil rights in the South encouraged SNCC in late 1961 to launch a program which went beyond the objectives of demonstration politics like the staged sit-ins. Its new program involved the protracted undertakings of process politics. Its objective was to prepare southern blacks for full participation in electoral politics as an instrument of basic social change. Full-time workers were sent into the rural communities of the South to induce black adults to register as voters and to see to it that they actually registered.

The registration effort was still in its first months when events began to shake the assumption that a nonviolent grass roots movement among blacks could count on the moral sensibilities of white Americans and on the protective power of the federal government.[5] The stepped up efforts of student civil rights activists were met by stepped up physical violence on the part of some southern whites. In Mississippi, NAACP leader Medgar Evers was murdered. In Birmingham, four little black girls died when their church was dynamited. In Montgomery, Freedom Riders were beaten by mobs. In Birmingham and Selma, civil rights demonstrators were hosed, clubbed, and set upon by unleashed dogs. Later on, during the summer of 1964, three civil rights workers were murdered in Neshoba County, Mississippi. These cases received national attention, but other early cases of brutal assault, murder, or attempted murder went unnoticed by the nation.

Other grave doubts were raised by the response of federal government officials—whether in Washington or in the field— to white southern terror tactics. Officials in Washington confirmed the reports that terror tactics were being used, regretted their use, and sent messages of condolence to the families of the victims. Yet when the pattern of violence became clear, the Kennedy administration—the first Democratic administration in two decades that failed (until the spring of 1963) to submit a civil rights bill to the congress—stuck to the seemingly ambiguous position it had assumed from its first days in office. It said in one breath that no new civil rights legislation was necessary —executive orders issued under existing legislation could handle the situation—and the next breath, that the use of executive action alone imposed a harness of constraints on its efforts to alter the southern situation.

In addition, Kennedy administration spokesmen periodically explained to White House reporters in "off the record" briefings that the president was deeply engaged in defusing explosive situations in the world arena—Laos, Berlin, Vietnam, Cuba—and that he needed a united nation behind him. He could not risk dividing the South from the North by pushing hard on the civil rights front. The spokesmen later explained that the president was deeply engaged in promoting measures of vital importance to world peace—the Trade Expansion Act of 1962 and the Nuclear Test Ban Treaty. He could not chance the loss of southern congressional support for these measures, and the loss of southern votes in the Senate, by introducing potentially divisive civil rights proposals. As for the charge that federal officials in the field—and F. B. I. agents specifically—were derelict in protecting the lives of civil rights workers, the Justice Department's reply, presumably approved by Attorney General Robert F. Kennedy, was that "maintaining law and order is a state responsibility."

With vital human rights at stake, it was difficult for student civil rights activists to swallow this dry legalism which made strict construction of the Constitution an excuse for nonaction. They saw that civil rights demonstrators who picketed a grocery store in Albany, Georgia, were prosecuted by the federal government, while local police officials who attacked and severely beat the demonstrators were not prosecuted under available federal law. The double standard of federal justice prompted SNCC leader John Lewis to ask: "Whose side is the government on?" Other black student civil rights activists—especially those working to bring more black adults into the electoral process by getting them registered as voters—began to echo Lewis. Their direct experiences could readily lead them to believe that the federal government had abdicated its responsibilities to defend the Constitution in the Black Belt; that despite existing civil rights legislation and legal support for integration, it had abandoned southern blacks to the local police; that local law and order officials remained at liberty to enforce caste systems of justice; that all the hallowed features of liberal democracy—local rule, trade unionism, the referendum, the local school—showed themselves to be the meshed gears of an engine of racism designed to crush aspirations to equality; that the jury system—the ultimate sign and symbol of liberal democracy in its local domain—was geared to reach not guilty verdicts in cases where white racist terrorists murdered blacks.[6]

Growing doubts among black student activists about the tactic of nonviolent resistance to racism led directly to doubts about what could be gained by more civil rights bills. Early in the summer of 1963, for example, a national coalition of Negro leaders and their white liberal allies set in motion a massive march on Washington to back a new civil rights measure President Kennedy had belatedly sent to the Congress. On the site of the march itself, Dr. King was cheered for his speech, "I have a dream." Yet John Lewis of SNCC signaled the growing Negro student disillusionment both with King's dream and with the hopes entrusted to more civil rights bills. "This bill," he said tartly, "will not protect young children and old women from police dogs and fire hoses for engaging in peaceful demonstrations."

Still, many blacks clung to a belief in meaningful legislation. As if in obedience to a positive duty to hope—and in an optimistic atmosphere set by the signing of the nuclear test-ban treaty, the new civil rights legislation introduced in Congress, and the near religious exaltation that was part of the massive march on Washington—many student activists launched new civil rights projects of their own and, of these, priority was again given to electoral politics as it bore on the work getting of southern blacks to register as voters.

IV

While the foregoing events were shaping up on the civil rights front, other issues took hold of groups of white student activists in universities, (especially in the elite universities of the North) starting at the University of California's Berkeley campus.

In 1960 national attention was first focused on Berkeley students when they protested the execution of Caryl Chessman, and later when they joined with other San Francisco Bay area students in demonstrating against a hearing in San Francisco by the House Unamerican Activities Committee. The committee responded by distributing nationally a film of the protest, in order to expose "Communist influence" among youth. Student viewers of the film, however, saw in it not only a self-caricature of the committee, but convincing evidence that demonstrations and direct action could pose a serious challenge to hostile authority.

The black student sit-ins had already taught white student activists the techniques of nonviolent action. Encouraged by the example of the successful Bay area protests in the face of hostile authority, in late 1961, some students around the country began to use marches, vigils, and pickets to protest aspects of American foreign policy. Then, as a trans-Atlantic companion piece to England where the student-inspired New Left launched a campaign for nuclear disarmament, some American students helped organize the Washington Peace March of February 1962, to express their concern about the nuclear arms race, nuclear testing in the upper atmosphere, and the newly launched program of civil defense against a nuclear strike. It was the first national student demonstration since the eve of World War II.

By the start of 1962, some white student radicals were well into a process of intense introspection concerning their duties to themselves and the motives behind their own social and political behavior. In this same spirit, they groped for a path to a radical ideology that would avoid the tendency of old-line radical youth groups to deify doctrine and grant it more importance than flesh and blood. The new groups wanted an ideology of radicalism that would make personal commitment, not abstract ideas, the stuff of radical politics—a personal commitment that could meet and master the problem of alienation as it appeared in its fundamental modern form. That form, as they saw it, was not the institutional alienation that the modern industrial regime—capitalist or communist—tends to intrude between the worker and the psychic rewards of production. It was the alienation that appears as the deadening of man's sensitivity to man, and the denial of man's right to his own humanity.[7]

In this groping for a new ideology of radicalism, white student radicals appear to have been influenced by the writings of diverse men—Martin Buber, Albert Camus, and Jacques Maritain among the existentialists, by C. Wright Mills among the sociologists and, later, by the Freudian-Marxism of Herbert Marcuse and the Gestalt-therapy anarchism of Paul Goodman. Yet, if there was a single decisive example of practical radicalism they were attracted to, it was the community organization work begun in the 1930's by Saul Alinsky in Chicago's "Back of the Yards" and extended to other depressed neighborhoods in other cities through his Industrial Areas Foundation. The ideas underlying Alinsky's approach to his community organization work, along with the tactical devices he used to achieve his ends, were set forth by him in his book, *Reveille for Radicals,* published by the University of Chicago Press in the late 1930's.[8] The effect of its rediscovery by white student radicals

50

at the start of the 1960's was to be reflected in the genesis of SDS.

But at the start of the 1960's, the National Student Association (NSA) was the most important student organization in the United States. It had a small national staff that dealt with matters of special concern to students as students—from the negotiation of special travel rates to the mustering of support for federal programs of aid to higher education. The staff also arranged an annual convention where student leaders of campus organizations around the country were brought together to elect national officers and to pass resolutions whose application (or nonapplication) was left to the discretion of component student groups.

In essence, the NSA was a loose and changing collection of student leaders. Until the start of the 1960's, it seldom if ever went on record in connection with political issues other than those having a direct and explicit bearing on the condition of the student in the American university. Moreover, only a handful of its leaders knew that the Central Intelligence Agency provided the NSA with funds to send American student delegations to the international youth conferences where they could counter the anti-American polemics and tactics of assorted youth delegations from other countries. In 1967 the relationship between the NSA and the CIA was exposed, compromising the NSA in the eyes of many students—all the more so because the NSA as an organization had previously been virtually invisible on the campuses of the nation.

The NSA was to remain virtually invisible in the eyes of most students even at the height of the two great "within the system" climacterics of student political activism in the 1960's —the 1968 bids of Senators Eugene McCarthy and Robert F. Kennedy for the Democratic presidential nomination, and the 1969 anti-Vietnam Moratorium and Mobilization efforts. Yet many of the young people who initially had a major hand in the

McCarthy campaign and the Moratorium and Mobilization projects were former principal NSA officers who apparently summoned each other to a common task.

Among them were Allard K. Lowenstein, Gloria Steinem, Curtis Gans, Sam Brown, Verne Newton, Jeff Greenfield, Ken Bode, and John O'Sullivan—each of whom later became prominent on the American political scene.

At the start of the 1960's meanwhile, the old and hereditary left still had campus affiliates which engaged sporadically in electoral politics in support of a candidate. They included the DuBois Clubs, the Young Socialist Alliance and Progressive Labor. These, however, either seemed chained to dogmatic ideologies, or were torn from within by controversies over fine points of doctrinal purity. There were also the slightly left of center traditional liberal groups, like the College Young Democrats, American Civil Liberties Union and SANE. To the right of center were conservative campus groups like the College Young Republicans and the Young Americans for Freedom. The main body of American students belonged to none of these political groups.

In June 1962, a new student organization—Students for a Democratic Society (SDS)—came to a formal birth.[9] The first leaders of SDS were a small group of white student intellectuals based mainly at the University of Michigan. Prominent among them were Tom Hayden and Paul Booth, who had been approached by the League for Industrial Democracy to help in reconstructing the League's moribund student sector.[10] By the spring of 1962, the Michigan leadership had organized likeminded student groups on 11 campuses, and in June of the year, 59 representatives met at the FDR Labor Center at Port Huron for the founding convention of the Students for Democratic Action, where they also issued *The Port Huron Statement* that had been drafted by Hayden.

Although the founders of SDS were students, the paramount

accent of *The Port Huron Statement* was not on student issues in relationship to their immediate university environment, but on the need to organize students into a radical new movement that could help them prepare themselves intellectually within the university for the work awaiting them outside. The main work was to invigorate American democracy by a process politics that would activate large numbers of people at the grass roots level politically and bring them together as a cohesive force—civil rights groups, antiwar groups, established reform groups in the labor movement, in liberal organizations and religious bodies. If this were done, students would be in a position to offer new policy alternatives to local and national electorates. Conceivably, they might be instrumental in realigning the Democratic Party from within to make it the instrument of a social movement that could swing the country away from the Cold War and toward a policy of disarmament—a relaxation of international tensions and a domestic program to end poverty and racial inequality.

There was not a syllable in *The Port Huron Statement* that advocated or justified a resort to violence as an instrument of social change. On the contrary, the statement argued that wherever nonhuman elements—whether revolutionary doctrine or material goods—assume greater importance than human life or well-being, man becomes alienated from man and the way is open to the self-righteous use of others as objects. Revolutionary terrorism was thus viewed as the mirror image of capitalist exploitation. In this connection *The Port Huron Statement* proclaimed:

We regard *men* as infinitely precious and possessed of unfulfilled capacities of reason, freedom and love. . . . We oppose the depersonalization that reduces all human beings to the status of things. If anything, the brutalities of the twentieth century teach that means and ends are intimately related, that vague appeals to "posterity" cannot justify the mutilations of the present. . . . Loneliness, estrangement, isolation describe the vast distance between man and man today. These dominant tendencies cannot be overcome by better personal management, nor by improved gadgets, but only when a love of man overcomes the idolatrous worship of things by man.

To the latter end, the SDS founding convention held aloft the ideal of a society based on participatory democracy. The argument behind the phrase was that as society was becoming increasingly centralized and as more power was being delegated to officials who were increasingly remote from the governed, men were losing control over the decisions affecting their lives. Technological developments and mass education could, however, create new forms of decentralization and local democracy in neighborhoods, factories, schools and other social organizations. SDS urged disenfranchised and powerless people to organize themselves and press their interests in opposition to the already powerful. The immediate effect of local insurgency—so it was hoped—would be to generate a climate for the reform of national policy. The long-range effect would be to teach the possibility and the meaning of participation.

SDS itself meant from the outset to be a model of the participatory democracy it preached. Being nondogmatic, it was open to students of all beliefs. Being decentralized in structure, it gave every local group—at the height of its prestige it had but 227 campus chapters, representing a ten percent coverage of all campuses [11]—full freedom to decide what initiative it would take and the tactics it would use. The only unifying bond among SDS members of the first generation was a shared sense of moral outrage and a joint commitment to work for the social changes envisioned in *The Port Huron Statement*.

After its founding convention, SDS leaders from around the country—like the leaders of the National Student Association —came to know each other fairly well. In this special sense, they could be said to form a national network, just as student activists who concentrated on civil rights formed a national network through personal contacts with each other, and as would the leaders of the anti-Vietnam War, Moratorium, and Mobilization efforts of the future. This is not the same as saying that SDS was part of a centrally controlled national or international "conspiracy." A local SDS chapter or a local affiliate of the Mobilization Committee might borrow the tactics of the civil rights movement, or be goaded into imitating the tactics of the newly militant black radical students simply to prove their credibility as agents of social change. Similarly, student eruptions that would soon break out in a number of countries almost simultaneously might show a striking conformity in ideology, symbols and tactics, but these sudden developments did not mean that there was a hydra-headed plot that had a single nexus. The apparent symmetry in the conduct of student political activists in different countries was due either to a similarity in local conditions or to the cross-fertilization of ideas and experiences rising from informal contacts or the reportage of the mass media.

As part of their on-campus educational work, the first generation of SDS leaders, in common with other radical white students, either worked through the normal channels of student government or invoked conventional means of protests such as petitions, picketings and public meetings. Many students expressed sympathy with the use of civil disobedience and other forms of direct action in behalf of racial equality and peace, but a resort to these techniques in a campus context was decidedly uncommon. When employed by student radicals, they were viewed merely as the means of bringing issues to public notice, with the resolution of the issues being entrusted to the conventional political process. What was said earlier bears repeating. The white student radical movement—like the black student civil rights movement—began with a firm commitment to nonviolence and with considerable optimism regarding the responsiveness of authorities.

Among white student radicals, the high point of optimism was reached in the summer of 1963—or at about the same time that some leaders of SNCC were becoming disenchanted with the prospects for a grass roots nonviolent movement. This was the time when the Nuclear Test Ban Treaty was signed, and when the civil rights march on Washington augured well for the passage of significant legislation. White student activists projected new civil rights works, particularly in the area of voter registration. Also, books like Michael Harrington's *The Other America*—which showed young activists the reverse side of John Kenneth Galbraith's *The Affluent Society*—awakened them to the reality of economic as well as racial inequality. During that summer, SDS began to mobilize students for community organization work among poor whites and other minorities, in much the same way as the southern civil rights movement had been working among poor Negroes. The hope was that if this new commitment to off-campus work in poverty areas resulted in an organization of the poor in their own interests, then the national climate of reform could be moved beyond the issues of segregation and voting rights to an effective attack on poverty and unemployment.

The assassination of President Kennedy in November 1963 was keenly felt by student activists, black and white, but it did not break their momentum. In 1963–1964, the student movement engaged in an effort to draw students into volunteer and full-time work in northern urban slums, in Appalachia and in the southern Black Belt. By the summer of 1964, thousands of students were involved in such activities, their legitimacy bolstered by President Johnson's announcement of a "war on poverty." In Mississippi—a focal point for the efforts made in the summer of 1964 to register black voters—nearly a thousand student volunteers aided in the effort to build the Mississippi Freedom Democratic Party as an instrument of electoral politics. The immediate objective was to have it send a delegation of its own to the 1964 Democratic Convention in Atlantic City where it could challenge the all-white segregationist Mississippi delegation.

The Mississippi experience was to mark the crossing of a psychological Rubicon for many students, white or black, who had come from outside to work in that state. The murder of three young men working on the Negro voter registration drive brought many students from the North face to face for the first time with the brute force behind southern racism. Worse, the communal absolutions offered the murderers provided the shocked students with an object lesson about how the whole of white-dominated local order was an accomplice to the violent repression of Negroes. White students who returned North from the Mississippi experience brought back with them to their campuses a newly urgent sense of social and legal justice for Negroes. In common with returning black students, they also brought back two more things: one was a gnawing discontent with the bland indifference and banalities that seemed to permeate white middle-class life—including collegiate life. The other was a strengthened conviction—which they broadcast to other students on campus—about the need for direct action and confrontation as the only way imperative social and political changes could be brought about.

Their convictions were reinforced by the fate of the Mississippi Freedom Democratic Party (MFDP) at the 1964 Democratic Convention. In Mississippi proper, the MFDP initially represented a rejection of the absolute southern white monopoly of Democratic party politics. In Atlantic City, white liberals refused to support wholeheartedly the bid of the MFDP to unseat the segregationist Mississippi delegation. The most they could offer the MFDP was a compromise whose terms would give the latter two seats in the otherwise segregationist delegation. It was especially disappointing to the MFDP that they failed to win support from Senator Hubert H. Humphrey, a

57

long-time champion of civil rights. Humphrey, in his bid for the vice presidential nomination, did not want to arouse southern opposition and took the lead in negotiating the compromise seating plan. To the then leaders of SNCC and to some of their black and white student supporters who had risked their lives to create an electoral foundation on which the MFDP was launched, the compromise appeared to be of a piece with the reluctance of the federal government to enforce existing laws protecting civil rights workers in the South.

The consequent onset of disenchantment among white student radical activists was expressed by SDS in the fall of 1964. While announcing that it supported Johnson in preference to Goldwater, the SDS issued a button—"Part of the way with LBJ"—to signify both continued fidelity to the conventional processes of electoral politics, and distaste over its latest turn. The disenchantment among the young black leaders of SNCC was even more marked. The Atlantic City experience gave the spur to their pre-existing tendency, which got underway during the Kennedy years, to distrust the good offices of liberal Democratic politicians and white liberals generally.[12]

In the aftermath of the 1964 Democratic Convention, SNCC leaders began to reappraise the history of their organization. In doing so, they would conclude that the white liberals who provided SNCC with its principal funds had used the purse strings to control SNCC's ideology, program, and tactics. SNCC, therefore, had not been able to do any more for black people than the white financial patrons wanted them to do. It did not include working for self-determination for the black community; rather it meant securing for the blacks a few concessions from the white power structure. The reappraisal, cast in some such terms, would presently close a vicious circle of distrust. The more the leaders of SNCC scorned their white financial supporters, the less funds they received from them; the less the funds they received, the more they were persuaded that they had even stronger grounds for raising the pitch of their scorn.

In a parallel motion, SNCC leaders began to turn away from the assimilationist objectives of Dr. King and his doctrine of nonviolent civil disobedience. The new voice they listened to was that of Malcolm X, who had risen from the lowest depths of the black urban ghettoes to become an articulate lieutenant of Elijah Muhammed, the head of the Black Muslims. In the months between Malcolm X's break with the Black Muslims in 1964 and his assassination in 1965, he attracted increasing attention as a forceful theoretician of black consciousness, black pride, black unity, black separatism, and black liberation. His concept of black power would first be amplified by Stokely Carmichael when he became the new head of SNCC, and later, in a more inflammatory way, by Carmichael's successor, H. Rap Brown.

The increasing emphasis placed on black self-reliance by black student political activists, leading to increasingly frequent rebuffs of offers of help from white liberal and radical students, would soon bring to a close the era of white student participation in the black student civil rights movement. But in the fall of 1964, when the latter development was still in prospect, a protracted series of episodes at Berkeley—extended from the start of the fall term to December—had a profound effect on the course white student radical activism would subsequently take.[13]

The series of episodes, which acquired the collective name of the Free Speech Movement, began as a student protest against the decision of the school administration not to permit the use of campus facilities for any political meetings related to the 1964 presidential contest. Students elsewhere were profoundly effected by events at Berkeley where the Free Speech Movement culminated in a paralysis of the university, a mass student strike in December 1964, and a victory where students won the right to stage on-campus political meetings that had off-campus political implications.

The Free Speech Movement took place at almost the mathematically exact moment when American higher education was posed for a quantum jump in the size of its student population. Five years previously, at the start of the 1960's, students in all American colleges and universities totaled 4.6 million. But between the mid-1960's and the end of the decade, the college-bound surge of children born during the peak period of family formations after World War II raised the total to 7.4 million —an increase of 60 percent in only five years. One-fifth of these students attended universities whose enrollment ranged between 15,000 and 35,000—a figure larger than most towns in the world. The aggregate national size of the American student body exceeded the total national population contained in some of the most industrially advanced nation-states in the world, and in most of the Third World countries in the United Nations.

The realities of this mass told on the perceptions of the students who comprised it. When their daily experiences were largely confined to their encounters in a university context, when they saw their own life duplicated on all sides in an environmental student sea, students who would differ on other matters—including the issue of the Vietnam War—would come to share either or both of two views. In one view they comprised, as students, a distinctive kind of class in American society. They had distinctive class interests as students, and those interests were covered by the laws of inevitability associated with the concept of class. In the second and larger view, they formed a Republic of Studenthood that was coextensive with the American Republic—or at least, was the keeper of the national conscience in the American Republic.

The consequences flowing from these two conclusions would become known in due course. More immediately, some white students—without regard to their general political orientation —were seized by what they thought was the cardinal lesson taught by the Berkeley Free Speech Movement. The lesson, in

60

their view, laid bare the fact that the university, as an institution, was hostile to humane values, to the traditional principles of civil liberties, and to any kind of education that did not serve the productive needs of the controlling industrial regime. This thesis was advanced in the following statement issued by the Free Speech Movement, to the effect that the university:

made the student a mere mercenary, paid off in grades, status and degrees, all of which can eventually be cashed in for hard currency on the job market. . . . Credits for courses are subtly transformed into credit cards as the multiversity inculcates the values of acquisitive society.

Other white students—liberal or radical in their political orientation—drew a further lesson from the Berkeley Free Speech Movement. These students had previously maintained that campus issues were trivial compared to the civil rights struggle—that white students in particular could prove their professed dedication to social change only if "they laid themselves on the line" by working off campus for the cause of civil rights on behalf of southern blacks. In their new view, however, the Free Speech Movement underlined the need to recast in a major way, if not to reverse altogether, their central tenets about student political activism. The movement, said they, showed that large numbers of students could be mobilized for direct action tactics on campus; that the campus itself could be made a battlefield for immediate goals that were politically worthwhile; that a local campus uprising, though focused on an issue that was seemingly bounded by the local university environment, could have national political importance by opening the eyes of students everywhere to the existence of the same issue in their own midst.

If some such arguments had been advanced at another time, perhaps the effects would have been as self-limiting as a gust of wind sweeping the drift of dust and feathers up against a stone wall. The arguments sounded in an hour when groups of white

61

student activists—centered mainly in elitist private and public colleges in the North—were psychologically ready to see the campus become an arena for political battle. The two main off-campus issues that had been the focal points for their interests and efforts up to that time—civil rights for southern blacks and the dangers of nuclear war—were undergoing a change of face.

The change in the case of civil rights has already been alluded to. It needs only to be repeated that though the emergent idea of black power had not yet been fully articulated—and would not be until April 1966—the force of its spread even in inchoate form among black students, registered on the nerves of some white student activists and foretold the approaching end of the era of white student participation in the cause of civil rights for southern blacks. In the case of the second issue, the danger of nuclear war had appeared to recede when the Nuclear Test Ban Treaty was signed and a subsequent U. S.-Soviet agreement reached early in President Johnson's Administration to cut back on the production of fissionable materials for military uses pointed to a continuing U. S.-Soviet interest in checking the nuclear arms race. Liberal and radical activists began to search for new programmatic directions.

NOTES

1. Martin Agronsky, et al, *Let Us Begin, The First 100 Days of the Kennedy Administration* (New York: Simon and Schuster, 1961), p. 73.

2. Jerome Skolnik, A Staff Report to the National Commission on the Causes and Prevention of Violence, *The Politics of Protest. Violent Aspects of Protest and Confrontation* (Washington, D. C.: U. S. Government Printing Office), p. 101.

3. Agronsky, *Let Us Begin,* p. 15.

The Politics of Hope

4. Walter Laqueur, "Reflections on Youth Movements," *Commentary* 47(June 1969).

5. Skolnick, *The Politics of Protest,* p. 102.

6. Howard Zinn, "The Limits of Nonviolence," *Freedomways IV* (First Quarter, 1964), pp. 143–148.

7. Theodore Roszak, "Youth and the Great Refusal," *The Nation* (March 25, 1968).

8. Saul Alinsky, *Reveille for Radicals* (Chicago: University of Chicago Press, 1939).

9. Paul Jacobs and Saul Landau, *The New Radicals* (New York: Vintage, 1966); Mitchell Cohen and Dennis Hale, *The New Student Left: An Anthology* (Boston: Beacon Press, 1966).

10. Richard F. Peterson, "The Student Left in American Higher Education," Daedalus (Winter 1968), p. 294.

11. Richard Blumenthal, "SDS: Protest Is Not Enough," *The Nation* (May 22, 1967).

12. Stokely S. Carmichael and Charles V. Hamilton, *Black Power: The Politics of Liberation in America* (New York: Vintage Books, 1967); Loren Miller, "Farewell to Liberals," in *Black Protest* (March, 1965), pp. 349–356; Lee Rainwater and William L. Yancey, *The Moynihan Report and the Politics of Controversy* (Cambridge, Mass.: M. I. T. Press, 1967).

13. S. M. Lipset and S. Wolin, eds., *The Berkeley Student Revolt* (New York: Anchor, 1965).

4

The Politics
of Transition

I

Since the birth of SDS in June 1962, its members had carried on local polemics, formed some new chapters, and launched community organization projects in the white and black ghettoes of northern cities. But coincidently with the December 1964 climax in the Berkeley Free Speech Movement, and largely under the stimulus of the lessons drawn from the event, a new proposal was discussed and adopted by SDS representatives when they met in Chicago during the Christmas vacation. They agreed that SDS, in its action program, should no longer confine itself solely to off-campus tasks of community organization. It should also initiate action programs involving students on campus. They did not have in mind a mobilization of students for a frontal assault on the universities. The first step in the action program, announced in the last days of December 1964, was a national student march in Washington, called for April 15, 1965, against the Vietnam War.

When the announcement was made, SDS had no more than 1,200 national dues-paying members spread thin in 30 campus chapters in the north. Yet the timing of the call was to endow SDS with a moral authority among students that eclipsed the prestige of all the hereditary student groups—far left, left of center, center, right of center, or far right. It would be fanciful to suggest that the leaders and members of SDS had probed deep into the Vietnam War and emerged with a comprehensive theory that enabled them accurately to foretell future developments. Their call for a demonstration in favor of peace stemmed from a kind of reflex pacifism. The Vietnam War, which had not as yet engaged American combat forces in direct action against the Viet Cong and the North Vietnamese, was not by itself a burning concern to them.

By now, of course, the genesis and course of the American involvement in the Vietnamese conflict have become a story many people know by heart, and hindsight makes it easy for some to claim that they were among the children of light who saw at the outset where events would lead and raised warning voices based on an accurate calculus of consequences. The truth is something else. When SDS issued its call for a student protest against the Vietnam War, the fund of knowledge about Vietnam was then, in the language of Abraham Lincoln, "as thin as soup made from the shadow of a pigeon that had starved to death." SDS leaders had no secret information about Vietnam policy talks that had divided national security officials in the Johnson administration. Their main source of information was nothing more or less than an accumulation of newspaper clippings dating back to the early days of the Kennedy administration.

But in the days immediately after SDS had issued its call there were the Vietcong terror attacks on American marine bases, followed in turn by the decision of the Johnson administration to start bombing North Vietnam. These events, all coming before April 15, had two retroactive effects. They transformed SDS's call for an orthodox peace demonstration—like a demonstration in favor of virtue—into a specific intent to prevent the conversion of a guerrilla war among Asian peoples into an American war in Vietnam. They also endowed SDS leaders with the aura of prophets who, seeing the end of things from the beginning, deliberately set out to move against history in order to alter events before they actually occurred.

Meanwhile, the bombing of North Vietnam by American planes spurred support for the SDS-organized student march in Washington on April 15. There were two other sharp spurs. First, in March, SDS at the University of Michigan, on the suggestion of Professor Arnold Kaufman and others, organized the first teach-in ever held on an American campus devoted to the subject of Vietnam. Here was a new political-intellectual entertainment invention in academic life, and students on 50 other American campuses (and others in Canada and abroad) quickly organized Vietnam teach-ins of their own. Also in March, the teach-in movement and the build-up of support for the April demonstration in Washington were both spurred by the injection of U. S. forces into the dim "war of the presidential succession" in the Dominican Republic.

On April 15, an estimated 20,000 students from across the country demonstrated in front of the White House in the first nationally visible protest against U. S. policy in Vietnam. SDS, as an organization, had previously received campus news coverage where it had been the sponsor of teach-ins. Now, however, the organization and its leaders were catapulted into national prominence by the extensive coverage they received from the communications media on the site of the Washington protest. By June 1965, when the academic year came to an end—coincidently with the time when 23,000 U. S. advisers in South Vietnam were committed to a combat role and the first wave of U. S. army reinforcements landed in South Vietnam—SDS was acknowledged as the nationally organized expression of the student antiwar movement.

In the near future, its membership would double, then double again until it attained its maximum strength of 6,200 national dues paying members.* At its maximum strength, its chapters never represented more than 10 percent of all campuses in the United States, but wherever an SDS chapter did take root, its initiatives would tend to dwarf those of other student groups. In the new code word of American student speech, a local SDS chapter was generally referred to as "relevant," while other student groups, by comparison, appeared otherwise. The organizations of the hereditary left, for example, seemed to be congealed in ideological inertia. The centrist clubs of Young Democrats and Young Republicans seemed but a collection of fledgling ward-heelers, careerists indifferent to issues, mouthing the platitudes and beatitudes of their parties. Student groups of the far right, like those that had come into prominence in connection with Goldwater's 1964 campaign, seemed preposterous.

From today's perspective, it is possible to see in the SDS call for the Washington March of April 15, 1965, the small seed that would eventually burgeon into many impressions, illusions, and hard set attitudes. Because students staged the first national protest against the Vietnam War, it would come to be thought that all students and only students opposed the war. Because students were presumed to be congenitally radical, it would come to be thought that only the radicals and no other group of students ever provided effective leadership in the antiwar movement. Because some radical students saw themselves in that very light, they would elevate themselves into an elite, privileged by the higher law of their own perfection to be bitterly scornful of liberals, to test all elected officials by the standards of moral absolutism and find them wanting, and to be

* The number of nondues paying students who participated in SDS activities has never been determined. *Life* magazine, in its issue of October 18, 1968, estimated that 35,000 students regularly participated in the activities which the SDS sponsored. Richard E. Peterson places the estimate at a higher level in his study, *The Scope of Organized Student Protest in 1967–68.* (Princeton: Educational Testing Service, 1968).

contemptuous of the inarticulate laboring man who did not take time off to join in demonstrations. Yet while all this was evolving—along with an increase in the number and size of student protests against the Vietnam War—the emergence of two other significant sources of opposition to the Vietnam War was seldom noted. One was composed of people who never went to college and in many cases never completed high school. The other was composed of a miscellaneous assortment of middle-aged or older people.

The round of teach-ins prior to June 1965, when colleges recessed for summer vacation, was an expression of hesitation between respectful inquiry and protest. The campus setting emphasized that objections to the war were still mostly on the intellectual plane. It was appropriate to a period when little was known about the origins of the conflict in Vietnam or about the nation's involvement in it. The most eminent professors were not fully informed about the matter, but those who had a driving interest in reconstructing and analyzing the story of Vietnam were generally to be found at the elite universities. It was on their campuses that previously ignored facts were marshalled, given a hearing, and forged into thorny questions to be hurled at administration spokesmen. The more the latter brushed the questions to one side, equivocated, failed to appear as scheduled on a campus, or escalated their own justifications for the American involvement in Vietnam, the more they eroded the legitimacy of their own authority.

From a constitutional standpoint, there was no declaration of war by the Congress, nor even a declaration of national emergency by the president. In committing U. S. forces to a combat role in Vietnam, President Johnson based his action on the general powers of the president as Commander-in-Chief of the Armed Forces, on the Tonkin Resolution and on an interpretation of some of the provisions in the SEATO treaty. A formal declaration of war by Congress, or even a declaration of a national emergency by the president, might have rallied the sentiments of patriotism, unleashed impulses for an all-out war effort, and perhaps might have worked to keep the critics of the president at bay. Yet precisely because President Johnson did not have an all-out war in mind—and never activated all the forces that make for emergency powers—he was to become, paradoxically, vulnerable to the charges of Caesarism that some eventually leveled at him.

The charges, however, did not sound in the first round of teach-ins before the school recess in June 1965.[1] The main things said at that time were addressed to simple issues of the past. For example, when President Johnson described the aim of U. S. policy as "observance of the 1954 agreements which guaranteed the independence of South Vietnam," some professor at a teach-in might note that the Geneva accords did not mention South Vietnam, but rather set a timetable for the reunification of the northern and southern parts of the country. When administration spokesmen claimed that the object of U. S policy was to guarantee the right of self-determination in Vietnam, some participant in a teach-in might point out that Premier Diem had explicitly refused to follow the election procedures laid down in the Geneva Accords, and in a State Department 1961 Blue Book, he was praised for avoiding the well-laid trap of the proposed elections.

When the State Department White Paper of 1965 claimed that the North Vietnamese had for five years massively intervened militarily in South Vietnam, students at the teach-ins could hear in rebuttal that at least 98 percent of the Vietcong were indigenously South Vietnamese. When administration spokesmen insisted that the guerrillas in South Vietnam were all communists carrying out a master plan drawn up in Peking, students at the teach-ins could be reminded that the majority of Vietcong were nationalists, and that even communist North Vietnam, while dependent for supplies on communist China, took care to avoid the role of a Chinese communist puppet. When administration spokesmen cited the obligations of the United States to come to the aid of South Vietnam by the terms of the SEATO pact, it could be noted that the pact did not justify the unilateral measures taken in defense of South Vietnam. So it went, item by item, in point-counterpoint.

All students who picked up local, regional, or national broadcasts of the teach-ins were not instantly converted into doves. Vietnam, for a while, remained an abstraction to most students. Especially in the early period when the burden of the U. S. combat role in Vietnam was carried in the main by professional soldiers, most students did not directly associate their own lives with the course the far-off conflict was taking. Dovish sentiment grew only slowly among students and—contrary to popular belief—did not become a majority sentiment among students nationally until very late in the history of the conflict. In fact, a broad strain of student antiwar sentiment had its roots in a hawkish instead of dovish outlook; hawkish students who spoke of the Vietnamese war as a mistake disapproved of the government's policies only because they were not successful. A grand success, especially if quickly attained, would in their eyes have purified any means used. They would have welcomed more intense application of American armed might if it resulted in a swift and conclusive victory.

Perhaps the main effect of the first round of teach-ins prior to the summer of 1965 was that it gave some students a new set of eyes trained on their immediate environment. Previously, when the vanguard of white middle-class students who first entered American political life in the civil rights movement of the early 1960's wished to act out their conscience, they could do so only by moving outside the normal orbit of their lives and onto the unfamiliar battlefields of the Deep South or the northern ghettoes. The Vietnam conflict, by contrast, would eventually become visible to many students on their own turf—the campus.

In Congress at this time, despite uneasy private discussions among groups of representatives and senators, dissent was as ill formed and hesitant as it was elsewhere. In May 1965, when the chance arose to oppose Vietnam with a vote—the issue was a supplemental appropriation of $700 million, the first of a string of presidential requests for more money for the war—only seven representatives and three senators voted against it. Senators Eugene McCarthy and Robert Kennedy were among those who voted for it. President Johnson at the time said:

This is not a routine appropriation. For each member of Congress who supports this request is also voting to persist in our effort to halt communist aggression in South Vietnam. Each is saying that the Congress and the president stand united before the world in joint determination that the independence of South Vietnam shall be preserved and the communist attack shall not succeed.[2]

During the summer recess, students could read news reports that more units of the U. S. Army had been shipped to Vietnam. They could also note that fresh offers to negotiate were followed by fresh escalations in the level of violence, that fresh reports of Vietcong defeats were followed by fresh Vietcong attacks, by more bombing strikes by U. S. aircraft, by more civilian refugees, by more civilian dead, and by an expansion of Vietcong control over the countryside.

Meanwhile, some students who spent the summer working on community projects related to the "War against Poverty" became vocal in their disillusion with it. When the antipoverty program was launched in 1964, Washington officials had explained that the program marked the start of significant social, political and economic reforms; that they would facilitate the political organization of deprived groups; that the "maximum feasible participation by the poor" in the design and management of the new program would help emancipate the poor from their bondage to political machines and bureaucrats. But, it soon appeared to some students that local political machines and other established agencies used federal funds allocated to

71

the poverty programs to preserve and extend existing power relationships. The poor had no real say in the design and management of the new programs; public bureaucracies remained as callous as ever toward the poor; and the local police were used to attack legitimate protest activities by indigenous organizations of the poor. As if all this were not bad enough, while programs launched to the sound of a coronation fanfare were under-financed from the start, their funds were now being held back or cut back further for diversion into the war in Vietnam.

These student criticisms seemed to be starkly confirmed when the Watts section of Los Angeles erupted in a riot extending for 144 hours in early August 1965.[3] The staggering statistics of the Watts riot exceeded all previous ones in the story they told of death, destruction, looting, and arrests. The psychic impact and political consequences of Watts were on an equally large scale. Watts—and later Newark—riveted attention on the presence of racism outside the South. It deprived most established civil rights leaders—black or white—of a vocabulary for expressing the deepest problems of northern ghettoes and raised questions whether those leaders could or would speak to the kind of issues raised by the riots. The slogan "Black Power," articulated by Stokely Carmichael of SNCC, would signal the full turn in the direction of black militancy away from the integrationist and assimilationist spirit of the pre-1965 civil rights movement toward a stress on black self-sufficiency and liberation.

The civil rights movement was largely middle-class and interracial; the liberation movement rejected white leadership and tried to fuse middle- and lower-class blacks into a single racial whole.[4] The civil rights movement was directed against the explicit and customary Jim Crow forms of racism; the liberation movement focused on the deeper and more intractable sources of racism in the structure of American institutions. The civil rights movement was guided by the concepts of nonviolence and passive resistance; the liberation movement stressed self-defense and freedom by any means necessary even if this meant toppling the whole system of laws and values of society. Finally, while the student component of the civil rights movement was largely drawn from among blacks who were in college or had gone to college, the liberation movement reached down to embrace high school youth and dropouts. When some of these in due course went on to college under a sudden proliferation of scholarships offered to them, they brought their militancy with them.

The fires of Watts were still burning when some black militant leaders began to point to a painful contradiction between the growing U. S. governmental commitment to protect the Vietnamese from the Vietcong and its failure to guarantee the freedom of oppressed citizens within America's own borders. Immediately after the Watts riots, some local blacks formed a community action patrol to monitor police conduct during arrests. In Oakland, other blacks carried the process a step further. They instituted armed patrols organized on an *ad hoc* basis and oriented to the single issue of police control. The Black Panther Party for Self Defense came into being in this way. Though its title would be contracted to the Black Panther Party, the idea of self-defense nonetheless remained basic. Three leaders of the Black Panthers—Huey Newton, Eldridge Cleaver, and Bobby Seale—were to become folk heroes who captured the imagination of a number of white radical student activists.

II

At the start of the academic year 1965–1966, a new round of teach-ins—more of them at more institutions than during the first round—brought students abreast of events in Vietnam, and connected them with "Watts." A Berkeley Vietnam Day Com-

73

mittee formed in the fall of 1965 set the pattern for a new wave of campus antiwar demonstrations. In some places, local demonstrations were organized by *ad hoc* student committees to end the war in Vietnam. But where an SDS chapter existed, its members not only tended to be the prime movers behind the antiwar protest, but set constraining boundaries for the protest that were generally accepted by other students. As a result, expressions of opposition to the Vietnam War in the fall of 1965 conformed to the legal norms for dissent. Instances where draft cards were burned or where some Berkeley students tried to stop troop trains were exceptions to the rule.

Public expressions of antiwar sentiment ceased to be a student monopoly after November 27, 1965, when 20,000 people —some from as far away as the state of Washington—met in the nation's capital to take part in what was called a March on Washington for Peace in Vietnam. Although the publicity was focused on the students, the event drew its tone not from students, but from an advance guard of the kind of people who would ultimately rally around Senator McCarthy and be the mainstay of his bid for the presidency. As Richard L. Stout has written,[5] the advance guard was comprised of people who were educated beyond the conventional B. A. degree, of the middle- or upper-middle class, neatly attired, subdued in manner, flanked by monitors to deal with disrupters and to make sure that only authorized signs were carried. Orderliness was their way of life. At the end of an afternoon of speeches at the foot of the Washington Monument, the protestors dutifully deposited their signs in specially fenced-off enclosures prearranged to prevent unnecessary littering.

Nationally known sponsors of the demonstration included authors Saul Bellow, John Hersey, and Michael Harrington; playwrights William Gibson and Arthur Miller; James Farmer, then national director of CORE; John Lewis, then of SNCC; Dr. Benjamin Spock, Erich Fromm, Norman Thomas, Bayard Rustin; actors Robert Ryan, Tony Randall and Ossie Davis; and cartoonist Jules Feiffer. The sponsors also included the leaders of a number of peace groups whose origin predated the movement against the war in Vietnam. Among others, there was Mrs. Dagmar Wilson of Women Strike for Peace, Dr. Bernard Feld of the Council for a Livable World, Dr. Dorothy Hutchinson of the Women's International League for Peace and Freedom, Edward P. Gottlieb of the War Resisters League, Stewart Meacham of the American Friends Service Committee and Dana McClain Greeley of the Unitarian-Universalist Association.

With notable exceptions, few of these sponsors had previously been active in radical politics. They were mainly a product of American liberalism. This strong liberal vein was equally true of people who, behind the scenes, carried the main burden of organizing the march. Three of these in particular were to play a major role in the McCarthy campaign—Sanford Gottlieb of SANE, the coordinator of the march; Curtis Gans, a former president of the National Student Association who subsequently joined the staff of the Americans for Democratic Action; and Jack Gore, an economics professor at the University of Colorado who was active in SANE and the teach-in movement. Personal contacts growing out of the march were later to be useful in the formation of what McCarthy would call the "government in exile." The march, however, had a more immediate political meaning that was generally overlooked at the time and would continue to be overlooked while press attention was centered on the rise of radical student activism. The meaning of the march was that moderates and liberals off or on the campuses were moving in nationally to take over the still small antiwar movement.

At the end of December 1965, when American troop strength in Vietnam stood at around 170,000, agitation against the war seemed to have had some effect on President Johnson's management of the conflict. On Christmas Eve, he called for a 30-hour bombing pause, and then extended the pause into January; concurrently, U. S. envoys were sent to several countries in a widespread diplomatic effort to open the door to peace talks. In mid-January of 1965, when it appeared that the peace offensive was failing and that the bombing would be resumed, 77 members of the House of Representatives sent President Johnson a letter urging him to continue the peace effort despite its lack of results to date. In a matching move on the Senate side of the Congress, 15 Democratic senators, led by Indiana's Vance Hartke, signed a letter urging the president to continue the bombing halt.

Senator McCarthy's name was on that letter. Robert Kennedy, while tempted, declined to sign it. As attorney general he had shared in the responsibility for Vietnam policy and had once declared, "We are going to win and we are going to stay [in Vietnam] until we win." He had come to have some doubts about the war, but he still shied away from an open breach with President Johnson and was not markedly unsympathetic with overall policy. Besides, he viewed much of the peace movement with a disdain like that of J. Edgar Hoover who described the small, but highly vocal anti-Vietnam demonstrators as being for the most part, "halfway citizens who are neither morally, mentally nor emotionally mature." [6]

When President Johnson at the end of January disclosed that the bombing of North Vietnam had been resumed, further escalation of the war seemed inevitable, and the immediate result was a buzz of talk in the Senate. On February 1, after a strategy meeting of Senate doves, Senator J. William Fulbright, as chairman of the Senate Foreign Relations Committee, disclosed that the committee would hold televised hearings on the subject of Vietnam. Fulbright and other committee members were not hostile to President Johnson personally, nor to the broad principle of executive leadership in national security matters. But they sensed that the United States was backing into a major conflict without being fully aware of all its implications. If the hearings generated an outpouring of public sentiment against the administration's policy in Vietnam, President Johnson might refrain from further steps which the committee members feared would lead to a direct confrontation with Red China, World War III, or nuclear holocaust.

Kennedy was not a member of the Foreign Relations Committee. But on February 9, a proposal he publicly voiced extended a little noticed proposal that McCarthy had made three weeks previously, saying that in advance of negotiations, the Vietcong should be guaranteed a role in a coalition government. The hawks denounced his statement as a sell-out; some doves saw in it something short of a U. S. pull-out; when liberal friends urged Kennedy to ally himself with Fulbright and move to the front of Senate Vietnam dissent, he remarked, "I'm not their Wayne Morse." [7] Yet he was increasingly viewed in antiwar circles as the authentic voice of those to whom he had once derisively referred to as "the people with the picket signs and beards."

In the televised hearings of the Senate Foreign Relations Committee, for the first time, a national audience saw elected officials in a legislative context expressing doubts and airing alternatives to current American policy in Vietnam. The hearings also made visible a group of Senate Democrats, joined by a smaller group of Senate Republicans, who had begun to function as a loyal opposition. The hearings, however, did not generate any tidal wave of antiwar public sentiment. Least of all did they stop the escalation of the American military involvement in South Vietnam. The bombing and ground fighting intensified. More and more troops were shipped from the United States to Vietnam. By the end of 1966, U. S. troop strength in Vietnam was 389,000, or roughly twice what it was at the end of 1965.

Yet the hearings had a special impact on some students who were engaged in anti-Vietnam War protests. Members of any subcultural group whose daily contacts are mainly confined to people like themselves and who tend to meet their own ideological outlook on all sides, can easily conclude that they form a majority. Such was the case with some antiwar students, especially after the views they expressed in their protest demonstrations were echoed by eminent senators on the Foreign Relations Committee. Precisely on this count, when they also saw that successive escalations of the war continued nonetheless, they began to insist that President Johnson was "defying the will of the majority." In their view, something was profoundly wrong not only with the president personally, but with the structure of government that permitted a president to define "the national interest" as he pleased, "unilaterally" to plunge America into a war in support of that definition, and to persist in widening that war in defiance of "the majority will." Student adherents to this view would presently mount an assault on the person of Lyndon B. Johnson, and on a constitutional order which allowed a president, as they saw it, to usurp personal power. A version of this antipresidential attitude would eventually emerge in the antipolitics approach to electoral politics that characterized part of Senator McCarthy's support in his bid for the presidency. It would have a special appeal to young people.

NOTES

1. *New Left Notes* (1965–1967).

2. Richard T. Stout, *People* (New York: Harper and Row, 1969), pp. 46–47.

3. Shalom Endleman, ed., *Violence in the Streets* (Chicago: Quadrangle, 1968), pp. 319–357.

4. Jerome Skolnick, A Staff Report to the National Commission on the Causes and Prevention of Violence, *The Politics of Protest. Violent Aspects of Protest and Confrontation* (Washington, D. C.: U.S. Government Printing Office), p. 100.

5. Stout, *People*, p. 43.

6. Stout, *People*, p. 45.

7. Stout, *People*, p. 45.

5

The Politics
of Confrontation

I

To meet the growing manpower needs of the armed forces in Vietnam, General Lewis Hershey, the head of Selective Service, had an announcement to make in the spring of 1966. Some students, said he, would have to be drafted, and student deferments would be terminated for those whose class standings were poor or who failed to reach a certain level of performance on a soon-to-be-administered Selective Service Qualification Test.

Campus reactions were immediate and sharp. Professors and students alike—whether prowar or antiwar—protested the use of grades for Selective Service purposes. In the case of professors, they could foresee that every examination would be another time of torment for them. If they gave a student a low mark because he deserved nothing better academically, they might be sending him on his way to war. If they gave him an unearned high mark simply to spare him from the war, they were corrupting the standards of academic excellence they professed to live by. As for students, they could foresee that every examination would be another time when they would be competing with their classmates in order to avoid the draft. Faculty members and students resented the cooperation of university administrators in supplying class standings and facilities for the administration of the Selective Service Qualification Test, and demands were at once heard that universities withhold such cooperation.

At the University of Chicago, 500 students led by SDS, staged an antiranking sit-in in the administration building and held control for three and one-half days.[1] This was the first time students anywhere had succeeded in closing a university administration building, and the first time SDS had undertaken on the "Berkeley" model a direct confrontation with a university administration. But the University of Chicago was not "Berkeley." Many things about it—the composition of its board of trustees, the nature of its chief administrative officers, the legislative organization, and unity of its faculty—would make it one of the few elite universities in the nation that was to be spared scarring episodes of violence in the 1960's. At the time of the SDS-led antiranking sit-in the university deliberately avoided a direct confrontation with SDS, and the latter eventually abandoned the building they had seized. No punitive measures were taken against the students involved, but the faculty senate voted to support punitive action if any future "disruptive protests" threatened the academic integrity of the university as an institution of higher learning. The sit-in had no immediate effect on university policy with respect to the draft, although later the faculty senate voted to end the transmission of "male class ranks" to draft boards. This demonstration sparked a nation-wide debate on the draft, led some schools to withhold class rank information from the draft boards, and helped popularize a refusal to cooperate with the draft as a means of resisting the war.

II

Among the watershed events in the history of white radical student activities in the 1960's, the SDS convention of June 1966, is of critical importance. Before coming to the reasons, one point that is often overlooked in assessments of student political trends must be underlined. It is that an on-campus generation of student leaders generally lasts no more than two or three years—corresponding roughly to the period between a student's sophomore year and the time when he ordinarily graduates. In the last half of the 1960's, this general rule was altered. The Vietnam War stimulated more students to protract their period of studenthood by going on to graduate or professional schools and, as a result, on-campus student leadership was often retained by graduate students, some in their late 20's, while their rank and file followers were undergraduates between the ages of 18 and 20.

Moreover, there were cases where political activists retained a student status of some kind merely to provide the necessary cover for the pursuit of their real interest—the political organization, mobilization and leadership of students. Sam Brown, a former head of the National Students Association, was to be, successively, an organizer of the Vietnam Summer where students rang doorbells to convey an anti-Vietnam message, the head or "Chief Kid" of the student sector of the McCarthy bid for the presidency, and the organizer and head of the Moratorium movement to end the war in Vietnam. Yet throughout the four years covered by these time-consuming and demanding projects, he carefully maintained his status as "a student" in Harvard's Divinity School where he ostensibly concentrated on the subject of ethics. It was as effective a cover as any concocted for CIA agents.

By the time of the SDS convention in June 1966, most of the original founders of the organization were no longer in college and made no pretense of being students. Paul Booth, for example, an original founder who had served as national secretary of SDS, had gone to work for the Meat Packers Union where he was engaged in workers' education projects. Tom Hayden, also an original founder and a "traveler" who stimulated the formation of campus chapters of SDS, had also concluded his formal education. He would continue to be identified with SDS, yet his theatre for action—and his extraordinary influence—would extend into realms covering the broad front of dissent and protest in the last-half of the 1960's.

Beginning with the June 1966 convention, the operational leaders of SDS nationally were men like Greg Calvert, Carl Davidson and Carl Oglesby. These men had moved far beyond the founding ideals of Hayden and the *Port Huron Statement*. They were far more radical in their analysis of American institutions and had no faith in the liberal tradition. They felt that working within the system could never change the basic antihumanist nature of corporate liberalism. Oglesby, then still a student but later a poet and political theorist, described the American corporate system as an "awesome organism . . . with about five percent of the world's people consum(ing) about half the world's goods, tak(ing) a richness that is in good part not our own and put(ting) it in our pockets, our garages, our split-levels, our bellies and our future." [2] The leaders of SDS in 1966 saw the need for a radical humanist movement and wanted to set about building it. The rank-and-file on-campus members were students who had joined SDS after the start of its anti-Vietnam program in December 1964. They were without ties to the original founders and did not view SDS as an organization engaged in antiwar work or in work on general political programs without special reference to the campus. In their view, the greatest promise of SDS lay in reaching uncom-

83

mitted students on issues which concerned them as students—
issues like those which emerged in the Berkeley Free Speech
Movement, in the antirank protests, in promoting the anti-Vietnam "We Won't Go" statements and in the beginnings of direct
resistance to the draft.

Their position was reinforced by an event that occurred in
April 1966—three months before the SDS convention. At that
time, Stokely Carmichael of SNCC completed the transformation of his organization away from reform and toward "revolution," first by articulating his militant interpretations of Black
Power and, second, by expounding the connection between racism and war. SDS itself, in its stand on the Vietnam conflict,
had undergone successive transformations of its own since December 1964. It had gone from propeace to antiwar, from antiwar to pro-Vietcong, from pro-Vietcong to anti-imperialism,
and from there to pro-Third World revolution. It would presently move from anticapitalism to prosocialism.[3] Yet the enunciation of the doctrine of Black Power meant that white student
radicals were irrevocably excluded from the black civil rights
movement. They could no longer find their constituencies for
radical action by going outside themselves into the black communities of the South. They must build their own radical movement in their own circumstances.

The delegates to the SDS convention of June 1966 included
a number of white students who had gone south in 1964 to aid
in the building of the Mississippi Freedom Democratic Party.
They had drifted into administrative roles in the headquarter
offices of SNCC because, as Staughton Lynd once put it, they
"were obviously better able to write press releases and answer
the telephone than to approach frightened black people in remote rural communities." [4] The objective result, however, was
that black SNCC field secretaries returning to their headquarters after beatings and imprisonments found more white than
black faces there. When the philosophy of black control of
black organizations was announced, the white students at the

SDS convention who had been in Mississippi during the summer of 1964, although pained by Carmichael's announcement, recognized from personal experience the force of the logic behind the doctrine of Black Power. They took the lead in winning from the SDS convention a formal endorsement of that doctrine. As they argued, they must not manipulate the lives of others who ran risks which they personally did not share; instead, they must put behind them the role of missionary to the oppression of others—the role of auxiliary to a radicalism whose center of gravity was in the lives of other people.

On the other hand, these same members of SDS were in quest of a new cause. They were in need of something to do which would have the same spirit, would ask as much of them, and would challenge "the system" as fundamentally as had the black voter registration drive in Mississippi in 1964.

These white student veterans of the Mississippi experience would be foremost among the students who helped prepare the ground for the "classical period" of the draft resistance movement. In the summer months of 1966 following the SDS convention, they took part in a series of small meetings held in places like Yale and Cornell, where they faced up to the fact that the kind of opposition to the draft which they contemplated would be considered illegal and would invite a punishment of up to five years in prison. They not only accepted that risk, but formulated the first steps for public and collective noncooperation with Selective Service by a resistance that would be radical, outside the law, unpleasant, and sustained.

The "classical period" itself began almost simultaneously on the Atlantic and Pacific coasts in the month of April 1967 when about 150 young men burned their draft cards in New York's Central Park. At about the same time in the San Francisco Bay area, David Harris, Dennis Sweeney, Lenny Heller and Steve Hamilton named themselves "The Resistance," and in its name called for a mass return of draft cards on October 16. There followed a series of dramatic acts of illegal resistance

85

to the draft where the violators of the law remained on the site of their violation and without resistance submitted to arrest. From there they were turned over to the machinery of criminal justice which brought them to trial, conviction, findings of guilty and a prison sentence. The "classical period" ended a year later, when in April 1968, President Johnson announced a partial bombing halt in Vietnam and withdrew from the presidential campaign, while a third day of draft card returns brought the number of noncooperation to approximately 2,500. Within that same week, Martin Luther King was assassinated.

To return to the chronological sequence. When the enunciation of the doctrine of Black Power forced the new leadership and members of SDS at their convention to consider how they could build a radical movement of their own based on their own circumstances, the action program they formulated was first called student syndicalism, a term borrowed from the student movement in Western Europe with its tradition of organizing students along trade unionist lines. But when it was observed that the student was not really a worker in an industrial sense, since his condition of studenthood was only a transient one, the action program was renamed student power—a term which was first sounded in Göttingen University in 1920 and later was revived by the Nazi student movement. In the SDS usage, however, student power meant the organization of student unions or parties which would work for reforms in university structures and would take the lead in arranging the confrontations that could bring about the reforms. A theoretical underpinning for the thrust of student power was needed, and the one devised and popularized on what Carl Oglesby called an experimental basis was largely the work of Greg Calvert and Carl Davidson. Briefly stated, their theory of student power made the following points: [5]

All advanced industrial societies have an imperative need for large numbers of highly trained professional and technical cadres; indus-

The Politics of Confrontation

try, government, communications, and education are rapidly expanding the demand for intellectually skilled manpower; and the swift rate of technical and scientific advance in the last two decades has created for the first time the beginnings of mass intellectual labor. Higher education is the servant of this process. It is meant to train students to be alert and intelligent within their narrowly defined discipline, and yet be numbed and inert outside it. Students must not apply the intelligence they are being urged to develop, either to the institutions where they are studying or to the society that produces them.

Higher education, realistically viewed, is the means by which monopoly capitalism produces the new social category of an intelligentsia without ideas. Students are its trainees. They are massed together in increasingly large and bureaucratized institutions, where they often experience with unprecedented intensity the contradictory demands made upon them by capitalist society. They are exhorted to think for themselves, yet their colleges are authoritarian complexes run by a small clique of professors, bureaucrats and lay governors. The official liberal ideology goes on claiming that the student should acquire knowledge for its own sake, while the relentless pressures of examinations remind the student that grades are what count. Examinations will label him with a quantified assessment of his success in absorbing the accepted syllabus of his subject. The student has virtually no control over this process. Courses, rules and results are determined by others.

To break out of this trap students must demand democratic control over the content of education—over the people who teach, over course patterns, reading lists, syllabi, and methods of assessment. They must desanctify the authoritarian institutions of higher education, strip them of their legitimizing authority, and have them reveal themselves for what they are—raw coercive power. People will not move against institutions of power until their legitimizing authority has been stripped away. Confrontations should be staged in ways that are likely to provoke over-reactions from the university authorities, with a consequent increase in the radical consciousness of students who had previously been apolitical.

In line with this theory, SDS sent out teams of traveling campus organizers to assist in giving local expression to the meaning of student power. The effects became visible when

87

school resumed in the fall of 1966. On some campuses, SDS leaders running on platforms advocating student power were elected as student body presidents or, perhaps more importantly, as the editors of local campus newspapers. Across the country, there were demonstrations in support of demands for the liberalization of rules affecting dormitories, grading systems and the rights of free speech. These demands had sounded before on many campuses, but the intervention of SDS appeared to have enhanced the skill and energy with which the demands were pressed on university authorities.

The concept of student power was congruous with SDS's original orientation toward participatory democracy. Yet a program addressed to students as students could not by itself come to grips with the continued escalation of the Vietnam War and the intensified black rebellion in the cities. Some members of SDS came to feel that it was futile to try to change the universities until there was a basic change in society as a whole. Other members argued that the university was in fact a microcosm of society, and that if students mounted a frontal assault on the structure of their respective universities, they could begin to change society. The struggle between these two views within SDS was still unresolved when in November 1966, Berkeley activists tried to set up an antidraft literature table next to a Navy recruiting table in the Student Union. The administration ordered the removal of the student table, claiming that as a state university campus, Berkeley had to offer government agencies special privileges. When the activists refused to comply with the order, the police were called in to eject them. They arrested first one student and then four nonstudents from the sit-in that was formed in protest. The arrests dramatized the fact, as Michael Rossman expressed it, that "students do not control the Student Union—which students have paid for and supposedly run." [6] By midnight, 3,000 students voted the school out on a protest strike which brought studies to a virtual standstill.

The Politics of Confrontation

The episode at Berkeley was followed by one in January 1967, at Brown University, where SDS members organized the first protest against the on-campus presence of job recruiters from the napalm-manufacturing Dow Chemical Company. The example of Brown was picked up on other campuses and in the ensuing months scores of increasingly militant demonstrations and sit-ins were staged, protesting the presence on campus of recruiters for the armed forces, the CIA and Dow Chemical— as well as university involvement with the R. O. T. C. and war-related research.

SDS, after several years of oscillating between general political issues, and alternatively, student power and university reform, now found an issue—the military connection of universities—that could bridge the distance between students concerned primarily with general politics and those concerned with campus matters.

Hence, from the spring of 1967 on through 1968, the central purpose of SDS became organization for on-campus confrontations over a university's involvement with military agencies. In the reasoning of SDS leaders, the confrontations were meant to have a disruptive effect on the military machine by impairing the ease of its relations with the university. They were also meant to affect uncommitted students by bringing home to them what general protests against the war did not—namely, that the war was a student concern, since university-military connections were undertaken without consulting students.

Some universities proved vulnerable to the new line of the SDS attack. University administrators could argue that the university was politically neutral—that as a community of scholars dedicated to objective teaching and research, it could not, as an institution, take a stand on political issues. Yet the university could scarcely maintain that it was not of service to some very specific social interests. Whether by choice or acquiescence, it was forced to involve itself in the life of ever wider segments of

89

the community, and in doing so, was much more fully in the service of some social interests than others. The impression that universities and some of the most eminent professors were involved in the Vietnam War effort was underlined by disclosures that faculty members at Michigan State University had worked with U. S. intelligence agencies in South Vietnam to bolster the Diem regime; that faculty members of other universities had been engaged in a Defense Department project known as "Camelot," designed to study and develop counterinsurgency tactics suited for Latin America; that the University of Pennsylvania was conducting an extensive research operation for the development of biological warfare; that the CIA sponsored assorted research projects under the cover of bona fide or paper organizations; that the CIA covertly subsidized various student, labor, religious and educational organizations in their overseas operations; and that some of the most prestigious universities like the Massachusetts Institute of Technology and the California Institute of Technology depended on the Defense Department for large portions of their budgets.

Many members of the academic community were deeply troubled by the effect this dependence had on the intellectual life of the universities and on scholarly enterprises in general. For student activists, that state of dependence provided further evidence of the untrustworthiness and bias of the universities, and provided ready targets for politically effective protest against university authorities. The more these authorities insisted on their own nonpartisanship, neutrality, and values of academia, the more they encountered students who seized on even the smallest detail in the routine of university life and enlarged it into a new indictment where the authorities were charged with being frauds, and their academic values judged bogus.

III

The commotions generated by radical student activists produced a bizarre piece of Epic Theatre—humorous, motley, audacious, ironic, full of actors and actions marked by a detached awareness of their own deeds. Theatrics were employed when an anti-Vietnam army of saints and sinners besieged the Pentagon on October 20, 1967. The besiegers had their small triumphs, but were finally routed by several thousand paratroopers, military police, and federal marshals. On the six o'clock news, the seizing of the Pentagon looked like a mindless spectacle. Nonetheless, the event ushered in the start of radical dramaturgy as an instrument of protest—a dramaturgy that was to be developed further by the media-conscious Abbie Hoffman and Jerry Rubin—leaders of a nonexistent organization they called Yippies.

The commotions weren't lessened by the intervention of such major political events as McCarthy's announcement at the end of 1967 that he would seek the 1968 Democratic presidential nomination; his "victory" in the New Hampshire primary; Kennedy's entry into the race for the nomination; or President Johnson's speech on March 31, 1968, which coupled a new bid for Vietnam peace negotiations with an announcement that he would not seek or accept renomination in 1968 as the Democratic presidential candidate.

The one immediate effect of President Johnson's announcement was a decline in the coherence of the resistance movement against the draft. High draft calls for college students in the summer of 1968 did not materialize. In the absence of dramatic single acts of escalation, the resistance lost its initial momentum and began to dissolve into irreconcilable splinter groups. On meeting with insurmountable opposition from other groups, some factions who advocated a multi-issue program and a long-run strategy for fundamental change, began to drift into SDS—which was itself about to break up in fierce factionalism. Concerns that were previously secondary to the war—drugs, diet, communes—became increasingly prominent among those who remained active in the resistance. As individuals began to put their energies into coffee houses, free schools, and other enterprises distinct from draft resistance work, the old resistance became even more fragmented.

Yet, although resistance to the draft abated, 1968 was the year when everything seemed most out of joint on the campuses. One of the worst episodes occurred at Columbia University in the spring.[7] The small campus chapter of SDS had long agitated for an end to university ties with the Pentagon-guided Institute for Defense Analysis (IDA). It also sought reversal of the university's decision to build a new gymnasium in adjacent Morningside Park. SDS argued that the park should be developed to benefit its surrounding community—Harlem. The chapter, however, made little progress through its leafletting, dorm talks, and small protests. The administration remained aloof, and the issues of the IDA and the gymnasium were not compelling to most students.

The situation changed after Mark Rudd, a bright radical, won the presidency of the Columbia SDS chapter. Episodes were staged over the days between March 27 and April 23, building up campus tensions and interest in attempts to confront President Grayson Kirk with a heavily-subscribed petition against the IDA. The tensions were compounded by black militant students who constantly challenged the commitments and seriousness of the white radical students who claimed to be their allies. Finally, tensions exploded when a cordon of Columbia fraternity men and athletes blocked Rudd's way as he tried to enter Low Library for an encounter with President Kirk. Rudd then led his group of around 200 supporters to the proposed site of the new gymnasium, where they tore down the fences protecting the property. Several policemen attempted arrests and were resisted. The group then doubled back toward Low Library, but finding a cordon of fraternity men and athletes guarding it, entered Hamilton Hall where they confronted a dean and discouraged him from leaving. The militant black students later that night chose to entrench themselves in Hamilton Hall and to eject the whites. The ejected white students, led by Rudd, entered Low Library where they occupied Kirk's offices, rifled files, made a shambles of the place, and prepared a number of statements arguing that, in its racist, reactionary policies, Columbia was a microcosm of society.

Columbia, at that time, had no faculty legislative body where debates about university policy could be staged and where a decision could be made representing the main weight of faculty opinion. In the absence of such a body, faculty members responded in a scatter-pattern. The university administration, after discrediting itself by its own manifest confusion, accepted the SDS's own definition of the university as a microcosm of society. It called in the police and imposed its authority on the campus by resorting to force. The effects on other students and on faculty members who had previously been unsympathetic with SDS's goal were described by Daniel Bell:

In all, about a hundred students were hurt by the police. But it was not the violence itself that was so horrible—despite the many pictures in the papers of bleeding students, not one required hospitalization. It was the capriciousness of that final action. The police simply ran wild. Those who tried to say they were innocent bystanders or faculty were given the same flailing treatment as the students. For most of the students, it was their first encounter with brutality and blood, and they responded in fear and anger. The next day, almost the entire campus responded to a call for a student strike. In a few hours, thanks to the New York City Police Department, a large part of the Columbia campus had become radicalized.[8]

In addition to Columbia, 145 campuses in 1968 experienced at least one protest incident involving violence, and an additional 379 institutions experienced a nonviolent but disruptive protest. The incidents went beyond the unfurling of Vietcong flags and the burning of draft cards and the American flag. They included episodes where students abused college presidents, locked up deans and held them as hostages, drove liberal professors off lecture platforms, rifled university files, wrecked computers, blocked a continuation of defense-connected research work, roughed up recruiters of personnel for jobs in corporations, burned down R. O. T. C. buildings, battled lines of police and National Guardsmen, and confronted school officials with non-negotiable demands—demands for a student-designed, revolution-oriented or Black-Power-oriented curriculum, and for student-hired revolutionary or Black-Power-minded professors.

As these episodes crowded against each other on the televised evening news, it seemed that academic life all over the nation was back to a Hobbesian state of nature, where there was no common power able to make laws and enforce peace. Even in places that had not been disrupted by physical violence, there appeared to be no agreement whatever—not between students and their professors, not between student-faculty coalitions and their administrations, and not between academic institutions and an intellectual tradition. What seemed to prevail instead was a war of all against all, for as Hobbes observed to be in a state of war it was not always necessary for men to exchange actual physical blows; it was to be in a state where a constant threat of combat extended over a tract of time, where every man indicated his disposition and readiness to fight, and where he could fight whenever he thought it would be advantageous to him.

In the same period, another image of American youth—on and off campus—was repeatedly featured by the televised evening news. It was the image of the American youth who, as the child of middle-class affluence, was committed to a sweeping cultural revolution against everything associated with his middle-class origins—its concern for appearances, its materialism, its sexual mores, its pious homilies and moral ambiguities, its drive for success, its science, technology, trade, industry, and administrative structures. Whether the cultural rebel was called a dropout, cop-out, hippie, or flower child, he was bent on retreating into a subcultural community that would be the antithesis of the one from which he seceded. His community was to be free of all coercive controlling organs. It would be based on natural love, shared possessions, handicraft work, mind-blowing psychedelic pleasures, ecstatic utterances and visions, appeals to humanity, and on music whose beat, twang, and blare would induce ineffable feelings of freedom and union as sovereign soul copulated with sovereign soul with no calculus of consequences.

These two pictures of American youth—one a campus revolutionary primed for violence, and the other a flower child destined to wilt from the consumption of drugs—gave currency to the macabre conclusion that the United States as a whole was moving inexorably toward an apocalyptic abyss, either by route of violent overturn, or by route of cultural decadence. Much of this picture was based on an illusion that was to persist beyond the 1968 presidential campaign or, rather, an illusion that was to be augmented by other illusions about the electoral role of youth in the respective campaigns of Senator Eugene McCarthy and Robert F. Kennedy for the 1968 presidential nomination.

NOTES

1. Vern Visick, "Rank Protest of 1966–1967," University of Chicago Divinity School, 1967, mimeographed.
2. Paul Jacobs and Saul Landau, *The New Radicals* (New York: Vintage, 1966), pp. 263–264.

3. Carl Oglesby, "Notes on a Decade Ready for the Dustbin," *Liberation* (August / September 1969).

4. Staughton Lynd, "The Movement: A New Beginning," *Liberation* (May 1969).

5. Carl Davidson, "A Student Syndicalist Movement," *New Left Notes* (September 9, 1967); Carl Davidson, "Toward Institutional Resistance," *New Left Notes* (November 13, 1967).

6. Michael Rossman, "Look, Ma: No Hope," *Commonwealth* (April 12, 1969).

7. Marvin Harris, "Big Bust on Morningside Heights," *The Nation* (June 1969); A. Barton, "The Columbia Crisis: Campus, Vietnam, and the Ghetto," Bureau of Applied Social Research, Columbia University, July 1968; Daniel Bell, "Columbia and the New Left," *The Public Interest* (Fall 1968).

8. Bell, "Columbia and the New Left," p. 95.

6
McCarthy
vs. Kennedy

I

In their campaigns for the 1968 Democratic presidential nomination, Senators McCarthy and Kennedy personalized the recurrent clash in the American political psyche—a clash between the impulses that repel Americans from power and those which attract them to it; a clash between the shame of power and its glory; between power gained by self-abnegation and power gained by a direct reaching for it; between a conviction that those who wield power abuse it and a conviction that nothing can be changed without first acquiring power. McCarthy appeared the embodiment of the first side of this dualism, Kennedy the second.

This general line of difference between the two men was the basis for particular differences in their respective bids for the Democratic presidential nomination. Yet, after Kennedy was assassinated and McCarthy's candidacy had run its course, post-campaign legends tended to amalgamate the two into the picture of a single race whose impressions passed in certain circles as self-evident truths. A number of students, for example, came to believe that people like themselves were responsible for the McCarthy and Kennedy candidacies, that students dominated the command decisions made in all campaign headquarters, that unaided students comprised the electioneering forces in the field, and that in both places—at headquarters and in the field—students had invented a new politics. They also came to believe that all participating students—whether at headquarters or in the field—dropped out of school for weeks and months on end to electioneer full time on behalf of McCarthy and Kennedy, and that in doing so they were solely motivated by their opposition to the Vietnam War.

To question the claims of these postelection legends is not to disparage the worth of what students actually did—particularly for McCarthy. In the critical New Hampshire primary alone, they were not only of vital strategic importance, but their work there on his behalf marked a new development in the evolution of youth participation in American electoral politics. Over the course of the nineteenth century, youth participation in electoral politics had steadily expanded. That expansion, continuing in the twentieth century, cast up its emblems in the persons of young people who appeared as a matter of routine on the staffs of incumbent presidents, of candidates for party presidential nominations, and of party nominees for the presidency. The novelty of the New Hampshire primary lay in the fact that for the first time in American history, students and other young people effectively mobilized themselves behind an insurgent candidate for presidential nomination from within a party, in direct opposition to the presidential incumbent of that party. This phenomenon itself, was striking. The postcampaign legends, however, exaggerated the role of students and other young people in the McCarthy candidacy. Their exaggerated claims, coupled paradoxically with the actual achievement of students in the context of the 1968 New Hampshire presidential primary, gave rise to some of the false analogies underlying the frontlash assumptions made in the spring of 1970 about the impending congressional election.

II

The McCarthy candidacy had its beginnings in the period between 1965 and the spring of 1967, when the anti-Vietnam marches and the sporadic efforts to elect peace candidates to Congress in 1966 resulted in a loose grass-roots communications network among antiwar people. With several exceptions, the key antiwar individuals, while drawing on student support, were not themselves students. They included ᴄANE's Sanford Gottlieb; Professors Arnold Kaufman of Ann Arbor and Jack Gore of Colorado (two veterans of the teach-in movement); Bella Abzug of the Women's Strike for Peace; David Hartsough, who directed the Washington staff of the Friends Committee on National Legislation; Paul Gorman, a young staff man for a number of liberal Democratic congressmen; Allard K. Lowenstein, the 38-year-old former President of the National Student Association; Curtis Gans, then 30; and Edward Schwartz, both former leaders of the National Student Association. Other key links in the network were represented by the leaders of new national committees of doctors, lawyers, businessmen, clergy, and laymen in opposition to Vietnam. Their numbers would grow significantly the next year, but in 1968 they were in search of a presidential candidate.

The dream candidate for most of these people was Robert Kennedy. Only the members of the "Stevenson crowd," (composed of the late Adlai E. Stevenson's political associates and financial backers) looked elsewhere. The Stevensonians—resenting the treatment Stevenson had received from the Kennedys and the New Frontiersmen—were as much anti-Kennedy as they were antiwar. They did not contemplate a future in which a candidate would directly challenge President Johnson for the nomination, but they did not want to be left with Kennedy as the only alternative if Johnson died in office, retired, or if a contest for the nomination should suddenly develop.

Against this background, McCarthy was invited to a quiet dinner of leading Stevensonians on March 22, 1967, in the Manhattan apartment of Thomas K. Finletter, a former Secretary of the Air Force in the Truman administration who had played a major role after the 1956 election in organizing the issue-oriented Advisory Council to the Democratic National Committee. The purpose of the dinner meeting, as originally conceived, was not related to the rising clamor over the Vietnam War. It was to provide an occasion where a number of prominent Stevensonians could try to persuade McCarthy to use his Senate platform to become better known nationally and a larger voice in the Democratic party, thereby putting himself in a better position to exploit any opening toward a presidential candidacy which might conceivably materialize. If McCarthy fell in with the plan, the Stevensonians, as they had already agreed among themselves, were ready to finance the costs of the added staff he would need.

Perhaps McCarthy had sensed what was in the wind. In any case, he took command of the table talk at the outset of the dinner by launching into a long analysis of President Johnson's handling of the Vietnam War. No matter what the Senate might do, he said, Johnson would not change the course he was on unless he were directly challenged for the 1968 Democratic presidential nomination. If no one else was ready to mount that challenge, McCarthy added abstractly, he just might do it himself. Some of the Stevensonians, on cue, now pressed the proposal for a McCarthy build-up, saying they had already sounded out a young but experienced professional who appeared qualified to head an expanded staff. McCarthy seemed receptive.

Before the meeting broke up, a call was put through to Richard Goodwin, who was at the top of his class at Tufts and Harvard Law, had successively been a law clerk to Justice Felix Frankfurter, served on the Commerce Committee and the Senate staff of John Kennedy, and worked as research director of the 1960 presidential campaign staff of Kennedy—all before he turned thirty. As a White House aide under Presidents Kennedy and Johnson, he, like other staff members, publicly defended Administration policies in Vietnam. His second thoughts about the matter were voiced only after he left the White House. Garry Wills describes Goodwin as "an especially important man to watch, since he has a discriminating feel for where the action is going to be, and a gift for focusing everyone's attention on it." [1] Goodwin confirmed his availability when McCarthy called.

Subsequent to the meeting in the Finletter apartment, McCarthy had some second thoughts of his own. He contacted several participants in the meeting and expressed the view that perhaps the time wasn't right to start the build-up. "Play it by ear," he reportedly said. "Live off the land, and let's see what happens." [2]

When President Johnson called General Westmoreland home from Vietnam in April 1967 to state the administration's case before Congress, McCarthy spoke out against the move, saying it was as "dangerous an escalation of language, methods and emotions" as would be an escalation of the war itself. He questioned the propriety of using "a field commander on active duty to make a case which is not only military but also political." In his strictures against the appearance of General Westmoreland before Congress he sounded a keynote theme for the months ahead. The theme was President Johnson's abuse of power and his misuse of the institutions of government.

During this period, there was more turmoil on the campuses and in ghettos, and there were more antiwar demonstrations the leaders of which became progressively more radical in their denunciation of the administration and American society generally. While these events held headlines, the elements of traditional protest in the form of a challenge at the polls were quietly beginning to take form.

First, in late April 1967, the issue-oriented "amateur" Democrats who comprised the California Democratic Council—which had been praising Kennedy—adopted a resolution calling for a special convention to determine whether to run a special slate of peace delegates in the 1968 California primary. Their intention was to challenge the Johnson administration's war policy, rather than challenge the president personally. But, with the formation of the Michigan Conference of Concerned Democrats, there materialized a challenge to both the person and the policies of the president.

Next, in June 1967, while the California and Michigan ideas were still in the air, a number of antiwar leaders met in Washington, D.C. with David Hartsough of the Friends Committee on National Legislation to decide on a course of action before the impending 1968 presidential election. Some persons proposed to form a slate of peace delegates to the Democratic National Convention—just as the California Democrats planned to do. This approach, in their view, was politically more realistic than was the proposal to start a Dump Johnson movement. The conventional wisdom held that it was virtually impossible for a political party to deny an incumbent president a renomination he wanted. Most of those present, however, agreed that Dump Johnson organizations, modeled generally after the Michigan Conference of Concerned Democrats, should be set up across the country. They argued that a dislike for Johnson personally could be as potent a force in a Dump Johnson movement as specifically focused antiwar sentiment. Allard Lowenstein, a participant in the meeting who argued in this fashion, offered to try to find a presidential candidate who would oppose Johnson.

While Lowenstein was engaged in his search, a loosely struc-

102

tured antiwar effort known as Vietnam Summer was undertaken by local citizens and college students in about 200 communities. As the project was launched, Dr. Benjamin Spock said: "We have in this country today a large number—millions —who are disenchanted with the Johnson administration because of the war. This group could well make the difference at the polls." [3] In three respects, the effort foreshadowed the McCarthy campaign. It introduced the slogan: "Everyone does his own thing." It introduced a house-to-house canvass by doorbell ringers with an anti-Vietnam message to convey. It provided the context in which Sam Brown, who would eventually become a leader in the McCarthy campaign structure, first gained a measure of public prominence. Brown saw in the Vietnam Summer a means "to translate demonstrations into a strong political force."

On August 17, while doorbell ringers were doing their work in connection with the Vietnam Summer project, McCarthy, in disgust, walked out on the testimony being presented by Undersecretary of State Nicholas Katzenbach before the Senate Foreign Relations Committee. Katzenbach had asserted that the speed of events in modern times gave the president the right to make war—if not to declare it—without consulting Congress, and that Congress was compelled to support administration foreign policy. "This," McCarthy was quoted in *The New York Times* as saying, "is the wildest testimony I ever heard. There is no limit to what he says the president can do. There is only one thing to do—take it to the country." But he himself was not yet ready to tap himself as the man who should take it to the country.

In the ranks of Americans for Democratic Action, meanwhile, some regular staff members including Curtis Gans wanted to reject the prospective 1968 candidacy of President Johnson. But the ADA Executive Board was not ready to go that far. It adopted a compromise proposal put forward by former Chairman Joseph Rauh—who had provided legal guidance to the Mississippi Freedom Democratic Party at the 1964 Democratic Convention—to push for a peace plan at the 1968 Convention and to back slates of peace delegates where that seemed appropriate. "If," said Rauh, "the effort can be made on the peace issue alone without any personal overtones of any sort, there are very real possibilities of success." [4] Events, though, were in the saddle. They moved in directions other than those of Rauh's compromise proposal.

On September 1, Curtis Gans joined Lowenstein in launching the official Dump Johnson effort under the Michigan-inspired name of the National Conference of Concerned Democrats. A cooperating student group, called the Alternative Candidate Task force for 1968, or ACT-68, was formed after a rousing appearance by Lowenstein at the 20th Annual Congress of the National Student Association. Its purpose was to begin the mobilization of students for the 1968 election.

The new student group never became the organizing force Lowenstein envisioned, but it did establish a loose network of contacts and Dump Johnson Chapters. ACT-68's leader, Sam Brown, was helped by other people whom he had come to know through the National Student Association. They included Stephen Cohen, a former Amherst student-body president who had gone on to the Harvard Law School; Cindy Samuels of Smith; Marge Sklencar, Mundelein College student president; David Hawk of Union Theological Seminary; Clint Deveaux, a one-time State University of New York at Buffalo student body president; and Sue Hester, formerly of Wheaton College. None of them had previously surfaced in any of the radical, SDS-type farragos; rather, they were antiwar student leaders who had come to the front on their respective campuses by the traditional route of student government. They would later have places on Senator McCarthy's staff.

Kennedy-in-'68 organizations had been sprouting around

the nation despite Kennedy's own insistence that he had no plans to run. Lowenstein, had kept Kennedy informed of plans of the antiwar movement and had spoken to him frequently about a potential Kennedy candidacy. But the Senator repeatedly foreclosed the possibility of his running against Johnson. As time passed, Lowenstein put it squarely to Kennedy: "I've got to let you know you're destroying everything by hovering. It keeps us from doing anything else." [5] Lowenstein went to others—General James M. Gavin, John Kenneth Galbraith, Representative Don Edwards of California, Senator Frank Church, Senator George McGovern, and Senator Lee Metcalf. All of them, for different reasons, either were unavailable or flatly refused. When Lowenstein first met McCarthy in September, McCarthy did not say no, but suggested that Kennedy would be the strongest candidate.

In the speeches McCarthy had been giving around the country in the immediately preceding months, he had advanced a proposal that the United States should disengage from an area in Vietnam as a test to "see what happens." This did not imply that the United States "should cut and run." It should merely ease its military efforts to see if the situation in Vietnam could be stabilized.

In answering criticisms of the Vietnam policy at his press conference on October 12, 1967, Secretary of State Dean Rusk warned that within the next decade or two there would be a "billion Chinese on the mainland, armed with nuclear weapons, with no certainty about what their attitude toward the rest of Asia will be." Four days later, in one of his rare full dress statements on the floor of the Senate, McCarthy criticized Rusk for obscuring the Vietnam debate. Vietnam, said McCarthy, "may well be a costly exercise in futility." He attacked Rusk for raising the "ancient fear of the Yellow Peril" in his mention of Chinese with nuclear weapons: "If this is the specter that is haunting Asia, it is difficult to see how we will rid Asia of it

105

even though we achieve an unpredictable and total victory in South Vietnam." In the course of the same speech McCarthy paid his sardonic respects to the earlier Katzenbach testimony, describing it as "nothing short, really, of a kind of prescription for a four-year, we hope benevolent, kind of dictatorship in foreign policy." Further, said McCarthy, there was the "erosion of institutions" for which Johnson was held responsible: "As majority leader, he used his power to destroy the Democratic National Committee . . . to turn the Senate into another House of Representatives . . . the Senate Foreign Affairs Committee into a sort of stock pen." There was also the revival of the Yellow Peril which brought McCarthy to the conclusion that the cause of peace would be better served if Dean Rusk would tender "a quiet resignation."

In Berkeley on October 26, 1967, McCarthy spoke of these things, but more importantly, for the first time publicly declared that the issue of Vietnam ought to be put to a political test within the Democratic party. "We have to be prepared," said he, "to send instructed delegates to the Democratic National Convention, if one has any power to influence these choices. We should be prepared to support favorite sons who may be committed to a position on Vietnam and on some issues that concern the country. And be prepared, I think also, where there are primaries, to support those men who may be willing to carry the flag against the incumbent president of the United States." In answer to the questions raised after his talk, he did not say who should challenge the incumbent president. He seemed to suggest Kennedy, but intimated that he might have to be the challenger himself. "I am not prepared to nominate anybody today," said McCarthy, "but I think we have to establish that this responsibility does exist." "Times arise in politics," he continued, "when an individual, like Bobby Kennedy has no right to calculate that things will be better for him personally if he waits until 1972. Everyone in high office in the Democratic party has to, at least theoretically, accept the possibility that there may be a call that he may have to answer."

Kennedy was certainly hearing the call. In a Louis Harris poll of that year, 71 percent of the American public agreed with the statement that Kennedy was courageous and unafraid to follow his convictions. But at a time when courage was important, he was torn by opposing advice he received from people close to him. His young staff aides—Adam Walinsky, Jeff Greenfield, and Peter Edelman—wanted him to run. So did the Kennedy women. But his brother Ted and the pros who had been vital to the successful candidacy of John F. Kennedy were opposed. They told him that he couldn't win, that he couldn't knock over an incumbent president from within his own party, that he would be ripe for 1972 and shouldn't "louse up his chances" by any premature moves that were doomed to fail.

On October 26—the same day that McCarthy addressed the students at Berkeley—Curtis Gans dropped in on a Democratic party workshop at Colby College in New London, New Hampshire. His visit, unrelated to any prospective McCarthy candidacy, was part of his effort to promote the Dump Johnson movement. At Colby, he spoke to David C. Hoeh, 30, who had worked in a number of New Hampshire campaigns and was currently at odds with Democratic Governor John Knight, a Johnson man. Gans also spoke to Hoeh's wife, Sandy, Second District Democratic chairman; Gerry Studds, 30, a master at Saint Paul's School; Dr. David Underwood III, Concord Democratic chairman; Vincent Dunn, state banking commissioner; and Charles Sheridan Jr., an attorney. Would they like to take part in an anti-Johnson effort? Hoeh and his wife answered with a straightforward yes. So did Gerry Studds. The others, with variable degrees of assent, indicated that they would at least consider the prospect of joining. Gans subsequently traveled the state talking to people Hoeh suggested, and in this way, the New Hampshire branch of the Dump Johnson movement was formed. It would soon be converted into what appeared to be the nucleus of the McCarthy organization in the state.

On November 2, McCarthy publicly confirmed that he might seek the Democratic presidential nomination. "You must take Vietnam to the people," he said. "When you say who's going to do it, I have to say that I don't know, but I might have to respond myself." This public intimation that he might run gave the spur to both the organization of his opposition and that of his supporters. In New Hampshire, the State Democratic Committee voted November 17 "to take all steps necessary to bring about the renomination and reelection of Lyndon Johnson." That same night, 13 people, headed by Hoeh and Studds, met in Bedford and formed the New Hampshire McCarthy for President Steering Committee.

By the end of November, some 30 states had the nucleus of a pro-McCarthy organization. Individual students—law students in particular—were involved in the effort, but in general, a typical nucleus was comprised of local ADA leaders, SANE members, former workers for Stevenson, persons who had spoken out against Johnson, and some lawyers and professors who were also Democratic county chairmen. McCarthy himself was under no illusions about the strength of his political position. He knew that despite the rise of sentiment in support of his candidacy, he could not win the nomination in a contest with President Johnson. He confined himself to the hope of being able to generate pressures that would result in a change of Johnson's policies. He was also aware of the possibility that if he did well in some of the primaries, Kennedy would enter the race. But he was not concerned, since he had already met with Kennedy and, as he later recalled, put the case to him as follows: "I told him I was considering entering the primaries. I didn't ask him what he was going to do. I just said, 'I'm not worried as to whether I'm a stalking horse for you,' meaning that if Bobby entered later on I would not say I've been tricked. I left it open to him. He didn't give me any encouragement or discouragement. He just accepted what I said." [6]

Kennedy's time to act decisively one way or another was at hand, but he continued to vacillate. He had previously affirmed his intention to support any bid Johnson might make for the nomination. He now stepped back from that endorsement and assumed a position of ambiguous neutrality. In successive remarks published in the press, he said that he thought a McCarthy candidacy would be a healthy development. Next he said that he expected the Democratic nominee to be Johnson—whom Kennedy was then leading in every major poll. Then in late November, he remarked cryptically: "I think I will remain out of the contest until the time of the nomination. Perhaps I'll have something further to say at that time." McCarthy, having waited for Kennedy or someone else to step forward as a challenger to Johnson, could wait no longer for whatever it was Kennedy might say later on.

At 10:07 A.M., November 30, 1967—eight months after his meeting with the Stevensonians in Finletter's New York apartment—McCarthy stood on the podium of the Senate Caucus Room to announce in a strangely worded way that he was seeking the presidency of the United States. "I intend," he began, "to enter the Democratic primaries in Wisconsin, Oregon, California and Nebraska. The decision with reference to Massachusetts and New Hampshire will be made within two weeks." He explained that he had talked to Democratic party leaders in 26 states and to candidates—especially Senate candidates—who faced reelection contests in 1968. His decision to challenge the president had been strengthened by recent announcements indicating that the administration seemed to have set no limits to the price it was willing to pay for a military victory in Vietnam.

The next day, McCarthy was in Chicago for a national meet-

ing of the Conference of Concerned Democrats—the Lowen-
stein-Gans organization. The meeting brought together some
450 people from 42 states—a heterogeneous mix of people that
proved to be an accurate representation of future McCarthy
supporters. They were neither youngsters nor peace freaks.
Rather, they were mature, responsible citizens like those who
had marched on Washington in November 1965. Other aspects
of the gathering anticipated added features of the McCarthy
candidacy. The delirious disorganization of his campaign was
foreshadowed by the fact that written pledges for contributions
of nearly $1 million that were made in Chicago never material-
ized. When McCarthy spoke to the Conference of Concerned
Democrats however, he made no play—verbal or otherwise—
to the pent-up emotions in the room.

It would become clear only in retrospect that McCarthy personally was almost incidental to the movement that bore his
name. He never established himself as the charismatic leader of
a cause, or the central figure of a cult, as did Adlai Stevenson,
Barry Goldwater, George Wallace or the Kennedys. The people
who rallied to his side had come to their views before he announced his candidacy, and his personal task, pursued in his
own personal way, was to give a common meaning to their
common voice.

III

Prior to McCarthy's announcement, John Safer, a former neigh-
bor in Washington, D.C., opened a small campaign office for
him in Washington's Colorado Building, hired a secretary, and
waited for things to happen. Safer, then in his early 40's, was a
Harvard Law School graduate and very successful real estate
developer in and around the Capitol. (As a man of diverse intellectual interests, he would soon emerge as a talented sculp-

tor.) He had begun to find money-making almost too easy to hold his full-time attention, and was increasingly drawn to the alternative of public service work. He assumed general charge of McCarthy's campaign financing, but fell deathly ill in mid-December, and didn't recuperate in time to rejoin the campaign.

On other fronts, latent sources of support for McCarthy were slowly being energized. Among these supporters were the politically experienced wives of some dove members of Congress—such as Senator Philip Hart of Michigan and Representative Henry Reuss of Wisconsin—whose husbands would not themselves openly break with Johnson to endorse McCarthy; and other women who were graduates of elite colleges and universities, and made extensive personalized political contacts with their fellow alumnae across the nation. The techniques they developed were later to be expanded to special groups such as teachers, lawyers, doctors, ministers, and accountants.

Other latent sources of support for McCarthy included hawks who wanted out of the Vietnam War by a quick victory, as well as doves who simply wanted out. They included Democrats and independents who were more antiadministration than antiwar. Some hawks, would later shift to Wallace, or would first shift from McCarthy to Kennedy, and then to Wallace. There was also a mix of Republicans—antiwar, antiadministration or anti-Nixon—who had no immediate vehicles for expression within their party after Governor George Romney of Michigan withdrew from both the New Hampshire primary and the Republican nominating contest. Still other sources of nonstudent support for McCarthy are alluded to in *We Were the Campaign,* by Ben Stavis, the best book extant focused on the feature of youth participation in the McCarthy candidacy. Stavis wrote:

We certainly were frustrated by the needs occasionally to blunt the issues of imperialism and racism to get votes. We guiltily worked with conservative businessmen, party hacks, party dissidents, Uncle

Toms, and former supporters of conservative Republican Barry Goldwater, to develop a broad base of support. To retain our own integrity and our respect for the voters and at the same time to get votes was a perpetual challenge.[7]

The best review of the McCarthy campaign as a whole, rather than just its youth feature, is Richard L. Stout's *People*. In his introduction, Stout—a *Newsweek* reporter who covered the McCarthy candidacy—put his finger on a reality of that candidacy by explaining an error that he and other reporters shared in covering the McCarthy campaign. He wrote:

It was known that a large volunteer army had risen around McCarthy, yet few of us reporters told of it in any depth. Most often we pictured the army as composed almost solely of college students and young people. This was only part of the truth. To try to correct this, I later went over the paths I had missed during the campaign.[8]

Tens of thousands of people across the nation participated in the McCarthy campaign at some point and in some fashion. Among these, some 800 people stood out as the principal volunteer McCarthy leaders on either the city, county, district, or state level. Stout's analysis of the replies he received to a questionnaire he sent to these leaders after the campaign—more than half of them replied—showed that 5.3 percent were between the ages of 15 and 20; 3.9 percent were between the ages of 21 and 25; and 14.8 percent were between the ages of 26 and 30. The main body of McCarthy leaders were evenly distributed among each of the five-year blocs of age groups between 31 and 50, for a total of 58 percent, with the balance composed of people who were 51 or over. In his analysis of their educational background, Stout found that 60.5 percent had two or more college degrees; 24.2 percent held a bachelor's degree, and 10.8 percent had attended college for an indeterminate period or were in college at the time of the McCarthy candidacy. Many of these were involved in some aspect of education, with law ranking second highest on the list of vocations.

These percentages certainly do not warrant the view that the McCarthy candidacy was carried forward by a "Children's Crusade." As for previous political involvement among its leaders, Stout concluded from his analysis that 38 percent had often participated in political activity, 29 percent had participated to only a slight extent, and 33 percent had never participated in political activity of any kind. More significantly, the fact that diverse motives—and not just an antiwar motive—induced the people to work as McCarthy volunteer leaders appears to be substantiated by a salient finding Stout made. It was that a shade over 50 percent of these leaders had never been members of any antiwar organization—not even of a moderate organization like SANE.

The financial heart of the support for the McCarthy candidacy, as analyzed by Stout, was based on the data provided by Herbert E. Alexander, director of the Citizen's Research Foundation of Princeton, New Jersey, which conducts a quadrennial study of presidential campaign financing. The data, in its own way, adds massive emphasis to the fact that the McCarthy candidacy was far from a "Children's Crusade." McCarthy had expected to spend about one million dollars. But his campaign eventually cost more than 11 million dollars—a sum far beyond the capacity of students and other young people to raise. It can readily be granted that students and other young people were among the exceptionally high number of individual contributors to the McCarthy campaign—250,000 in all—whose contributions ranged anywhere from one dollar to 25 dollars. Yet a dozen individuals alone contributed a total of more than $2 million, and the same group of individuals raised even more than they gave.

Aside from the office expenses John Safer initially absorbed prior to the official announcement of the McCarthy candidacy

—or similar expenses subsequently absorbed by June Oppen Degnan, a wealthy Californian and a rabidly anti-Johnson member of the ADA executive board—the roll of major contributors was headed by Howard Stein, the 41-year-old president of the Dreyfus Fund, and the company's retired chairman, Jack Dreyfus. A number of executives of other mutual funds were also among the major contributors. Other contributors included Martin Peretz, a young Harvard professor, and his wife, who was rich in her own right; Blair Clark, McCarthy's 51-year-old campaign manager, and a member of the Clark Thread family; Stewart R. Mott, a 31-year-old philanthropist from Flint, Michigan, and New York City, whose family owned a substantial amount of General Motors stock; William Clay Ford of Detroit, largest stockholder in the Ford Motor Company and owner of the Detroit Lions; Ellsworth Carrington, a New York stock broker; Bruce Robert Gimbel, of the New York department store family; Henry Niles, a Baltimore insurance executive; Martin Fife, a New York leather-goods manufacturer; Alan Miller, a retired patent attorney; Harold Willens, a Los Angeles manufacturer and real estate developer; Arnold Hiatt, chief executive of the Green Shoe Company of Boston; Dan A. Kimball, of Los Angeles, a former Secretary of the Navy, husband of the liberal columnist Doris Fleeson, and chairman of the executive committee of Aerojet-General; and Martin Stone, a Los Angeles manufacturer.

"A number of other major contributors were relatively young men who had created successful businesses of their own," Stout wrote. "Their giving was essentially altruistic. Some may have thought McCarthy had a chance of winning, but all knew he was a desperate long shot. It was not the kind of giving that expected a tangible benefit. These new contributors filled the void in the lagging early stages of the campaign and were the financial heart of it throughout."

IV

Ben Stavis, in his study, reckoned that almost a thousand young people worked at various points for variable lengths of time in McCarthy's national campaign headquarters in Washington; another 5,000 to 10,000 worked part time in storefronts in the primary states, campus headquarters and nonprimary states; and some 50,000 students joined in canvassing around the nation. Within the segment of the 800 McCarthy volunteer leaders across the nation, it was possible for Richard L. Stout, in his own study, to focus on 150 young people who held important positions in the McCarthy campaign structure. His key findings about them were these:

Their I. Q. was well above the national average. Their average age was between 24 and 25, generally placing them, if they were students, in graduate studies or in the professional schools—or, in the case of nonstudents, as recent entrants in the professions or in the business world. A strong presumption existed that they could personally bear much of the financial cost of working for McCarthy or could do so with the help of their families; they came from families having an average income of $31,500—or twice the income of the older leaders of the McCarthy campaign spread across the nation. While the professions of their fathers ranged from policemen, to members of the Congress, to very successful writers, to symphony orchestra directors, nearly a third were businessmen, and a high proportion of these were executives. Many of the young leaders had been involved in National Student Association activities, in the civil rights movement, or in antiwar protest, although most did not become especially concerned about the war until late 1966 or early 1967. Only a minority took part in the April 15, 1967, peace marches in New York City and San Francisco and in the Pentagon demonstration the following October.

McCarthy's appeal was to quieter students, rather than radical demonstrators. Students on the verge of radicalism may

115

have been induced by his candidacy to "work within the system," but the committed radicals followed a law of their own, being without regard to the effects their actions had on the McCarthy candidacy. For example, the demonstrations by young people on the site of the Chicago convention drew their organizational drive from the peace issue, not from the McCarthy candidacy. In their encounters with young McCarthy workers, many of the demonstrators vehemently argued that the latter were wrong-headed for wasting their time in electoral politics.

As for the students who actually worked for McCarthy, only a handful suspended their studies for months on end to work full time on his behalf. A larger number moved in and out of the campaign picture over several weekends of work. A still larger number may have devoted several hours a day for several days to campaign chores of variable importance, not the least of which was their sudden appearance along with older people at ward meetings where they voted out the regular Democrats and voted in people pledged to McCarthy. A great many students, of course, made the fate and tactics of the McCarthy candidacy—and later of the Kennedy candidacy—the subject of nonstop discussions in campus haunts; and the discussions added to the politicization of students just as the demonstrations of the antiwar movement gave them a mutual vocabulary. But it would be false to claim that there was a mass uprising of students who devoted themselves for sustained and protracted periods of time to electioneering work.

It would also be false to claim that all the young people involved in the McCarthy candidacy were motivated solely by a desire to end the Vietnam War. Although this held true for an indeterminate number of volunteers, there were those who worked for purely social reasons—it was fun, or exciting, or simply an easy way to meet members of the opposite sex. Other young people gravitated to McCarthy simply because they hated Johnson, or because they had an aversion to anything bearing a Kennedy name. Still others regarded the McCarthy candidacy as an opportunity to learn how people can be organized to work politically at the grass roots level. (Careerist motives were to be found principally among the students who were to work for Robert F. Kennedy, and who wished to be part of the Kennedy story with its aura of wealth, power and glamour.)

To note this diversity of motives is simply to restore to students the right to their own humanity, rather than force them to conform to exalted images of wisdom and nobility. The efforts of the students who worked for McCarthy in the specific context of the New Hampshire primary were impressive enough on their own terms and need no gilding. With the direct and indirect contributions of nonstudent sources—including the blindness of New Hampshire's regular Democratic politicians in opposition to McCarthy and the psychological shock of the Tet offensive—students transformed McCarthy's academic exercise into an authentic struggle for power within the Democratic party.

Some sense of the matter can be gained by noting McCarthy's position in the period right after his November 30 announcement. His only staff member with experience in the dynamics of presidential politics at the time was Richard Goodwin—who would eventually leave the McCarthy campaign, join Robert Kennedy, and then rejoin McCarthy after Kennedy's assassination. McCarthy's campaign manager—Blair Clark, a man of independent means—had had a successful career in newspaper and television work, but virtually no practical political experience; and his low key, undemanding ways inspired little confidence in his ability to deal with the tasks he faced. He would be attacked from all sides; however, it would become clear only in retrospect that Clark, was the only kind of campaign manager suited to McCarthy's own temperament.

In the weeks following his announcement McCarthy seemed listless, and this impression was especially marked when he was viewed alongside George Romney. Romney, who in his quest for the Republican presidential nomination exhibited all the signs traditionally associated with a serious candidate, was the focus of press attention. He was full of hustle and bustle, radiated kinetic energy, was trailed by an extensive staff, made himself the center of any group of people, and was always accessible to the press. None of this was true of McCarthy.

When it appeared that the McCarthy candidacy was going nowhere, pressures on Kennedy to either become a candidate or to announce his support for McCarthy increased. On college campuses he was met by signs taunting him as a cop-out, while some of the leaders of the RFK-'68 organizations drifted away from him and into an uncertain position in the McCarthy camp. Kennedy, for his part, was persuaded that not only could he not win the nomination, but by entering the contest would split the party and cause the defeat of some of the liberal senators who might support him. Still, partially because of personal dislike, and a conviction that McCarthy was doomed to fail Kennedy did not support the McCarthy candidacy. If Johnson defeated "Kennedy-McCarthy instead of just McCarthy," said he, "Johnson would have destroyed all his opposition in the Democratic party." [9]

One of the sources of the miasma that seemed to envelop McCarthy's candidacy was his continuing indecision on the question of whether he should enter the New Hampshire primary. The case for avoiding New Hampshire was a strong one. The Democratic party there—with little more than 80,000 registered Democrats—was relatively small, and it was presumed that a high percent of the party workers were controlled by either of two pro-Johnson men, Governor King or Senator McIntyre. It also was uncertain what the results of the Kennedy write-in movement (then underway in New Hampshire) would

118

amount to. Nor was it clear what President Johnson meant to do. It was unlikely that he would make a direct personal entry in the New Hampshire primary, followed by a personal campaign in the state, yet the regular Democratic organization could mount a write-in campaign on his behalf. Alternatively, either King or McIntyre, acting as surrogates for Johnson, might offer themselves as favorite son candidates. In either case, McCarthy, by entering the New Hampshire primary, would not be in a position to make a clear cut test of the peace issue. On the basis of all of these factors, it seemed best to skip the New Hampshire primary and wait for the later primary contest in Wisconsin to test his strength. He could then take part in the Massachusetts contest. Wisconsin was a midwestern state, not unlike Minnesota, where his appeal was unquestioned. In Massachusetts, assuming Kennedy out of the race, McCarthy had a politically sophisticated state of increasingly dovish sentiment—in contrast to New Hampshire's reputation for hawkishness. Besides, in Massachusetts he could count a broader base of financial and organization support than appeared available in New Hampshire.

But while McCarthy was indecisive, Sam Brown had been calling from Cambridge to Washington in an effort to reach somebody in the McCarthy entourage with whom he could talk about the student role in the campaign. The persons closest to McCarthy at the time gave him no encouragement. They were fearful, as was McCarthy himself, that a large-scale student involvement in the McCarthy candidacy would backfire, and they urged Brown and others like him to stay in school rather than drop out to work in the campaign. Brown, however, would not be put off. For ten days he tried to reach someone that would give him encouragement, and finally drove to Washington in the third week of December to put the case squarely to Blair Clark. "I told him," Brown later recalled, "what was happening with the students of America, that they were about to rise up against their president and that he needed me. I was ready to go to work that day. I told him there was a conference in Cleveland of the University Christian Movement coming up and that McCarthy should be represented." Clark listened, then reached in his pocket and pulled out $200 which he handed to Brown. In avuncular but passionate tones, Clark said: "Go, my son." [10]

By the end of December 1967, McCarthy changed his mind about the primary contest in New Hampshire. Five points in particular had been impressed on him. First, there existed in New Hampshire a pro-McCarthy nucleus of an "experienced, broadly representative, and committed organization," plus a large volunteer stock to draw on for canvassing and envelope-stuffing. Second, the populous southern part of New Hampshire contained bedroom communities for people who worked in Boston, with large numbers of new, independent voters. Third, since the media always focused on New Hampshire, the exposure McCarthy would get would assist his later efforts. Fourth, a New Hampshire campaign made in the teeth of the opposing Democratic regular organization, would reaffirm the seriousness of the McCarthy candidacy and lay to rest the many doubts that had been voiced. Finally, it was claimed that the campaign could be financed at bargain basement prices. The initial estimate came to about $50,000, but the ultimate cost was to be close to $300,000.

McCarthy's announcement that he would enter the New Hampshire primary excited the corporal's guard of people around Hoeh and Studds. Beyond that, it drew a trickle of out-of-state students to New Hampshire. The first of these was Eric Schnapper, 24, a student at Yale Law School and the son of a Washington publisher. Schnapper did not get involved in the campaign for purely idealistic motives. His candid intention was to get some political experience. Besides, his personal political loyalties ran toward Kennedy, and he eventually moved to the Kennedy camp.

McCarthy vs. Kennedy

Schnapper left school for a while and became the original full-time McCarthy staff member in New Hampshire. His first task was to help set up the McCarthy headquarters in Concord, the state capital, in time for the candidate's scheduled arrival on January 26 when he would file his candidacy papers at the State House. Schnapper, who had never done anything of this sort before called his girl friend at the Connecticut College for Women and had her recruit student volunteers for the McCarthy effort. Schnapper drove to New Haven to pick up the first three student volunteers—Ann Kibling, Lee Van Kirk and Naomi Fatt. In the meantime, Dan Dodd arrived in Concord from Union Theological Seminary and got to work on recruiting students from New Hampshire colleges. Dianne Dumanoski, a Yale graduate student in literature, arrived in Concord and, joined by Cindy Samuels, organized a number of students from Smith and other campuses. Other arrivals included Nicki Sauvage, Sue Solenberger, and Sara Elston from Smith, and Chris Howell from the Connecticut College for Women.

There was no centrally coordinated master plan that brought the first students to Concord. The first arrivals acted very much on their own initiative, and for a variety of personal motives. They showed up in New Hampshire either because they spontaneously responded to an issue and to a situation, or because they wanted to be with someone who was already at work for McCarthy. The initial group of students who comprised the staff of the McCarthy New Hampshire campaign were mainly graduate students whose class schedules gave them a greater mobility than undergraduates. Moreover, as Stavis later wrote, a staff member, in its New Hampshire meaning:

was essentially anyone who worked during the week. He prepared materials to be used on weekends, then supervised the people who came to Concord—or elsewhere—on weekends. To be on the staff, one only had to come to the office during the week, even part of the week. If he arrived on Thursday, he would know enough about

121

procedures on Friday to supervise people on the weekend, so he was a staff member.

Hoeh, the State chairman of the McCarthy campaign in New Hampshire, was an administrator at Dartmouth University, and could not devote full time to the McCarthy candidacy; nor could Studds, considering the demands of his own work as a master of St. Paul's School. Since they could not be away from their regular work for extended intervals, the personal staffs they recruited were drawn mainly from Dartmouth and, for the sake of convenience, were based in Hanover. Since Hoeh had all he could do to merely attend to the details which fell within his own broad area of responsibility—the media, McCarthy's schedule, and his own relationship with the state Democratic party—he could not attend to the hourly crises in the McCarthy state headquarters in Concord.

In this way, the state headquarters, throughout the New Hampshire effort, was dominated by outsiders, and the New Hampshire headquarters and field staff combined—which eventually became the core of McCarthy's national campaign staff —formed its work habits in an atmosphere of isolation from the local political leadership. Stavis later wrote:

We did not have in New Hampshire, an opportunity to work with a strong, imaginative, resourceful local committee that could organize its own campaign and give us accurate information about the local political situation. Failure to learn how to work creatively with the indigenous state and local McCarthy committees turned out to be a major problem when we moved to Wisconsin and California, for example, which had organized strong campaigns.[11]

New Hampshire, however, taught the young McCarthyites a lesson about the importance of locating the state headquarters in the main population center. Concord, the state capital, was fairly central in location, but the main population center where roughly a third of the state Democratic vote was concentrated was in Manchester. The separation of the state headquarters

122

from the Democratic stronghold of Manchester kept the head-quarters people in a dangerous condition of ignorance about the McCarthyite needs in that city, and was a contributing factor to McCarthy's loss of Manchester, a loss that tipped the state to Johnson.

With every passing day, more students showed up in Concord volunteering their services. But the build-up of strength was not as swift as postcampaign legends would have it. As late as the second week in February—six weeks after McCarthy had announced his intention to enter the New Hampshire primary—there were less than a hundred out-of-state students working for him there. The press had not, as yet, fully discovered the existence of the so-called "Children's Crusade," and Romney continued to monopolize press attention. On January 26, when McCarthy appeared in Concord to file his candidacy papers in the State House, he paid a courtesy call on Governor King, and the latter—as evidence to the lifelessness of the McCarthy campaign—greeted him with hearty affability. Like other self-confident pro-Johnson regulars in the Democratic organization, King was convinced that McCarthy would be lucky if he got as much as 10 to 12 percent of the primary vote.

It would later come to be said of the student workers for McCarthy in New Hampshire that they were "like the Vietcong" and could not be fought by the traditional methods of political warfare. It would be closer to the truth to say that the regulars of the New Hampshire Democratic organization walked into an ambush because they failed to credit students with the one capacity students are supposed to have—a capacity to learn. It was the speed with which students mastered the techniques of the Old Politics and the thoroughness with which they applied them in New Hampshire's electoral context that made the regular Democratic professional politicians of the state seem, by contrast, inept.

This was all the more true of the student effort after the arrival in Concord of a triumvirate of leaders who had been—or were still—closely connected with the National Student Association and Allard Lowenstein. The first of this triumvirate was Stephen Cohen of Harvard. On February 6, Cohen, while still in Cambridge, shaved off his mustache, put on a neat blue pin-stripe suit, drove over to Radcliffe to pick up Arlene Popkin and Mary McCarthy, (daughter of the candidate) and headed for New Hampshire. Sam Brown, the student coordinator, arrived in Concord five days later, and Curtis Gans about a week after that to direct all the work centered in the Concord state headquarters. All three men brought their experience with fairly large-scale political operations to the monumental tasks they faced.

And they were not alone. Ann Hart, 21, the daughter of Senator Hart, moved from a McCarthy office in Washington she had been managing to New Hampshire, where she helped manage student volunteers. John Barbieri, 23, just back from the Peace Corps in India where he had dealt with fairly large scale undertakings involving political organization had originally come to New Hampshire to help Romney, but the Republicans had no place for him specifically or students generally. So he showed up instead at the McCarthy headquarters in Concord, became Brown's assistant, and quickly began to organize a mass mailing campaign.

Ben Stavis, a 26-year-old Ph. D. candidate at Columbia, who found that he had a block of free time made a bus and train trip to New Hampshire with his wife and was put to work. He helped annotate voting lists with party affiliations so as to avoid the wasted effort of canvassing or sending mail to Republicans. He presently came to be known as the "map man," because he obtained detailed maps of every city and town to be canvassed from the state highway department. He cut the maps into sections and duplicated each section so that canvassers, also armed with street directories, would be able to find their assigned

124

areas with no difficulty. In a matching effort, Joel Feigenbaum, 25, a Cornell graduate student in nuclear physics, supervised canvassing, dispatching thousands of students throughout the state.

Three weeks before the election over 500 students went to New Hampshire, but it was not until February 28, when Romney dropped his bid for the Republican nomination, that the press turned its full attention to the "Children's Crusade." The reports sent out over the country brought around a thousand students in for the final weekend surge, and it was said that more than twice that number were told not to come because there was neither housing nor work enough for them.

An estimated 5,000 students were involved for varying lengths of time and in varying capacities in McCarthy's New Hampshire campaign. In all, students and young people canvassed some 60,000 New Hampshire homes—about two-thirds of the total—got out twice that many pieces of mail, and distributed untold numbers of leaflets. As the election neared, homes not yet visited were telephoned and the political inclination of the voters were again noted. The day before the election, sample ballots were distributed to every doorstep in the state. Then on election day, an intensive effort was made to pull all potentially favorable voters to the polls.

But the student effort was only one of four main elements in the conduct of the campaign. The first was McCarthy himself. He toured the state, met potential voters at large receptions and small parties, greeted workers in factories, was interviewed by newspaper editors, and walked the streets and entered stores introducing himself to people. The second was an intensive media effort—full page newspaper ads and radio and television commercials were most concentrated in the final days of the campaign. The third element was the use of prominent professors, generals, show business personalities, and local business and religious leaders.

There was nothing intrinsically novel about any of these elements. They were all drawn from the Old Politics—the same source of the techniques students used in their own area of involvement in the campaign. But there were some extrinsic novelties in the New Hampshire picture. The McCarthy campaign demonstrated that Old Politics techniques could be effectively used by outsiders on a statewide basis. Another and more subtle novelty carried a concealed price-tag lucidly expressed by Stavis when he wrote:

The campaign was unusual in that it ignored most secondary groups that are the cornerstone of American party politics. We did not pay too much attention to bargaining with leaders of ethnic groups. We did not negotiate with union leaders although we did leaflet plant gates. We formed no specific religious committees to support McCarthy. In fact the religiously oriented literature was deliberately withdrawn. We did not avoid issues at the request of a businessmen's organization. . . . Our tendency was to ignore the fundamental patterns of association and go directly to the voter. Perhaps this tendency was politically naive and eventually meant we could not get delegate votes. But the student organizers simply had no desire to bicker with leaders of these types of secondary groups. We were students, schooled in research and judgment, not negotiation and compromise. And McCarthy wanted this sort of campaign. When Kennedy later entered the race, his experience in manipulating special groups more than made up for his failure to have a significant student campaign.[12]

New Hampshire marked the classical—or golden age—of the McCarthy volunteer effort. Various young people, like those mentioned in this account, were assigned areas of responsibility as leaders or coordinators. But the demarcation between the leaders and the led was obscured. Everyone pitched in to do anything, and the once-fumbling effort went off with a professional precision that was unthinkable just weeks earlier. Later, after some of the young people who had worked together in New Hampshire either shifted their base of action to McCarthy's national headquarters in Washington or spread out over the country to participate in state primary contests, they formed a "blood brotherhood" where they gave first priority to each other's requests. At the same time, many among them jarred local people by their brash air of superior knowledge, by their tendency to keep at arms length any late-coming volunteers. Some among them, in their own naked struggle for power and prestige, went for each other's throats with the cold ruthlessness of the children in *The Lord of the Flies*. But in New Hampshire, their high order of selflessness—regardless of the motives that originally prompted them to join the McCarthy campaign —had the kind of fresh and charming innocence that is prior to experience.

The charm that the press saw in the student effort was amplified by contrast with the performance of the professional politicians in nominal command of New Hampshire's Democratic party. The regulars had four months in which to mount a powerful administration effort before the votes were cast. Yet they faltered at every turn. For example, the New Hampshire regulars distributed a pledge card to be signed by registered Democrats asserting they would write in the president's name on the primary ballot. In this way they gave McCarthy a gift issue which he effectively exploited, saying that the pledge card was "the closest thing there could be to denying people the right to a secret ballot."

Next, the regulars abandoned their original strategy of ignoring McCarthy and extolling Johnson as "A Strong Man for a Tough Job." Instead, they attacked McCarthy directly, and in the course of the attack, the increasing violence of their rhetoric served only to reveal their own mounting sense of panic. They accused McCarthy of being a spokesman for the forces of appeasement, of advocating a policy of surrender, of representing the noisy and unruly voices of extremism in the land, or of recommending that draft dodgers go scot-free. One Adminis-

127

tration radio commercial blared: "The Communists in Vietnam are watching the New Hampshire primary. Don't vote for fuzzy thinking and surrender." Since McCarthy was not guilty of any of the things of which he had been accused, his mildly phrased replies made his accusers seem noisy, unruly, and worried.

As March 12, election day, drew near, no one on the McCarthy staff could confidently predict the size of the vote he would get. The staff guesses ranged from eight to 60 percent of the total. There was a tendency to rely on the judgment of the press to determine whether or not a vote estimate was respectable. If the press called 25 percent a strong showing for McCarthy, then it would be so. If the press called 40 percent a decisive loss for McCarthy, then it would be so. In point of fact, McCarthy polled 42 percent of the total Democratic vote to 48 percent representing a write-in for President Johnson. The vote on the Democratic side was 23,280 for McCarthy to 29,021 for President Johnson. All the newscasters called this result a great victory for McCarthy.

But there was more to the story. A Republican write-in-vote of 4,063 for McCarthy, when combined with his Democratic vote, brought him within 230 votes of beating Johnson. The fine points of detail in these figures were ignored by McCarthy's young supporters when the votes came in. In their minds, the proposition that McCarthy had won a great victory in New Hampshire, ceased to involve a metaphoric use by newscasters of the word "won." In the minds of McCarthy's young and exuberant supporters it became a proposition that he had literally won the primary.

The New Hampshire mystique spread its contagion over developments that had been underway in other states prior to March 12. In Wisconsin, Nebraska, Florida, and Pennsylvania, McCarthy leaders met all the local requirements to have his name placed on the primary ballot. In Massachusetts, the

March 5 deadline for President Johnson to decide whether he or any Democrat designated by him would run in the April 30 primary came and went; McCarthy, by default, was assured the entire 72 votes of the Massachusetts delegation on the first ballot at the convention. In Connecticut, inroads were made in the traditional strongholds of the regular Democratic organization when an adult crusade of McCarthyites—led by the Reverend Joseph Duffy, 35, a Protestant theologian; Stephanie May, a member of the National Board of SANE; Anne Wexler, wife of an eye surgeon; Geoffrey Cowan, a Yale law student; and many starred names among American writers and actors—took control of party organizations in a string of small-town caucuses, a first step in selecting delegates to the national convention. In other Connecticut towns, McCarthyite adult crusaders circulated petitions to force primaries in their communities, a device discovered by Cowan in his research into Connecticut election law.

Much the same sort of thing happened in Minnesota on the evening of March 5 when members of the Democratic-Farmer-Labor party gathered at precinct and ward caucuses held across the state to elect delegates to the county and district conventions which in turn would select representatives to the state DFL convention in June. Each of Minnesota's eight congressional districts would select five national convention delegates, and the state convention would choose 20.

Long in advance, the McCarthyites, led by people like John Wright, 34, a child psychologist at the University of Minnesota and chief spokesman of the Minnesota Concerned Democrats, DFL Vice Chairman Forrest Harris, Twin Cities legislator Elpha Samby, and law students Vance Opperman and Howard Kaibel began to prepare for the conventions. They had students canvass door-to-door and by phone in the third, fourth and fifth congressional districts, encompassing the Twin Cities and suburbs. They held precinct caucus schools for people who do not

129

ordinarily attend precinct caucus meetings. On the night of March 5, DFL regulars found themselves confronted by battalions of students, nuns, citizens of all economic levels and colors who outvoted them. Among those defeated were Secretary of State Joseph Donovan, St. Paul Mayor Tom Byrne, Hubert Humphrey's son Robert, his son-in-law, Bruce Solomonson, and Robert Short, the perennial finance chairman of Humphrey candidacies.

The McCarthy forces did not mount efforts in rural districts and thus were unable to control the delegation to the national convention. But what happened that night in the Twin Cities, Richard L. Stout later wrote:

was a portent of the exclusionary tendency that developed in many McCarthy organizations; veteran party workers who had realized the importance of political involvement long before an issue came along were tossed out on their ears simply because they were old guard, even in many cases, when they might have worked with the McCarthy effort.[13]

The same night in California, nearly 500 parties were held to get the 13,746 signatures necessary for placing McCarthy's name on the ballot for the June 4 primary election. The first candidate to file the requisite number of signatures would get his name placed at the top of the ballot which could mean perhaps an extra 5 percent of the vote. By law, the gathering of signatures couldn't begin until the first minute of March 6, and so the parties were scheduled for late in the night of March 5. Across the state beginning at midnight, some 28,000 persons signed their names, and at 9 A.M. the next morning, campaign leaders Gerald Hill, Edmund G. Brown Jr., Mrs. Jo Seidita, and a number of aides, bore cartons of petitions into the Los Angeles Register of Voters office. They were the first to file.

All this, to repeat, was underway prior to the voting in New Hampshire on March 15. But the results in New Hampshire achieved with the help of students and other young people—

and the new-born legend that McCarthy had "won" the Democratic primary in that state—suddenly invested the efforts elsewhere with a new significance. It appeared that all the petitioning, the caucusing, the jockeying for position on the part of McCarthy's supporters in different parts of the country, was something far more than the eccentric twists to be expected in the politics of a nation of 200 million. He had won a major test at the polls in New Hampshire; he was a serious candidate for the presidency; he was a person around whom major forces in the nation could coalesce; and all that had formerly seemed but wayward expressions of local political accidents, now appeared to be part of an inexorable national groundswell of support for McCarthy.

V

This sense of the matter was not initially shaken by the entry of Kennedy into the nominating contest. Although Kennedy generated some excitement, in the eyes of McCarthy supporters he appeared to be an opportunist who waited for McCarthy to show Johnson's vulnerability before risking a contest with the president. Indeed, it was after Kennedy's entry into the contest that McCarthy for the first time began to talk about the presidency as though he were personally running for the office itself, rather than just spoiling it for Johnson. Since Kennedy's strength had not been tested in any primary prior to March 31—the day President Johnson announced he would neither seek nor accept the Democratic presidential nomination—McCarthy's young staff, blooded in New Hampshire, could claim that they had "knocked Johnson out of the presidency." The claim, of course, would be disputed by Johnson, by the Vietcong in Vietnam, by radical blacks in the ghettos, and by radical students on the campuses of America. Yet it nonetheless gained widespread currency, particularly after Wisconsin went to the polls for the Democratic primary and gave McCarthy 412,160 votes or 56.2 percent to 253,696 or 34.6 percent for Johnson. The fact that the vote was cast on April 2, two days after Johnson withdrew from the race, was seldom taken into account.

After Johnson withdrew his name the campaign nominating contest took on a progressively more ugly aspect. It became not a contest over principles, but a straightforward power struggle between McCarthy and Kennedy, two men who opposed the Johnson administration but who differed in their tactics and were as one in their intense dislike for each other.

In the McCarthy camp, the network of youthful workers who functioned with éclat in New Hampshire, were not adaptable to local conditions in the primaries that came after Wisconsin. McCarthy was the victor in only one of these—Kennedy was the victor in others. But there was no longer a "hate Johnson" motive to keep the young workers for McCarthy united or dedicated to the hard grind of campaigning. The youth component among his workers became sharply divided against itself, and their contributions to the campaign receded in importance while the older people—who had been the real mainstay of his candidacy all along—continued to do what they could to advance his cause and keep it alive.

The Kennedy camp, in the meantime, claimed the support of youth, though his campaign was run by family members, by the professionals associated with John F. Kennedy's political career, and by Robert Kennedy's Senate office staff. Efforts were made to mobilize students for canvassing, and various inducements from the offer of free transportation to the totem symbols of authority were broadcast widely, but there were relatively few takers. Students wanted to work in a campaign that was their own, and did not wish to be tools of middle-aged professionals.

Instead of organizing students and citizens to form committees, raise funds and carry out programs, the Kennedy campaign had a simple field program for young people. They were to form the crush of bodies at his campaign rallies, where their smiling faces, cheering, flag-waving, screamers, and jumpers, would form images suited to the television camera. These rallies, broadcast nationally on the six o'clock evening news, conveyed the sense of a majoritarian surge of support for Kennedy, and gave him two minutes of cost-free exposure that was worth $40,000 of television time. Otherwise, the Kennedy people worked closely with local politicians and power brokers for interest groups.

Yet as was said at the outset of this chapter, powerful post-campaign legends tended to amalgamate the McCarthy and Kennedy candidacies into the picture of a single candidacy—a picture of the irresistible strength of students when they are organized for participation in electoral politics.

NOTES

1. Garry Wills, *Nixon Agonistes* (Boston, Mass.: Houghton Mifflin, 1969), p. 456.

2. Richard T. Stout, *People* (New York: Harper and Row, 1969), p. 60.

3. Stout, *People*, p. 62.

4. Stout, *People*, p. 64.

5. Stout, *People*, p. 65.

6. Stout, *People*, p. 77.

7. Ben Stavis, *We Were the Campaign. New Hampshire to Chicago for McCarthy* (Boston: Beacon Press, 1970), p. 107.

8. Stout, *People*, p. 7.

9. Stout, *People*, p. 143.

10. Stout, *People*, p. 137.

11. Stavis, *We Were the Campaign*, p. 172.

12. Stavis, *We Were the Campaign*, p. 12.

13. Stout, *People*, p. 174.

133

7

From Chicago
to Kent State

I

The McCarthy candidacy was the apogee of youth participation in process and electoral politics in the 1960's, but it did not by any means displace participation in event politics—demonstrations and protests. By August 1968, on the eve of the Democratic National Convention in Chicago, circumstances were taking shape that would eventually contribute to the illusions that bred the 1970 springtime theories of backlash and sidelash.

For example, the Black Panthers had emerged as the arch symbol of black militancy. They claimed to be against black cultural nationalism, against black racism, and for revolution on behalf of all the poor people in the nation regardless of color. Their theory of revolution, as enunciated by a handful of their articulate leaders, was a mish-mash of fragments drawn from Marx, Lenin, Mao, Guevera, and Fanon. Yet it was not the Black Panther theory of revolution—nor their shakedown of merchants—that enraged many whites. It was what Huey Newton, the Oakland founder of the Black Panthers, had taught his small band of followers—that, ostensibly in self-defense against black as well as white policemen, they had a constitutional right to carry a gun. Mutual hatreds and fears led to Panther-police shoot-outs with a loss of life on both sides, while a pall of gunsmoke and counter claims often made it hard to determine whose finger pulled the trigger first. The Panther claims that 29 of their members had been "assassinated" were carried across the country by the mass media and widely accepted as fact. Months after the string of deaths, Jay Epstein, a Harvard professor, produced evidence that only in one case did the police, in fact, shoot to death an unarmed man.

In August 1968, the position of national chairman of the Black Panthers was held by Bobby Seale, 31, but he was eclipsed in celebrity by Eldridge Cleaver, 33, the Black Panther "minister of information." Cleaver was virtually unknown before his autobiographical *Soul On Ice,*[1] (written while he was imprisoned in California for assault with intent to kill) was published after his parole. With the publication of the book and the wide acclaim it won for its stylistic brilliance, Cleaver became an overnight folk hero to politically active white students. They packed the halls where he spoke and, regardless of how they reacted to his arguments, were fascinated by him personally. He appeared to be wound tight with hair-trigger tensions, demon-haunted, full of the bitter rage of an Ahab shaking his fist at the white whale—a man reconciled to the likelihood that as a revolutionary he would meet a violent end in the course of fulfilling history. Cleaver, the 1968 presidential candidate of the Peace and Freedom Party, was wounded in a Panther-police gun battle. His parole was rescinded, and rather than return to prison, he fled the country, going first to Cuba and then to Algiers.

While white student extremists made noise and Black Panther leaders excited fear, the Yippies as of August 1968 were the source of both noise and fear. The Yippies, founded by Abbie Hoffman, 30, and Jerry Rubin, 30, were a rhetorical stunt—not a political organization. The most it amounted to was some scattered communes of young people living according to their own cultural styles. They were magnified to the size of a threatening political force only because Hoffman and Rubin had an authentic flair for theatrics and a shrewd insight into the workings of the mass media. More clearly than most people they saw that the news media will always play up the bizarre —the pimping son of a hard-nosed puritanical cop on the vice squad, or the pacificist son of a five star general. Hoffman and Rubin deliberately marketed themselves as chaotic, outlandish personality models for younger people to emulate. Though they pretended to be deep and fertile theorists and practitioners of revolution, they were in fact make-believe players in a theater of the absurd featuring pot, put-on costumes, wild pronouncements, fornication, and hell-raising for the hell of it. They assumed, correctly enough, that those in high places would take the Hoffman-Rubin clowning seriously, panic, and overreact.

It was a time when odd-lot groups of young people who wanted no part of electoral politics were vocal in their advocacy of revolution and in their confident predictions about the inevitability of revolution. They appeared to assume, or at least led many nervous people to believe, that the noise of rebellion was the same as a planned revolution, that all who talked of revolution had the same revolution in mind, and that the revolution being talked about was near at hand. They also contributed to a climate where some jittery politicians and officials mobilized the forces at their command and seemed prepared to physically crush the revolutionaries.

It was in this climate and on the eve of the Democratic convention that the steering committee of the National Mobilization to End the War in Vietnam (MOBE) applied to Chicago city officials for a permit to stage an antiwar demonstration during the convention. MOBE was the organization that had brought together demonstrators for the Pentagon March on October 21, 1967. It was a loose coalition of autonomous local and national antiwar groups that secured permits and made other logistic arrangements necessary to the success of a mass demonstration. Its principal leaders in 1968 were David Dellinger, 52, an old-line pacifist, editor of *Liberation* magazine, and chairman of MOBE; Rennie Davis, 28, national coordinator of MOBE, and son of one of President Truman's top economic advisors; and Tom Hayden, 28, a New Left spokesman, and one of the founders of Students for a Democratic Society.

These men were advocates of the politics of confrontation—but not of violence. They set out—like Martin Luther King and his followers in the civil rights movement—to expose the violence of their adversaries. With respect to their own cause, all had spoken out against violence as a tactic. But while MOBE was applying for a permit in Chicago to protest the Vietnam War, Hoffman and Rubin were publicizing a theatrical proposal of their own. They wished permission to stage a "Festival of Life" in Chicago's Soldiers Field and described their plans in terms that suggested a protracted public orgy. Theatrical projections on the expected size of the invasion of Chicago by the forces of MOBE and the Yippies cited figures in the range of several hundred thousand young people. These estimates alone ignited panic buttons in Chicago officialdom. The Yippies efforts at the politics of the put-on and their effects on law enforcement officials are described in the comprehensive account of the 1968 campaign, *The American Melodrama,* coauthored by Lewis Chester, Godfrey Hodgson and Bruce Page of the *London Sunday Times.*

The list of Yippie projects, by no means exhaustive, included ten thousand nude bodies floating in protest in Lake Michigan; the mobilization of Yippie "hookers" to seduce delegates and slip LSD into their drinks; a squad of 230 "hyperpotent" hippie males assigned to the task of seducing the wives and daughters of delegates; releasing greased pigs in the Loop area; a mass stall-in of beat-up automobiles on the expressways; the insertion of LSD into the city's water supply; Yippies dressed in black pajamas to dispense handfuls of rice to the citizenry; and the infiltration of the right wing with crew-cut Yippies who, at an opportune psychological moment, would exclaim, "You know, these Yippies have something to say."

They did have something to say, of course, but they were saying it in a code that the literal-minded security authorities could not hope to break. If it were not for its consequences in Chicago, the spectacle of the Yippies' irreverent balderdash being pored over by hard-nosed investigators in the FBI, the Secret Service, and Daley's police department on the hunt for clues to revolutionary intentions might have seized the nation with a paralyzing bout of mirth. The mind of the Chicago police department, however, remained studiously unblown. An emergency guard was placed on the city's LSD-threatened water supply, just in case.[2]

There were also rumors of an internal uprising among the demonstrators culminating with the Black Panthers directing an extravaganza of burning, looting, and shooting. Ironically, when the Chicago Black Panthers heard of the role that rumor had assigned them, the known members either left town or went into hiding inside the city.

The rest of the story has been told many times.[3] The deliberately overblown projected mass descent of several hundred thousand young people on Chicago for a protest demonstration against the war in Vietnam never took place. While McCarthy was urging his own young supporters to stay away from Chicago, more generalized advice to the same effect appeared in the news stories Chicago officialdom issued about the planning for the Democratic Convention. The stories, stressing the preparations being made to ward off assaults, made it clear that the city would be a very dangerous place for young people. When the daily confrontations between the antiwar protesters and the police eventually came to a head in the "police riot" in Grant Park, the ghettos of the city were quiet. The Black Panthers, save for Bobby Seale, were nowhere in sight. As for the Yippies, neither Hoffman nor Rubin were directly involved in the act that led to a clash with the police. Yet after the clash, they seemed driven by the aesthetics of their make-believe to present themselves as the stars of the chaotic event.

Despite all the violence that flared in Lincoln Park and in Grant Park, no one was shot or killed; but the pervasive atmosphere of violence invaded the hall of the convention—as it did the homes of television viewers across the nation—to convert the convention hall into a field of battle where delegates who supported McCarthy or Humphrey seemed like mutually hostile scorpions sealed in the same bottle. On the eve of the convention, Nixon seemed an easy man to defeat. At the end of the convention, the Democratic presidential nomination won by Humphrey seemed worthless. The Democratic party itself—Old Indestructible, the oldest political party in the world—seemed to have seen its last days as an institution. True, the Democratic Convention had approved several reforms in response to the clamor McCarthy forces raised about its unrepresentative, boss-ridden procedures. It approved the creation of a commission on delegate selection and party structure, and a commission on national convention procedures to formulate and propose new ways to promote more democracy within the party at every level. Yet it was widely believed that the foregoing amounted to no more than cosmetic touches on a corpse suffocated under the arch symbols of the Old Politics—Mayor Daley, his machine and his police.*

At the end of the convention, an eavesdropper on the talk among young people who had worked for McCarthy, Kennedy and McGovern (whose presidential campaign began three weeks before the convention) could easily have gained two impressions.

* The obituaries did not take into account the state of opinion within the city of Chicago itself. Some 70 percent of the townspeople fully approved of the conduct of the police; Daley won reelection by an overwhelming majority to an unprecedented fourth term as mayor.

Some of the young people meant to leave the Democrats and form a new party based on a new coalition of progressive forces. Others now agreed that SDS extremists had been in the right all along, and that electoral politics was foolish and wasteful—that violent revolution was the only way America could be purged of its vices. This was not McCarthy's own view, yet he was not at liberty to urge his young followers to give their support to Humphrey. He had often said during his campaign that he had "set the people free." So he did, but in so doing he became a prisoner of events that either pushed him in directions he didn't want to go, or prevented him from moving where he did want to go.

McCarthy, for example, had worked with Humphrey since young manhood, and there was enough space in Minnesota for both of them to spread their wings as U. S. senators. He never wished to attack Humphrey personally, and certainly hadn't contemplated a time when they would be directly pitted against each other for the Democratic presidential nomination. He didn't relish in the pain he caused—any more than Humphrey enjoyed his own counter-attacks on McCarthy. Yet the logic of McCarthy's stand on the issue of Vietnam made him Humphrey's harsh accuser, and the binds of Humphrey's position as vice president, and as the presidential candidate of the party in power, forced him to reply in kind to McCarthy.

Still, on the eve of the convention, McCarthy confided to friends that he would not flatly refuse to endorse Humphrey if the latter won the nomination. He meant to hold back for two or three weeks, either to give Humphrey a chance to shift on the issue of Vietnam or to make the endorsement of his candidacy a *quid pro quo* for his shift. There might have been an immediate endorsement if a compromise plank on Vietnam as agreed to by the Humphrey camp and various camps of doves before the convention met had not been vetoed by the long distance intervention of President Johnson, who insisted on his own draft of a plank. In any case, prior to the latter development, it was McCarthy's view that George McGovern and Edward Kennedy had lost their bargaining power with respect to the Vietnam plank when they prematurely announced that they would actively support the party choice for the presidency. Then, in a direct reference to himself McCarthy added, "The problem I have is with the young people. I've been more insistent than I really wanted to be about not supporting the ticket. Because they'd figure this is a sellout. They're ready to accuse me of a sellout, anyway." [4]

After the riot in Grant Park, McCarthy had added reason to be concerned about the charge of sellout. Humphrey was too absorbed in nailing down the presidential nomination to grasp the full meaning of the riot—which climaxed in the same hour when the convention delegates made him the Democratic presidential nominee. The young McCarthyites who witnessed the violence learned concurrently that the McCarthy candidacy officially died before the first convention ballot had run through the roll call of the states. They also heard a rumor to the effect that when the police were in the full tilt of their attack on the Grant Park demonstrators, Humphrey merely closed a window in his hotel suite because the tear gas outside began to drift in. Without inquiring into the truth of the rumor young McCarthyites denounced the window-closing as the gesture of a man who had a stone where his heart should be—a man who, if elected president, would base his administration on clubs and tear gas. They soon began to wear blank white campaign buttons, indicating that they would never work for Humphrey.

There was more to the dim, weird, and afflicted drama that had yet to be played out. Early in the afternoon on the day following the balloting for the presidential nomination, McCarthy gave his valedictory address to the army of his young workers massed before him in a room in the Hilton hotel. He recalled again the goals of his campaign—an end to the war in Viet-

141

nam, a reassesment of America's priorities, and the raising of basic questions about the processes of American government and American politics. The campaign, he said, attained its goals in all these respects. McCarthy urged his volunteer army to adhere to a faith in "the potential of the American system to respond in a time of need such as this." There was, of course, the question of what was to be done next.

What we do [said he] is to go on, to continue to present to the people as best we can for judgment between now and November the issues we have been raising for nine months in this country. We will continue to demand explanations from the candidates. But more important than that, we will proceed as best we can to support those candidates, particularly for the United States Senate, who have stood with us, and to identify those issues with our candidates.[5]

He did not on this occasion refer to the presidential nominee of the Democratic party. But a short time afterward, McCarthy walked over to the battlefield of Grant Park, stood under an elm tree and, with microphone in hand, addressed the young throng as "the government in exile." There were shouts of "No" when he urged them to continue to work within the system. But he shot back his own "Yes," and in an allusion to the Democratic and Republican nominees for the presidency, quickly added: "I will not endorse either of them. I am prepared to stay with the issues so long as I have a constituency, and I still have a constituency." There was neither bitter denunciation of the victors, nor self-pity. On the battlefield of defeat, his note continued to be one of hope and optimism. He said in his peroration:

Let us be prepared to make mistakes, if we must make them, on the side of trust rather than on the side of mistrust in our fellow men or in other peoples around the world. Let us be prepared to make mistakes on the side of hope instead of on the side of despair and fear, whether we look to the present or whether we look to the future. This should be your spirit. This has been the spirit of my campaign. And we can, I think, make it the spirit and the basis of action in the United States of America and in those things around the world in which we have some influence and some force. So let us go from here to do the thing we can do, and not worry about what we cannot do; here this afternoon, to make the kind of commitment, as I made it to you and as you have made it to me.[6]

If McCarthy still had in mind an early endorsement of the Democratic nominees for the presidency and vice presidency, an event intervened at 5 A.M. on the morning of the next day which foreclosed that possibility. Between 20 and 30 McCarthy staff members in a suite on the fifteenth floor of the Hilton were having a party, reminiscing about the campaign, while others sat in the corridor singing or playing bridge, and still others were asleep in nearby rooms. A handful of policemen suddenly entered the room where the party was underway. They ordered everyone to leave, claiming that objects had been thrown from the windows of the rooms. During the Grant Park violence, debris had in fact come from windows on various floors of the Hilton, including the fifteenth, but subsequent inquiry showed that no objects were being hurled out of the window of the room when the raid started. An argument ensued—and was on the wane—when National Guard troops, followed by more policemen and a hotel security man poured onto the floor. In the tumult, the police snapped again. A brush led to a blow, a blow to a fall, to hysterical screaming, clubbings, Mace, and an escalation of force until a raid on one room became a general physical expulsion of people from the floor.

A desperate phone call asking Humphrey to help never reached him. An overprotective aide who took the call refused to awaken Humphrey to inform him of the latest lunacy. The existing bitterness toward him was compounded. McCarthy, meanwhile, had risen early. In a hotel corridor, he encountered an aide whose face was covered with blood from a scalp wound

143

sustained during the police clubbing. McCarthy asked questions, learned what had happened, searched for his workers and found them herded into the lobby and sitting on the floor. He asked for the police officer in charge. When there was no response, he ordered his workers back to their rooms in groups of three and four. He would not himself depart from Chicago until most of his young campaigners were safely out of the city. "We are leaving Prague," the pilot of McCarthy's campaign plane said over the intercom as the aircraft took off from the Midway Airport.

II

Two weeks later, some of the young members of McCarthy's national staff met in Martha's Vineyard to decide their next move. What if they aligned their emotions, energies and newly acquired skills behind Humphrey's candidacy in a "stop Nixon" drive? At the Martha's Vineyard meeting, the young staff members listened to the pleading of Vermont's Governor Philip Hoff—a dove friendly to the McCarthy cause but now on a mission from Humphrey. He urged the McCarthyites to work for the Democratic ticket. They were promised a budget of a million dollars if they joined the Humphrey effort. The young people decided that they were not representative enough to act collectively. Moreover, they feared that an attempt to take any clear position would fragment the diverse elements of the staff. They endorsed neither Humphrey nor revolution, but encouraged McCarthy supporters to work in the campaigns of peace-oriented senatorial and congressional candidates. Many former staff members did precisely that.* The main corps of McCarthy

* They joined the senatorial campaigns of Morse in Oregon (lost), Cranston in California (won), Gilligan in Ohio (lost), McGovern in

workers, however, did not actively participate in the local campaigns. Perhaps they were too physically and emotionally exhausted. Those who went back to school, however, like the youths who went back to school after the Mississippi Summer, found the pastoral quiet and peace of academic life hard to endure.

As for the presidential campaign itself, there are so many barriers to sight and sound in America's continental democracy that a man in New York who wishes to be heard in California often has to raise his voice and shout. Humphrey had to shout, partly because during the first months after the convention there was no money for talking in a normal voice over television. Yet, the more he shouted, the more he confirmed the will of some young people to believe that he, along with Mayor Daley, was the essence of everything wrong about the Old Politics. It was seldom admitted that, except for McGovern, all the contenders for the 1968 Democratic presidential nomination—Humphrey, McCarthy, Robert Kennedy—initially took similar positions at the outset of America's deepening involvement in the Vietnam conflict. Humphrey lacked the freedom that the others had to change their minds and speak their views openly as they saw fit. Any crisis flowing from opposition of Democratic senators to the Vietnam policy of a Democratic president would affect only the Democratic party. But if Humphrey as vice president opposed President Johnson vigorously and openly, or resigned as vice president in protest against a policy with which he disagreed, the consequence could be a profound constitutional crisis affecting the very foundations of American government.

South Dakota (won), Hughes in Iowa (won), Ribicoff in Connecticut (won), Clark in Illinois (lost), and O'Dwyer in New York (lost). The congressional campaigns of Lowenstein (won), Koch (won), and Scheuer (won) in New York, Hoeh in New Hampshire (lost), and scores of others also had help from former McCarthy workers.

145

Humphrey was stuck with Johnson. He was stuck with Vietnam. He was stuck with the student hecklers who dogged him in his campaign. Few of these hecklers knew or cared to know anything about the role Humphrey had played for two decades as a leader of American progressivism and as legislative midwife to many of the landmark political achievements since 1948. They saw him as Johnson's accomplice who went to any lengths, including attacks on their heroes, to demonstrate his loyalty to Johnson's Vietnam policy. In the eyes of the hecklers he was another war criminal, and they felt they had a clear right to prevent his being heard during the campaign whether he spoke on or off campus.

Nixon, on the other hand, as a virtual unknown to the student hecklers, was virtually ignored. Their fury and frustration with Johnson and the Democrats led them to concentrate their rage on Humphrey—Johnson's hand-picked successor—rather than the more shadowy figure of Richard Nixon.

For his part, Nixon was careful to play to the hilt the politics of reverse images. It is a politics where an aspirant for the presidency coolly estimates the worst things people suspect about him, and then frames a line of controlled personal conduct in which he will appear to be the exact opposite of his suspected nature. In this system a five-star general aspiring to be president, for example, will allay the suspicion that he is a Caesar-minded militarist by talking like a self-abnegating pacifist; an aristocrat will deal with the suspicion that he is a class-conscious snob by affecting to be a man of plebeian tastes; a plebeian will affect the elegance of an aristocrat in order to quiet the suspicion that he is a simmering revolutionary; and a Catholic aspirant for the presidency, conscious of the suspicion that he is under the control of the Vatican, will try to show himself to be more Protestant than Martin Luther. In Nixon's case, he knew that many people who had come of political age in the late 1940's or in the 1950's thought of him as a gut-

146

fighting political vendettist. So, in the 1968 presidential contest he affected to be a model of sweet reasonableness, tolerance, restraint, compassion, and forgiveness. He went so far as to state that "In a Nixon administration, students will have a better alternative than to take to the streets in protest. They are going to have a piece of the action." [7] Student hecklers generally left him alone to concentrate on Humphrey, and Wallace.

Wallace seemed to welcome the student hecklers. He adeptly manipulated their heckling to his own political advantage, yet some student members of the New Left escalated their banter for reasons of their own. If they were to inherit the American earth—so their theorizing ran—traditional American liberalism had to be destroyed, and the forces of the American extreme right had to gain a monopoly of all the levers of political power. When that happened, the failures and repressions that would ensue would create a classical revolutionary situation from which the New Left would inevitably emerge as the decisive victor. To promote the cause of progress through disaster, the New Left must continue its disturbances in order to augment Wallace's strength—the more he captured the traditional sources of Democratic party strength, the more he would either increase the prospects of Nixon's victory or produce an Electoral College deadlock in which he would be in a position to pick the next president of the United States. Either way, the results would set in place all the elements needed for the revolutionary situation that would usher in the ultimate triumph of the New Left.

Other students were less sure. They began to ask questions about the deep inroads Wallace threatened to make on traditional sources of Democratic strength in the urban north. How was it, for example, that some of the rank and file voters who had originally preferred either McCarthy or Kennedy indicated that they intended to vote for Wallace? How was it that blue-collar workers cheered Wallace to the rafters every time he mounted another of his attacks on students? Although Humphrey would win back a substantial portion of the ethnics and hard-hats who gravitated to Wallace at one point in the 1968 presidential campaign, questions about the Wallace phenomenon would continue to haunt students with a reflective turn of mind.

If Nixon had defeated Humphrey by a massive majority, or if the McCarthy candidacy had been seen for what it really was —an adult crusade, and not a "Children's Crusade"—perhaps the postelection reaction against peace-minded students on the part of some liberal Democratic political leaders would not have been as pronounced as it turned out to be. Yet because Nixon won by only a hair, it appeared in retrospect that the seemingly worthless Democratic presidential nomination had been worth something after all. It was claimed in retrospect that a Democratic victory which could have been won—despite the shambles of the Chicago Convention—had been lost because the student supporters of McCarthy wanted it to be lost.

It would have been more plausible to maintain that since people of mature years were the original source and leaders of the McCarthy candidacy, Humphrey lost the election because of a postconvention sit-down strike among them. Or, to put the matter more directly, most of the rank and file voters for McCarthy eventually came around to supporting Humphrey, but the sizeable minority that did not switch, may have been crucial in the loss of some states—especially where there was a deliberate do-nothing policy among local McCarthy leaders. Nixon carried several states (California, Illinois, and New Jersey) in which the active McCarthy committee refused to help Humphrey by only a very narrow margin. If California alone had gone to Humphrey, Nixon would have been denied a majority in the Electoral College. In addition to California, Nixon carried all the other states that had critical Democratic primaries—New Hampshire, Wisconsin, Indiana, Nebraska and

148

Oregon—some of which had been bastions of McCarthy strength.

Chicago, however, had made it impossible for McCarthy to issue an early endorsement of Humphrey's candidacy. He removed his own name from the ballots of 25 states, but waited until October 29, 1968—a week before the election—before issuing a tepid statement to the effect that he meant to vote for Humphrey. He had been urged to act sooner, and the pressure built up after Humphrey's September 30 television statement on Vietnam was construed to mean that the Democratic nominee had broken free of Johnson's stranglehold on his campaign. To McCarthy though, Humphrey's statement on Vietnam was no more than "good openers for twenty-five-cents poker." [8] In any case, he held back his endorsement until the senatorial candidates he campaigned for announced that they were going to vote for Humphrey. Perhaps more to the point, McCarthy— who had not told his supporters what to do in the case of his own candidacy—could not have dictated their action concerning Humphrey. He had, he said, set people free.

III

In mid-September 1968, when the presidential campaign was just beginning to heat up, the Steering Committee for MOBE —David Dellinger, Rennie Davis and Tom Hayden—met in Washington with a hundred other people representing groups that covered the entire spectrum of MOBE's membership. The result was an announcement sent out nationally to all active antiwar groups urging them to "descend on Washington" on Inauguration day, January 20, 1969.

At all subsequent meetings held to discuss strategic plans for what was presently called the "counter-inaugural protest,"

MOBE officials—with the scars of the Chicago riot in mind—made it clear that they were planning only peaceful protest activities. Dellinger, supported by Davis, insisted that MOBE make the protest a political, not a physical confrontation, designed to show the new president how deeply divided the American people were over the war. "To get into a street fight with the police," said he, "is simply to focus on the wrong issue."

Washington officials had drawn a moral from the Chicago experience and calmly assessed the alarmist FBI data dumped on their desks. Their own political intelligence revealed no potential for any serious security threat, although some commotion might take place. Washington officials had also learned much from the confusion in Chicago—as analyzed in Daniel Walker's report, "Rights in Conflict"—and after negotiating in good faith with MOBE, granted the permits to march in time to get the instructions out to the demonstrators.[9] They agreed to the installation of the facilities that were requested. By meeting all reasonable demands consistent with security, they hoped to curtail provocations for violence.

The so-called underground press was quick to respond to this version of Chicago played backwards, and a festive mood among the planners of the protest replaced the bitterness left by the Democratic National Convention. The spirit of the preparations had its effect on staid antiwar groups, such as the Women's Strike for Peace, the Committee for a Sane Nuclear Policy, and the University Committee on Problems of War and Peace. When all these groups decided to participate in the counterinaugural activities, their presence restored a more moderate balance to the roll of demonstrators.

Two days of demonstrations preceding the inauguration on January 20 passed without incident. MOBE's marshals and the police worked with each other to keep all protest activities within the limits set forth in the permits. Flare-ups did eventually occur, involving some 100 demonstrating youths who felt that "kids in conflict with cops, in violent conflict with cops, will have a taste of blood and know true revolution." They hurled objects and obscenities at President Nixon and others during the Inaugural parade, and tried to provoke the police. Some police broke discipline and cracked under the taunts, with results that led to localized clashes. But the ground rules fixed in advance, and the mutual resolve of MOBE's officials to stick to the rules, effectively isolated the "crazies." The police kept the good will of most demonstrators while the disruptive elements gained few recruits and lost the moral support of many. It seemed, as President Nixon himself said in his Inaugural address, that the country wanted everyone to lower their voices and come together again in support of the articles of peace between majorities and minorities. This was not to be.

Antiwar protesters were prepared to mark time until the Nixon administration organized itself and tipped its hand on Vietnam policy, but Nixon lost little time in exposing his attitudes about two provocative matters. The first was his commitment to a southern strategy, revealed first in his reluctance to apply the full force of those civil rights laws which required him to cut off federal funds to southern school districts that refused to integrate. The second was his strictures against student protesters, revealed in the letter of praise he wrote to the Reverend Theodore Hesburgh, president of Notre Dame, who had warned students that demonstrators at Notre Dame would be given ten minutes to disperse—if they failed to do so, they would face instant suspension or expulsion.

President Nixon's strictures fell on the deaf ears of black students in his native California. Immediately after the election, they had launched a strike against San Francisco State College in support of a list of ten "non-negotiable demands." In the following weeks, the college was the scene of violence unmatched in the history of American higher education, and was the first

151

ever to be occupied by police on a continuous basis over several months. By the end of the semester on January 31, 1969, there had been 731 arrests on campus, more than 80 students were reported injured in the course of their arrest, and others were hurt but not arrested. Thirty-two policemen were injured on campus. Aside from unnumbered small fires and a major one in a vice-president's office, eight bombs were planted on campus and two firebombs were hurled into the home of an assistant to the president. In mid-February, a campus guard received head injuries from a bomb that exploded at the entrance to the administration building. Three weeks later, on March 5, 1969, a 19-year-old Negro sophomore was partially blinded and maimed when a time bomb—which police said he was installing—exploded in the Creative Arts building.[10]

An uneasy peace eventually came to prevail at San Francisco State, but student shock tactics exported from the college were adopted elsewhere. In April, 300 militant Harvard students, mostly white, got into the swing of things. While the Puritan founders of the college turned over in their graves and Boston Brahmins were numbed with shock, the militants seized University Hall, the main administration building, kicked eight deans out of their offices, chained up the doors, and began a sit-in. The next day, Harvard, the original fount of the liberal arts in America, was wounded in its innermost being when Harvard President Pusey overreacted as the militants hoped he would. At his call, more than 400 state and local police descended on University Hall, used their night sticks with the zest of uninhibited rage, broke up the sit-in, and arrested 197 students.

Not long afterward, another ivy-league college was the source of photographs that sent shock waves across the country. At Cornell, militant black students armed themselves with guns and bandoliers of ammunition, holed up in a building they had seized, and conveyed the impression that they were prepared for a death stand rather than submit to whatever it was they claimed threatened them. Photographs broadcast to the nation showed the armed black militants in the role of look-outs hugging walled openings to escape detection while they watched for any approaching enemy force. Cornell seemed a horror story come true.

At the same time, a group of young white extremists who had been known as "the crazies" during the counterinauguration demonstration against the war in Vietnam, extended the scope of the tactics perfected by militant members of the Black Students Union at San Francisco State. After June 1968, the crazies became known as the Weatherman faction of the SDS. Under either name, when they found themselves isolated from the main phalanx of organization that belonged to MOBE, they concluded that their only natural allies were violence-prone black militants. To prove their own worth as allies, they embarked on a stepped-up program of urban guerilla warfare, marked not only by the bombing or burning of university structures and other public buildings chosen as symbols of corrupt capitalism, but by destruction for its own sake.

Meanwhile, a criminal prosecution begun in September 1969 reawakened memories of the raw confrontations between youthful antiwar demonstrators and police that had convulsed the city of Chicago and appalled the nation during the 1968 Democratic Convention. Subsequently eight activists had been indicted for "conspiracy to incite a riot"—meaning the riot at the time of the convention.[11] They were brought to Chicago for a trial in a federal court presided over by Judge Julius Hoffman, 74. Taken together, the eight represented virtually the whole spectrum of American dissent from pacifists to hard-line radicals to cultural revolutionaries. Six of the eight have already been mentioned: David Dellinger, Tom Hayden and Rennie Davis of MOBE's Steering Committee, Abbie Hoffman and Jerry Rubin of the mythic Yippies, and Bobby Seale of the Black Panthers. The remaining two were John Froines, 30, as-

153

sistant professor of chemistry at the University of Oregon, and Lee Weiner, 30, a teaching assistant in sociology at Northwestern University.

Their prosecution was the first of its kind under an antiriot rider to the Civil Rights Act of 1968, which had been tacked onto the bill by Senator Strom Thurmond as a weapon against "outside agitators." The Chicago Eight—as they had come to be called—were charged with conspiring to travel across state lines with the intention of inciting a riot; to teach the use of incendiary devices to be set off during the riot; and to obstruct firemen and law enforcement officials in the performance of their duties during the riot. Each defendant was also charged with an individual overt act—making a speech, or attending a meeting or training session.

Student political activists across the nation paid close attention to the ramifications and pyrotechnics of the trial, and helped raise funds to cover the costs of the defense. Many were bemused by the antics of Hoffman and Rubin. Froines and Weiner were "followers" more than leaders, and as such not well known to student political activists nationally. Seale had become better known since August 1969, when he was held in $25,000 bail on charges involving the murder in May of a former Black Panther in Connecticut. But Dellinger, Hayden, and Davis, were all key figures on the student scene. Student political activists saw themselves on trial with these three and, in their eyes, the outcome would go far toward determining how much dissent would be permitted in America under the Constitution.

The trial was to make Judge Hoffman a favorite among that segment of the American population that was outraged by any kind of disorder. Many legal specialists, however, took a different view of the indictment, the trial, and the way Judge Hoffman conducted the proceedings. If the defendants were guilty of acts of incitement to riot, why, they asked, considering that federal law recognized the primacy of state jurisdiction over riotous conduct, didn't the state government prosecute? Why was conspiracy alleged? Was it not enough to allege illegal acts of violence and incitement? Why these eight defendants chosen out of the many people who took part in the demonstration? Why was Bobby Seale indicted, considering that he had attended only at the last moment and made speeches in the vein of those made a thousand times before by scores of other black militants, none of whom were indicted?

As the trial proceeded it presented a vivid paradigm of attitudinal conflict—the defendants, scornful of the accepted standards of American life, and the elderly judge, mystified and horrified at their disbelief, fearful that the American system was being threatened by a new breed of hedonistic or anarchic youth.

Hoffman's mystification was mirrored by many people who identified the defendants with their still fresh memory of what they had read in mid-August about the four-day Woodstock Music and Art Fair in Bethel, New York. More than 300,000 participants from all over the country—despite massive traffic jams, drenching thunderstorms, and shortages of food, medical facilities, and water—braved campgrounds of mud to share in the extraordinary event. Judge Hoffman's horror was also shared by many people when the defendants on trial were connected (falsely) in the public mind with the events that had occurred in Chicago's most fashionable shopping and apartment hotel district on October 11, 1969. In the course of an antiwar parade moving through the area, a group of Weathermen ran wild, shouting and breaking expensive store-front windows. The result was a brief and bloody battle with the police, a broken neck suffered by City Corporation Counsel Richard Elrod, and the arrest of 100 persons. There was, on this occasion no police provocation; the destruction of property and the attacks on persons were deliberate, calculated acts by the Weathermen, flowing from their philosophy of social change. What they brought about instead was a consolidation of the popular conviction that Mayor Daley and his police were absolutely in the right during the riot the previous year in Grant Park.

From the outset of the trial, Bobby Seale seemed the most forceful of the defendants. He wanted the trial postponed until his attorney, Charles R. Garry—a white California lawyer for many Black Panthers—recovered from a gall bladder operation. Judge Hoffman refused. Seale then demanded the right to defend himself and to cross-examine witnesses who tied him to the alleged conspiracy, but Judge Hoffman insisted that Seale was adequately represented by William M. Kunstler, one of the defense attorneys. Seale proceeded to escalate his protests, calling the judge a "racist," then a "fascist" and finally a "pig." Judge Hoffman ordered Seale shackled and gagged in court. But after some days of the distracting and evocative sight of a black man bound and gagged in an American courtroom, the judge suddenly declared a mistrial for Seale and separated him from the proceedings.

While the long trial was in progress, politicians and the mass media grossly exaggerated the confrontations between the defendants and the judge. The behavior of the defendants was described as violent and anarchic—part of a new conspiracy to stop the courts from functioning. The Yippie defendants—Hoffman and Rubin—did in fact deliberately feed this over-reaction. They spent much of their courtroom time analyzing trial coverage in the papers, plotting press conferences, arranging for "Yippie witnesses" to get on the stand in time for deadlines, even calculating which of the defendants was getting most of the media attention. They knew that the smallest unconventional act would goad the court into over-reaction, would be fixed upon by the press, and would spread an image of defiance and disorder in the country—along with the impression that the nation had raised a generation of sybaritic revolutionaries.

At the end of the long trial, the jury found that none of the defendants were guilty of conspiracy. Five of them—Dellinger, Hayden, Davis, Hoffman and Rubin—were found guilty of inciting to riot. The remaining two—Froines and Weiner—were found not guilty of any charge. Judge Hoffman, however, proceeded to mete out contempt citations for all the defendants, their principal lawyers, and Bobby Seale. Each alleged act of contempt was assigned a weight of its own on a tariff schedule of punishment, and each carried a sentencing to a certain number of months in prison. So it went from defendant to defendant, each accumulating his own measure of punishment on a certain number of counts. Hoffman found Seale guilty of contempt on 16 counts, and sentenced him to three months imprisonment on each count—four years in prison in all.

Lawyers construed this move as an attempt by Judge Hoffman to evade a Supreme Court ruling that a trial judge may sentence no one to more than six months for contempt. It was, at any rate, an astonishingly heavy sentence of a man who was not convicted by a jury and was in fact separated from the trial. It was equally disconcerting that lawyers for the accused should end up with exceptionally heavy sentences for contempt, and that two of the defendants who were found not guilty of any of the charges on which they had been brought to trial were nonetheless sentenced to jail for their own alleged contempt of court. All the defendants, however, were released on bail pending an appeal of their respective cases to a higher court.

IV

Before the Chicago trial MOBE dissolved and was replaced in June 1969, by two new organizations which often appeared to be interchangeable in function and personnel. One of the two

—the New Mobilization Committee to End the War in Vietnam—was composed mainly of leaders and cooperating organizations who had taken part in the demonstrations planned by the old MOBE. The second organization was the Vietnam Moratorium Committee. Its principal leaders—Sam Brown, David Mixner, David Hawks and Marge Sklencar—had led the student sector of the McCarthy campaign.

The antiwar forces were generally quiescent during the previous months when the opening rounds of the Paris peace talks coincided with the staffing of the new Nixon administration. But beginning in March, and for the spring, summer and autumn months that followed, a swirl of concurrent events combined to renew vocal opposition to the military establishment, to the war, and to "things in general." For example, the administration's request for funds to construct the Safeguard ABM system led to months of debate in the nation and in the Senate, where the request was eventually approved by a razor-thin margin. Then, there were the successive commotions caused when it was disclosed that the Pentagon had made a heavy investment of funds in the development and production of weapons for biological warfare, that the army had made a regular practice of shipping large containers of nerve gas by rail, and that under the terms of a "secret contingency plan," American forces were stationed in Thailand where they provided combat support to Thai troops engaged in anti-Communist military operations across the border in Laos.

In Vietnam, meanwhile, fierce fighting continued on the ground and the bombing, though restricted in scope, became more concentrated. In Paris, the peace talks appeared to be congealed in mutual intransigence. In the Senate, on March 17, the Nixon administration's Vietnam policy was attacked for the first time by a Democratic dove when Senator McGovern castigated the administration for its lack of "strength and courage to genuinely reverse our course." Later, on May 9, in what was considered the most blunt criticism of the president by a Republican Senator since Nixon took office, Senator Jacob K. Javits of New York attacked the president's policy of Vietnam peace talks as insufficiently flexible in dealing with the Vietcong and North Vietnamese. Still later, on September 25, Republican Senator Charles E. Goodell of New York proposed legislation requiring withdrawal of all American troops from Vietnam by the end of 1970. This proposal reopened a full scale congressional debate on the Vietnam War that had been suspended to give President Nixon a chance to develop his policy.

President Nixon himself had not been idle. In a television speech delivered in May, he had proposed a phased withdrawal of most outside allied and enemy troops from South Vietnam over the period of a year. The next month, after a meeting at Midway with President Thieu of South Vietnam, he announced that 25,000 American soldiers would be redeployed by the end of August. When Ho Chi Minh, the 70-year-old president of North Vietnam died in Hanoi on September 3, President Nixon ordered a suspension of B-52 raids over the various battlefields to see what effect this would have in de-escalating the war. Although the raids were resumed at the end of the three-day cease fire that was initiated to mark the funeral of Ho Chi Minh, President Nixon in mid-September announced that an additional 35,000 American troops would be brought home by December 15, thus raising to 60,000 the number of troops that were to be withdrawn from the war zone. He followed this with a further announcement that draft calls for the remainder of 1969 were to be cut by 50,000 men—a move that amounted to a suspension of the draft in November and December.

Despite these actions antiwar protests continued to mount, and demands were amplified for a speed-up in the rate of withdrawal. President Nixon appealed to the nation for support, and insisted that the other side would bargain seriously to end

159

the war in Vietnam only if it knew that Americans were united behind their president's policy. "I understand," he added, "that there has been and continues to be opposition to the war in Vietnam on the campuses and also in the nation. As far as this kind of activity is concerned, we expect it. However, under no circumstances will I be affected whatever by it." [12] The echo of his remarks still hung in the air when the Faculty of Arts and Sciences of Harvard University on October 7 voted to call for an end of the Vietnam War and the withdrawal of American troops; the action was thought to be the first time in Harvard's long history that its faculty—as a collective body— ever took a political stand in opposition to government policy. Five days later, the presidents of five of the eight ivy league colleges and of 74 other colleges and universities, speaking as individuals appealed to President Nixon for a "stepped-up timetable for withdrawal from Vietnam." [13]

Amid the cross-tensions of fear and hope rising from all such events, the Vietnam Moratorium Committee unveiled the protest strategy it had in mind. On the 15th day of each month, starting in October, it would call for a cessation of ordinary work in order to protest the Vietnam War; the successive monthly protests would stop only when the war stopped.

On October 14, the White House tried to discredit the Moratorium by challenging its leaders and supporters to repudiate expressions of support given them by the Hanoi government. At the same time, the leadership of the House of Representatives choked off a planned all-night debate scheduled by anti-war congressmen. Yet the two moves could no more stop what was in motion than a pitchfork can hurl back the sea. Millions of Americans joined in protesting the war on the first Vietnam Moratorium Day. Black armbands, prayer vigils, candlelight processions, and speeches to huge assemblies marked the occasion. Other protesting Americans briefly halted the routine of their life, whether in offices, factories, shops, or the bustle of the traffic on city streets. A number of colleges suspended regular classes in favor of a day and night-long teach-in devoted to Vietnam. Students also fanned out from their colleges to ring doorbells in surrounding neighborhoods, to pass out antiwar literature, to get signatures on antiwar petitions, and to discuss the issues.

Washington was not meant to be the focal point of the first Moratorium. Nonetheless, tens of thousands of demonstrators marched past the White House on October 15—while President Nixon appeared to ignore them. That he was fully aware of the protest march, however, was revealed by two White House actions which bracketed it.

First, Vice President Spiro Agnew was now assigned much the same kind of role which Nixon himself, as vice president, had played under President Eisenhower—the role of the administration's ambassador to the right wing of the Republican party and hatchet man on the prowl against administration adversaries. President Nixon, after the model of President Eisenhower, affected to be infinitely compassionate and forgiving toward all who disagreed with him. In an October 15 speech to a Republican fund-raising dinner in New Orleans, Agnew sharply attacked the participants in the Vietnam Moratorium Day, saying that they were "encouraged by an effete corps of impudent snobs who characterize themselves as intellectuals." [14] A phrase was born.

Second, in a television speech to the nation on November 3 —the eve of scattered elections around the country— President Nixon reported on his search for peace in Vietnam and declared that he had a plan to bring home all American ground forces in an orderly way under a secret timetable. Immediately after he completed his televised remarks, a number of television commentators analyzed the substantive merits of his policy statement. Their instant criticism jarred the White House, beset as it was by the strains inherent in the complex task of negotiating an orderly retreat from Vietnam that would

161

also meet with the approval of the Pentagon. So the next day, newsmen summoned to the President's White House office were shown a large stack of telegrams which he claimed were full of praise for his speech on Vietnam. The messages, said Nixon, proved that the "great silent majority of Americans" backed him in his search for peace.[15] The "silent majority" was more than just a phrase. It was partially rooted in the state of public opinion at the time—depending on the kind of questions the polls asked. It was also rooted, in part, in the continued prevalence of a post-World War II political tendency on the part of a majority of Americans to agree that the national interest in the world arena is what the president says it is.

The Moratorium set for the weekend of November 13–15, unlike the one held in October, planned to make Washington the focal point for the antiwar protest. Its organization was a cooperative venture of the Moratorium Committee and the New Mobilization Committee. But as the weekend of November 13–15 drew near, the administration tried to blunt in advance any impact the antiwar demonstrators might have. On November 10, Agnew signaled the start of a counterattack by denouncing the demonstrators as a strident minority performance —a "carnival in the streets." [16] The next day, Veterans Day, "the great silent majority" with backstage administration encouragement, took to the streets in a show of support for President Nixon's policies. Many of the traditional Veteran's Day parades were described as larger than usual, and many marchers attributed the increase to the fact that people were fed up with all the noisy dissenters.

These proadministration marches, however, were eclipsed in size by the Washington-focused second Moratorium. Aside from the many demonstrators who lobbied their home-base congressmen and senators, the Moratorium program on November 14 featured a continuous stream of individuals—each representing a member of the U. S. armed forces killed in Vietnam

—who moved around the Lincoln Memorial, past the White House (where there was a requiem roll call of the dead) and onto the Capitol lawn. The next day witnessed the largest mass march ever held in Washington. An estimated quarter of a million people, who at midday formed a solid moving carpet of humanity extending from the foot of the Capitol to the Washington Monument, demonstrated for an immediate withdrawal from Vietnam. The massive size of the crowd and the experiences shared by its members over the Washington weekend infused the marchers with a poignant sense of community and potency.

Except for two flurries where small groups of self-styled revolutionaries—only marginally linked with the antiwar demonstration—indulged in a politics of violent confrontation, it was a peaceful demonstration. The agitators tried to march on the South Vietnamese embassy. They threw rocks and bottles at the Justice Department, and twice ran up the Vietcong flag, but tear gas and arrests eventually quelled their activity.

The disruptions, however, did not hide from general view the nonviolent conduct of the rest of the crowd of a quarter of a million people. When the marchers in Washington finished their program in the national capital and packed for a return to their points of origin, congratulatory notes were heard on all sides. The main body of marchers and their marshals were congratulated for conducting themselves with dignity and restraint. The Washington police force was congratulated for its professionalism in handling crowds and in defusing potentially explosive episodes. The American Constitution was congratulated for its guarantee of the right of petition. American education was congratulated for having reared a generation of students who— despite the hippie drop-outs and despite the revolutionary polemics and guerilla tactics of a handful—still chose to seek its political objective by working within the system.

The one major exception to the chorus of official praise for

163

the conduct of the demonstrators sounded in a strong statement by Attorney General John N. Mitchell. Previously, so reported *The New York Times,* the Justice Department had taken a hard line against granting a parade permit to the demonstrators, but city officials had urged the White House itself to issue the permit, fearing that a refusal could itself prompt violence. Now, however, as if to prove that he had been right all along, Mitchell flatly stated that the weekend peace activities were by no means peaceful. "The New Mobilization Committee," he said, "aided this violence through a combination of inaction and affirmative action." [17] The attorney general's hostility to administration critics was echoed four days later by Vice President Agnew who responded with panegyrics to Nixon's November 3 statement of policy on Vietnam. Speaking before the Chamber of Commerce in Montgomery, Alabama, Agnew challenged the news judgment and the fairness of the press. In particular, he singled out *The New York Times* and *The Washington Post* as examples of newspapers that suffered from lack of competition. Agnew, by now, was indeed a household word.

V

In the weeks that followed, a round of meetings between a group of former campaign workers of McCarthy, Humphrey, and Kennedy came to a head in an announcement issued in Washington on January 5, 1970. The group, which called itself Referendum '70, had as its honorary chairman John Kenneth Galbraith, Harvard University economics professor and former Ambassador to India during the Kennedy years. Members of its advisory committee included Fred Dutton, former adviser to President Kennedy and Robert Kennedy; Richard Goodwin; Ted Van Dyck, former assistant to Humphrey; Mayor Charles

Evers of Fayette, Miss.; Gloria Steinem, writer; Andrew Young, vice-president of the Southern Christian Leadership Conference; and Vernon Newton, executive director of the New Democratic Coalition of New York. Other members included individuals who had been prominent in the Moratorium Committee to End the War in Vietnam.

The purpose of the group, according to its announcement, was to start a campaign to make the 1970 congressional elections a referendum on the Vietnam War. Members of the group would use their political expertise to elect candidates—Republicans, Democrats or Independents—who shared their concern over the war and the myriad of ills affecting the United States. Aid would come in the form of field organizers to assist candidates in campaigns, training sessions for candidate's staffers, and research on political issues. Financial support would be left to others, though the group's own budget was put at $500,000, to be raised mostly through appeals to individuals.

An idea was now in the air. Yet the antiwar movement itself seemed to enter a period where it did little more than discharge steam, like an idle locomotive switched to a side track. There were several reasons for inaction. Recent changes in the draft law, followed by the first draft lottery in a generation, had partly removed a motive for student protests against the Selective Service Law. The reduction in the number of young men called up monthly for the draft, coupled with the slow but steady withdrawals of American units from Vietnam, made for a propaganda more persuasive than any of Nixon's speeches concerning his avowed resolve to scale down and eventually end the American embroilment in Vietnam.

When the Christmas Eve Peace Vigil sponsored by the Moratorium Committee mustered little support, the coordinators of the committee, led by Sam Brown, reconsidered their position. At a press conference held in Washington's Ambassador Hotel on January 6, 1970, they announced the general terms of the new plans they had in mind and the central thought behind them. "President Nixon in his November 3 speech," said Brown, "had stated a policy for continuing the war, not for ending it, but," he added, "it will become clear by March or April that the people have been deceived." [18] The Moratorium Committee, therefore, would not sponsor any major demonstrations in the next three months. It would concentrate instead on the task of rekindling the antiadministration fervor that was so evident during the October rallies and the November massive march in Washington. The period between January and April 1970, would be spent on the organization and canvassing of neighborhoods by persons opposed to President Nixon's Vietnam policy. After that, the committee would promote a fast on April 13–15, and would urge those fasting to donate the money they would otherwise spend for food "to relieve the suffering of the victims of this war both in Vietnam and at home." On April 15 itself, the deadline day for filing income tax returns, persons opposed to Nixon's policy would rally at local Internal Revenue Service offices. The taxpayer rallies would center on the issue of high taxes due to disproportionate military spending.

At the same January 6 press conference in the Ambassador Hotel, David Mixner, another coordinator, indicated that the Moratorium Committee—in line with the announcement made the previous day by spokesmen for the newly formed Referendum '70—would start a campaign service for antiwar political candidates. It planned to generate thousands of volunteers for the campaigns, to provide experienced consultants to advise on campaign strategy, and to organize entertainers and speakers for fund-raising performances. In this way, they would help "doves running for re-election and doves running against hawk incumbents." [19] The Moratorium Committee expected to have the resources to aid 50 to 60 candidates for the Senate or the House of Representatives who sought assistance.

166

But the April fasts fizzled, as did the April 15 tax rally. Soon afterward, the Moratorium Committee and the new MOBE announced their own dissolution. Brown was not yet ready to publicly disclose his private assessment of the antiwar movement with which he had been associated from the beginning, yet he had come to see no future in an antiwar movement based solely on students. In an article he wrote for the August *Washington Monthly*, he explained why:

Not enough students have the stature, capacity, or inclination to run a tightly disciplined peace movement, which would be required to make them effective and keep them moving toward Middle America. Even if such an organization were possible, students alone would be unable to attract a majority of the American people to any politically effective peace position. Students can have an impact since most Americans still don't want to hate their own children. But you must have strong leadership off the campuses to set the tone and direction of the antiwar effort and to give it hope. . . .

Most American voters make political decisions largely on issues of tone and style rather than on the basis of vigorous foreign policy analysis. . . . They don't like long hair, campus protests, or, in short, class values. They may dislike the war, but they dislike radicals far more. Moreover, they inherit this country's anti-intellectual legacy, so that if the President calls for "team spirit" for them, "communal solidarity" smacks of the red specter and academic snobbery.[20]

Other people also began to argue that the deepest yearning for peace lay in Middle America—that there is where the true antiwar majority was to be found. There, too, were people concerned with the deadening sameness of the assembly line, with inflation, with the problems of buying a home, with unemployment. They were not the hard-hat stereotypes that had been applied by the media and the New Left to people who worked with their hands. They wanted an end to the war in Vietnam; they wanted a healthy environment, and, like youth in the colleges, they wanted to play a significant role in the political process. Yet Middle America shunned the peace movement because they associated its aims with anarchy, juvenile delinquency, flag burning, and alienation from one's parents. They disliked these things even more than they disliked the war, and unless the peace movement turned away from the "crazies," unless it reached out for an alliance with Middle America, it would suffer from self-inflicted wounds.

At the same time, academicians, intellectuals, and antiwar politicians associated with the left wing of the Democratic Party, began to call more loudly for an end to violence, delinquency, and confrontation. There was also among them a growing willingness to acknowledge a hard truth that, while opposition to the war was a matter of highest principle to some young people—a principle for which they were willing to face beating, imprisonment, and a lifelong handicap to their careers —many had opposed the war for entirely selfish purposes and were not at all concerned for the problems of others. These students wished only to maintain their student deferments, and were insensitive to the fact that wartime service was to be the lot only of those too poorly educated to avoid it. This new criticism rising from the left wing of the Democratic party lay behind a sidelash twist in a significant remark by Senator Edward Kennedy when he said that the Democratic party could not allow a love affair with campus youth on the issue of war to weaken or obscure the close tie the party always had with the labor movement and the working man.

VI

During spring semester psychological pressures on a campus are at their peak. It is a time of reckoning. Term papers are due; the student has to catch up with all the work he hasn't done over the quarter or semester or, in some cases, the year; final examinations are in the offing; and graduating seniors begin to look for jobs or nervously await word from graduate and professional schools.

As April 1970 neared its end, many college officials and professors held their fingers crossed in a mixture of hope and fear. The academic year that had begun in the fall of 1969 was not altogether free of violent or potentially violent protests. California students continued to suggest the picture of a powder keg with a lit fuse. The latest explosion occurred in the spring of 1970 when University of California students at Santa Barbara burned a branch structure of the nearby Bank of America, and when a student was killed in an ensuing clash with the police. Concurrently, Yale students demonstrated in New Haven for a fair trial for Bobby Seale. (Seale was indicted on charges growing out of the murder of a former Black Panther member.) A number of campus demonstrations and protests had also been staged in support of the defendants in the Chicago "conspiracy" trial.

In the main, however, the nationwide picture suggested a marked reduction in the frequency and scope of student disorders. If the calm held until June, perhaps it could be said that students had finally negotiated a full psychic turn away from protests as a way of life. The apparent calm—even on campuses that had formerly been the main centers for student demonstrations—could be ascribed to a number of different reasons: to the mass media's boredom with the subject of campus unrest; to changes in the draft laws; to the signs that the Nixon administration was in fact withdrawing American forces from Vietnam; or to the growing tendency among college administrations to take a firm stand against disruptive dissenters and to make a fuller use of court injunctions to forestall protests.

Another reason could be added to the list, based on the findings made in a survey during the spring of 1970 for the League of Industrial Democracy (LID). According to the LID's survey the radical left-wing student movement had collapsed into fragmented, embittered, competing organizations. What had formerly been a fairly unified movement with a widely accepted leadership and common goals had become a melange of grouplets, projects, and styles, "with no shared sense of direction, and very often with profound and even bitter internal differences." Why the disintegration of the New Left? The answer the League gave, based on its survey, corresponded with what various people associated with the left of the Democratic party had come to say about the student antiwar movement generally. The New Left's disintegration, LID declared, was due at least in part to its growing isolation from the mainstream of American political and social thought that is identified with organized labor, middle-of-the-road black groups, and traditional liberals. In so isolating themselves, the New Left adherents "lost the possibilities of ever winning major support for their program of change. By provoking the opposition of labor, the representative black groups, and the traditional liberals, the New Left destroyed its possibilities of becoming a mass movement."

Still, whether or not the splintering of radical groups (and the isolation of the guerillas among them) or any other reason cited to explain the apparent calm on the campuses, was the decisive factor in the picture, student political activism by late April 1970, appeared to be turning in peaceful ways to a new set of national issues—pollution control and prevention, consumer protection, elimination of poverty, compensatory educational programs for the disadvantaged, control of firearms, and abortion-law reform.

But then, in a White House broadcast on April 30, President Nixon announced that as part of a design related to the safe withdrawal of more American troops from Vietnam, a combined American and South Vietnamese armed force had en-

170

tered Cambodia to destroy the Communist bases in that country. The logic of President Nixon's announced intention of trying to reduce the level of the American involvement in the Vietnam War by an action that seemed to enlarge the scope of American operations in Southeast Asia was a line of reasoning many people had difficulty in following.

The first reflex action among students came the next day in New Haven. A mass meeting of Yale students had already been scheduled to protest the criminal prosecution of Bobby Seale. The meeting, when held, was swiftly transfigured into a mass discussion of the Cambodian incursion. A resolution was put and passed, calling for a nationwide strike of students in protest against the latest turn in the Vietnam conflict. That same weekend, the national apparatus of the antiwar movement which had been dismantled was hastily reassembled in preparation for a new march of war protesters on Washington. Beginning on Monday, May 3, some students on politically-active campuses and on those with a previous history of unrest echoed the Yale call and went out on strike.

Not all the campuses that went out on strike right after President Nixon's announcement did so for reasons directly related to the Cambodian invasion. Some went out on strike simply as a release from springtime pressures. At Iowa State, for example, a student water fight led to a fracas, to a call to the police to break it up, to a clash between the students and the police —and then to a call for a strike in the name of a protest against Cambodia. In any case, as later studies showed, the strike tended to be limited in scope up to the moment on May 5 when the news was broadcast that four students who had been bystanders at a Kent State protest had been killed by the Ohio National Guard.

The trauma in the news drew at least some of its force from the previous anonymity of Kent State. Nothing about the place —its administrative leaders, its faculty, or its student body—

171

had ever drawn national attention. If anything newsworthy happened on the campus, reports of the event were confined to the local press, or at the most, to the Ohio press. So it was in the case of the tangle of events that had run their course at Kent State in the spring days immediately preceding May 5. There had been rising tensions between some of the students and the merchants of the city leading to police arrests of students on what the latter charged were petty misdemeanors used as pretexts for harassment. The students reacted to the arrests by setting up road blocks that interfered with the flow of commercial traffic in the city and brought more law-enforcement agents to the scene.

Independently, rising antiwar tensions led to a rally at Kent State where a splinter group set fire to the campus R. O. T. C. building, and then cut the hoses of the firemen called to combat the blaze. Still another group called another antiwar rally for May 5, but university authorities, fearing a resumption of the violence that had issued from the previous rally, denied the student group permission for the rally. Students who had assembled on the appointed rally ground found themselves facing detachments of the Ohio National Guard and were ordered to disperse. Many students, obedient to the order, did disperse. Others remained where they stood, and some of them hurled epithets and rocks at the guardsmen. Consequently, the students found themselves surrounded by the guardsmen, one of the platoons dropped into a fire position, and triggers were pulled. Among the students killed were some who were merely passing by on way to their classes and who happened to step into the paths of wild bullets.

Very little of the previous tensions at Kent State were known to students elsewhere, and it is not too much to suggest that if students nationally were polled before May 5 and asked if they knew where Kent State was—or had they as much as heard of the place—the overwhelming majority would have responded

172

in the negative. It was this very facelessness, the blood that was suddenly streaked across the cipher, that gave the phrase "Kent State" its purity and power as a rallying cry. Kent State was studenthood in the abstract, and the four who had died there were representative of studenthood itself suddenly slain. Subsequent news that students at Jackson State had been killed by Mississippi police was received as the Kent State story in black face. White students could relate personally to the Kent State deaths as they could never relate to other violent deaths— whether in Vietnam or in Watts, Detroit, Newark, Miami— where the dead were mainly black inhabitants of the ghettoes.

Following Kent State national attention focused on a transcontinental strike of students—the largest in American history —which brought the teaching of the regular curriculum to a standstill in over 400 American institutions of higher learning. It was not noticed at the time that 70 percent of all college institutions in the United States did not go out on strike but remained open despite Cambodia, Kent State, and Jackson State. But the 400 striking schools included institutions of higher learning that were publicly or privately supported, secular or religious in orientation, elitist or mass-based in clientele, urban or rural in setting, more than a century or but a few years old, the scenes of previous student disturbances or undisturbed islands of calm. In any case, it seemed that any institution that amounted to something beyond a mailing address had a local strike committee. Every institution with a claim to leadership in American higher education seemed to have a cadre of students who formed themselves as a regional strike center or as the headquarters of a National Committee, Union, or Movement —each claiming a mass following, and each designed to coordinate a major countrywide activity that would come to a head —in what?

No answer to the question, however fanciful, lacked its earnest adherents. Every college closed by a strike seemed to be a grand assize of all the discontents and aspirations of the age. All now found expression in a theatre crowded with youthful strategists and tacticians who brought to the polemics of the hour the echoes of lessons learned in academic studies of the American Revolution, the French Revolution, the Russian Revolution, the Chinese Revolution, the Algerian Revolution, and the Cuban Revolution. Some objective-minded bystanders might have wondered aloud, as Emerson did when he looked from afar at the 1848 French Revolution, whether the results would be worth the trees that went into the barricades. Yet any wondering aloud in this vein was muted, especially when it appeared that the hard core of young revolutionaries who had but recently been isolated on politically active campuses—or expelled from school—reappeared at the center of the turmoil like Lenins returning from exile and exhorted students to turn strike into a resumption of the unfinished student revolutionary war against "the system"—beginning with the university itself.

NOTES

1. Eldridge Cleaver, *Soul On Ice* (New York: Dell Publishing Company, 1968).

2. Lewis Chester, Godfrey Hodgson, and Bruce Page, *An American Melodrama* (New York: The Viking Press, 1969), pp. 579–580.

3. Daniel Walker, *Rights in Conflict: The Violent Confrontation of Demonstrators and Police in the Parks and Streets of Chicago during the Week of the Democratic National Convention of 1968, A Report of the National Commission of the Causes and Prevention of Violence* (New York: Bantam Books, 1968).

4. Richard T. Stout, *People* (New York: Harper and Row, 1969), p. 376.

5. Stout, *People,* p. 370.

6. Chester, *An American Melodrama,* p. 656.

7. Garry Wills, *Nixon Agonistes* (Boston, Mass.: Houghton Mifflin, 1969), pp. 348–349.

8. Stout, *People*, p. 375.

9. Daniel Walker, *Rights in Conflict*, The Response to the Counterinaugural Protest Activities in Washington, D. C., January 18–20, 1969. A special staff study submitted to the task force on law and law enforcement, The National Commission on the Causes and Prevention of Violence (Washington, D. C.: U. S. Government Printing Office) p. 79.

10. William H. Orrick, Jr., *Shut It Down! A College in Crisis*, San Francisco State College, October, 1968–April, 1969. A staff report to the National Commission on the Causes and Prevention of Violence (Washington, D. C.: U. S. Government Printing Office).

11. *Transcript of the Contempt Citations, Sentences, and Responses of the Chicago Conspiracy Ten*, foreword by Ramsay Clark, introduction by Harry Kalven, Jr. (Chicago: Swallow Press, 1969); Mark L. Levin, George C. McNamee, and Daniel Greenberg, eds., *The Tales of Hoffman* (New York: Bantam Books, 1969); Bobby Seale, *Seize the Time* (New York: Random House, 1969); Tom Hayden, *Rebellion and Repression* (New York and Cleveland: World Publishing Company, 1969).

12. *New York Times*, September 27, 1969.

13. *New York Times*, October 12, 1969.

14. *New York Times*, October 20, 1969.

15. *New York Times*, November 5, 1969.

16. *New York Times*, November 12, 1969.

17. *New York Times*, November 17, 1969.

18. *Washington Post*, January 7, 1970.

19. *Washington Post*, January 7, 1970.

20. Sam Brown, "The Politics of Peace," *The Washington Monthly* (August 1970).

8
The Unlikely
Tiger

I

An idea first voiced in January by Referendum '70 was brought to life at Princeton University four days after President Nixon's April 30 speech on the Cambodian offensive. The university community, alarmed and angered, met in Jadwin Gymnasium, where it decided by a vote of 3,800 to 22, to approve a university strike in protest against the war. Subsequently, under the spur of the news about the killings at Kent State, the community, again by an overwhelming vote, decided that the most effective and nonviolent way for students to help end the war and reshape America was by electing congressmen who would push for programs of peace at home and abroad. It also was agreed, following many faculty meetings, that the university schedule for the fall term would be rearranged to give students a two week recess immediately before the November elections so that they could devote full time to electioneering for representatives and senators. This decision, whose objective was to "give the system one last chance," was the origin of what presently came to be called the Movement for a New Congress (MNC), and the idea of a two week recess came to be called "The Princeton Plan."

176

The peril that Princeton had survived was recalled by Robert Goheen, its president, in his October 1970 report on *The State of the University*. He wrote: "When deep emotions are aroused, institutions and communities, like individuals, find it hard to hold to reasoned and reasonable courses. We saw strong evidence of that last May. No one should minimize the intensity and extent of the feelings aroused here following the Cambodia decision and then the Kent State and Jackson State tragedies." It was therefore the more significant that "most elements of the university community retained as much of a sense of balance as they did; that the lapses in policy did not go farther or reach deeper than they did." A large majority of both students and faculty "saw the importance of avoiding coercion and violence in expressing their urgent feelings and concerns about national policy in Southeast Asia and their desire to strike strongly against it."

Goheen's estimate of the dangers inherent in the turbulent days of early May was shared by presidents of other universities, among them Chancellor Alexander Heard of Vanderbilt University, in his capacity as President Nixon's special adviser on campus unrest. He later reported to the president on June 22, 1970, that it would be wrong to think of the campus upheavals as "a temporary, aberrational outburst by the young, or simply as a campus crisis or a student crisis." He went on to say:

Because of its immediate and potential consequences the condition we face must be viewed as a national emergency, to be addressed with the sense of urgency and openness of mind required by national emergencies. . . . The Cambodian action (followed by the Jackson State and Kent State killings) sharply intensified feelings among students already protesting the war and showing disaffection with society generally. More important, Cambodia provoked and exposed antiwar and societal discontents among large numbers of students of *normally moderate and conservative* political viewpoints. Before Cambodia, many of us on the campuses believed that

177

deep disaffection afflicted only a small minority of students. Now we conclude that May triggered a vast pre-existing charge of pent up frustration and dissatisfaction.[1]

II

The reactivated New Mobilization Committee hastily conjured up another mass descent of young people on Washington to protest the Cambodian invasion. Though it was cynically described as "the greatest mass ego trip in American history," earnest new groups of protesters who were obviously "square" showed up in Washington. Fifty students from the University of Minnesota School of Law, appeared on the Hill to lobby against extending the war into Cambodia and for an administration understanding of the depth of student unrest; their fares had been paid by $5,000 raised in the Minnesota and St. Paul legal community. Funds raised among merchants and citizens in Northfield, Minnesota, made it possible to send to Washington a peace lobby of four students and two professors from the anything-but radical St. Olaf's College. Then again, Mike Brewer, vice-president of the Ripon Society, an organization of young Republican liberals, teamed up with Sam Brown to start an organization called "Project Pursestrings." Its aim was to bring pressure on members of Congress to support an amendment to the military procurement bill, sponsored by Senators McGovern, Hatfield and others, that would cut off funds for U. S. military operations in Cambodia and Laos and require a complete pullout from Vietnam by mid-1971.

Of special interest was a party from New Haven led by Yale's President Kingman Brewster, Jr. Brewster had previously raised questions about the adequacy of the existing electoral process, and had voiced skepticism about how fair a trial black men could get in the U. S. courts. In the eyes of Vice-President Agnew, Brewster and the students who shared his views were the "rotten apples" who should be thrown out of the barrel of American society. Agnew wanted to see Brewster fired as Yale's president in a general dismissal of the "hard core of faculty and student" protesters from the colleges and universities. Agnew seemed unaware that while "Harvard is the mother of movements, Yale is the mother of men"—and that it was Yale men, more than those from any other single university in the nation, who were represented in force in the House, the Senate, and the Executive itself. Whether or not they agreed with Brewster personally, they needed no gratuitous advice from outsiders about how Yale men should deal with the President of Yale. Least of all did they need that advice when the party Brewster led to Washington at this time included Yale trustees who would ordinarily be thought of as the embodiment of an establishment that had an intransigent hostility to the younger generation.

The descent of the "squares" on Washington had its counterparts all over the country as students invaded state capitals from California to Illinois, from Wisconsin to Massachusetts, urging state legislatures to enact bills that would prohibit local residents from fighting in undeclared wars.

So many university dominated peace organizations came to birth—or rebirth—in the days immediately following Cambodia and Kent State that a National Coalition for a Responsible Congress was quickly formed as an umbrella for all campus-based peace groups. At the same time, the organizations with representatives on the Washington scene were brought together into a single lobby comprised of inter-related organizations housed on the fourth and fifth floors of an office building at 815 17th Street, N.W. The desks were makeshift or rented; the old folding chairs were uncomfortable; coffee urns sat on the floor; irreverent political cartoons, newspaper clippings, and

interoffice memos were taped to the walls among posters protesting war, pollution, and racism. The offices had the atmosphere of a campaign headquarters two days before election,
and they were maintained by a small flow of contributions from
private donors and by staffs of young volunteers. Nearly 200
staff members, mostly students, but also former government
lawyers, ex-Peace Corps volunteers, and professional secretaries, worked in these offices for either no money at all, or for a
subsistance allowance of little more than $30 a week. Their im-
mediate project was to try to persuade Congress to pass the
McGovern-Hatfield amendment. The interrelated organizations
were:

Continuing Presence in Washington: This organization established by Dartmouth students to supply data on congressional
voting records was hooked into a computer in Hanover, New
Hampshire. It armed visiting groups of war protesters with data
on how each representative and senator from their own home
base stood on the war and other issues, and arranged congressional audiences for those visiting groups. Continuing Presence
became the largest-staffed of the components in the peace lobby
with 40 full-time members and 30 to 40 part-time volunteers.

Law Students against the War: Apart from assisting in
lobbying work, this organization tried to place law-student volunteers in selected campaigns as speech writers, advance men
and strategists.

Referendum '70: This was the organization that had been
formed back in January 1970, by people who had been associated with the political fortunes of Humphrey, McCarthy,
Kennedy, and McGovern. Its young staff, composed mainly of
veterans of the political bids made by the men just named, did
in-depth research on the voting records of incumbents, and
planned to provide free technical assistance on campaign strategy to antiwar candidates.

Bipartisan Congressional Clearinghouse: This organization

owed its birth to Mark Talisman, an aide to Representative Charles A. Vanik, Democrat of Ohio. It was designed to guide volunteer students to candidates needing help. It also kept files on the services offered by various antiwar and new priorities organizations throughout the country and disseminated the information gathered.

These organizations did not exhaust the peace groups on the national scene. Scarcely a day passed when the American genius for "private association"—noted by de Tocqueville back in the 1830's—did not lead to the birth of a new *ad hoc* peace group. One such group was the National Petition Committee, based at the University of Rochester and largely student coordinated. As of May 15, it claimed to have more than 230 campus and other local chapters in its campaign to gather 20 million signatures on petitions against military involvement in Indochina. Students and other signers of the petitions were asked for a donation of 50 cents or more, and it was hoped that the movement nationally could collect $10 million. The effort in the spring of 1970 managed instead to raise $80,000 for antiwar causes.

Another fund-raising organization—the Universities National Antiwar Fund—came to birth in Boston on May 11. Initial sponsors of the effort included six Nobel Prize winners on the faculties of either Harvard or M. I. T., as well as Mary I. Bunting, President of Radcliffe College; Jerome B. Wiesner, Provost of M. I. T.; Albert Ullman, Provost of Tufts University; Lionel Trilling, author and critic; Professor Abram K. Chayes of the Harvard Law School; Dr. John H. Knowles, Director of the Massachusetts General Hospital; David Reisman, sociologist at Harvard; Bruno Rossi, Professor of Physics at M. I. T.; Albert M. Sacks, Associate Dean of the Harvard Law School; and other members of the Boston academic community. While most other fund raising groups had modest goals in mind, the Antiwar Fund aimed at major contributions that could result in a kitty of 15 million dollars to be used in helping peace candidates get elected in November. The idea was that professors across the nation would be asked to contribute at least a day of their salary to the Antiwar Fund.

Professor Jule Charney of M. I. T., chairman of the funds organizing committee, observed that "it was too simple a gesture for a professor to dismiss his classes and let his students go out on strike. The professors should be willing to contribute a substantial part of their salaries to elect peace candidates." Harvard's Professor George Wald, a Nobel Prize winner in biology, added that scholars should treat the fund like the income tax: "One of the biggest difficulties of democracy is how expensive it is to get elected to any office. We need big money." Professor Wald was an expert on vision. But the professors at 100 universities who were eventually brought into a network for the support of the Antiwar Fund apparently did not see things as he did. As of mid-September, the Fund had raised only $85,000 instead of the hoped-for 15 million.*

Then there was the Princeton-born Union for National Draft Opposition. As of May 18, it claimed to have member chapters on more than 100 campuses, all aimed at developing a program of legal obstructions and challenges to the Selective Service system in order to deny the government manpower for the war. In its specifically Princeton context, it was a "within the system" activity that won broad support from almost all elements of the Princeton community. Through it, conservatives from the so-

---

* The sum was eclipsed by the $400,000 collected at that time through a direct mail campaign organized by Sen. George McGovern for liberal Democratic Senators up for re-election. Some antiwar activists resented the McGovern drive's success because they considered it to be ideologically impure. For example, hawkish Sen. Gale McGee of Wyoming shared in the McGovern raised kitty because he was a domestic liberal, even though the Universities National Antiwar Fund contributed to the unsuccessful campaign of his dovish primary opponent, State Senator D. P. Svilar.

182

cially elite Prospect Avenue dining clubs, liberals from the politically oriented Stevenson Hall, and left activists who had recently blockaded the building at Princeton which houses the Institute for Defense Analysis, could make common cause against the war.

In this same period the Democratic National Committee tried to be "relevant." At a May 14 news conference in Washington's National Press Club, Democratic Chairman Lawrence F. O'Brien announced that he would establish a clearinghouse to which young people and other persons interested in participating in the political process could apply on a more or less bipartisan basis. The clearinghouse would send the names of volunteers onto a candidate for governor, senator, representative or state legislator with whom their views seemed compatible. Though Mr. O'Brien insisted that such volunteers would be interested in a wide range of issues, it was clear that the motivating force behind the program would be the eagerness of young critics of the war in Vietnam and Cambodia to work for dove candidates in the 1970 congressional elections. It was indicated that the services of the clearinghouse might even be made available to Republican candidates in special instances when an individual Democratic nominee was a supporter rather than a critic of the Nixon administration's foreign policy.

In addition, said O'Brien, he had invited the Republican national chairman, Representative Rogers Morton, to join in co-sponsoring the campaign to broaden public participation in the fall elections. He did not, however, explain how both parties could simultaneously operate a common clearinghouse for volunteer workers. Could the Democratic National Committee, for example, be instrumental in actually wedding volunteers to antiwar Republicans or Democrats contesting the seats of incumbent Democrats? Could the Republican National Committee actually be instrumental in wedding volunteers to antiwar candidates, Republican or Democratic, who were hostile to the policies of the leader of the Republican party, President Richard M. Nixon? The entire proposal struck many students as implausible.

As often happens in a time of great commotion, an organization that was destined to surface as one of the most effective youth-dominated activities in the 1970 election—Frontlash—gained very little notice during this period. Frontlash was formed in 1967 to mobilize the energies of youth to help build a broader, more conscious electorate by sparking voter registration and get-out-the-vote drives. In 1970 about 10,000 volunteers from hundreds of campuses, high schools, and youth and student organizations joined in these projects in ten states. Their efforts were backed by the Committee on Political Education and AFL-CIO affiliates, the UAW, the A. Philip Randolph Institute, the League of Women Voters, the Voter Education Project, the League for Industrial Democracy, the United States Youth Council, and grants from the Stern Family Fund and the Leonard Sperry Research Center Fund.

On politically active campuses, the Princeton-initiated Movement for a New Congress (MNC) provided a focal point for organizational work in the remaining weeks of the spring term. No one can say precisely how many MNC chapters were quickly formed only to have a life as brief as a mayfly, and how many actually stayed alive and did some work. Nor can anyone say precisely how many regional centers actually coordinated campus activities in an assigned area. The habits of event politics based on demonstrations and protests did not readily yield ground to the discipline and details of process politics. It can be said only that the gross figure usually given for the number of MNC chapters was "over 400" plus 35 regional centers.

National headquarters for the MNC was the basement storeroom of a physics building on the Princeton campus. MNC's national leaders were William Murphy, 28, a Princeton University doctoral candidate in politics whose father was a six-term congressman from Chicago, and Professor Henry Bienen of Princeton, who did his Ph.D. work in African politics at the University of Chicago. Neither man had any illusions about what was needed to elect good politicians. Nor did they have any extravagant expectations that their regionally-organized student groups would turn certain defeats into victories. They did contend that their organized manpower could help candidates in races where there was a reasonable hope of victory.

It's the daily work of the campaign that counts [said Murphy]. First, the students will be canvassing—going into precincts and finding out what the voters think in relation to the candidate's thinking. Then he can go in and talk directly to them in specific terms. It will be bad news to a lot of students, but canvassing doesn't mean ringing a doorbell and starting an argument about Vietnam. The second crucial thing is to get the people who agree with our candidate registered and to the polls. This is basic machine politics. If it wins elections, why not use it? More good men have been blocked from serving in Congress, not because they lost to better men, but because the candidate's team didn't get the voters to the polls. Practical politics is often the last thing anyone thinks of—except the guy who wants to win bad enough.[2]

Bienen, agreeing, stressed the value of careful planning. "Simply providing a large number of volunteers is not enough" he explained. "The students have to be exceedingly well-organized, and the local campaigns have to be organized to receive them. Everything has to be done in a systematic fashion; it can't be half-baked." It would not make sense, for example, to send students down to South Carolina to battle Mendel Rivers; his position was so strong that he merely had to give a slight hint that he was alive on election day to get voted in by a landslide. The MNC's efforts would be concentrated on those races where peace candidates were given a good chance of winning. As Bienen said, "It would be a sin to lose a marginal race because the kids are working for a lost cause somewhere else."

The initial "no nonsense realism" of MNC's national head-

185

quarters was reflected in the instructions handbook it sent to student volunteer workers. "We need hard facts, not hopes," the text read. Canvassers were urged not to be argumentative, snobbish, or too noisy:

You are not canvassing for an antiwar referendum, you are selling a candidate. Doors will be slammed in your face, dogs will growl, children will cry, old ladies in tennis shoes will question your ancestry and patriotism. Forget it. Get the facts. Bring them in.

In this spirit, MNC's leaders viewed much of the student lobbying in progress in Washington as amateur street theater. Most politicians, they said, saw so many lobby groups that they quickly dismissed—either from their front offices or from their minds—the lobbies that could not deliver votes or money. Fifty students spending an hour talking to a congressman on the fence about Vietnam might be fun for the students, but it was just one more yawn for the politician in his Washington sleep. The same 50 students could have done more to change the nation if they had spent that hour working in their local precinct back home to defeat the congressional fence-sitter.

The rush of early decisions made at MNC headquarters were both clear-cut and sensible. It was decided that MNC would concentrate on some 50 to 60 contests for House seats and seven senatorial races out of a total of about 460 congressional contests in 1970. The areas of concentration were all swing districts where the liberal vote in the 1960's either won or came within five to ten percentage points of victory. It was hoped that student electioneering manpower could hold these marginal districts for incumbent doves or win them for doves who were challenging hawkish incumbents. To this end, district voting patterns in the 1960's were analyzed and computerized along with the voting records of incumbent congressmen. Various swing district contests identified in this way at Princeton were then sent to the regional centers, as in the case of the regional center established at the University of Chicago for contests in the Middle West. The regional centers in turn, transmitted the information they received to campus chapters of the MNC. At the same time, the regional centers transmitted to Princeton the names and summer addresses of students who had volunteered to support candidates; this information was computerized and a tape of names was then provided to MNC endorsed local candidates. By this means, volunteers and candidates were presumably brought into contact with each other.

Other things went forward on many campuses in the days and weeks immediately following Cambodia and Kent State. On the assumption that the war in Vietnam would be the issue in the 1970 election, and that students would work for peace candidates, faculty members in various colleges and departments arranged workshops where students could be armed intellectually for the electioneering tasks they would face. Professors of history or international relations, for example, provided material bearing on the genesis of the Vietnam conflict and its evolutionary turns. Professors of economics provided material bearing on the costs of the Vietnam War—this, for use in student approaches to businessmen and workers. Professors of political science conducted special drill sessions on the mechanics of the electoral process from canvassing voters to guarding the polls on election day. Professors of speech conducted their own kind of special drill sessions designed to train students in the arts of winning voters over to an anti-Vietnam War stand. All this, in lieu of strike-bound classes, could be justified as a form of educational activity worthwhile in itself.

Still, it was one thing for students to create a campus MNC chapter or to prepare themselves for electioneering chores, and it was another thing for that college or university, as an institution, to decide whether or not it would adopt the Princeton Plan in which class schedules would be rearranged to provide a two-week recess in the fall for students to campaign for candidates of their choice. The Princeton Plan was debated in hundreds of university and college senates, in departmental meetings, over luncheons in faculty clubs, and in hastily summoned caucuses. No proposal like it had been put to colleges and universities in the entire history of American higher education; and its full implications could not be grasped by analogies to past experience. At Princeton itself, the proposal was the subject of ten special faculty meetings convened between May 4 and May 27.

Elsewhere in the nation, only 23 institutions—most of them private colleges—ultimately adopted the Princeton Plan in toto, although an indeterminate number seemed to permit students to take a "long weekend" immediately prior to election day.

Several reasons were commonly cited for adopting the Princeton Plan. First, no time would be lost from the teaching term. The total days of recess in the year would simply be rearranged so as to open up the two weeks before the election in exchange for days taken out of the summer, Thanksgiving, and Christmas recess. During the two-week break, as during other recesses, students would be entirely free to engage in political activities or not as they saw fit. Those who wanted to work against peace candidates would have as much opportunity to do so as those who wanted to work for them. Those who wanted simply to take a vacation and those who wanted to get on with their upper-class independent work in the library or the laboratories could do so, just as much as they could in any normal Christmas recess. No coercion of individuals was involved, nor was there any commitment of the institution to any form of partisan political activity. Academic calendars have always been adjusted for religious and economic needs, or for the convenience of an individual faculty member. It was inconceivable that adjustments for democratic electoral politics should be considered out of order—particularly when young people specifically sought the time to increase their participation in the electoral process, and were willing to sacrifice vacation time for the opportunity.

Second, education in the classroom was strengthened by the many opportunities for personal development and growth through the pursuit of varied interests and talents beyond the classroom. In the same way that this consideration led to many campus publications, preprofessional associations, athletic teams, musical and theatrical groups, and so on, encouragement of an interest in public affairs and the furthering of a sense of social responsibility are important elements of a liberal education. Adoption of the Princeton Plan would allow students to gain more first-hand experience with the electoral process. It would join practical experience to the study of theory and, by adding an immediately relevant activity, would permit students to prepare themselves better for adulthood.

Third, the adoption of the plan would channel student political activity into the established electoral process and would thus give students their right to influence political outcomes in legitimate activity, rather than in explosions of frustration. By directing campus tensions toward national issues and away from internal campus concerns, the plan would buy peace for the campus. Moreover, by granting an officially approved block of released time, students could be active in electoral politics without penalty, while faculty members could also do so without ignoring their professional responsibilities. The recess for political activity would allow students and faculty to have a direct, constructive influence on the political process and—in the words of one university faculty resolution—would help "to restore the university to a position of American leadership and . . . restore its strong voice in the councils of government."

Finally, the Princeton Plan as conceived and stated by Princeton, did not imply any direct politicization of the university. All that was entailed was a two-week recess in which individuals could act according to their own convictions. No institutional sanction was accorded by the recess to any particular view or ideology, and no member of the university was in any way bound by any institutional political stand to which he could take exception. The plan was laid in such a way as to preserve academic integrity and facilitate the expressions of individual conscience in a manner which reconciled the moral imperatives of some with the academic rights of all.

The reasons why most institutions rejected the Princeton Plan—if they considered it at all—included everything from a business-as-usual mentality to simple inertia, from a predominant prowar sentiment of the trustees and administrative heads to a fear of a cut-off in alumni gifts. Some institutions, though, rejected the Princeton Plan on the formally stated ground that it violated the traditional principle of institutional neutrality with respect to political and moral issues—a principle which in theory assures the individual member of the academic community the unquestioned right to advance his own dissenting views.

One of the fullest developments of this line of argument appeared in a position paper that Dr. Keith Spalding, President of Franklin and Marshall College, wrote and submitted to his college faculty on June 13. Copies of the paper were sent to other institutions. In stating his objections to the Princeton Plan, Spalding observed:

My own conviction is that those who argue that the college is part of an unresponsive system, that it must not be neutral, that colleges, their faculties and students must take concerted stances on political, social and moral issues, are inviting damage to the academic community. I prefer a commitment to higher education based on the belief that ideas are hammered out of the freedom for everybody, of every persuasion, to express those ideas. It is the obligation of the college or university to protect that freedom for all within its boundaries, and all at the same time, so that none is intimidated in his expression.

The reality in which American higher education has always existed, and has prospered, is that it is indeed a part of the system. The society has taken it on itself to establish within it, and to tolerate, institutions in which every aspect of that society can be criticized, and they have become the seedbeds of the ideas which generate the society.

It was enough, argued Spalding, for the college to stand for the indivisible freedom of expression for all. The college preserved itself protecting that common freedom. It could not protect it and become at the same time a politicized institution, since such a dual course was a self-contradiction. It followed, that if a college greatly violated its purpose as a seat of learning and a testing ground for ideas, if it engaged so directly in social or political action as to exceed the limits of the tolerance of that society, society could exercise its power to destroy it. More important, by giving up its cherished principle of freedom within itself, the college would destroy itself as a college. Spalding continued:

I have strong convictions that the services of colleges and universities should be offered for the benefit of society, but I am still impressed with Justice Holmes' declaration that the scholar cannot carry beneath his gown the flaming sword. His obligation is to seek the truth, to help others find truth by teaching, and to say the findings of his own investigations freely and without fear. His discoveries have more impact on civilization, because of the seriousness of his purpose and the superiority of his intellect, than all the doorbell ringing he might do in a lifetime. His right to citizenship is not to be denied, but despite all the sophistry which has accompanied claims of the role of leadership in America by scholars and the powers of universities in the councils of government, it is not demonstrated by history that scholars or those they teach are better equipped than others to govern. Theirs is, in fact, a quite different and in some senses a higher calling.

This view did not foreclose the right of students to participate in the fall campaigns. Students wishing to participate could do so on an adult basis—meaning on their own volition, their

191

own choice of time, and by accepting the consequences of their actions. There was no reason for a college to be asked to grant favors to students by offering them opportunities which were already theirs if they wished to take them. In most colleges, students determined for themselves the holidays they observed, the classes they attended or did not attend, the functions they patronized. They did so with the knowledge that the consequences of their actions were their own. As was expected of other adults in other fields of endeavor, they were free to make conscious decisions about the efforts which were most important to them, and to accept the implications of those actions. They could, if they wished, campaign for candidates on the basis of an individual decision—as many were already doing—and they did not need to be paternalized in the matter. Besides, said Dr. Spalding:

It is unseemly to argue at one moment in opposition to punitive legislation, loyalty oath proposals, and the like, that students and faculty should not be singled out for unusual treatment, and now at another time, to argue that students and faculty are entitled to some special privilege. Workers in a factory, generally speaking, do not receive time off for political activity. Other professionals do not take time for political action without the consequences of losing income. It is surely unreasonable to suggest that students somehow have a greater entitlement, or that being a member of a college or university faculty is a profession of such luxury that he should be given two weeks off without professional responsibility to commit his acts of citizenship.

Dr. Spalding and others also attacked the educational benefits claimed for the Princeton Plan. The views concerning those benefits, it was said, were far too simplistic, because the last two weeks of a political campaign form but a small slice of the political process. In the frenetic activity of the last two weeks of a campaign, there would be little or no opportunity for the candidate or his staff to orient an onrush of new volunteers to the needs or themes of his campaign. The most effective participation on the part of students would be running mimeograph machines, stuffing envelopes, answering telephones, and driving voters to the polls. This activity would be useful, but would hardly be equivalent to an effective and instructive look at the political process.

In addition, opponents of the Princeton Plan contended that since the public was intensely hostile to students, a mass descent of young people on the neighborhoods of candidates involved in war and peace issues would be unwanted by the very candidates they favored. Either that, or the mass descent would lead to an antistudent backlash and would create opportunities for demagoguery on the part of desperate candidates. Not only would the students be misled if it was suggested to them that they were likely to be effective in an assault on voters or candidates in the final days of a campaign; but the frustrations and disenchantments resulting from that experience would revisit themselves on the campus.

These consequences were considered in the light of other backlash sentiments observed in recent times. It was said that there was overwhelming evidence that the mass opposition to student radicals and to all they symbolized was far more intense than was the feeling against Communists back in the Joe McCarthy days, or against Negroes more recently; all students were lumped together regardless of how they conducted themselves, and were lumped together again as something indistinguishable with crime in the streets and ghetto riots. Office seekers in both parties would undoubtedly emphasize the need to observe college rules and local laws, to work within the system, and to keep protests peaceful. The temptation, however, would be to go beyond the rules and to seek to play on voters' fears by elevating the students and "the kids" into loathesome bogeymen. This tactic would be particularly enticing for candidates who thought they were losing or were failing to make headway in their contests; especially for conservatives running against

193

those liberals closely identified with the peace movement, civil rights agitation, and other student causes. There was an unparalleled opportunity for demagoguery in the fall election. If students found themselves to be the victims of it in the course of volunteer campaign work—if after having given the system "one last test" they found it to be a rotten mess—then, on their return to college, they would be determined to pick up the protests, demonstrations, and violence where they left off.

Another reason cited why student disenchantment with their campaigning experience would come home to roost on campus was the statistical fact that some 80 percent of the congressional districts were "safe" districts. Frustrations over failure to effect change by making their political citizenship a two-week-a-year matter would suggest to students that colleges were guilty of a shabby gimmick, and the institution which made an offer of a recess period "to allow students to vent concern and energy in another direction," would deserve the anger that would be directed at it. It would insult the intelligence of students by asking them to believe that they could solve great problems by tremendous bursts of energy. It would arouse expectations that would ultimately be shattered, and thus add to student discontent. It was more appropriate for the administrations and faculties of colleges to urge their student bodies to continue—through education—to equip themselves more fully for the responsibilities of citizenship. It was not irrelevant for them to acquire a knowledge of history, economics, political science, the nature of the human condition, and science, before they could expect to succeed in bringing sophisticated judgment to bear on the complex problems of society.

Then there were the practical objections to the Princeton Plan. A two-week recess for political activity would subtract from class time that would have to be offset either by starting the fall term earlier, or by extending it into the usual Christmas vacation. This shift could affect the vacation plans of faculty and students, the research plans of faculty members, and the employment plans of students—a factor of particular importance to many students in "commuter" colleges. The money they earned in summer or Christmas-time jobs often determined their financial ability to stay in school—and was the leading reason why most "commuter" colleges rejected the Princeton Plan. In such circumstances it seemed unjust to accommodate the political activity of some students at the expense of the rights and reasonable expectations of other students and faculty who, for whatever reason chose not to be political.

Finally, there were the legal and financial grounds for rejecting the Princeton Plan. The provisions of the Revenue Code under which colleges and universities enjoy exemptions from federal income tax status, describe exempt organizations as including corporations:

organized and operated exclusively for . . . educational purposes . . . no part of the net earnings of which inures to the benefit of any private shareholder or individual, no substantial part of the activities of which is carrying on propaganda, or otherwise attempting to influence legislation, and which does not participate in, or intervene in (including the publishing or distribution of statements), any political campaign on behalf of any candidate for public office.

Under a strict construction of this definition, some privately endowed universities had already forced political clubs, including Young Republicans and Young Democrats, to move off campus. It was explained that the colleges where they were located would lose their tax-exempt status as educational institutions if they provided such clubs with office space or other services. The strict constructionists argued that any college would surely lose its tax immunities if, by a decision of its administration and faculty, it ceased to function for two weeks as an educational institution and became a staging area for political campaigns. Colleges and universities were already in an acute financial bind; they could not afford to risk losing their tax-exempt

195

status because they permitted the use of their educational facilities for propaganda and political purposes. Fear of running afoul of the tax laws led Princeton itself to withdraw from the MNC headquarters the right to rent-free use of the university computer facilities. This loss crimped operations until a local businessman made his own computers available to the MNC. On the same ground, Columbia and M. I. T. each ordered its campus chapter of MNC to get off campus and locate itself on a nonuniversity site. The search for new quarters led to time-consuming delays; moreover, with the removal of MNC from the immediate flow of student traffic, the task of recruiting student volunteers was greatly complicated.

Guidelines developed by the American Council on Education, however, were endorsed as "fair and reasonable" by the commissioner of internal revenue and finally helped clarify the issue of the tax-exempt status of educational institutions. These ACE guidelines then formed the basis for the guidelines laid down by universities adopting the Princeton Plan. Those issued by Princeton University itself on July 30, governing the use of its facilities and services in connection with political activities, corresponded in the main to those issued by other institutions. They provided that:

1. Neither the name nor the seal of the university or of any of its schools or institutions should be used on letters or other written material intended for political purposes, including the solicitation of funds for political purposes or activities.

2. No university office and no faculty or staff member's office should be used as a return mailing address for the solicitation of funds for political purposes, or the solicitation of endorsement of candidates for public office, or support for proposed legislation.

3. In political correspondence, the university title of a faculty or staff member should be used only for identification and

only when accompanied by a statement that the individual is speaking for himself and not as a representative of the university.

4. Whenever university duplicating machines, computers or other equipment or supplies are used for political or other non-university purposes, their use must be fully compensated for from private funds.

5. No office employee nor other employee should be asked to perform tasks in any way related to political activities while on regular duty.

6. In no case should any action be taken which might implicate or be thought to implicate the university in any political activities.

One more thing remains to be said.

A springtime Harris Poll [3] which covered 80 percent of the campuses where there had been protests after Cambodia, showed that 75 percent of the students in those colleges favored and supported the protests, with half of the student body actually participating. A substantial 65 percent of the students interviewed wanted to "change the system from within," and agreed that the "most effective" way "to bring about real improvements in problems facing the country" was by working "to elect better public officials." Sixty-three percent rejected a resort to violence as a tactic that could bring about changes in the system. Thirty-nine percent of all college students interviewed reported that they intended to participate in the fall campaigns to elect peace candidates to Congress and to other public office. "This intention," said Harris, "would come to over two million students working in the 1970 election, if they go through with plans they formulated as the school year ended."

Further, the students wanted help from their colleges in carrying out their political plans. Harris reported that fifty-seven percent maintained that campus administrators should give the students time off to participate in the fall's political campaigns for two weeks in October. When asked how effective they thought they would be in this massive infusion of student power into the political mainstream, students showed a fair degree of realism; only 22 percent said that they would be "very effective," and a much larger 60 percent expressed the view that they would be "somewhat effective." Only 27 percent said that they intended to work for an organized protest group in the coming autumn—though 62 percent believed that if the students' efforts to elect peace candidates failed, the participants would "become disillusioned and turn to renewed protests and demonstrations."

NOTES

1. Robert Goheen, *The State of the University*, October 1970.
2. Ned Schneier and William Murphy, *Vote Power, The Movement for a New Congress* (Englewood Cliffs, N.J.: Prentice-Hall, 1970).
3. *New York Post*, July 20, 1970.

PART II

Promise and Performance

9
Great
Expectations

I

Many of the young people who had raised their voices in protest and frustration during the spring and summer of 1970 were unable to vote in November because they had not yet reached the statutory age of 21, or because they were disenfranchised by restrictive residency requirements. Still, of those who were eligible to vote both in 1968 and 1970 their turnout rates were unimpressive. In the 1968 presidential election, the 11.1 million persons between the ages of 21 and 24 represented, according to the Bureau of the Census, 9.6 percent of the total voting age population. Of this group, 5.7 million—or 51.1 percent—reported that they had voted. In the 1970 congressional election, again according to the Bureau of the Census, the 12.6 million persons between ages 21 and 24 represented 10.4 percent of the total voting age population. Of the group 3.8 million—or 30.4 percent—reported that they had voted.

Beyond the act of voting, there is no count on how many young people actually participated in the 1970 congressional elections. In the specific case of students, some worked in the summer primaries on behalf of a candidate, but not in the fall election. Some, who worked for a candidate in the fall election, did not take part in the summer primaries. Some, either in the spring or fall, worked for no more than a day or weekend. Some stayed the course of a contest from start to finish. Moreover, many different kinds of student-run organizations injected some of their leaders and rank-and-file members into local campaigns. There were enterprising, laissez-faire students who shopped around individually in the free competitive market and attached themselves to a particular campaign or candidate that struck their fancy. This campaign could be that of a conservative and hawk as easily as that of a liberal and dove. Yet the media—and the public—tended to see only the movement of students to the side of liberal-dove candidates and to ignore the not insignificant movement to the conservative-hawk side.

Virtually the only effort of young people that lent itself to a direct nose count involved the ten-state Frontlash voter registration drive in which 10,000 participating youths helped add a total of 180,000 new voters to the electoral rolls. Yet even here it is not certain how many of the participating young people were students and how many were nonstudents, and of students, how many were drawn from the colleges and how many from the high schools. Nor is it certain whether the participating youth were involved in the fall contests beyond the voter registration limits of the Frontlash undertaking. *Congressional Quarterly* has estimated that around 75,000 students worked for peace candidates in both the primaries and the elections. But the figure still leaves out of account the young campaign workers who were not students and those who enlisted in campaigns for hawk candidates.

This study's data, presented in the chapters that follow, leave open the question of how many young people took part in the electoral politics of the 1970 congressional contests beyond the mere act of voting. But an attempt will be made to assess the actions and effects of young people's participation in the 1970 contests. The data bearing on this point come from four main sources: extensive interviews with candidates, party managers and young people in selected parts of the country; material supplied by reporters assigned to follow thirteen specific congressional contests; a survey made for this study by Professors Jack Dennis and Austin Ranney of the University of Wisconsin, comparing and contrasting the 1970 electoral participation of students at representative groups of Princeton Plan and non-Princeton Plan colleges; and another survey made for this study by Professors Henry Bienen of Princeton University and William T. Murphy, now of Brown University, focused on the electoral response of voters to student canvassers in five selected congressional districts.

The data from these four independent sources differ in points of detail, yet most of the material indicates that the dominant characteristic of youth's response to the 1970 congressional election was apathy. We maintain that this apathy, while real enough, seems greater than it really was because the springtime expectations of massive armies of young workers for "peace candidates" in the 1970 elections were so exaggerated. The extent of student apathy can best be put in perspective through comparisons of student participation in previous congressional elections with the one in 1970 and, again, through comparison between student participation in the 1970 campaigns and participation by the general population. Above all, the significance of student participation or student apathy appears more clearly when one takes into account the effectiveness of relatively small numbers of students in certain specific electoral contexts—whether the results took the form of a victory or the inroads that even a losing candidate made in the traditional sources of his opponent's strength.

But these perspectives were not available, to the advocates of the frontlash, backlash, and sidelash in the spring of 1970. Most of them based their perceptions on a particular vision of what the last half of the 1960's and the first months of the 1970's were like.

II

The Vietnam War was certainly a deeply divisive issue in the last half of the 1960's, and the commotions flowing from it certainly conveyed the impression of a nation swept by a universal tornado. Yet a different national picture of the matter appears in a 1970 study titled *Vietnam and the Silent Majority* by Milton J. Rosenberg and Sidney Verba of the University of Chicago, and Philip F. Converse of the University of Michigan.[1] The three authors are not only known by their peers in the academic world to be among America's most eminent university-based specialists in the study of political public opinion and the attitude change process, but they frankly identified themselves as doves on the Vietnam War. They also frankly acknowledged that their purpose in preparing the study was to illuminate both the nature of the tasks of persuasion and the means of persuading the American people to reject the Vietnamese War, and to call for its rapid termination through a political settlement. In undertaking their analysis, they drew on their own work and on a critical appraisal of the best known public opinion polls, to "tell it like it is"—whether the message was reassuring or depressing.

One of the studies they drew on was made in the spring of 1967 by Sidney Verba in collaboration with Richard A. Brody of Stanford University.[2] The time was well after Vietnam had become a major public issue, and the study found that while most people were seriously concerned over Vietnam—it was identified as the most important issue facing the American people—relatively few had taken any active role with respect to the controversy about it. Only about 2.5 percent of those interviewed in a sample of 1,500 said that they had ever written a letter to a government official or to a newspaper on the subject of Vietnam. Less than one percent—or eight out of 1,500—said they had ever taken part in a march or demonstration in relation to the war. It is true, of course, that a small percent in a nation of over 200 million may mean a great number of people. But the fact that only a small percent was politically active in the agitation over the issue of Vietnam, indicated —as of that time at least—that perceptions about the reality of the American public were distorted by the acts of a relatively small and highly visible group. More to the point, it by no means followed, as some of the student leaders of the agitation against the war in Vietnam appeared to believe at that time, that they represented the voice of the majority which President Johnson willfully chose to ignore.

There was a change in the picture after the Tet offensive of the Vietcong in early 1968. Whereas 22 percent of the American people polled in 1965 believed that America's entry into the Vietnam War was a mistake, the number climbed to over 50 percent in 1968. But not all of those polled favored a withdrawal of American troops as a way of ending the American involvement in the conflict. The finding of a 1968 study made by the University of Michigan's Survey Research Center, cited in *Vietnam and the Silent Majority,* was instructive. Among those who viewed the war as a mistake, almost as many favored escalation as withdrawal. All told, a five-to-three majority regretted the original intervention, but at the same time those calling for a "stronger stand even if it means invading North Vietnam," outnumbered those advocating complete withdrawal by about as large a margin.[3]

The findings of a spring 1970 Gallup Poll, also cited in *Vietnam and the Silent Majority,* were no less startling. Young people and college graduates were somewhat more sympathetic to student strikes against the war than the average American, but they were still strongly opposed. The young people (those between the ages of 20 and 29) condemned strikes by 73 percent to 25 percent while college graduates condemned them by 73 percent to 24 percent.[4] What is more, the findings of a 1968 study by the Survey Research Center indicated that 63 percent of the people who believed the war was a mistake nonetheless viewed protesters negatively, and even of the group favoring complete withdrawal from Vietnam, 53 percent had a negative reaction to the protesters.

Two more astonishing findings to come out of the studies of public opinion in relationship to the issue of Vietnam, involved the "hawk-dove" divisions according to educational background and age.

First, by 1966 the male and female products of elite American universities had moved sharply in a dove direction. They were, in the main, holders of two or more degrees. But the vast majority of college students neither come from elite universities nor possess graduate degrees. They come rather, from quasi-anonymous colleges and, as Professor Verba's studies showed, they not only "remained decidedly hawkish throughout the war," but it "was fair to say that they supplied the very backbone of popular support for the war." On the other hand, Professor Verba's studies also give evidence that from a quantitative standpoint, the greatest concentration of dove opinion was found in the nurseries of the so-called "hard hats"—that is, it was found in the 20 percent of the adult population with education limited to grade school.[5]

Second, other sets of figures drawn from different polling sources failed to record signs that the generation under 30 had fixed dovish responses in sharp opposition to a hawkish older generation. The reverse was true in the last half of the 1960's. Whites under 30, particularly males, were in the aggregate quite hawkish in their expressed desires to solve the Vietnam problem through escalation; they also favored the most harsh penalties for draft evaders. People over 60—many of whom never went beyond high school in their education—were relatively dovish advocates of a pull-out policy. The broad mass of the nation's adult population between the ages of 30 and 60 tended to sway between these two poles.

If all this was true, then some of the assumptions underlying the spring 1970 predictions about a student frontlash, and some of those underlying the predictions about a backlash, were of questionable validity. On the side of frontlash, it was dubious whether any great mass of students in colleges across the nation —or recent graduates from those colleges—would volunteer for work in electoral politics on behalf of congressional candidates solely because the latter were identified as doves on the issue of Vietnam. On the side of backlash, it was doubtful whether any great gain could be made among hard-hats by attacks on the lack of student patriotism with respect to the Vietnamese War, when the hard-hats quantitatively comprised the greatest concentration of dove opinion in the nation.

Other assumptions appear as dubious when examined in the light of the general picture of student political activism in the last half of the 1960's. It is true that after 1964 student political activists tended increasingly to focus their efforts on event politics in either of its two most common forms—the demonstration and the disorder. The disorder was more frequent than the demonstration although the demonstration was more visible nationally. Demonstrations were usually addressed to a national issue like the Vietnam War; they often called upon national leadership to resolve the issue and it stressed that the participants—like those who took part in a March on Washington—came from all over the nation. Demonstrations renewed the participants' sense of mission and community, and these were vital to the larger student movement. They also helped that movement by creating the illusion that students were a nationally organized political force. But demonstrations were expensive, time consuming, and difficult to organize. They could be circumscribed by astute maneuvers on the part of the opposition, or even by inclement weather. Worst yet, their political effect was at best uncertain, and repetition only tended to reduce their impact.

The disorder as a political event was far more frequent and far more popular among students because it was generally confined to the campus. As such, it was a local rather than a national event, and was more easily organized. But what was the most common specific issue in the campus disorders?

It was not the Vietnam War. Only four percent of the colleges as colleges ever took a position on the war—either pro or con. Nor was the most common specific issue the dependence of the university on the federal government for secret funds for research and teaching. In 1966–1967, the government contributed 13 percent of the direct instructional costs of higher education, but when the indirect costs were added, the U. S. share shrank to only four percent. While the federal government provided the lion's share of research funds—about 87 percent of the 2 billion dollars spent by universities on research in 1967—by the end of 1969, only 1.89 percent of the federal research grants were classified because of their defense implications. Moreover, secret research work with defense implications was confined to a handful of universities that were equal to the demands of high technology—and in 1970, one of the most celebrated of these, the Massachusetts Institute of Technology, announced that it was terminating its involvements in secret research. Most federal research grants, like most business contributions to higher education, went into areas that were little involved with politics. It would be hard for even the most inflamed student revolutionary to make a convincing case that federal support for training research workers concerned with the control of cancer or pollution was part of a reactionary plot linking universities to the war machine.

The most common theme in campus disorders was student power—not peace. The most common specific issue of the campus disorder was race, and even more specifically, race as it related to institutional practices. The most common use of disorder in an attempt to change things was focused on matters like dormitory rules, admissions policies, the curriculum content, and the presence of an R. O. T. C. unit—issues that clearly were more institutional than national, calling for solutions that were local and not national by definition. Precisely on this account, it was difficult for the federal government to legislate controls over campus disorders. In the few instances where such controls were ventured, it was left to the discretion of local institutions to apply them locally.

What was true of the period between 1964 and 1968 was also largely true of the period between 1968 and 1970, except that in the latter case, campus disorders tended to wear a more violent face than before. Yet, that violence served only to sharpen the point of the question mark opposite the frontlash predictions in the spring of 1970 about what effect a mass uprising of students to work for peace candidates in congressional contests would have on the voters.

Notwithstanding the involvement of students in the McCarthy campaign, the history of student political activism in the last half of the 1960's suggested that it would be very difficult to mobilize great numbers of students for electoral work because: first, their political experiences were with event politics, not with process politics; second, their experiences in event politics were more with disorders than with demonstrations; and third, because their experiences with disorders were confined to the campus where the main point at issue was race or an institutional practice, not the Vietnam War. It would be even more difficult to mobilize black students for that kind of work, when the doctrine of Black Power carried with it a lack of interest in black involvement in white electoral politics. It would be just as difficult to mobilize Spanish-speaking students—the Chicanos —for that kind of work, because they too were beginning to exhibit a counterpart to the Black Power attitudes.

At the same time, to admit that the disorders focused on local campus issues were more frequent than the demonstrations focused on national issues is not to imply that all forms of campus protest were disorderly. A mound of evidence to the contrary appears in important studies by individuals such as Kenneth Keniston of Yale and his Yale associate Michael Lerner, and by agencies like the American Council on Education and the Carnegie Commission on Higher Education. Taken in the aggregate, the studies showed that while incidents occurred in two-thirds of America's 2,500 colleges and universities during the last half of the 1960's, the overwhelming majority of protests were peaceful, orderly and clearly within the bounds of dissent protected by the First Amendment to the Constitution. Besides, well over a thousand campuses passed through the last half of the 1960's in so tranquil a state, without a peaceful protest of any kind, (let alone a violent one) that they seemed to be under deep sedation. This is all the more remarkable when one considers how many grounds exist for justifiable criticism of many American institutions of higher education.

Protests involving property damage or personal injury occurred on fewer than seven percent of all campuses or, more precisely, tended to crop up at intervals at a small group of campuses. Institutional reactions to protests that were disorderly were far firmer than all the talk about permissiveness would lead one to believe. The American Council of Education's report on campus tensions found, for example, that in the academic year 1968–1969, the police were called in by 55 percent of all institutions that experienced student disorder. At 75 percent of all institutions having violent protest and at about 25 percent of those having nonviolent protest, major civil or institutional action was taken against the students involved. In every case of the most publicized campus disorders like those at Berkeley in 1964, Columbia in 1968, Harvard in 1969, and the

University of Chicago in 1969, students were either convicted by the courts (almost 800 at Berkeley) or suspended or expelled by the university (123 at Chicago).

This nonpermissive response, supplemented by additional evidence assembled by Keniston and Lerner, warranted their conclusion that "when it comes to protecting their own turf, most faculty members are very conservative." They observed that in fewer than two percent of campus protests were any faculty members involved as leaders of disruptive or violent actions and, in most such cases, faculty leadership consisted of one or two men in a faculty community overwhelmingly opposed to their actions. Faculty members, however, frequently supported nonviolent protests against the war and social injustice. But even the most radical faculty members were as committed to nonviolence as they were committed to basic social change.[6] According to the Carnegie Commission on Higher Education, 81 percent of faculty members agreed that "campus disruptions by militant students are a threat to academic freedom," while 79 percent believed that "students who disrupt the functioning of the college should be expelled or suspended."

Here again, what was true of the period between 1964 and 1968 was largely true of the period between 1968 and 1970, except that in the latter case, there was a marked stiffening of student attitudes against disruptive campus demonstrations. Research on student protest and campus unrest had indicated that the best way to predict—with up to 83 percent accuracy—the presence or size of protests on any given campus was to study the characteristics of incoming freshmen. On these grounds, beginning in 1966, the American Council on Education— supported partially by a research grant of the National Institute of Mental Health—started to study the attitudes of entering freshmen toward selected issues. The studies made in 1967, 1968 and 1969, showed the following:

In 1967, less than one half of the 185,848 freshmen surveyed at 252 institutions agreed that college officials were too lax in dealing with student protests. In the survey of 1968, covering 243,156 first year students at 358 institutions, 55 percent agreed. And in 1969, of the 168,190 students surveyed at 270 institutions, 60 percent agreed that college officials were too lax.

In 1967, 5.1 percent of the male, and 4.2 percent of the female entering students in all institutions estimated that they would be likely to participate in a protest activity of some kind. The proportion dropped to 4.2 percent and 3.9 percent respectively in 1968. In 1969, the question asked about protest activity was broken down into three more specific questions: 7.2 percent of the men and 5.6 percent of the women said they might protest U. S. military activity; 6.3 percent of the men and 6.4 percent of the women said they might protest ethnic racial practices; but only 2.2 percent of the men and 1.8 percent of the women said there was a good chance that they might protest college administration policy.

There were, however, marked turns of a different kind with respect to other matters. In 1967, two-fifths of all entering freshmen thought that college officials had the right to ban persons with extreme views from speaking on campus; in 1968–1969, less than one-third took this position. Again, in 1967, 85 percent of the entering students agreed that the faculty had greater competence than students for designing the curriculum; in 1968 and 1969 almost 90 percent thought that students should have a major role in shaping the design. In 1966, less than one-fifth of the entering freshmen rated themselves above average on political liberalism, but their subsequent trend toward liberal political preferences appear in Table 1.

Along with this trend toward liberalism, the last half of the 1960's witnessed a sharp decline in the importance of party identification for the future electorate. Or to restate the matter,

212

TABLE 1

*Political Outlook of Entering College Freshmen:
1969 and 1970*

CURRENT POLITICAL PREFERENCE	1969	1970
Liberal	32.6%	36.6%
Middle of Road	44.4	45.4
Conservative	22.9	18.1
TOTAL	99.9%	100.1%
Expected Preference in 4 Years		
Liberal	39.0%	44.6%
Middle of Road	29.5	31.3
Conservative	31.5	24.1
TOTAL	100.0%	100.0%

Source: American Council on Education, *ACE Research
Reports,* vol. 4, no. 7 (1969); vol. 5, no. 6 (1970).

the 1960's witnessed a sharp rise in the tendency of young people in college to identify themselves as independents. This
trend appears in the studies made since 1966 by the Gallup organization about political partisanship among college students.
Yearly since then, representative samples of college students
have been asked: "In politics, as of today, do you consider
yourself a Republican, Democrat, or Independent?" The trend
of the answers to this question appears in Table 2:

TABLE 2

Party Identification among College Students

YEAR	REPUBLICAN	DEMOCRATIC	INDEPENDENT
1966	26%	35%	39%
1967	29	29	42
1968	19	37	44
1969 (May)	23	33	44
1969 (November)	21	27	52
1970 (May)	18	30	52

Source: *The Gallup Opinion Index,* no. 60 (June 1970): no.
55 (January 1970).

213

On the basis of these realities, some of the conclusions drawn in the spring of 1970 from the immediately preceding history of student on-campus protests should have been the opposite of those that underlay the backlash and the sidelash assumptions.

In the case of the backlash, it should have been observed that any line of electioneering attack by Republicans designed to portray students collectively as vandals, bums, effete snobs, and spoiled brats, carried two inherent dangers—one immediate, the other long range. With respect to the immediate danger, the line of attack would proclaim its own injustice to the mass of students who knew from direct personal experience that their conduct on campus had been orderly. Some of these students —along with some parents and teachers—who might otherwise have been indifferent to the election contests could consequently be goaded into volunteering for electoral work on behalf of candidates opposed to the slandering Republicans.

The long-range dangers were more subtle, but their potentialities were no less real. They were rooted in the element of truth contained in the observation of Louis M. Seagull, of the University of Pennsylvania, that "the importance of the existence of a political generation is that the patterns established in formative youthful years tended to persist. The impact of events then lingers even if the events themselves do not." In other words, the outlooks, habits of thought, and reactions formed in late adolescence and early maturity can have consequences extending into the future, independent of the events which caught a generation of young people in their periods of political crystalization.

If so, there was a high order of probability that any party or political figure identified with an unjust attack on students during their political formative years could bring down on itself a hostility that might extend into the future and outside the college environment. It would be one thing if such a party or political figure deliberately meant to invite that kind of ongoing

214

hostility on the basis of a calculation that it would gain more in other quarters because of it; but it would be another thing if no compensating gains were in sight, or if the party or political figure meant to retain the support of the college-educated segment of the population but proceeded blindly to alienate it.

In the specific case of the Republican party in 1970, it faced a reverse situation of the one that prevailed during the New Deal-Fair Deal years. Prior to 1952, more of the better-educated voters identified themselves as Republicans than as Democrats. After 1952, while the Democratic proportion of the college-educated population tended to remain constant, the Republican proportion declined—with the losses spinning off in the form of an increase in the number of voters who identified themselves as independents. The changes in party identification among college students, as they appeared in the Gallup studies, cited in Table 2, underlined this trend. Unless the Republican strategists in 1970 deliberately meant to write off the college-educated vote for the future, it was hard to see the logic of the White House attack on students.

The sidelash assumptions of liberal Democrats which developed later in 1970 were no less open to question. When the evidence of the last half of the 1960's indicated that the overwhelming number of students were never a party to violent protests, nor looked with favor upon them—when the evidence indicated to the contrary that the overwhelming majority of students were self-disciplined—the fear some liberal Democrats had of bringing students into their campaign structures scarcely seemed warranted. It did not follow, as some liberal Democrats seemed to assume, that students would vote Democratic because they couldn't vote Republican. Given the 13 percent rise between 1966–1970 in the number of students who regarded themselves as independents—and who by May 1970, comprised in the aggregate 52 percent of all students polled by Gallup—many students could very well look upon the Democrats as being part of the same picture they saw in the Republican party: a sum of things which did not have much meaning in terms of their own political values and perceptions.

The case studies which follow attempt to gauge the metabolism of the electoral blood flowing through the body of American politics—to determine whether that metabolism remained constant throughout the nation, as well as the reasons for any local variations.

Each of the campaigns that were monitored by our field reporters had previously been chosen by the Movement for a New Congress as a target area into which young volunteers would be channelled. In each contest selected the opposing candidates were considered electable. By observing the activities of young campaigners and the general voter's reactions to the work in different regional areas, local contexts, and partisan frames, we sought to determine whether the young could elect a new Congress and force the president to end the war, and whether or not the rest of the voting public turned against the efforts of the young.

NOTES

1. Milton J. Rosenberg, Sidney Verba, and Philip F. Converse, *Vietnam and the Silent Majority. The Dove's Guide* (New York: Harper and Row, 1970).

2. Sidney Verba and Richard A. Brody, "Participation, Preferences and the War in Vietnam," *Public Opinion Quarterly* (Fall 1970).

3. Rosenberg, *Vietnam*, p. 37.

4. *The Gallup Opinion Index*, no. 60 (June 1970).

5. Rosenberg, *Vietnam*, pp. 53–58.

6. Kenneth Keniston and Michael Lerner, "Campus Characteristics and Campus Unrest," *The Annals of the American Academy of Political and Social Science*, 395 (May 1971).

10
The Stevenson
Landslide

T HE city of Chicago and the state of Illinois are logical places in
which to test the theory of an antistudent and antiyouth backlash. Chicago is the capital city of the Midwest—a region celebrated in political folklore as the heartland of right-thinking,
right-living Americans. It is, additionally, the capital city of the
hard-hats and ethnics—both endowed, according to political
folklore, with conditioned reflexes that are antipermissive and
antistudent. Above all, Chicago is governed by Mayor Daley,
the "boss" of the regular Democratic organization.

After the clash between the Chicago police and the young
demonstrators at the time of the 1968 convention, Daley stood
out on the American political stage as a larger-than-life plac-
arded figure in a morality play. To his admirers, he incarnated
the courage to resist any accommodations with permissiveness
and lawlessness, and to insist on the preservation of law and
order. To his critics, he incarnated everything that was repressive in American life and everything corrupt in the "Old Politics." If the two placards—one of super-human virtue, the
other of inhuman vice—corresponded to the reality of politics,
Mayor Daley should have been "more Catholic than the Pope"
in stressing the law-and-order approach in the 1970 election
campaign, going beyond the Nixon administration and the

217

like-minded congressional candidates whom they supported. He should have been foremost in catering to backlash sentiment, and in "slating" candidates for the regular Democratic organization to support in 1970, he should have excluded from consideration all except grim-faced law-and-order types, but he did the exact opposite.

Chicago's Democratic organization has been in power for four decades. It is not immune to the iron law of decay. But whether or not it is overtaken by that law in the emergent future, its survival in power has thus far exceeded all other major urban political organizations in modern American history. During its lifetime, political machines elsewhere, which once seemed invincible, have ceased to be. In Boston, James Curley and his junta heard their last hurrah; in New York City, the imperial tribe of Tammany was reduced to a junk pile of warpaint and ceremonial feathers; and in Jersey City, the bully-boys of Mayor "I am the law" Hague, were weakened to a point where they seemed incapable of fighting their way out of a paper bag. There were other casualties: the Pendergast freebooters in Kansas City, and those of F. H. "Boss" Crump in Memphis became a foul memory; with the assassination of Huey Long, his Louisiana machine dissolved into a swirl of warring fragments.

In Chicago, control of the Democratic machine has never been the permanent, unbroken monopoly of a single man. In the last four decades, leadership has passed from Anthony Cermak to the dual team of Edward J. Kelly and Patrick Nash (with Jacob Arvey in a strong advisory role), and then to Richard Daley. The machine, moreover, never dominated the entire state of Illinois. Within the Democratic party, it has often been challenged by "downstate" Democrats and forced to give ground before them; within a lively two party system in Illinois, it was often defeated by the statewide Republican party in contests for major offices. But the Chicago machine did not con-fuse its frank interest in the fishes and loaves of political power with lofty ideological pretensions. It periodically provided a space in the public realm where Democratic contenders for office it could scarcely understand, got a chance to have their say, to do their work, and to excel at it. Among those who stood outside the machine yet had its backing for high office were certified liberals like Governor Adlai E. Stevenson and Senator Paul H. Douglas.

Like urban machines elsewhere, the Chicago machine over the last forty years has had its thieves, scandals, and other not so original sins. But it has survived most other machines because it has the wit to know and do several things that the rest did not. It knew early in the depression that its "Christmas baskets" and tons of coal could no longer cover the needs of people in distress, that no matter how much money it collected for "social services" through its "take" from the rackets, from upper-world contractors, or from upper-world businessmen who wanted franchises and monopolies, it could never get enough money to pay for the alleviation of misery in exchange for votes. So it recognized that it must join the New Deal and, through it, openly secure from public sources authorized funds to be spent on social programs established by law.

It also made itself a kind of ombudsman mediating between the persons for whom the social programs were intended and the bureaucratic administrators of the programs. Its vast network of precinct captains became more than just a downward channel of communication designed to get out the vote according to instructions. It provided people with a feeling of access to the governmental system. It learned not to approach people with waspish moralism, passionate self-righteousness, or sniffish sermons about how immoral it is for someone to ask and for someone to answer a demand for a "piece of the pie." Instead, its recurrent argument was that the network could be of help in meeting their concrete and pressing needs for jobs, sidewalks, police protection, legal counsel, lighted streets, transportation, housing or recreational facilities. On a *quid pro quo* basis, it asked for and got votes in return.

Above all, the Chicago organization survived because it knew that every political interest in the city—ethnic, racial, economic, religious, cultural, or political—when placed alongside all the others, was a minority interest. Minorities could form an electoral majority only if they coalesced with other minorities. To that end the organization became the mediating agent—according to its own ideas about "distributive justice." By indirection, informally and always gradually, it arranged compromises among the various power elements within the city which the individual groups could not achieve. The organization made certain that no minority group would lose all that it had, that none would get all that it wanted, and that each would give something and take something—but not automatically as a matter of routine justice. The "balanced ticket," timing, and evidence that a group had some clout, were the essence of the brokerage business performed by the organization.

This record does not mean to dismiss or condone the organization's cruelties, blindness, and arrogance.[1] In regard to Mayor Daley personally, an apostle of the bitter truth would be strongly inclined to point to him as the examplar of a hard reality about American politics—that if you want to get anything done, you must entrust it to the wrong man who stands for the right thing for the wrong reasons. The right thing he does will not be ascribed to any altruistic motive, but rather to his felt need "to get elected." As a result he is "safe," unlike the right man who stands for the right thing for the right reasons, and is likely to be considered a subversive threat to community morals. Yet, even the most severe critic of Mayor Daley and his machine is compelled to give both of them high marks for professional competence in their chosen tasks.

The machine has no articulated "unified field theory" of urban politics. Mayor Daley would probably stammer if asked to state systematically the guiding philosophy underlying the decisions he makes. But the patterns of action that he and other ethnic politicians around him exhibit in concrete situations also reflect the ideas that account for the inner life of their organization.* It is an uncoerced congery of disparate people with uncommon ends, held together at the center by logrolling and by a "constitutional morality" which blends something of the old watchwords of fraternité and egalité with Calhoun's notion of a "concurrent majority." [2]

According to the organization, its broad patterns of conduct assume that no significant economic, racial, religious, ethnic, or private political association in the community can be ignored. If an election is won either by ignoring any such group, or by making it a scapegoat for an attack by others, it may be impossible to govern after the election, and would surely foster a politics of revenge with each group pulling apart from the whole until only fragments remain. What is more, in any victory it is essential to know how to "conquer but spare." The majority that has coalesced must not use the weight of its numbers to crush the minority's claim for equitable considerations; this means it must stop short of insisting that the majority takes all. Conversely, the minority must not frivolously or vengefully use its veto power over the desires of the majority; it must stop short of insisting that "nothing be allowed the majority except by the consent of the minority." If the organization is to be the broker for orderly social changes, the changes it promotes must neither be too fast to repel conservatives, nor too slow to repel reformers.

Prior to 1968, the organization—in its usual indirect and in-

* I am indebted to Father Andrew Greeley of the National Opinion Research Center, University of Chicago, for his helpful comments about the inner life of "ethnic politicians."

formal way—had arranged compromises among the various power elements in the city that gave a place in the sun to the representatives of each major group. Without fanfare, for example, Irish aldermen and congressmen were slowly phased out and replaced by representatives of other ethnic groups. (After 1970, the Chicago delegation in the House of Representatives included one Irishman, three Poles, two Jews and two blacks; after the 1971 aldermanic and mayorality election, blacks held 30 percent of the seats in the city council.) But prior to the 1968 turmoil at the Chicago convention, the organization had little experience with youth culture and was unprepared to cope with it. The immediate response was to stand on the letter of the law; which led to a stand backed by brute force.

The immediate public reaction in Chicago, measured by the polls, overwhelmingly approved of the police actions against the demonstrators. Publicly also, Daley and the other ethnic politicians in command of the organization insisted on the correctness of their stand behind the police. Privately, they reappraised the whole affair and its consequences, and reached conclusions that went beyond what the opinion polls indicated. They knew that a significant number of independent voters and independent Democrats in and around Chicago were repelled by the use of force and were straining for a chance to strike back at the organization, which they held responsible for the convention-time shambles. The hierarchs of the organization also knew that they could not govern the city if they confined their appeal to the segment of the electorate that favored a politics based on fear, bigotry, and the settlement of issues by repressive violence, for the electorate also contained a liberal human strain that was hopeful, rational, and sympathetic to victims of a malfunctioning social, economic, and political order. It was this liberal strain—and not the blacks in the ghettos— that had to be appeased in order to avoid serious political rebellion against the machine.

The Stevenson Landslide

The liberal wing of the local electorate had coalesced around the oldest son of Adlai Stevenson. Adlai E. Stevenson III, had served for a while in the Illinois House of Representatives and subsequently became the state treasurer in an election where he led the Democratic ticket in the number of votes amassed. Stevenson had wanted the 1968 endorsement of the regular Democratic organization for the party's nomination to the U. S. Senate, but was denied it on the ostensible ground that he refused to pledge his support for President Johnson's Vietnam policy. The real reason for the denial was Daley's decision that Adlai III was not needed on the ticket at that time. Instead, the 1968 senatorial endorsement went to Illinois Attorney General William Clark, who in the course of the campaign against the incumbent Republican Senator Everett Dirksen, made himself over into a dove and, despite his ultimate defeat, did much better than expected at the polls.

After the 1968 elections Stevenson, in measured but pointed words, frontally attacked not only Mayor Daley's handling of the young demonstrators during the Chicago convention, but his rule of the Democratic party in Chicago. This anti-Daley move was followed by signs that the insurgent forces behind Stevenson were beginning to organize themselves in two areas which Daley's Chicago machine had never been able to penetrate— the suburbs of Chicago and downstate Illinois. It seemed evident that liberal sentiment was growing for a challenge to the organization, particularly for party nominations for vital Cook County offices, for the U. S. Senate, and for governor. It was, in a sense, a prospective attack in imitation of guerrilla warfare theory where the countryside is won before a siege on the urban center is undertaken.

There is no telling whether the insurgent forces gathered around Stevenson could have succeeded. The challenge never came to pass, and history, as Lord Acton once observed, never discloses its alternatives. In fact, Daley managed to head off his undoers at a giant picnic of independents and Independent Democrats held on Adlai III's farm at Libertyville, Illinois. The crowd was anti-Daley; the featured speakers were identified as anti-Daley men. One, Senator George McGovern of South Dakota, in the course of his work as the head of the Democratic party committee appointed to consider reforms in national convention procedures, had recently reopened the wounds of 1968 by a public clash with Daley. Unknown to the people in the crowd, however, the mayor decided to appear at the picnic and voice a plea for "party unity."

His motives were not unmixed. He meant to seek the mayorality of Chicago for an unprecedented fourth term in 1971. If "Paris was worth a mass," the avoidance of a possible costly primary fight for the Democratic mayoralty nomination was worth a gesture of public reconciliation with insurgent Democrats. Daley was in close contact with Professor Richard Wade of the University of Chicago, a member of the Chicago Housing Authority. Wade, in 1968, had acted as a field marshal organizing and directing the Indiana forces in support of Senator Robert F. Kennedy's bid for the Democratic presidential nomination; he had subsequently become a "McGovern man" and was anxious to promote his interests in advance of the 1972 Democratic presidential primaries. In his own appraisal of the political terrain he was convinced that the Democratic party nationally would again suffer a serious self-inflicted wound if "reformers" like McGovern and "regulars" like Daley kept alive the hostilities of 1968. To promote McGovern's interests primarily—and Adlai III's interests only incidentally—Wade persuaded Daley to show up at the Libertyville picnic and make his peace with the senator from South Dakota.

There were further implications to the truce. At the time that Daley left Chicago for the drive to Libertyville, Everett Dirksen, the incumbent Republican senator, was on his death bed. Daley knew about Dirksen's condition, and it could be expected that upon Dirksen's death—which in fact occurred that afternoon—Republican Governor Richard Ogilvie would appoint a Republican to replace Dirksen until the 1970 election. The Democrats had to decide who they should nominate for the 1970 senatorial contest that would strengthen the rest of the Democratic ticket for county and state offices. In Daley's pragmatic reckoning, Adlai III was that man. He could tap suburban and downstate votes that were beyond the reach of the regular Democratic organization. Less tangibly, Daley also knew from his own days as a member of Governor Adlai Stevenson II's State Cabinet, that to have an aristocratic Stevenson at the head of the Democratic ticket would please many of the ward heelers of the Daley organization for much the same reason that "hillbillies" of Arkansas take pride in being represented in the Senate by the scholarly and aristocratic J. William Fulbright.

The appearance of Daley at the picnic held on Adlai III's farm was a surprise to the crowd. Some booed when Daley appeared on the speaker's platform, and when he was introduced to speak. Daley chose to ignore this hostility. He made his plea for party unity, shook hands all around, and left. He gave no indication of any plan he had in mind for an alliance with the Stevenson forces. Later that night, when the picnickers were home listening to the news, they heard the report of Daley's presence at Libertyville in almost the same breath that they heard the report of Senator Dirksen's death. They could now put two and two together and see the shape of things to come. Months later, Daley's regular organization officially endorsed Stevenson as the Democratic nominee for the Senate. His Republican opponent was Senator Ralph T. Smith, whom Ogilvie had appointed to Dirksen's seat.

Senator Smith was to be one of main beneficiaries of the Nixon administration's strong backing: the president and the vice-president each made three campaign visits to Illinois on his behalf: as many as 14 Republican senators campaigned around the state for Smith on one day; and campaign dollars flowed into Smith's coffers from Republican National Headquarters. The Smith attack pressed home by the various visitors focused on Adlai E. Stevenson as an "ultraliberal," a captive of the "permissive philosophy," and an "unpatriotic leftist." The message of the campaign was that while Smith would stand firm against the young radicals and their threats against the social fabric, Stevenson would pander to them while they tore the nation apart.

The machine's precinct captains in the hard-hat and ethnic neighborhoods know their people better than any pollster. If their people were poised for an antiyouth, antistudent backlash as the Nixon political operators had assumed, nothing was more likely to stir up an underground protest by the precinct captains than the regular organization's endorsement of the senatorial candidacy of Stevenson—a man whose name symbolizes American liberalism. There was no such rebellion, any more than there was 22 years previously when the regular organization once again, out of need, endorsed Adlai Stevenson II for the governorship of Illinois. If the precinct captains in 1970 had any deep concern, it was that Stevenson would not be "fiery enough." But they otherwise welcomed "a strong ticket" that included not only Stevenson, but a number of other attractive young liberals for important state offices. Among these was Professor Michael Bakalis, Assistant Dean of Liberal Arts at Northern Illinois University, who was nominated for the post of state superintendent of instruction—which he was to win by over 400,000 votes.

The real difficulty in the situation was not the response of Daley's precinct captains after he endorsed Stevenson, but the reactions in the Stevenson camp after he accepted the endorsement. Some of the insurgents who had previously supported him claimed he had "sold out" to Daley and the Chicago machine. If he were elected, they feared that his victory with organization support would be a catastrophic blow to the cause of political reform in Cook County. He would bring in with him "every bum the party chose to put on the slate," [3] and thereby end up their captive.

Students in Chicago's 25 different colleges were concerned not only by Daley's endorsement of Stevenson, but by another development in the actual campaign. They had looked with favor on Stevenson's choice of Daniel Walker for his personal campaign manager. Walker was the author of the celebrated Walker Report, which stamped the phrase "police riot" on the conduct of the Chicago police at the time of the 1968 demonstrations in front of the Conrad Hilton Hotel. But as the campaign progressed, Stevenson had brought into his Daley-Walker combination another apparently clashing element in the person of Thomas Aquinas Foran, the federal prosecutor in the trial of the Chicago Eight. Foran was used as a speaker before small-town audiences downstate where he effectively helped neutralize the law and order issue.

In a meeting of extremes, neither the Agnewites who earlier saw Foran as the great avenger of permissiveness, nor the students who saw in him the full proof of Stevenson's "sell-out to the machine," bothered to take the whole man into view. Students seemed unaware of the fact that Foran had earlier obtained indictments of the Chicago police for the convention disturbances; that he was deluged with hate mail for prosecuting a school integration case in a Chicago suburb; that he had vigorously pushed faculty integration in the public schools; and that Foran, in fact, had always been a liberal on racial and economic matters. They also seemed unaware that Foran in the course of his work for Stevenson in the 1970 election, upstaged Jesse Jackson on a TV talk show with ploys like, "I agree with you completely Reverend Jackson, but I'd want to go further and take an even more radical stand."

While many students cited Daley's endorsement and Foran's

227

participation in the campaign as the reason for not working for Stevenson, the three-way campaign stretch from Daley to Walker to Foran did not alienate all students. A number did useful work for him at points where the Daley organization had no strength. In vote-rich Cook County, of which Chicago is a part, the most impressive youth work was carried out in the affluent "Gold Coast" towns along the north shore of Lake Michigan. The main Stevenson work force here combined university educated housewives—of the League of Women Voters variety —and students from private colleges. From all of these private schools, the most effective student workers were those from Bard College in Lake Forest. Bard, a fashionable Catholic girls' school, and the young workers it contributed to the foot-slogging tasks of the Stevenson campaign, are of special interest because they are representative of the post-Vatican II products of Catholic higher education.

Politicians who fail to recognize the effects Vatican II has had on the Catholic teachers of the Catholic young in the United States may continue to make their appeals to Catholic youth on the assumption that they are conditioned by an authoritarian training to sound "Hail Mary's" and to take rigidly rightist political positions. The reality is something else. The leading post-Vatican II products of Catholic higher education are surfacing in the national population as a phalanx that has shaken off the pre-Vatican II "siege mentality," and that no longer huddles together as if to make everything stand still; on the contrary, it is outgoing in its world view, and committed to heroic humanism. If they seem "heresy minded," it would be closer to the truth to suggest that they see in a figure like the late Senator Joseph McCarthy the ultimate heresy against reason, honesty, and Christian fair play.

The foregoing to one side, although the Stevenson candidacy failed to bring out the number of student workers expected in the spring of 1970 under the frontlash theory, the campaign from start to finish flew directly in the face of all backlash and sidelash assumptions.

When Senator Smith mounted an expensive television campaign that suggested Adlai III to be soft on student radicals, the regular precinct captains either dealt with the impact of the ads in their wards, or shrugged them off, knowing that the student issue would not win the Republicans votes. The precinct captains also made the most of the disclosure that Smith's campaign managers and his advertising agency had tried to discredit Stevenson by paying some hippies to pose for fake TV pictures in which they endorsed him—a gambit that backfired when one of the hippies confessed. Again, the precinct captains rejoiced when Agnew arrived on the Chicago scene and fatuously accused Stevenson of disgracing his father's name by his permissive attitude toward student violence, crime, and other allegedly explosive issues; the captains knew what the polling data used by the White House failed to reveal—that Chicago's hard-hat and ethnic voters would resent Agnew's attack on one of "Chicago's own boys." Finally, the loudest cheers of the campaign came from the captains in the hard-hat and ethnic neighborhoods when, at one point in the campaign, Adlai III departed from his habitual moderation to pull out all the stops and struck back hard at Vice President Agnew and Senator Smith.

Adlai E. Stevenson III won the Senate seat by 2,065,154 against his opponent's 1,519,718—a majority of 500,000. He had neutralized the "law and order" issue not so much by putting an American flag in his lapel, but by previously having sponsored, as a member of the Illinois legislature, anticrime legislation long before it became fashionable.

The typical American voter who is supposedly central to the backlash and sidelash theories did not make himself felt in Chicago or in Illinois in 1970. Apparently, the Dayton housewife whose husband is a mechanic, whose cousin is a policeman, and who is deeply worried about the "social issue," was detained in Dayton. Given the myth of the machine, can it be claimed that Stevenson's 500,000 majority was stolen, purchased, or brought to the polls by a disciplined patronage army? Votes are certainly stolen and bought in Chicago, but it is simply impossible to buy or steal half a million of them. The patronage army, while effective, is minute compared to the size of the city. The simple fact is that in defiance of all the assumptions about the makings of an antistudent backlash, Adlai III not only won three-fourths of all black votes in Chicago, but three-fourths of all Polish votes as well.

Other attractive, young, liberal Democratic candidates joined him in leading the first major success for the Democratic organization in previously solid Republican suburbs of Chicago. As a result, the Republicans lost virtually every office of any significance in Cook County. The Democrats also made impressive gains in the Illinois Senate. They had never controlled the Illinois Senate in this century, not even during the high tide of the New Deal, and went into the 1970 election with a 19–39 deficit in seats. But, after upsetting all six incumbent Chicago Republicans in the Senate, they came out of the election with a 29–29 tie—which meant that Democratic Lt. Governor Paul Simon, as president of the Senate, had the deciding vote in case of ties.

If the student issue was not a handicap to Stevenson, student workers were not a strong positive force. They did help in selected areas, but they did not make a major contribution to the victory. The returns suggested, however, that young voters did cast their ballots for Stevenson even though the number who took an active part in the campaign was reduced by his alliance with Daley.

Though Daley himself was subsequently re-elected mayor by a landslide majority in 1971, the anti-Daley bias of young people was revealed in the 1972 Illinois Democratic gubernatorial primary. Paul Simon, who made his political mark as a "downstate" reform-minded member of the Illinois State legislature, was slated for the nomination by Mayor Daley's regular Democratic organization. Many young people turned against Simon on that account and allied themselves with Daniel Walker, who sought the gubernatorial nomination as an independent Democrat. Walker, for his part, first won the countryside and the university communities and then laid seige to the urban center of Cook County, where a cross-over vote of Republicans into the Democratic primary gave him the margin of votes he needed for victory. It remains a subject of local dispute whether it was the same cross-over or a sit-down of Daley precinct captains that was also responsible, in Cook County, for the nomination as district attorney of Edward V. Hanrahan, a "law and order" incumbant who ran as an independent Democrat after he had been slated and then dropped by the Daley organization.

NOTES

1. Mike Royko, *Boss, Richard J. Daley of Chicago* (New York: E. P. Dutton and Co., 1971).

2. Theodore J. Lowi, foreword to *Machine Politics,* Harold F. Gosness, 2nd edition (Chicago: University of Chicago Press, 1968).

3. *Chicago Journalism Review* (November 1970).

11

Hartke and the Corporal's Guard

Eᴀᴄʜ major election contest is unique. They differ in the ways candidates have been personally identified with past issues at the focus of national attention, and in the way they propose to deal with current ones. There are differences in the histories of their respective parties; in the hopes and fears stirred by the party banners they fly; in the way the nominees won their nomination; and in how the scales balance the advantages and disadvantages of incumbent and challenger. There are further differences in the way names are listed on the ballot; in the qualities of the other candidates whose names appear on the party ticket; in the number of people who vote one way because someone they hate is voting another way; and in the weather over the farms and the cities on election day.

All such variables were at work in the 1970 senatorial contest in Indiana—the state due east of Daley-land. All of them, in their interrelationship, determined how the sum of 1,627,180 ballots cast were ultimately divided between Vance Hartke and Richard L. Roudebush, the two main contenders. Yet the contest is illuminating because the hairline closeness of the vote makes it possible to isolate the source of a small bloc of votes that became the "tipping point" in the election outcome. More to the point, the direct connection between that small bloc of votes and work performed by students underlines an important truth that was often overlooked amid postelection talk of student apathy—that great swarms of student volunteers need not be the determining factor in the success or failure of a candidacy. The Indiana senatorial contest demonstrated that a corporal's guard of students injected into a campaign picture at a critical point in time to perform a specific function they are uniquely fit to do—and coming on top of a foundation of work performed by many other people—can squeeze out the critical handful of votes that lead to victory.

The contest in Indiana matched Representative Roudebush, a hawk, against Democratic incumbent Senator Vance Hartke, a dove. Hartke had first gained national prominence as a dove in mid-January 1966, by initiating a letter signed by seventeen senators that urged President Johnson to continue the bombing halt despite the lack of results in the administration's "peace offensive." Although Roudebush, who had spent many years in the House, was a celebrity of sorts in his own congressional district, he was virtually unknown outside it. In 1970, however, he gained national prominence by conducting a campaign based on such inflamed zeal for the backlash theory, and pitched at such a sustained screech, that it made Vice President Agnew seem almost a flower child by comparison. On the public platform, in leaflets, and in television, radio and newspaper ads, Roudebush sought to exploit all the assumed public hostility to students and to young people.

Evidently Roudebush felt that the marked inroads George Wallace had made in Indiana in 1968 pointed to the certainty of victory for anyone who embraced the backlash theory and carried it to its furthest extreme. The air of Indiana has never been altogether cleansed of the endemic suspicion which gave the state the name of Hoosier—a contraction from the frontier day call for recognition: "Who is there?" Indiana at one time was hospitable to the Ku Klux Klan, and today Indianapolis houses the national headquarters for the American Legion. On these counts, Roudebush's campaign based on an anticipated backlash seemed a logical strategy for victory. In fact, he almost succeeded. He was tripped up in the end by no more than 20 University of Chicago students who had gone to Indianapolis to lend a hand to the Hartke cause.

The story can be told in a few words. In Indiana during a normal off-year election, the outcome of a state-wide contest generally depends on the pattern of voting within two rival strongholds, one Democratic, the other Republican. The Democratic stronghold is Lake County along the southern shore of Lake Michigan, which includes industrial towns like Gary, Hammond, Whiting, and East Chicago. The Republican stronghold is Marion County in the center of the state, which consists largely of the city of Indianapolis. In a normal off-year election, Marion County will go Republican by around 18,000 votes. In 1970, however, Roudebush hoped to pick up the bloc of Democratic voters in Lake County who had defected to Wallace in 1968. It thus became all the more imperative for Hartke to do what he could to hold the normally Democratic areas and to make a special effort to reduce the normal Republican majority in Marion County. His success required the support of the many blacks who lived in that county. Yet the overall voter turnout of Marion's blacks in an off-year election had been 60 percent of the turnout in a presidential year compared to an overall white turnout of 75 percent.

Against this background, Matthew Reece, an independent political consultant based in Washington, D.C., had advanced the idea—which Hartke's managers ultimately adopted—of reaching every regular Democratic voter in Marion County who had voted in both a presidential and off-year election to ask if he was willing to serve as a Hartke block captain. If the answer were yes, he would receive the names of voters on his block. The lists turned over to the captains would be composed mainly of Democrats who had voted in the presidential election of

1968 but not in the off-year of 1966, plus all new voters who had registered after 1968.

In places where Hartke block captains were to function, an effort was made to keep individual volunteer work to a minimum. A total of 4,000 volunteers proved available in the county, which meant that most of the inner city precincts in Indianapolis, black or white, could be well covered. Each of the block volunteers was to be given a card for distribution to individual homes saying that sometime between 2:30 and 5:30 in the afternoon on election day the volunteer would call and ask the people within if they voted. If they hadn't, they would be urged to do so at once. A determination would be made beforehand as to which persons on the block were likely to be Republicans, and their names would be crossed off the list of the people to be approached. In the actual mechanics of the matter, a single block volunteer would, on the average, be responsible for contacting around 15 homes.

On the Thursday morning before the election, the regular Democratic workers in the Marion County Democratic headquarters awakened to the fact that their well laid plan had a flaw. They had a list of 4,000 volunteers and they had a list of all the voters within each precinct. The flaw was that they had to match each of the names on the precinct lists with the 15 homes that were to be indicated on the cards guiding each volunteer to his targets. Since there were 800 precincts in all to be covered, and since the identity of the Democrats had to be established on the basis of previous participation in party primaries, it was a time-consuming business to differentiate between likely Democratic or Republican prospects and to transpose the Democratic names to the cards. It was calculated, for example, that doing the job in a single precinct would require between three and four hours. Yet the entire operation had to be completed by Friday if the cards were to be available to block captains by the Monday before the election.

It was quickly obvious to the Marion workers that they were

losing in a race against time. At the present pace, the task in hand could not possibly be finished. But five University of Chicago students who were on the scene appraised the situation for what it was and flashed a signal for help to their friends. By six o'clock that evening, 15 student reinforcements arrived from Chicago and plunged into the exacting work of culling and collating. They labored, with growing expertise until after midnight, flopped down for a few hours of rest on cots that were brought in for them, resumed work early the next morning and by one o'clock on Friday afternoon had completed the seemingly impossible. The cards went out to the block captains, with consequences that told on election day.

But there was more to what the Chicago students accomplished. Earlier in the year, the Republican-dominated Metropolitan Governing Council in Indianapolis had redistricted the precincts in the city—especially the black precincts in the inner city. As a result, some 75 percent of all the registered blacks were forced to cast ballots, if they voted at all, in places other than those in which they had been accustomed to voting over the previous ten years. The Marion County Democratic Committee urged the ward chairmen of the black inner city precincts to instruct each voter on where he would find his new polling place. But the ward chairmen balked at the suggestion, saying they lacked both the workers and the time to do so.

On Friday afternoon before the election, the problem of reaching these inner-city blacks was put to the small group who had just successfully completed the crash job of getting out the cards to the block captains. They promptly volunteered to cover some 15 precincts in two wards which held 9,000 registered black voters. Normally 5,200 could be counted on to vote in an off-year election, but in 1970 the student campaigners, whose goal was to increase the percentage of black votes cast, had not only to get those who were registered in a frame of mind to vote, but also had to let them know where to cast their ballots.

236

Hartke and the Corporal's Guard

The students worked the precincts for the remainder of Friday, Saturday, Sunday, and Monday, talking to people in the wards and giving them instructions on the location of the new polling places. On Tuesday, election day, they went back to the same precincts to pick up nonvoters and bring them to the polls.

Their extra effort paid off. The precinct turnout on election day was considerably higher than what it normally was in an off-year election. The small band of 20 University of Chicago students was credited in the end with getting out some 2,300 votes for Hartke that might otherwise not have been cast. Those extra votes cut down the usual Republican majority in Marion County, enabling Hartke to emerge the victor in the senatorial contest by a hairline majority. The final vote was Hartke 865,439 to Roudebush 861,741, a margin of just 3,800 votes.

It is idle to speculate whether much greater participation by students would have produced a more comfortable margin for Hartke. Conceivably, Roudebush's backlash campaign might have succeeded if students had been more visible and vulnerable. What is unchangeable is the success that students achieved in Marion, performing a task that students are preeminently equipped to carry out.*

* As these pages go to press, a decision of the U. S. Supreme Court on February 23, 1972, has opened the door to a recount of the votes cast in all Indiana counties in the 1970 senatorial contest. If Roudebush actually seeks a recount, Hartke's margin could just as well be increased as it could be wiped out. This would not, however, undercut the main point being made in this short chapter—namely, that a handful of students can be as strategically important as a great battalion of them.

12
Tunney: A Winner and a Question of Character

I N his *Rhetoric,* Aristotle analyzed the means by which a speaker persuades an audience, and assigned to them an order of importance. First in importance, according to Aristotle, was the impression a speaker conveys of his character; for when issues are complex and the lines of action to be taken are not self-evident, the audience will naturally give its trust to a man whose character it deems just and wise rather than to one it deems wicked and foolish. Second in the order of importance was the speaker's skill in the arts of oratory, in his capacity to arouse the emotions of pity and fear. What the speaker actually has to say about the issue in dispute was ranked third.

In making these observations, Aristotle may well have had in mind a situation not unlike the 1970 California senatorial contest in which the incumbent, Republican Senator George Murphy, was challenged by Democratic Representative John V. Tunney.* Tunney, in the end, decisively defeated Murphy, yet

* Mrs. Steven Roberts of Malibu and Tom Dove of Oakland monitored the 1970 U. S. senatorial contest in California for the present study. I am in debt to them for the raw material they assembled for my use in the writing of this chapter.

relatively few university students or other young people who might have been expected to do so, worked for him. It was not that the young wanted Murphy to win; they did not. Nor did they find fault with Tunney's general record and campaign utterances; his record in the House of Representatives was acceptable, for the most part, to students, and with several critical exceptions, his campaign utterances were equally acceptable and were expressed with passable eloquence. But students remained apathetic to Tunney in his campaign and joyless in his hour of victory.

The reason for this apathy amounts to a cautionary tale for political leaders who think that they can endear themselves to students and young people in general by saying "most of the right things." In the 1970 senatorial battle in California, John Tunney learned that students, even students who have never studied Aristotle, demand character above all in a politician. That quality, the students decided, was lacking in Tunney.

Tunney, the six-foot-three son of Gene Tunney (one time heavyweight champion) and heir to a steel fortune, had coasted through his student years until his junior year at Yale. Then he became ambitious. In 1955, he received a B.A. in anthropology from Yale; he attended the Academy of International Law at The Hague in 1957 and went on to the University of Virginia Law School, where he roomed with Ted Kennedy and graduated in 1959. He was admitted to the bar in Virginia and New York, where he briefly practiced; did a tour of military duty in California, and ultimately settled there. He opened a law office in Riverside, and taught a course in law at the University of California's Riverside campus before he got involved in politics.

Born in New York City and raised in Connecticut, Tunney had been a Republican until 1960 when he switched to the Democratic party to vote for John F. Kennedy. As a Democrat he won election to Congress in 1964 at the age of 30 and was returned in 1966 and 1968. Tunney looks like the Kennedys, sounds like the Kennedys, and made liberal use of Kennedy-like campaign techniques. An extensive media effort featured him romping on the beach with his beautiful Dutch-born blonde wife and three little boys, along with a legend designed to remind voters about his father: "Put a fighter in your corner." In 1970, still only 36 and with credentials as a political liberal and a dove on Vietnam, he entered the Democratic primary for the seat held by Murphy.

In winning the nomination, Tunney defeated Congressman George Brown, Jr. and Los Angeles County superviser Kenneth Hahn. Hahn, a white man who had strong support from blacks, was unknown outside of Los Angeles County, but Brown was a formidable contender within the statewide party. He was the first California congressman to speak out against the Vietnam War, was one of the leaders in the 1967–1968 Dump Johnson movement, and had supported Cesar Chavez' United Farm Workers Organizing Committee in their boycott against the California grape growers. Understandably, Brown's record made him a favorite of the more liberal wing of the California Democratic party—especially of the young people and students who had worked for McCarthy in 1968. Although some former McCarthyites had since joined the "turned off generation," those still active in politics rallied to Brown's side. They worked diligently for him, with the result that, in some parts of the state, he gave Tunney a close race. According to some analysts, Brown might have won if Hahn had not been in the race and if he had won more support from liberal Democrats who refrained from voting—or cast votes for Tunney—because they did not think Brown would stand a chance in the fall against Senator George Murphy.

After the primary, Brown set his sights on becoming California State Democratic Chairman. In a *quid pro quo* bid for Tunney's support he wholeheartedly endorsed Tunney for the Senate seat and worked for him in the general election. He could not, of course, transfer his own student supporters to his victorious opponent. Tunney and his campaign managers wanted student support but on their own terms, not the students'. Similarly, he was cautious in his approach to blacks. True, he solicited and received endorsements from the principal black leaders in Los Angeles and in the Bay area, but he refrained from campaigning actively for the black vote—a point that was not lost on young people. It was as if he meant to avoid all appearances of an overt alliance with the traditionally Democratic minority vote in favor of a suburban strategy. His sole appearance in "black" Los Angeles between the primary and general elections was a flyer into the Broadway Crenshaw Shopping Center, an affluent, black middle-class area.

Tunney's strategy was designed to cut into the support of George Murphy, the incumbent Republican. Murphy, born in New Haven, Connecticut, on the fourth of July, had, after a stint at Yale and working as runner on Wall Street, "made it" on the Broadway stage in the 1920's, then "made it" again in Hollywood following his motion picture debut in 1934 in "Kid Millions," a musical starring Eddie Cantor. In a reversal of the way in which Tunney, a Republican Catholic, converted into a Democrat, Murphy, a Democratic Catholic, converted in 1939 into a Republican. From that time on, he became increasingly identified with right-wing Republican politics in California. Like Ronald Reagan—another Democrat converted into a Republican—Murphy had served as president of the Screen Actor's Guild. Then he worked for Technicolor.

Murphy was working for Technicolor in 1964 when, at the age of 62, he won the California Republican nomination for the U. S. Senate. His Democratic rival in the general election was Pierre Salinger, President Kennedy's former press secretary who had been appointed by Governor George Brown to fill a vacancy in a California seat in the U. S. Senate. The results of the contest seemed to be another indication that California voting behavior defies analysis. Murphy emerged the victor despite President Lyndon Johnson's landslide victory as head of the 1964 Democratic ticket—just as in 1968, liberal Democrat Alan Cranston was elected to the Senate as the state sent Richard M. Nixon to the White House after having earlier rejected him decisively as governor.

Apart from the erratic element in California voting behavior, the tendency among Californians to turn against candidates who strike them as being "just politicians," worked in Murphy's favor in 1964. While Murphy could typecast himself as the innocent citizen untainted by deals, he could also typecast his Democrat opponent, Pierre Salinger, as a "walking smoke-filled room." But in 1970, it was revealed that Murphy had received a salary and other considerations from the Technicolor Corporation while serving in the Senate. This time around, it was he who seemed the less than scrupulous wheeler-dealer in his bid against young Tunney, the nice young man who romped with his family on the beach. Murphy suffered from another handicap in a contest that was billed as a clash between age and youth. A cancer operation left him with a permanently hoarse low voice, and while his physicians declared him completely cured, his health was an issue in the campaign. Moreover, Murphy's primary campaign, like Tunney's, had brought him into the general election in a somewhat battered state. Millionaire businessman Norton Simon had waged a belated but spirited primary battle against Murphy, and though a virtual unknown in California politics, won more than 30 percent of the Republican vote. His impact on the subsequent campaign, however, was even greater. His money had publicized the Technicolor charges against Murphy, split the liberal Republicans away from Murphy, and proved the latter's vulnerability.

The law and order issue was still of major importance in California in 1970. The student uprisings at Berkeley, Isla

Tunney: A Winner and a Question of Character

Vista, and other campuses was kept in the mind of the voters by Governor Reagan's continuing verbal assaults on "permissiveness," and by Murphy's echoing of the governor's rhetoric. In dealing with it, Tunney had to be wary of a blue-collar backlash at "youth-blacks-crime." Yet he also was wary of a "youth-black-liberal" reaction, which could lead to his defeat by nonvoters if he appeared too obvious in his courtship of the blue-collar vote. At first, he denounced violence in a straightforward way, but he always added: "Law and order does not mean repression. It does not mean the absence of civil liberties." As the campaign heated up, he placed increasing emphasis on law and order and a decreasing emphasis on civil rights; thereby alienating many blacks, Chicanos and young people. In his view, for instance, a Chicano riot in Los Angeles (which many locals thought to be a case of police over-reaction), was "Maoist" inspired; there was a "pogrom" against the police; the FBI was "the nation's frontline of defense against subversives, terrorist conspiracies, and interstate crime." At the University of Southern California (a traditionally conservative campus), he said it was time for students to "affirm a declaration of independence from the anarchists and arsonists who want to destroy our democracy." He asked students to reject pleas for amnesty and accept the fact that local police should be called on campus when violence threatened.

Tunney also exploited the Technicolor issue, calling for "law and order of the board room as well as of the streets." This issue proved something of an embarrassment when it emerged that Tunney's own father, as a member of the board of Technicolor, had voted to give Murphy the money—a fact that Tunney first denied, but later was forced to publicly recognize.

In other respects, Tunney's inflamed rhetoric on the law and order issue seemed to be part of a rhetorical match with Murphy. Murphy, for example, took out a full page ad in the state's major newspapers calling Tunney soft on crime because he

243

voted against the D. C. Crime bill. He accused Tunney of showing no concern for the problems of campus unrest and crime control until it became a necessity. Tunney, he said, "will say Angela Davis should only be tried for contributing to the delinquency of a minor," a position he called consistent with Tunney's attitude that the Chicago Seven "should be charged with littering the streets instead of conspiracy." Murphy repeatedly drew great rounds of applause when he said he favored firing faculty members who told students "if you don't go out and join the riot, you'll flunk my course."

The spirit of Murphy's campaign appeared in one of his ads, cast in the form of two dictionary definitions of the word *A-MER'ICA*. The first definition, with which Tunney was presumably identified, had a line crossed through it. It read:

> *A-MER'ICA* noun: war, hatred, bigotry, riots, bombing, segregation, burning, poverty, crime, intolerance, killing, drug addiction.

The second definition, with which Murphy was presumably identified, stood as the correct definition. It read:

> *A-MER'ICA* noun: freedom, opportunity, choice, hope, compassion, strength, change, brotherhood, courage, accomplishments, work, chance, progress, people.

The ad proved so embarrassing to the Berkeley chapter of the Young Republicans that they refused to allow the use of their name in connection with its publication in the student newspaper.

Paradoxically, the war in Vietnam, which was supposed to dominate the center of the political stage in California, appeared to be relegated to a minor, almost walk-on part, in the 1970 campaign. Tunney felt that American involvement in Vietnam should be ended by a pull out at an announced time. To Murphy, this was a policy of "cut and run." His own contribution was simply to call on the North Vietnamese to release the American prisoners they held. Undoubtedly students were in sympathy with Tunney's stand on Vietnam, but they questioned his low keyed approach as well as his positions on other issues. For example, students were upset by Tunney's neutrality on the grape boycott and did not take kindly to him even when Murphy went to the extreme of remarking that "wetbacks are built low to the ground so they should pick grapes."

For their part, members of the Tunney staff often spoke derisively of the 1968 "Children's Crusade" on behalf of McCarthy. They wanted nothing of the sort for Tunney. A "studenty" approach to politics, as they saw it, would not make for an effective campaign at a time when a suburban approach was called for. Nevertheless, Tunney staff members wanted some youth participation for some purposes. They initially seemed to assume that it was possible for them, at will, to turn on a faucet and a mass of young workers would gush forth to work for Tunney—that the only problem to be faced was how to control and channel the energies of the young enthusiasts.

Previous history seemed to warrant this assumption. After all, California's vast network of universities, colleges and junior colleges could be called the birthplace of student unrest. All the causes of student uprisings—unresponsive university administrations, R. O. T. C. courses, Black Studies programs, the Vietnam War, adverse living conditions, the firing of popular professors—had triggered violent commotions on California campuses. One event, occurring in the spring of 1970, was the burning of the Bank of America building in Isla Vista, where many students of the nearby Santa Barbara branch of the University of California resided.*

Tunney did in fact attract some 5,000 young workers to his

* George Murphy so wanted to remind voters of this incident that his headquarters featured a huge wall poster with a Bank of America check superimposed on a picture of the burning building.

campaign, who put in anything from one hour to many weeks of work on his behalf. Yet most of his young workers were 15-, 16-, and 17-year-old high school students, rather than college students—the ratio of high school to college students was seven to one. Moreover, the college component working for him was comprised largely of students from the smaller colleges. What is of interest is that so few students from the most prestigious California universities joined the Tunney campaign despite their antipathy for Murphy and the assumption that they could be enlisted with ease.

One of Tunney's chief problems was to "turn on" the McCarthy type of student activists who had worked hard for George Brown in the Democratic senatorial primary only to see him go down to defeat. Their very activism made it difficult to bring about a switch in their allegiance from Brown to Tunney. They wanted to believe in the rightness of their man and his cause, and they were not convinced by Tunney.

Another of Tunney's problems among students is best approached by an indirect route. Political professionals who admire craftsmanship in a detached way—even if they are its victim—could admire the relatively high order of technical skill with which Tunney intermixed the role of the fox and the lion in staging a winning campaign. They noted how he met the threat of the law and order issue by outshouting Murphy about it. They noted how he pursued a politics of net gain by giving little attention to the blocs of inner-city votes that were already in the Democratic camp and concentrating on the suburban vote. They noted his use of filmstrips designed to make him appear a reincarnation of the two slain Kennedys.

Yet the very ground on which political professionals admired Tunney's craftsmanship became the ground on which some disaffected students remained disaffected. As they viewed him, Tunney was a changeling and a manipulator—too clever by half. They would rather go down in heroic defeat fighting by the side of a man of uncompromising principles, than to win with a man who in their view seemed to assume that success itself—however won—would purify the means used. These students had railed at the packaged and contrived politics of the Reagans and Murphys on the Republican side of the party line. They could not be expected to go into reverse and exult when they saw the same packages and contrivances in the Tunney candidacy. It offended their sensibilities to see Murphy wrap himself up in the American flag. But it also offended their sensibilities to see Tunney wrap himself up in the ghost of the Kennedys—duplicating beach scenes that may have been authentic enough when lived out by John and Robert Kennedy, but which now seemed to have both a script and a media director setting up the lights, cameras, and angle shots on what appeared to be just another Hollywood stage set.

Students at leading California universities brought an absolutist moralism to their outlook on the campaign and were unforgiving of the slightest deviation from what they thought was the hygienically pure and mathematically exact moral syllable for Tunney to utter. They refused to understand why he snatched for his own use the law and order issue which had for so long been a monopoly of Reagan and Murphy. By the same token, they refused to understand why some things in the context of a campaign really cannot be explained in full, but are touched on only in shorthand forms. They were moral absolutists who regarded Tunney as a moral equivocator for failing to conform to what they would have done.

There was, in addition, a paranoid strain among some students. For example, a loud clatter of underground talk went to the effect that it was the policy of Tunney's managers to confine students to backroom jobs. In fact, there were some areas in California where youths—as a matter of policy—were not sent out to canvass, either because other groups were thought better suited for the job or because it was thought that young canvassers would lose more than what could be gained by their presence. Labor groups, for example, did the canvassing in most of the blue-collar districts in Los Angeles, while central Pasadena specifically refused to allow young workers in the area. On the other hand, in San Diego County, young people were used to recruit adult canvassers to work in their own neighborhoods, a novel innovation worth the consideration of political aspirants of the future.

While the complaint that Tunney did not want students to be either seen or heard appears unjustified, Tunney made himself vulnerable to the slings and arrows of scornful university students in other respects. From the standpoint of organization, for instance, the Tunney youth campaign suffered from the problems inherent in all California politics—the unwieldly size of the state and the endemic hostility between the political operators based in the Los Angeles central headquarters and those based in the San Francisco Bay area. At the Los Angeles headquarters, in particular, the tone of the youth staff was one of frenetic excitement. While this sense of participation gave the young workers a heady sense of involvement in the affairs of the great world, youthful nerves were shot—as early as three weeks before the election—with the result that the scatter-pattern judgments that were sometimes made multiplied the disorganization that accompanies any campaign.

Disorganization—and the brusqueness of manner which often goes with it—also worked against the Tunney campaign when it led to the rejection of some student volunteers. It was hard for the rejected to realize that even in the best organized campaign there are a limited number of places for volunteers and a limited number of functions they can perform. To the rejected, however, the phrase "we will call on you when we need you," sounded like a brush-off by an inside clique who were sure they were going to heaven with the candidate, and wanted to reserve it all for themselves. So the rejected became one of

248

the sources of the word-of-mouth advice to other students to "stay away from the Tunney campaign." The same kind of advice was sounded by students who were assigned at random to makework projects without any consideration of the interests of the volunteer or of their talents. Many of these square pegs in round holes were not content with their misfit. They looked around the campaign, saw where they stood, and without as much as a formal farewell, they walked out, trailing resentment.

Meanwhile, little love was lost between the youth workers in Los Angeles and San Francisco. Robert Klein, the Chairman of Youth for Tunney operating out of his Los Angeles base, tried to carry an inhuman work load, mainly—so it is said—because he did not trust the youth workers in San Francisco. At one point, the entire San Francisco youth staff was on the verge of rebelling because of Klein's alleged lack of trust in them. Students at the major universities learned about the conflict between Los Angeles and San Francisco, and drew hostile conclusions.

But the basic reason for student disaffection with Tunney was neither the conflict and disorganization of the campaign machinery, nor the distaste for the campaign's tactics. Rather, it was Tunney personally. From the beginning, the students suspected his strength of character. Later, they settled into a frame of mind where they were prepared to believe the worst about him. Incidents that served to confirm their belief were not lacking. In early September, for example, an aide in Tunney's Los Angeles headquarters telephoned various local radio-TV stations with a news release. One of the calls went to the manager of the largest black-audience radio station in Los Angeles. The station manager, who was very pro-Tunney, had endorsed his candidacy at an early date and was prepared to go out of his way to be helpful. After transmitting the message, he asked if the aide had any more information that the station could pass along to the black community. The aide replied, "Well no, we don't have anything for your people. After all, who else could they possibly vote for anyway? You're in our pocket." The station manager was shocked by this verbal straight-arm. The Tunney staff eventually found out what happened but waited for several days before dismissing the imperious aide, and even then failed to offer the station manager either a follow-up explanation or apology. The story quickly spread throughout the black media where students picked it up.

If this story had been an isolated incident, students might have dismissed it for what it was—a gross stupidity that could not fairly be charged against Tunney himself. A candidate for a major office, torn from every side by the demands of his campaign, cannot be expected to monitor every phone call or to be responsible for every turn of the tongue by subordinates. But students did not regard it as an isolated incident. Politically skeptical students, already disturbed by the slickness of Tunney's tactics, felt that it was emblematic of his whole campaign —a campaign based, as they saw it, on Tunney's hard-nosed calculation that other groups as well were "in his pocket" so that he had no need, or desire, to consider their sensibilities.

A later episode reinforced the conviction of students in places like Stanford. Apparently, Tunney was under the impression that he had the full support of the "concerned youth of California"—and no one on his staff wanted to tell him otherwise. Why not? Tunney, reportedly, was so sensitive to criticism, overt or implied, that in the words of one of his top aides, "We can't tell John that there might not be a good crowd at the next shopping center stop or we'd have an extremely upset man on our hands." As a consequence, his advisers subjected him to a regimen of artificial sunlight. Robert Klein decided to cancel a scheduled appearance at Stanford where it appeared that Tunney would be facing a critical panel of students. Tunney was not told the real reason for the cancellation; instead his staff resorted to a subterfuge. The storytellers, however, overlooked an upset member of the Tunney youth section who had taken offense because the headquarters staff in Los Angeles, unwilling to entrust the youth staff in San Francisco with the staging of the Stanford appearance, had commuted north to handle it; he leaked the real story of the cancellation to the Stanford campus newspaper, and it made Tunney out to be not "a fighter in your corner" but a man with the backbone of an over-ripe banana. Word spread to the nearby Berkeley campus, with the same negative effects. If the offended students could not vote for Murphy, they still had the choice of not working for Tunney. Many proclaimed "a plague on both your houses," and retreated into privacy.

Even those students from the leading universities who worked for Tunney seemed to have clothespins clamped on their noses. Howard Sall, for example, a UCLA junior who canvassed in Westwood, candidly stated that he wasn't really for Tunney, but thought it was more effective to work for the Democratic candidates than for the Peace and Freedom party. Reagan and Murphy, he said, were "even more tied into the establishment" than Unruh and Tunney, but that was the only difference he saw. He found canvassing depressing because the voters knew so little and because the more he thought about the candidates the worse he thought they were. "They're all beginning to sound the same," said he, "calling for more cops and all that."

But Tunney's calculated strategy and professionalized tactics worked. Without significant help from students, who found him deficient in character, he won with 3.4 million votes, or 53.7 percent, to Murphy's 2.8 million, or 44.4 percent. Even if students felt that Tunney differed only in degree rather than in kind from Murphy, his overall vote was impressive evidence that he succeeded in making big inroads in California's non-Aristotelean suburbs.

The Tunney plurality also included a significant number of

251

newly registered voters who were signed onto the voter lists as a result of a well-organized, hard-sell voter registration drive carried out in minority and working-class neighborhoods by the California branch of Frontlash. Although the registration drive was nominally nonpartisan, the voters who were reached and put on the rolls were almost exclusively Democrats.

James Wood, the organizer of Los Angeles Frontlash, found that the reaction in poor areas to student registrars was strongly positive, since the people of the area were "glad to see the kids doing something useful instead of turning on all the time." California Frontlash differed from most other politically active youth groups in several respects. It was not composed solely of students—college or high school—nor was it made up solely of middle-class whites, or blacks. It was a diverse coalition and, as such, was one of the few youth groups that effectively recruited both black and white working-class youth. Although its work was endorsed and assisted by a number of national organizations, it was one of the few groups whose main financial support and manpower came from organized labor. Its leadership in the main was drawn from members of the Young People's Socialist League. It also was one of the few groups whose youthful workers were singularly free of both histrionics and apocalyptic visions—one of the few that did not issue ukases to the effect that they were giving "the system a last chance." Its members preferred to work at the basic task of building a base for political power from which they could march at the head of events and determine for themselves what events would become. They had medium and long-term objectives as well as short-term goals. As a consequence their organization, which was involved in process politics rather than protest or demonstration politics, was not something that was here today and gone tomorrow. It was—and is—a continuing operation from one year to the next.

In the spring and summer months of 1970, California Frontlash produced an army of 2,000 young volunteers—from campuses, high schools, ghettoes, labor unions, churches, as well as youth and student organizations. They worked as "bird dogs" and registrars, signing up almost 100,000 new voters from poor neighborhoods. In the five assembly districts of California with the heaviest Frontlash drives in 1970, registration increased by an average of seven percent over 1968, as compared to only .01 percent statewide. Los Angeles Frontlash, together with its companion project Reachout conducted by the A. Philip Randolph Institute and Coalition for a Better Government in the Crenshaw district, registered 30,000 voters and ran a get-out-the-vote effort in 50 precincts on election day. San Jose Frontlash registered 19,000 voters and ran a countywide get-out-the-vote effort, assigning more than 1,000 volunteers into 150 precincts. Alameda County Frontlash registered 22,000 voters and mobilized about 250 high school and college students for bringing out voters in the sixteenth A.D. in Oakland. San Francisco Frontlash enrolled 16,000 voters and helped coordinate a large student-labor turnout drive; in San Mateo County, a joint Frontlash-Movement for a New Congress project registered nearly 6,000 voters and organized 350 election day workers. Hundreds of other students helped cover the precincts in Stockton, Modesto, and neighboring towns. Overall, despite heavy rainfall on election day, Frontlash turned out 3,000 workers in 15 cities. The increased voter turnout resulting from these efforts helped elect Tunney and various congressmen, and, by electing a new Democratic majority, helped to change the face of the state legislature.

13
Black on Black

I

If apathy marked the reaction of most California youth to the Tunney-Murphy clash, the nationwide apathy of young blacks is an even more striking feature of the 1970 elections. Youth participation tended to mean, primarily, white youth participation. Most young blacks seemed settled in the conviction that it would make no difference which of any two white candidates running against each other won a contest for a House or Senate seat. Each candidate would be racist to the marrow of his bones, and any candidate who won with the help of the black vote would invent a thousand excuses afterward why he could not make good on his campaign promises to blacks. Since one white candidate was as bad as any other white candidate, young blacks apparently concluded that there was no point in campaigning.

But there was a conspicuous exception to the general electoral apathy of young blacks—the election of Ronald V. Dellums to the House of Representatives from California's seventh congressional district.* It is a portent of what a well-organized,

---

* The 1970 contest in California's seventh congressional District was monitored by Tom Dove of Oakland. In the writing of this chapter, I made free use of his core material, supplemented by details drawn from the local press and the literature of the rival candidates. Any fault found with the perspective which informs the account, should be placed at my door alone.

strongly motivated group of young black militants can do for a candidate of their choice.

II

Frontlash and youth, particularly black youth, were major factors in Dellums' victory. Overall population statistics— 396,243 people in 1960, and an estimated 450,000 in 1970— convey little about the congressional district, but a breakdown is more revealing. Although the district as a whole is predominantly white, it has an inordinately large bloc of nonwhite minority voters for Northern California. The 1960 census figures, acknowledged to be on the low side, showed that 24.8 percent of the district's population was black, and 4.2 percent was Mexican. The median age of these minority groups was 27.1 years, as against the white median age of 34.5 years. Assuming an increase since 1960 in minority groups as well as in students, the 1970 census may show that relative to the seventh congressional district's total population, it now possesses one of the largest concentrations of "youth" found anywhere in the United States.

The district runs the gamut of the ideological spectrum. It includes the northwestern portion of Alameda County, a conservative bastion in the Bay area, whose town of Albany—which has a Democratic mayor—serves as the regional headquarters of both the John Birch Society and the Neo-Nazi American Party. It also includes Emeryville, a low property tax enclave for the protection of industry; Piedmont, the regional center of aspirants to upper middle-class status; roughly one-third of the city of Oakland; and the city of Berkeley—a heady brew of working-class Democrats, University of California liberals, radicals, assorted hangers-on, the California College of Arts and

Crafts, as well as the exclusive "Western 8th Sister," Mills College for Women. In essence, the district can be likened to a stage where sound tracks of almost all the clashing shouts in the United States are tuned up to their maximum decibel count and played simultaneously.

For twelve years prior to the 1970 primary, Representative Jeffrey Cohelan, a liberal Democrat, served the district in the House of Representatives where his record made him one of the nation's most respected congressmen. In six straight elections, his strong backing from the labor and academic communities, coupled with the chores he performed in Washington for his diverse constituents, enabled him to defeat his Republican opponents easily. In the elections of 1964, 1966, and 1968, he was re-elected by two to one margins.

The Republican hierarchy in the seventh district assumed that Cohelan would win the Democratic primary in 1970 by acclamation and then coast to victory in November. None of them saw any point in seeking the Republican nomination. So it went by default to John E. Healy, 25, the only person to file for it. Yet when the June primaries were held, the outcome was stunning. Cohelan was defeated by Ronald V. Dellums, 34, a trim, rangy, militantly black member of the Berkeley City Council, which meant that the Republican nomination won by Healy might be worth a good deal.

Dellums, a life-long resident of the district, was born in Oakland, spent two years in the United States Marine Corps and went on to acquire a bachelor's degree from San Francisco State College and a master's degree from the University of California at Berkeley. Following Berkeley, he was successively a psychiatric social worker for the California Department of Mental Hygiene, Program Director of the Bayview Community Center, Associate Director and Director of the Hunter's Point Youth Opportunities Center, a planning consultant to the Bay Area Social Planning Council and Director of the Concentrated

Employment Program of the San Francisco Youth Opportunity Council. Since 1968, he had been a senior consultant for Social Dynamics, Inc., a Berkeley-based venture to develop manpower and community organization programs on a nationwide basis. He was also a part-time lecturer at San Francisco State College and at the Graduate School of Social Work at Berkeley. Dellums had married the former Leola Roscoe Higgs and was the father of three young children.

Out of his diverse career, Dellums attracted young people as a magnet draws iron filings. With their help in early 1967, he bid for and won a seat in the Berkeley City Council. Once in politics he displayed some of the political schizophrenia that characterized Berkeley and the district as a whole. He regularly insisted that he was against violence overseas or at home, and just as regularly identified himself with local insurgency that sometimes spun-off violent episodes. His ambiguity was most marked in his role in spurring the local merger between the Student Nonviolent Coordinating Committee (SNCC) and the Black Panther Party. But there were other inconsistencies. Dellums identified himself as a man "who understood the human issues underlying heated confrontations," and "could deal with them while others do the shouting." Yet he took part in the strike at San Francisco State where naked coercion was used to back up non-negotiable demands. He was eloquent in denouncing police repression, but was silent about the physical intimidation of white liberals by black militants. He warned against setting the stage for fascism in America, but never condemned the black militant embrace of anti-Semitism.

These ambiguities, however, were put to one side by Dellums' adherents in Berkeley proper. They admired him for ethnocentric reasons. He had always sided with the Berkeley students in their recurrent clashes with university administrators. He joined the students in inveighing against the proposed tuition hikes in state universities and colleges, although many institutions of higher learning in the nation were being forced, like California itself, to increase their tuition fees in line with rising operating costs. He sided with the antiwar demonstrators, whether they used peaceful or violent means to protest against the Vietnam War. He sided with the diverse groups that created Berkeley's People's Park which was the cause of a violent dispute with state political authorities; Dellums also took credit for getting the troops off the streets of Berkeley at the height of the clash over the People's Park.

Dellums, of course, was hardly the first bundle of contradictions to become an office seeker. Nor was he the first office seeker to become a Democrat out of convenience; he could—and probably would—have identified himself with the Vegetarian party if Vegetarians comprised the majority in the voting constituency. Dellums was skilled in presenting himself as a figure incarnating the spirit of the New Left and the New Politics; yet he was no less skilled in applying the lessons he learned from the white masters of the Old Politics to win. In the language of one of his own political pamphlets, Dellums is "Black, radical, articulate and effective."

The mood of his campaign for the Democratic nomination appeared in one of his hard-hitting broadsides against a very vulnerable target. The broadside was captioned:

WHAT WE HAVE HERE
IS SOCIALISM FOR THE GUYS AT THE TOP,
AND CAPITALISM FOR YOU AND ME
AND EVERYBODY ELSE.

The text went on to note that "the people at the top"—the industrialists, the moneymen, the big growers—"preach free enterprise." But, it read, "we still have to realize, once and for all, that the guys at the top yelling the loudest about the virtues of free enterprise and competition are the ones who don't believe in it for a minute for themselves." They were the people whose businesses and farms ran on government subsidies. Dellums ticked off other "guys at the top":

The ones who pay a fraction of the income tax they're supposed to, while *we* pay higher taxes to compensate. The ones who live off stocks at *one-quarter* the tax rate you pay. The ones who make millions—millions—in bond income without *one penny* of income tax. The oilmen who get to write a quarter of their investment off their taxes every year—not just till it's paid off, but forever.

Nothing is going to change until we realize that *we* are paying for *them*—that just closing the loopholes they've engineered in the tax laws and getting them to pay the taxes they are *supposed to* would lower everyone else's tax by twenty cents on the dollar.

We have to realize they want capitalism and competition only for *us*.

We have to stop playing their game and fighting with each other.

Let's get organized.

His operational phrase was "Let's get organized," and he proceeded to do so. By the first of 1970 he had knit together a coalition of the working poor, student-faculty white liberals from the colleges and universities in the district, and Chicanos responsive to the leadership of Cesar Chavez. The coalition also included the younger members of the Black Caucus, and the activists of the Young People's Socialist League, who—as noted —were the main force behind the Frontlash voter registration drive in the seventh district as they were elsewhere in California.

Although Dellums had previously justified or sided with all student strikes, demonstrations, and protests staged in the area, he and his young black staff had strong reactions against the May-June explosion on local campuses. They privately cursed it for a number of personal reasons. First, it would increase the possibility of a backlash against students—a real problem for a

259

Dellums race that would have to depend heavily on students for most of the legwork his campaign would require. Second, they feared—on the basis of past experience—that following the explosion and the release of emotional energy, there would be the usual student letdown, and the bright shining moment when protest within the system was in vogue would give way to disillusionment on the part of young idealists. Third, it was feared by Dellums and his staff that the explosion would escalate into incidents of violence at a time when it was important not to revive memories that associated Dellums with eruptions of campus unrest.

Dellums and his staff could do little about the first two fears, but were well placed to clamp a lid down on the possibilities for campus violence in the district. The major concern to Dellums was Berkeley, where campus radicals had always been deaf to pleas from liberals for peaceful conduct. The radicals were contemptuous when liberals argued that the one major result of all the radical commotion in times past was the election of Reagan as governor. It was the radical view that Reagan's election was an indispensable step in the grand design of history where social progress would come about through calamity.

Whether or not Dellums and his staff had previously interposed themselves between that theory and its application in election contexts, it was different this time. With his own political prospects at stake, self-evident historical truths were subject to reinterpretation. Berkeley had been calm since April 1970; later, despite the May-June strike over Cambodia, Kent State and Jackson State, it was one of the few major campuses where the strike was a model of serenity. Why?

Dellums and his candidacy played a part. Some white students, radicals no doubt, reasoned that Dellums, after all, was their man, and should be treated as an exception to the historical rule of progress through disaster. With other white student radicals, however, reason apparently did not do its work un-aided. It was reportedly tied to the persuasive force of physical coercion: early in the Dellums' candidacy, militant young blacks in the district made it clear that they would consider it racism if any white radical group at Berkeley queered his chances by generating local disturbances. The message, cou-pled with ill-concealed threats of physical beatings, came through.

In Washington, Congressman Cohelan maintained his faithful service to liberal causes, unaware of the underground fears and ferments bubbling in his congressional district. In apparent con-fidence that his "record of twelve years of service would speak for itself," he barely campaigned at all for the Democratic nomination. His expectation that he would be easily renomi-nated was shared by many regular Democrats who had pre-viously supported him in the general election. On the assump-tion that his renomination was a certainty, they—a total of 54,000 registered Democrats in the district—did not bother to vote in the Democratic primary. The Dellums coalition, on the other hand, brought most of its own bloc of newly registered Democrats to the polls, and the consequences told when the ballots were counted. Dellums polled 42,619 votes, 54.8 per-cent of the total; Cohelan polled 35,137 votes or 45.1 per-cent.

While the Republicans added only 8,801 voters to their list prior to the primary and only 1,800 more in time for the gen-eral election, the chieftains of the Dellums coalition and their Frontlash assistants did not rest content with the number of new voters they had registered in the preprimary weeks. After the primary, they mounted another registration drive to pick up voters who had previously escaped their net. The result was an additional 15,000 newly registered Democratic voters on the rolls by election day. In all, Dellums' forces added a total of 30,460 new voters to the Democratic rolls, bringing total registration on the day of the general election to 143,572 Democrats and only 62,290 Republicans. This imbalance was to be the controlling factor when the vote was cast.

III

As noted earlier, a virtual unknown, John Healy, won the Republican nomination for the House seat by default. When Republican leaders learned that Cohelan had been defeated in the Democratic primary by Dellums, they concluded that Dellums in turn could be beaten, provided they could transform Healy's image from what nature made it to be into what politics demanded that it be.

And so the transformation attempt began.

Healy, a trainee for a loan adviser position in the Albany office of the Household Finance Corporation, had no qualifications to compare with the series of responsible positions held by Dellums, but this did not deter his new backers. In his campaign literature they saw to it that Healy was described as a "financial consultant for a national consumer finance organization." His campaign managers were even more forceful in changing Healy's marital status so he could compare more favorably with Dellums, a father of three. Healy, a bachelor, was persuaded that he would have a better image if he married. The woman chosen was Margaret Ingles, a friend of Healy's who had a master's degree in guidance and counseling and was employed by the California Youth Authority. It was suggested that she would bring to him an identity with the cause of California youth; besides, the fact that she possessed a master's degree— in a degree-conscious district—would help offset Healy's educational inferiority—two years at Merritt College, a junior college—especially when compared to Dellums' credentials.

Both Healy and his friend proved agreeable, so the marriage took place.

Healy was advised not to attack Dellums, who was a vigorous advocate of an immediate end to the war in Vietnam and an immediate withdrawal of all troops, as a "peace freak." The district, it was decided would not take kindly to an attack of this kind, particularly since Dellums had honorably served for two years in the Marines. Instead, the Republican stage managers thought it advisable to amplify Healy's service in the Army from 1966 until 1969, including a year as a cavalry sergeant in Vietnam where he had been "decorated for gallantry in action during the Tet Offensive." Heavy stress was placed on the fact that he was "the only congressional candidate in the nation who has served in the [Vietnam] conflict, and knows the problems first hand." As a result, it was pointed out that "when he talks about how we can get out of Southeast Asia he speaks with the insight of a man who has been there, tested under fire."

Healy's advisers decided that his stand on Vietnam should be moderately dovelike. "I feel," said Healy, "we could pass the responsibility for defending Vietnam to the Vietnamese by intensifying their training. We could be out of Vietnam in ten months and leave a better atmosphere for a just peace." They had somewhat more difficulty in shaping his position on student unrest, which he could not denounce because of the large student population in the district. His advisers had him speak in code language. "I share," said Healy, "the concern for this nation and the world so sincerely voiced by fellow members of my generation. But I believe change must come through peaceful means, and that campus violence and destruction by the violent radical minority must be curtailed. I will work to bring an atmosphere of peace and quiet to the campuses of this district. I believe in freedom from fear." Such mild rhetorical flights by Healy could hardly match Dellums' broadside manifestos, such as this one:

HARD-HATS, BLUE COLLARS,
STUDENTS, BLACK PEOPLE,
AND THE AMERICAN DREAM:

Working class people get told now that their enemies are young people and black people, when actually the enemy of *all* these groups is the same: A government which serves Big Power, Big Business, Big Money; the handful of powerful interests who are the "insiders."

So-called hard-hats have been ignored as much or more than any class of Americans. They believe in the American dream but have been turned away from noticing that the dream has only been realized by people in power. Workers are told it's the students and blacks who are responsible for their lives not working out; for the fact that they work harder and harder while getting deeper in debt. But the *real* reason is an administration and a Congress which can favor big oil companies with tax breaks, while blaming workers for inflation. . . .

Ron Dellums thinks the Nixon-Agnew-Mitchell-Republican movement to separate workers from their natural allies—the other people on the outs—is cynical, cruel, dishonest, immoral, and un-American. He's going to work to get workers, and poor people, and all other unrepresented people together where they belong.

Finally, Healy's campaign slogan was "Responsible Government." Yet his generally pallid and moderate positions offended hard-line Rightists who wanted to crush Dellums for his sympathetic association with the Black Panther party. At the same time his campaign had enough of a "law and order" overtone to offend the white liberal community which was not entirely happy with Dellums.

As the days went by, Healy or his Republican stage managers decided to appeal to disaffected white workers who feared Dellums, and to the dissident Democrats who backed Cohelan. He seemed to be making headway in both ways as election day drew closer. While the mass of organized labor could not be won, it could and did begin to back out of any direct part in the race. White liberals who had always voted Democratic began re-examining their position, and they too started to back-slide. But Healy's drive was checked on both fronts when Vice President Agnew was brought in to further his cause. In characteristic style, Agnew attacked Dellums' candidacy in language which made it seem that his election to the House would be the next worst thing to electing Bobby Seale to the White House. The effects on the black voters—as well as on liberals—in the district were disastrous for Healy.

What about the hierarchs of the national Democratic party? They were in no way unmindful of Dellums' candidacy. When he defeated Cohelan, they saw a new rising political star in the West and decided to hitch their wagon to him. They were not put off by the fact that Dellums had previously declared that he had "no allegiance to the Democratic party" and sought the Democratic nomination merely because the Democrats were a majority in his district.

Nationally known Democrats, who do not ordinarily take the stump for a first-time-around Democrat, came to the seventh congressional district at some time between the primary and the election to help give Dellums the biggest publicity build-up that any newcomer on the national political scene has known in many years. In between times, and aside from their personal political ambitions, they may have persuaded themselves that they were also helping the Democratic party—that by their efforts on Dellums' behalf they were beginning the process of his domestication, so that the Democratic party nationally could safely trot him out on showcase occasions in the future.

Dellums was not the source of profound thoughts or epigrams that will someday be inscribed on the pediments of public buildings. But he understood some things with mathematical precision, including the hyperthyroid temper of his district.

When his antennae told him that people in the district were beginning to grumble that the contest for the House seat was fast becoming an outsider's race, he sent word to the Democratic

265

party notables that the best thing they could do for him was not to come into his district before the election.

The second thing Dellums understood was the art of how to make a shared fear a cohesive force among otherwise disparate groups. He did not personally create the atmosphere of fear that hung like a brass curtain over the district, but he knew how to turn the atmosphere to his advantage. In a cascade of speeches and handouts, he drove home the theme that his candidacy was the "last real chance" the electorate had to avert the apocalyptic forces bearing down on them.

The third thing which Dellums understood was the decisive one—the leverage that comes with organization and enables a tight-knit, minority fraction of all the stockholders in a Leviathan industrial corporation to hire and fire the management, and to dictate all other policies. It is this principle that enables a small but internally united and disciplined force to rout a mob many times its size. Dellums' political talent enabled him to conjure up for his own purposes such an organization—internally united and disciplined.

These were the results in the general election: Dellums (Dem.) 88,737 votes, or 57.3 percent of the total; Healy (Rep.) 63,819 votes, or 41.3 percent of the total. Dellums became the first black man in the United States ever to be elected to the House from a predominantly white district.

Although Dellums faced a virtually unknown and inexperienced candidate, Healy bettered by 15,500 votes the record of the Republican challengers of Cohelan in the three preceding congressional contests. Healy's votes did not all come from registered Republicans, and the total cast for Dellums, which was 14,000 votes below the 1968 general election total for Cohelan, suggests that a sizeable number of these Cohelan-Democrats either voted for Healy or stayed home on election day; Healy was in fact endorsed and supported by the seventh district's only Democratic mayors—H. F. Call of Albany and Donald Neary of Emeryville. It also seems fair to assume that between 35 to 40 percent of Dellums' final vote came directly from the people whom he and his coalition allies had registered as new voters since the first part of 1970. He was, in a word, far more a people's candidate than the candidate of the regular Democratic party.

Part of the result can be ascribed to the identity—or lack of identity—of his opponent. But the greater part must be ascribed to Dellums' workers. The supreme achievement of Dellums as a black candidate for the Congress in a predominantly white district was his success in winning support among his fellow blacks. It is no easy thing for a black man with any pride to be an active participant in traditional electoral politics. There are too many voices of past experience shouting at him: "What's the use? It won't make any difference who wins or loses. The same betrayals and entrapments will follow." Nor is it easy for blacks to concert their strength on a single objective. Too many of them are caught up in the most desperate and tragic of all struggles—the struggles of the poor against the poor.

When these realities are born in mind, the full significance of Dellums' work defines itself more clearly. His victory was a black political victory. In California's seventh congressional district in 1970, Dellums was able to persuade the black community and the Black Caucus—a collection of loosely affiliated black organizations brought together for political projects—to put aside their internal differences. At the same time, he had the kind of ambiguity where the most embattled black militant could identify with Dellums as the outspoken radical, while the property-owning black moderate could identify with Dellums as the young city councilman. And if there was any gap in this convergence of extremes, it was closed by the ramrod thrust of Agnew's attack on Dellums, which outraged local blacks.

Interestingly, two groups of white students—the campus

267

Young Democrats and those who had been involved in May-June with the launching of a local Movement for a New Congress—were not involved in his campaign. By July, the exhaustion in these groups, as the Dellums forces had feared, materialized. It was impossible to rouse them for any kind or form of project, much less for an election, even though there were many—about 12,000—summer school students on the Berkeley campus. White student canvassers for Dellums came out only in the last days of his campaign as a direct consequence of his "last stand" and "last chance" pitch.

The one group of white students who did belong to Dellums' disciplined army already has been mentioned. They were pragmatic members of the Young People's Socialist League, who provided the bulk of the manpower for the district's Frontlash registration drive. They were kept at least one degree removed from the inner cadre of the army Dellums had whipped into organized shape, but they were a definite help to him.

Dellums drew on his white liberal supporters for money, canvassing, and votes, but everything else was black-oriented. His chief advisers were young blacks. His chief supporters were blacks and Chicanos (an equally disaffected political force). He ran a black campaign attuned to the needs and aspirations of the young blacks who were his friends and coworkers. In the end, his victory margin was black. The black community's support enabled him to outstrip the white labor vote for Cohelan in the Democratic primary; and it was the solid black vote, again cast on a previously unequalled scale, that enabled him to triumph in November over the combination of a Republican backlash, labor defection, and a low Democratic turnout.

The role of youth in the Dellums campaign was two-edged. It vastly increased the number of pro-Dellums voters; but it also stirred up an antistudent backlash. On balance, although Dellums almost lost because of youth, he could not have won without youth. Young people did not work for Dellums in overwhelming numbers throughout the campaign, but in its last days, enough were frightened into action by the "last-real-chance" argument both to work and to vote for him.

14
Hart:
Youth + Youth

I N California's thirteenth congressional district, a Democratic challenger, 27-year-old Gary Hart, a high school history teacher from Santa Barbara, ran against an eight-term incumbent, 61-year-old Charles Teague of Santa Paula.* With a final count of 127,120 votes for Teague to 87,646 for Hart, the victory margin was 37,500. Since a majority of one is enough to elect, it would be easy to conclude that Teague's victory amounted to a rout of Hart and of his very young, all-volunteer force of campaign workers. To call a result a rout, however, does not necessarily make it so. Doubts arise when the 1970 results are placed alongside those of 1968. At the time, Teague, with a victory margin of 73,000, received 63 percent of the total vote. In 1970, he dropped to 58.5 percent.

The differential between 1968 and 1970 can not be explained simply by noting that the district voted overwhelmingly for Nixon in 1968 or that 86 percent of the registered voters in the thirteenth congressional district went to the polls in that presidential election year, whereas 78 percent did so in the

* Donald MacDonald, editor of the *Center Magazine,* Center for the Study of Democratic Institutions, Santa Barbara, California, monitored the 1970 contest in California's thirteenth congressional district. Mrs. Steven Roberts of Malibu also assisted in this work. This chapter is based on the raw material they assembled for my use.

1970 election. In 1970, Teague still appeared to hold all the conventional trump cards of politics and able to top any card played against him by Hart. Yet the young challenger, with everything stacked against him, somehow mounted a spirited campaign whose long-range effects may be more significant than any intermediate defeat in 1970.

As an arena of battle, California's thirteenth is one of the largest congressional districts in the United States. It stretches almost 200 miles along the Southern California coast, from Santa Maria and Lompoc on the north to Malibu and Woodland Hills in western Los Angeles County on the south. It includes all of Santa Barbara and Ventura counties. There are no megalopolitan urban centers in the area; Santa Barbara, with about 90,000 people, is the largest city, followed by Oxnard, Ventura, Santa Maria, and Santa Paula. Since the turn of the century, Santa Barbara has attracted individuals of great personal and family wealth, many of them adopting it first as a winter-vacation retreat, and later as a permanent base. Agriculture is the dominant economic activity in the district, and the petroleum industry, and the tourist trade are important. An estimated 15 to 20 percent of the constituents are Mexican-Americans, and a lesser percentage are blacks.

The district contains four junior colleges, two colleges, and one university, whose combined registration in 1970 was 37,000, including 20,000 commuting students and 15,000 resident or boarding students; most of the latter, or 13,600, are at the University of California in Santa Barbara. The four junior colleges have open admissions, offer extensive vocational training courses, and accommodate many part-time and night students who work to support themselves. The two colleges—Westmont in Santa Barbara and California Lutheran at Thousand Oaks—are Protestant schools. In addition, the district is the home of several "think tank" establishments, such as the Center for the Study of Democratic Institutions at Santa Barbara. Six daily

271

newspapers are published in the district. A local television station in Santa Monica is an affiliate of the Columbia Broadcasting System. National television is fed into the district through Los Angeles stations and is received by either cable or external antenna.

In recent decades, registered Democrats have always outnumbered registered Repuʰlicans in the district—in 1970, the figures stood at 141,000 to 132,000. Yet the occupational, ethnic, educational, economic, and urban-rural mix of the area has made it moderate to conservative in its political preference. In 1954, it sent Teague, a self-styled progressive moderate Republican, to Congress for the first time and regularly re-elected him in two-year intervals after that. The district rejected the extremism of Goldwater in 1964 but voted overwhelmingly for Nixon in 1968.

Still, in this politically and ideologically moderate and nonflammable district, there occurred in 1970 in Isla Vista—the off-campus student enclave next to the University of California in Santa Barbara—a series of violent youth confrontations. These included the burning of the Bank of America branch, the death of a student trying to cool a disorder, police raids, curfews, and adults defying the curfew in a show of sympathy for the young.

A partial explanation for the violent disorder in a seeming paradise is that 98 percent of the students at the University of California at Santa Barbara (UCSB) come to it from outside Santa Barbara. Another part of the explanation is the nature of Isla Vista itself. It cannot be called a community. Very few adults live in it, but it has about 13,000 young people, including 9,000 UCSB students. The physical structures consist of apartment buildings (paperthin walls and high rents, say the students), a pool hall, several hamburger and taco joints, two bookshops (neither of them adequate) a record shop, several grocery stores and gas stations, a movie theater, and very little else, save hundreds of dogs and much boredom. All the postriot investigations of Isla Vista pointed to the clear need to change the place from a collection of young people into a community. Late in 1970, the University of California Board of Regents, by voting 350,000 dollars to achieve that objective, recognized the university's responsibility to provide a decent environment for the vast majority of students who prefer to live off campus in Isla Vista.

It was in the heated-up atmosphere of Isla Vista violence in the spring of 1970 that Gary Hart waged his youth-oriented campaign in a three-cornered primary for his party's nomination. Hart graduated from Santa Barbara High School in 1960, where he had been student body president, an all-conference football player on a championship team, and winner of the Outstanding Senior award. He attended Stanford University on a scholarship, studied abroad in Florence, Italy, traveled to the Soviet Union and Eastern Europe, and worked one summer as an intern in Congressman Chet Holifield's office. He attended Harvard University where he earned a master's degree in education, and then taught American history at Tougaloo, a black college in Mississippi, where he was also active in the civil rights movement.

In 1966, he returned to Santa Barbara High School where he taught world history and coached the basketball team. In the fall of 1967, he joined Lowenstein in the beginning stages of McCarthy's campaigns. Later, Hart worked in Lowenstein's successful campaign for a seat in the House of Representatives from Long Island. Hart studied Spanish and Mexican history, and taught English in Cuernavaca, Mexico, after which he returned to Santa Barbara where he taught at Laguna Blanca, a private elementary and secondary school. He married Cary Smith of Princeton, New Jersey, whom he had met during the McCarthy campaign.

After winning the three-cornered Democratic primary fight

273

for the nomination to the House seat from the thirteenth district, Hart began to feel that he had a chance of defeating the hitherto unbeatable Teague in the fall election. While he knew that many of the Democrats in the district were originally from the South, and both conservative and middle-aged or older, the new people in the district were for the most part under 40. Many were registered Republicans with no commitment to Teague, and Hart felt he had a chance to win over a sizeable number of them.

Teague comes from a ranching family in the Santa Paula area of Ventura County in the southern part of the district. He is a stockholder in the Lemoniera Corporation, a citrus ranch. His son, Alan, is mayor of Santa Paula. Teague himself is the ranking Republican on the House Veterans Affairs Committee and the second-ranking Republican on the House Agriculture Committee.

The six newspapers in the district, with one exception, favored Teague's re-election principally on the grounds of his experience and his seniority in Congress. But there were some significant differences on issues. On Vietnam, Teague favored the Nixon administration's "Vietnamization" policy and its withdrawal program; Hart proposed that a date be set within a year for the withdrawal of all U. S. forces. On military service, Teague favored continuing the present "random selective system" until such time as it is "practical to have an all-volunteer military force"; Hart proposed that the draft should be ended immediately in favor of an all-volunteer professional army, severely limited in size. On crime control, Teague favored extending the right of wire-tapping; Hart favored increased federal aid to upgrade prison personnel, and to pay higher wages to prisoners so as to rehabilitate rather than harden them. On campus unrest, Teague favored laws that would deprive students who engaged in violent activities of federal grants and loans; Hart favored the prosecution of all illegal actions whether committed by students or the police. On environment, Teague supported the Environment Protection Agency, but claimed that there were still not enough votes in the Congress to authorize the federal government's buying up the leases that would put a permanent stop to off-shore drilling for oil; Hart urged as a guiding principle that the burden of proof for any proposed development by commercial interests affecting the environment must be on those interests and not on the conservationists. On the unionization of farm workers, Teague favored the right of farm workers to organize, but believed that "strikes and boycotts should not be allowed during peak harvest periods"; Hart favored the right of farm workers to unionize as well as the picker's national boycott of grapes.

Hart and the very young people who comprised his staff were in accord on the main campaign problem they faced. If they were to hope for success in a district that was 200 miles long, they must conduct door-to-door canvassing through at least 90 percent of the district. They must try to see every voter, talk to every voter, find out how every voter thinks, identify favorable voters, discover the disenchanted Republican voters, and then call back on those leaning to Hart. The district had never really been canvassed; many people in the district did not even know who the incumbent was. Canvassing also happened to be best for Hart since he did not have any funds, and canvassing required the least expenditure of money— provided there were enough volunteers.

In the search for volunteers, Hart spoke on every college campus in the district as well as at the University of California at Los Angeles and Valley State College in San Fernando. He also talked at every high school that permitted political speakers. When asked why he spent so much of his time talking to high school students who were nonvoters, Hart explained: "When we recruit 10 precinct workers, that is worth 400 to 500 votes. Second, when I talk to a group of high school students, they will be going home that night and mention to their parents that I spoke at their school that day."

An effort was also made to recruit young people in the labor force; some of these were also students at the local city colleges. But they were generally so busy with their studies and work—and in a number of cases, with their families—that they had no time for the campaign. In Santa Barbara itself, where Hart was well known, a number of older people came forward as volunteers for canvas work. These included the new people from the think tanks. It was obvious, however, that the main canvassing burden in the district as a whole would have to fall on student volunteers. But students at the three residential colleges in the district—the University of California in Santa Barbara, Westmont in Santa Barbara, and California Lutheran at Thousand Oaks—failed to show up in the numbers predicted back in May-June at the time of Cambodia and Kent State. At UCSB proper, the campus newspaper was run by radicals who thought that Hart was "a jerk," and hence gave no publicity to student recruitment for his campaign.

At the same time, Hart's own youthfulness posed a special problem for a student-based campaign. Some voters saw an automatic link between the fact of Hart's youthfulness and the violence in Isla Vista. They asked the canvassers if "Hart identifies with students." The canvassers insisted that he was opposed to violence but not to lawful dissent. Other voters, on hearing the words "Gary Hart" slammed the door in the face of the canvassers. "At times," said Ernest Glover, a Vietnam veteran who was the UCSB representative of the Hart campaign, "being a student hurts, especially in neighborhoods where they're flying the American flag."

Hart's main organizational problem, to repeat, was finding enough students to do the volunteer work. He had attracted exceptional youth support in his primary contest back in June, but his successful bid for his party's nomination coincided with

276

the cresting of student strikes against American policies in Southeast Asia and the killing of students at home. He represented the liberal, nonviolent response to those policies and actions, and as such, was attractive both to the majority of young people who rejected violence, and the adults who feared and opposed it. But President Nixon had succeeded in cooling off student activism by promising to withdraw American ground forces from Cambodia by June 30 and by announcements of further American troop withdrawals from Vietnam.

As a result, when young people returned to classes in September, Hart—like other liberal antiwar candidates—encountered a quite different emotional climate in which youthful rage had been displaced by a kind of wait-and-see skepticism concerning Nixon's avowed determination to end the war in Vietnam. In these circumstances, Hart was faced with the infinitely more difficult political task of rendering other and more complex issues both clear and urgent. Yet such issues—congressional reform, inflation, economic recession, ecological deterioration, urban misery, and conversion from a wartime to peacetime economy—did not lend themselves to emotionally charged exhortations. They were more suited to reading and research, and to analysis in classrooms or dormitory bull-sessions than to political polemics and doorbell ringing.

Since the Vietnam issue was defused by the fall of 1970, Hart didn't dwell on it to the extent that marked the primary contest. As a result, campus radicals accused him of being a "cop-out." At the same time, he was hit from another side because of a story he had released to the press—namely, that back in 1967, when he had been granted a medical deferment from the draft, he had turned in his draft card as a gesture of protest against the war. His key aides were divided on the wisdom of making this fact public. Some favored the announcement on the ground that it would convince youth that Hart was not "a gutless dissenter." Others thought it was an obvious mistake for Hart to break the story. The ultimate decision to make a public announcement about the matter was based on the conviction that Teague knew that Hart had turned in his card, and that the congressman planned to spring the story too late in the campaign for Hart to make an effective explanation.

With the announcement, *The Santa Paula Daily Chronicle* published an inflammatory "How I Burned my Draft Card" editorial, which Teague picked up and published as an advertisement. By the time the ad appeared, it was too late for Hart to buy space in order to rebut it—although he did buy an ad after the election "to clear the record." Hart insisted that he could not have violated the law by turning in his draft card, since he had already been deferred from the draft on medical grounds. Teague, replied that the attorney general's office in Washington had informed him that such action was illegal, and went on to suggest that a candidate who flouted the laws was not fit to be sent to Congress to enact them.

It is difficult to determine just how badly Hart was hurt by the draft card issue. To suggest that it was a decisive factor in his defeat is to ignore the inherent difficulty of turning a long-entrenched Congressman whom no one hated out of office. But this does not suggest, conversely, that Hart was not hurt at all by the story of his draft card. It may have made the difference between losing with 40 percent of the vote instead of 43 percent.

But all of this was the negative side of the picture. There was a positive side to it as well. If the turnout of young people for Hart was far below that of the McCarthy campaign—and again, if the numbers did not approach the expectations at the time of Hart's primary victory in June—far more did work for him than had ever before worked for a congressional candidate in the district. Estimates as to the exact number of young volunteers vary. The high figure cited was "between 700 to 1,000." A more modest estimate places the number at 350 young people who "did something" for the Hart campaign—anything from spending several hours in passing out literature in a super-market, to working full time for six weeks, seven days a week on clerical or canvassing chores.

Of the youth who worked on the Hart campaign, relatively few came from the residential universities and colleges in the district. The majority were high school and junior college students. In Ventura County, for example, they comprised between 75 to 80 percent of the precinct-canvassers for Hart. Not everyone slammed the door in their faces when they mentioned the words "Gary Hart." In some areas, like the Simi Valley, the young canvassers met with an extraordinarily favorable reception. Apparently nobody had ever canvassed the valley before, and the warm reception given the young canvassers —even by householders who were to vote against Hart— suggested that the people in the valley "had been sitting around a long time waiting for somebody to come and talk politics with them."

It was also noted that Republican voters were often more open and friendly to the young canvassers than Democrats. Part of the reason, paradoxically, had something to do with the Isla Vista disturbances. Republicans, more so than Democrats, were likely to be struck by the contrast between young students working in a political campaign and those burning a bank. Republican parents seemed particularly terrified by the prospect that their children might be sucked into the drug culture. They were relieved to see "the kids" working in a political campaign, even if "the kids" were not their own. They could cite the young canvassers as an example to their own children about the good things to do—in contrast to the alternative of "sitting around and smoking pot."

Hart, a high school teacher, stressed the merits of his young canvassers who were high school students. He said

High school students are more valuable in a political campaign than college students. They're more political than they've ever been, and they don't have some of the radical hang-ups of college

279

students. They can influence their parents and their parents' friends, because they have community ties—whereas many students in the colleges are not from the community where they go to school.

At the same time, as a high school teacher, he remained concerned throughout the campaign of what would happen to the outlook of his canvassers if he lost. To forestall their possible alienation from electoral politics, he hammered away at the point that his young canvassers were not to construe his possible defeat as a proof that the system of electoral politics was a failure. There was the next time around to bear in mind.

Whatever blunders may have been committed by Hart and his young advisers in the course of the campaign, the paramount fact remains that Hart made politics a branch of the teaching profession for a considerable number of young people to whom it had previously been a closed book. In much the same way that a dark background brings out the sparkle of a diamond, what he taught his young volunteer workers even in defeat shines as a singular triumph.

15

Ottinger + Goodell = Buckley

I N the 1970 New York senatorial race, the liberal forces in the state were divided between Democratic Representative Richard L. Ottinger, and the incumbent Republican Senator Charles Goodell.* Each of the two was backed by hardworking and enthusiastic youthful supporters and campaign workers. Victory, however, went to a third party candidate, James Buckley, who was also backed by enthusiastic and hardworking young workers. Buckley won a minority of the vote—and with that minority, became the first third-party candidate elected to the U. S. Senate since 1940, when Robert La Folette, Jr., won as a Progressive in Wisconsin.

Prior to the onset of the 1970 senatorial contest, events pointed to New York as a good place to look, along with Chicago and Illinois, for evidence to support assumptions about an antistudent backlash. Nothing of the sort occurred. With three armies of young people working for the three contenders, there was no backlash against the young. Instead, there was a three-

---

* Stephen Schlesinger, editor of *The New Democrat,* was the principal monitor for this study of the 1970 United States Senatorial contest in New York. In addition to the fund of material which he assembled —and whose use I here gratefully acknowledge—I drew in this chapter on the perceptions of Professors Leon Cohen and Roy Speckhard of State University of New York at Albany.

cornered free-for-all in which the young blasted away at each other.

Politically, New York is divided into three parts, which every candidate for state or national office must bear in mind: upstate New York is basically conservative Republican; New York City is heavily Democratic; and the fast-growing suburbs of New York City and the upstate cities which are at present a mixed picture. In 1970, as the elections approached, New York's governor was a moderate Republican, Nelson A. Rockefeller of New York City and suburban Westchester County; its senior senator was a liberal Republican, Jacob K. Javits of New York City; and its junior senator was a Republican conservative-turned-liberal, Charles F. Goodell of upstate Jamestown. Rockefeller, who was running for re-election, forced the nomination of Goodell over strong conservative opposition.

On the Democratic side, the ideologues of the New Politics are contemptuous of and label as "cheap," Mayor Daley's "ethnic" politics. So, while Daley won the greatest triumph of his career in 1970, the ideologues of the New Politics in New York made up a Democratic slate in New York State consisting of four Jews and a black—all from New York City—and still expected the party to get the Irish and Italian support, and the suburban and upstate vote.

In New York, the slate prepared by the party leaders did not go unchallenged in the primaries. Arthur J. Goldberg, the former associate justice of the Supreme Court and ambassador to the United Nations, who was the regular candidate for governor, defeated his challenger, Howard Samuels. But in the four-way Senate race, Theodore C. Sorensen, the eloquent former aide to John F. Kennedy and a newcomer to New York politics, was snowed under by Representative Richard L. Ottinger of Westchester County, who mounted an expensive television campaign. Even Paul O'Dwyer, the beau ideal of the left wing of the Democratic party, got twice as many votes as Sorensen.

Ottinger + Goodell = Buckley

The net result of the Democratic primary maintained the unbalanced ticket of four Jews and one black on the state-wide ticket —Goldberg running for governor, Ottinger for senator, Basil A. Paterson, a black, for lieutenant-governor, Adam Walinsky for attorney general and Arthur Levitt for controller.

Despite the obvious internal fragmentation in the government and politics of New York—especially New York City—many outsiders view the place as a united, malign force, the source of every dark wind that blows across the face of the nation. In 1970, Vice President Agnew set out to flatter Middle America by playing on their fear and hatred of all he and they thought New York represented. All along the campaign trails, the worst charge Agnew could hurl at any man he sought to defeat for office was that he had tie-ins with the "radical-liberal Eastern Establishment"—meaning New York City.

Equally sinister references to "radical New York students" also contained, in New York itself, a full measure of irony. While Ottinger and Goodell had their young volunteers, the most ardent, dedicated, and numerically significant campaign workers were those who worked for James L. Buckley, the senatorial candidate on the Conservative ticket.

Meanwhile, the radical-liberal establishment of New York City was hopelessly divided between the Democratic and Republican nominees. Since his victory in 1959 in a special election, Charles F. Goodell, a Republican, sat in the House of Representatives. But until Senator Kennedy was assassinated and Governor Rockefeller appointed him to the vacant senate seat, he was just another upstate Republican politician who shared the prejudices of his constituents toward the city of New York and who conveyed the impression that his understanding of the world around him was confined to the maxims of Poor Richard's Almanac. The short stroll from the House side of the Capitol to the Senate side was his "Road to Damascus." Like Saul of Tarsus who fell on his face and rose as St. Paul,

Goodell on that short walk experienced a spectacular conversion.

He shed the anonymous style and abandoned the conservative stand on public issues through which he had maintained his place in public life in upstate New York. With a more diverse constituency to appeal to in his bid for election to a full six-year senate term, he dressed himself to their taste. His shirts turned rainbow; and his suits were wide lapel, double-breasted chic. More to the point, he suddenly became a leading voice advocating quick withdrawal from the war in Vietnam. This rapid shift in political identity amused some of Goodell's colleagues and jarred others, particularly some senior Republicans who resented what they said was Goodell's consistent opposition to President Nixon on so many key issues. In upstate New York, the reaction to the swift shift was not tinged with amusement. It was streaked with outrage over what they, the upstaters, considered to be a betrayal of their original support for him. When he appeared at a GOP state convention, he was greeted by catcalls.

Against this background, Agnew invaded the New York campaign to denounce Goodell as a "radical-liberal" who was hiding behind the Republican label. He accused Goodell of turning on his president and party and suggested that true Republicans in New York should vote for the Conservative party candidate, Buckley.

If Goodell's voting record were viewed as a single whole, it would be hard to explain the attack. Goodell was not a senator on whom the administration could always count, but in that respect, he was hardly unique. According to *Congressional Quarterly*'s study of 72 roll calls in 1969 involving presidential positions, Goodell supported the White House on 53 percent of them (compared to an average of 75 percent for the entire Senate) and opposed the president on 25 percent. But six other Republicans strayed as often, or more often, than Goodell. By

CQ's statistics, Senator Barry Goldwater (R-Arizona) supported President Nixon on only 39 percent of those 72 roll calls and opposed the White House 19 percent of the time.

Other Republicans with low "support" scores included Senator Karl Mundt of South Dakota, 53 percent; Senator Mark O. Hatfield of Oregon, and Senator John Sherman Cooper of Kentucky, 50 percent; and Senator Marlow Cook of Kentucky, 44 percent. Three Republicans—Senators William B. Saxbe of Ohio, Charles M. Mathias, Jr. of Maryland, and Edward W. Brooke of Massachusetts—scored only 57 percent. On foreign policy issues alone, moreover, Goodell backed the president 63 percent of the time, a better record than ten other Republicans. One of Goodell's fellow Republican freshmen, who was also up for re-election in 1970, had shown himself to be even less reliable on White House issues. Senator Ralph Smith of Illinois, appointed to succeed the late Everett Dirksen in the fall of 1969 voted with the president only 36 percent of the time. He raised his "loyalty rating" to 45 percent in 1970—which still placed him below Goodell—yet Agnew campaigned on his behalf.

It was obvious that for some reason, a special case was being made of Goodell. It is true that conservatives in the White House and in the New York Republican party had for months previously been denouncing Goodell's "liberal heresies," especially those with respect to the Vietnam War. But this does not explain why Agnew set out on the extraordinary course of attacking Goodell openly after he became the regular Republican nominee for the Senate. President Roosevelt, for example, tried in 1938 to bring about the defeat of several incumbent members of his own party, but the attempt, which failed, was made within the framework of the Democratic nominating primaries, not in the general election where a Democratic candidate faced a Republican rival.

The Byzantine mysteries of the matter do not easily unravel for analysis. One can only cite an intriguing underground theory which circulated among Republicans in Washington and was overheard and published by William Greider of *The Washington Post.*

The theory maintained that the clear front-runner for the Senate seat at the time was the Democratic nominee, Representative Ottinger. Goodell, though fighting on the same left-of-center turf, could not overtake him. If so, an Ottinger victory would strengthen further the hold of the Democrats on the Senate. New York, however, presented a special equation in which party nominations have a fractured influence. In 1969, New York's Mayor John Lindsay ran as a liberal independent and won re-election with less than a majority of the votes against two more conservative candidates who were wearing the regular party labels. The White House project in 1970, therefore, was to reverse the case as it applied to the Senate race. Since Goodell could not win, it might be possible to help engineer a minority victory for Buckley who, as a Conservative, was attracting substantial support from regular Republicans all over the state —especially in the counties of Nassau, Suffolk, Erie, Monroe, and Albany. But what could the White House do to help his cause along? It could send Agnew to New York to attack Goodell, and by that attack, win for Goodell a surge of liberal-independent sympathy. If Goodell's standing on the charts thus rose, it would be at the expense of Ottinger, since the two men were fighting for the same left-of-center constituency. The more votes Ottinger lost to Goodell on this account, the more Buckley's prospects would improve as a likely minority victor in a three-way race. If he actually won, he could be counted on to vote with the Republicans in organizing the new Senate.

Whether this theory was much too subtle to be the product of a thought-out plan, the vice president's attack on Goodell did, in fact, have the effect just indicated. There was a shift of sentiment away from Ottinger to Goodell, and no argument could awaken voters concerned to the perils of the trap they were walking into. There was a split down the middle of the peace movement and liberal vote. On October 13, for example, 40 prominent peace leaders who were much admired by New York liberals joined in a statement endorsing Goodell. They included Father Daniel Berrigan, Father Philip Berrigan, Rev. William Sloane Coffin, Jr., Jules Feiffer, Jane Fonda, Betty Friedan, Murray Kempton, Coretta Scott King, Stewart Meacham, David Schoenbrun, Dr. Benjamin Spock, Gloria Steinem, George Wald, and Cora Weiss.

Two days later the Movement for a New Congress endorsed Goodell, as did 60 student body presidents and editors from college and university campuses throughout New York State and the Northeast. Stephen Golden, New York regional director of the Movement for a New Congress, spoke for both the state and national groups. Speaking on behalf of the student leaders were David Hawk, national coordinator of the Vietnam Moratorium Committee, and Marge Tobankin, vice president of the student body at the University of Wisconsin, and Wisconsin state coordinator of the Vietnam Moratorium Committee.

The 60 student leaders—in endorsing Goodell on the first anniversary of the first Moratorium—declared: "Charles Goodell has become the foremost symbol of positive leadership and constructive dissent in the U. S. Senate." The Movement for a New Congress, in comparing Goodell with Ottinger stated:

It was our decision that the senator was the better of the two candidates. His stance on the war has been impeccable. His position on foreign policy has been well thought out and has been in the best interests of the United States and its citizens. . . . It is a case where the peace candidate, Senator Goodell, is running against a candidate who wants us out of Vietnam—sometime.

It was another example of the death-wish that has so often characterized young liberal idealists in New York politics; they would rather go down to defeat with their own choice, than win

287

with a candidate whose credentials were as good—or almost as good—but operated from an independent base. Ottinger, who had been elected three times to the House of Representatives from a heavily Republican district, was a rich young man with a hard-to-match liberal record. His district, which included Rockefeller's home in Pocantico Hills, bordered the Hudson River. The pollution of the river and the deterioration of its shoreline got Ottinger involved in ecological questions before ecology became fashionable, as well as in political conflict with Rockefeller. Although he was an early critic of the Vietnam War, unlike Goodell, he did not center his actions and speeches on the war; if anything, he specialized on environmental problems.

Ottinger spent almost a million dollars on television to win the primary campaign, and his spending was one of the major issues raised against him during the campaign. Most of the money was contributed by his mother, Mrs. Louise Ottinger, whose late husband had been a founder of the United States Plywood Corporation. On the night of his primary victory, Ottinger pledged to his youthful supporters a continuation of the tough kind of campaigning that had won for him—whirlwind tours of the state, hand-shaking visits to factories and shopping centers, local speeches and visits, in addition to television.

Ottinger's managers knew that their main opponent was Buckley; they even thought at one time during the campaign that Goodell, recognizing that he could not win, would withdraw in order to prevent a Conservative victory. It was clear to them, and to neutral observers, that Rockefeller, who had engineered Goodell's nomination, was becoming more and more neutral in favor of an accommodation with a possibility of a Buckley victory. Ottinger himself tried to maintain a central position between the Don Quixotes on the left who were faithful in their fashion to Goodell, and the Galahads of the right, who were obviously making advances as the campaign moved into its last weeks.

Ottinger + Goodell = Buckley

Spent emotionally and financially by his bruising primary campaign, Ottinger started to cut back expenditures as the campaign neared its end. As a result, even though heavy spending had been used as an issue against Ottinger, Buckley raised more money and outspent both his opponents. Just before the election, Buckley reported receiving $1.5 million and spending $1.1 million; the Ottinger figures were receipts of $687,000 and expenditures of $728,000. Goodell raised $533,000 and spent $516,000.

The Buckley campaign, which was managed by F. Clifton White, who had been campaign manager for Goldwater's presidential campaign in 1968, was built solidly around the "social issue," as defined by Wattenberg and Scammon, in three phases. Phase One was to introduce Buckley to the voters and the media. Phase Two was to emphasize the issues of campus and slum unrest, crime, pornography and shifting moral standards—and Buckley's opposition to them. Phase Three was to shift from issues that were not working to others that might work. Buckley never found it necessary to go into Phase Three. His emphasis on the "social issues" scored enough voters to give him a narrow victory in the three-man race. He received 2.3 million votes, or 38.8 percent; Ottinger, 2.1 million, or 36.6 percent; and Goodell, 1.4 million, or 24.6 percent.

The Buckley campaign set off sparks of excitement, not among the little old ladies in tennis shoes, but among "the kids." A caller at his senatorial headquarters on 38th Street and Madison Avenue would see ordinary youngsters, who loved the Mets, ate hamburgers, wore sideburns, blue jeans, and modestly long hair, working furiously at stuffing envelopes and making phone calls. New Yorkers also saw, with a great deal of amazement, small tables on the big street corners, brimming over with Buckley stickers, buttons, and literature—the tables all manned by youngsters.

They, in their fashion, were as particular a kind of young people, as were SDS followers. Sociologist Richard Braungart of the University of Maryland, who studied 1,246 students from ten Eastern universities, concluded that members of the right-wing Young Americans for Freedom (YAF) and the radical Students for a Democratic Society (SDS) tend not to get along as well with their parents as do the more moderate Young Republicans and Young Democrats. Whatever that labored conclusion is supposed to mean, the young people who worked at Buckley's offices—not all of whom were members of the YAF—had strong motives for working as hard as they did.

A representative expression of these motives could be heard from Steven Babcock, one of the youth coordinators on the older side. A Westerner transplanted to New York City, he ticked off Buckley virtues in the following order: He was a statesman, not a politician; he was a conservative who was "responsible"; he was "darn proud" of what America stood for; and most of all, he looked like a winner. Buckley's young supporters were incensed at "the gall" of Goodell for running as a Republican. "Why," one of them asked, "should I help a guy who's going to vote Democratic when he's re-elected."

Many of the young people had to work to support themselves in order to campaign for Buckley, and there appeared to be a direct correlation between the effort they put into their teenage jobs in answer to raw needs, between the discipline and self-control that kept them at their income-producing jobs, and the fervor of their devotion to Buckley's cause.

One example is the case of 15-year-old Michael Davies, a student at Regis High School, who helped set up Buckley tables in the Chase Manhattan Plaza, on Wall Street, and in some other financial centers. "The people who came up to the tables," he related, "expected to confront political hippies. When they saw our Buckley pins, it had a devastating psychological effect. They clapped us on the shoulders." But Davies had to work on part-time jobs to pay his transportation from Manhasset, Long Island, where he lived, to the Buckley headquarters for his two days at the tables. "I get up at 6:30 in the morning on Mondays and Thursdays to mow the neighbors' lawns. This way I can pay the $12 fare for my two round-trips weekly."

Davies and a freshman at St. John's College, Richard Delguadil, who served in the Buckley Youth, spoke rather bitterly about their need for self-support. "We couldn't pay for the transportation of the kids, or ourselves out of the campaign funds," said Delguadil. "All the money raised at the tables, maybe $100–$200 a day, went to defraying train costs from kids on Long Island. It also helped support storefronts in Queens and elsewhere. But kids were working on part-time jobs night and day so they could come in to the headquarters and paint the walls and send out letters. The Buckley kids have to work to support themselves. The young people who work for Ottinger and Goodell don't hold summer jobs. They don't earn money. Their parents pay for their vacations while they work for the candidates."

The Conservative philosophy, for all its inconsistencies, breeds on common soil. Most of the young people at Buckley headquarters lived at home with their parents because of convenience, and because it saved money. They all attended or were headed for local colleges because the tuition was low. Most of them lived on Long Island, in the Bronx, or Queens; very few of them lived in the "limousine liberal" atmosphere of Manhattan. Some proved to be more conservative than their parents—one of those reverse mirror-images to SDS radicals who rebel against their illiberal parents.

It was at college, though, that the "true grit" of the Conservative student was tested. Isolation and harassment constantly beset the fervent believer. SDS was a particular nemesis. Arnold Steinberg, a 22-year-old student just out of college, directed the news division of the Buckley campaign. He is bespectacled, small, and has an open dispassionate manner.

When I was at UCLA in 1966–1967, I worked for Ronald Reagan. I debated a lot of SDS people. I was even friendly with some of them. I debated Bettina Aptheker at Cal. Tech. in 1967. But I was always threatened. I got calls all the time. Once I debated Mike Lee, an SDS leader at San Fernando Valley State College. After it was over, he said to me, "If I had a gun, I'd shoot you." I can't be friends with a student like that. But, as in any organization, there are good leaders and bad ones.

Although the SDS and YAF represented the two extremes of the student spectrum, and though both often clashed in the colleges and at rallies, they had common linkages in philosophy. Each began from the premise that the Great Society domestically and the Vietnam War in foreign affairs were failures of liberalism. Each condemned the two main parties for their participatory roles in the debacles. Each group was highly individualistic, though its members were products of different family backgrounds. Steinberg may have at least grazed the truth when he said:

An SDS member is usually from an affluent background. A YAF'er usually has to work his way through college. If a YAF member were arrested at a Conservative rally, and a SDS member were arrested at a radical rally, their parents would also react differently. The YAF parents would be very firm on civility and respect for law. They would say, "That's wrong, I'm no longer going to support you, go to jail." The SDS parents would be more tolerant and supportive. They would automatically pay the bail and underwrite the court costs. They would try to keep the son out of jail.

It is with respect to the solutions to problems that the two organizations come to the fork in the road where they part company. The SDS advocated a basic, revolutionary alteration of society. YAF preached a sort of retrenchment, a cut-back of program, a return to laissez-faire.

It has been estimated that while Ottinger, as the Democratic candidate, made a respectable enough showing in attracting student helpers in the final days of the campaign—between

Ottinger + Goodell = Buckley

2,000–3,000 on a state-wide basis, of whom perhaps 700 were from out of state—it was the Buckley campaign in the "radical-liberal" stronghold of New York that attracted by far the largest number of dedicated youthful workers. The estimates here are in the neighborhoods of 7,000, of whom 400–500 showed up from out of state. Since it was these Buckley youth who helped carry him to victory—even though a minority victory—the result can scarcely be ascribed to an antiyouth backlash. It might be described as a case where one segment of youth lashed back at another segment—a situation, the possibilities of which very few people consider.

16
Brawling Bella
and Lord Melbourne

A belief that a candidate from a "safe" congressional district was assured of a victory in the general election was a factor in the attitude adopted by many young people toward the candidacy of Bella Abzug after she won the Democratic nomination in New York's nineteenth congressional district.* They may also have shared the sentiment voiced by Lord Melbourne when he heard that a celebrated poet had died. "Good!" said Melbourne, "Now we can have his works without having to put up with the man." Students and other young people who admired Bella Abzug's works found it hard to put up with her as a person.

Bella Abzug has some appealing qualities for youth. She is colorful, pugnacious, and committed. Shot through with a pushy, brawling, raw surge of physical energy, she was prodigious in expending it on social justice. Admittedly, she seldom showed any charity toward those whose opinions differed from her own, but that negative trait is common enough among reformers. The zeal requisite for great reforms in society is rarely

* In the writing of this chapter, I drew on the material Stephen Schlesinger made available to me after having monitored the 1970 contest in New York's nineteenth congressional district.

accompanied by a tolerance for views contrary to those for which the reformer is prepared to sacrifice himself.

In 1970, Bella Abzug surfaced as a candidate for the Democratic nomination in the nineteenth congressional district. As soon as she entered the primary, her ebullient personality, along with her abrasiveness and passion, were recorded in detail by syndicated columnists based in New York, and by reporters from around the country who quickly recognized her as a character. *The Washington Post* referred to her as "a Valkyrie, a hell raiser and a Jewish mother with clout." Gloria Steinem called her a "Shirley Chisholm who is white and who is Jewish." Pete Hamill, a columnist for *The New York Post,* said of her:

The final thing I admire about Bella is that she is a real New Yorker. New York is in her voice, which has a raw, street hoarseness; it is in the way she walks, with a bold swagger all of us picked up from Warner Bros. movies and watching guys who ran numbers in the 1940's. When she talks, she throws punches; she never whines, she never backs off.

Along with these judgments, went anecdotes like the one which Jimmy Breslin passed along to his readers:

On a night during the fall campaign, Michael Macdonald, an Abzug campaign aide, came into the Lion's Head Saloon, which was located next door to her campaign headquarters on Christopher Street. Macdonald was holding his side. He ordered a drink and talked to nobody. "What the hell is the matter with you?" someone asked him. "Oh that dirty effin woman, I'll never work for her again." "What's the matter now?" he was asked. "Do you know what she did to me?" Macdonald said. "What?" "She punched me." He clutched his side. It developed that a bit earlier, while riding in the back of the car with her, he began to argue about the schedule and as he argued she got mad. Finally, Mrs. Abzug gave him a whack in the side. Macdonald spent the remainder of the evening in the Lion's Head. The next day he received a telephone call from Mrs. Abzug. "Michael, I called to apologize. How's your kidney?"

295

Manhattan's nineteenth congressional district, an ethnic melting pot, encompasses a large portion of the West Side below 83rd Street, and runs from the luxury priced co-ops of Riverside Drive and Central Park West down to Greenwich Village, the East Village as well as the entire Lower East Side, a telling slum area that was first condemned back in 1906. By 1970, the nineteenth congressional district as a whole was in worse shape than Harlem. The median value of housing units in Harlem was three and one-half times the value of those in the nineteenth. Harlem had 28,743 housing units in which there were shared, partial or nonexistent bathrooms; in the nineteenth, there were 38,159. The unemployment rate in Harlem was 7.6 percent; in the nineteenth, it was 8.7 percent. The district also supplied 200 percent more men to the armed forces than any other Manhattan district.

The nineteenth is heavily Democratic, and for 14 years prior to 1970, was represented in the Congress by Leonard Farbstein, who also had the backing of the Liberal party. In that period, as the deterioration of the district became more pronounced, its politics shifted from moderately to militantly liberal. Farbstein's voting record reflected the change. He had once been a hawk on Vietnam and a supporter of military appropriations. By 1970, many families in the area, with the exceptionally high proportion of young men doing military duty, were making known their disillusionment over Vietnam. In response, Farbstein shifted to the side of the critics of military appropriations and Vietnam. He also emerged as a cosponsor of liberal domestic legislation. His general voting record in the Congress immediately prior to the June 25, 1970 Democratic primary received a 100 percent rating of approval from the Americans for Democratic Action.

In 1970, however, although Leonard Farbstein had turned into a model liberal, he was 68 years old. He spoke inaudibly to audiences, and was already drawing his pension from the

New York State Legislature where he had spent 23 years. The old-line Democrats were strongly in his corner, but there were many new Democrats who were not. Some 7,000 people in the district, a large majority of whom were Puerto Ricans, had been registered during the 1969 mayorality campaign of John V. Lindsay with no affinity or fealty to Farbstein or the old line Democrats. Moreover, about 60 percent of all Democrats registered in the district were women.

It was a setting which seemed made to order for Bella Abzug. The daughter of the owner of the Live and Let Live Meat Market, she had attended Columbia Law School, where the prejudices most law schools have against women students did not prevent her from breaking through the barriers to become an editor of *The Columbia Law Review*. She was admitted to the New York Bar in 1947 and spent the next twenty-two years fighting for liberal causes. Her announced intention to contest the Democratic nomination excited young people, women, reformers, liberals, and radicals. All were intrigued by the possibility that a woman with her background and concerns might reach Congress. And after that? They put themselves in her place, and like columnist Pete Hamill, fantasized the consequences.

She would not have to be polite to the senile mummies who rule that shabby body [Congress]. She would not have to be nice to Mendel Rivers. She would not have to be nice to Carl Albert. She could raise hell. If that means being dragged from the floor of the House, yelling against their dumbness, I'm sure Bella would risk it.

Enough people in her district were of the same mind, so that in a hard-fought Democratic primary, she defeated Farbstein by a margin of 2,700 votes.

Her hard-fought primary campaign, which came in the wake of the Cambodian-Kent-Jackson State uproar, was a fun-filled, exciting race for the large number of young people, women's liberationists, and peace activists who sprang to her call. Bella

297

used her coterie of energetic volunteers to blanket her district with literature and to climb the stairs of the thousands of tenements that comprise the district. Typically, it seemed that Bella was more ubiquitous than all her workers combined as she would appear at every street corner shouting her message in the accent that outsiders found harsh and strident, and her fellow west-siders recognized as their own. Most people who watched her campaign were reluctant to cite any other cause for her close victory over Farbstein than her own fight and drive.

Her opponent in the general election was Barry Farber, a frequent contributor to the *Saturday Review,* a professor of broadcast journalism at St. John's University, and the host of a radio talkshow on WOR-AM that is syndicated nationally and sent to 106 foreign countries via shortwave. Farber had grown up in North Carolina, where he had participated in the desegregation of the university stadium. He spoke with a slight southern accent—an anomaly in Manhattan's 19th District, and had shown considerable initiative in his work as a freelance journalist in covering the 1956 Hungarian uprising and the Castro revolution in Cuba. A self-absorbed man, with a long association in the advertising milieu and a flair for the mellifluous adjective, Farber received the Republican and Liberal endorsement. Since he had never participated in politics before, this double backing came as a surprise. The Republicans apparently believed that Farber had such a high recognition rating in Manhattan because of his long-time work as a radio host that he might overcome the heavy Democratic registration. The Liberals had more subtle reasons. They never regarded Abzug as a person whom they could control; or rather, Alex Rose, the head of the Liberal party, and Bella Abzug detested each other, and he chose to support her rival.

The Liberal party in New York is largely a paper organization with about 400 active members and some 109,000 registered voters. Originally created by the International Ladies

Garment Workers Union as a bargaining gambit in politics, it survived over the years because of the bargaining talents of its leader, Alex Rose. Liberal votes enabled John Lindsay to wrest City Hall from Democratic control in 1965; in 1969, after the mayor was beaten in the Republican primary, he won enough votes as the Liberal candidate to win the general election.

The party's top body, a 35-man committee that initiated the Liberal position on issues and endorsements, in 1970 was made up of aging members, and 72-year-old Rose. Many committee members failed to show up for key votes, but even if they had been present, it would not have made a difference; although he never fully tipped his hand as to what his ultimate aims were, they would have voted as Rose wished them to. With Rose laying down the doctrinal line, the liberal party frowned on even clubhouse discussions of U. S. policy in Vietnam until well into 1967, long after it had become a controversial issue in the major parties. Rose, who described himself a "terribly close friend" of President Johnson, asked that the party call for a bombing halt and immediate negotiations in September 1968. That was a month after the Democratic Convention in Chicago and five months after President Johnson announced that he would not seek re-election. It was the intervening pro-Vietnam stance of the Liberal party that apparently brought on the first frontal clash between Alex Rose and Bella Abzug.

Abzug's campaign as the Democratic nominee for the congressional seat was billed in advance as the archetype of a youth-oriented, issue-inspired race. On the face of things, it should have attracted a mass of youthful workers, especially since the entire City University of New York system was given a two-week recess just before the November election, freeing 180,000 students to participate in politics. Students at the city colleges were mostly in the liberal camp, although there were sizeable radical groups, many of which were sympathetic to Abzug's stand. Issues like peace in Vietnam, and Women's Liberation were still hot in New York City. If any problem could be predicted for the Abzug campaign, it was how to cope with a mass of student volunteers and to give them work to do where they could feel they were making a direct contribution to the outcome. But her campaign attracted a strikingly small number of students.

Every person pays some price for her native elements of strength. In Bella Abzug's case, all the strength she had in 22 years of brawling to see that justice was not only done but was visible as it was being done paid its price in her campaign. The toughness of spirit she had needed beforehand had the effect in the campaign of a pavement-breaking pneumatic drill, pressed hard against the exposed nerve of a tooth. Because of her stridency and sharp tongue, she lost much of her staff, alienated many men and women in the district, and kept many potential young volunteer workers at bay.

Douglas Ireland, a 28-year-old young man who muttered out of the side of his mouth, and appeared physically to be in his forties, was Abzug's campaign manager. He was one of two individuals who survived the entire Abzug campaign, the other being Marylyn Marcossen, 22, head of student volunteers. Most staff members could not put up with Abzug's constant demands, her savage changes in temper, and her unfailing complaints that things were not being done correctly. Ireland, however, was struck by Abzug's powerful egoism and driving presence. He placated her, dealt with her outbursts, and acted as a liaison with the ever-changing staff. "As far as students go," Ireland said, "we will win this because of Abzug alone. She doesn't need anybody else, only money. Students are not that crucial. I don't care about them."

The case was not that clearcut. After the primary, most of the wealthy New York Democrats who—from a distance— were caught up in Abzug's cause assumed she would win hands down in a traditional Democratic area and withheld the contributions she needed to meet the costs of offsetting Farber's well-financed, smooth-running, and hard-hitting campaign. He spread literature around the district charging her with "softness on Arabs" because she had once said in a Greenwich Village forum: "I would find it difficult to vote for planes for Israel." The effects began to damage Abzug in the solidly Jewish blocs in her district, especially after Farber distributed an excerpt from *The Jewish Press,* an Anglo-Jewish weekly newspaper, where an article by the right-wing columnist Victor Lasky associated Abzug with the Arabs and the Communists. A headline was imposed on the excerpt, reading: "A vote for Barry Farber is a vote for Israel."

Abzug was put on the defensive, and lacked the funds to counteract effectively. In a letter to *The Village Voice* (circulation: 140,000), she explained her views:

My basic campaign document . . . stated plainly that I favor sale of jets to Israel in her struggle for survival. . . . Granted that Israel needs and should get the jets, what next? Does anyone think that Israel's future lies with perpetual warfare?

Farber's smear campaign, plus his efficient public relations intensified the need for student support for Abzug. The students could provide free work in a campaign that was already in debt and unlikely to receive further assistance; they could counter the Farber tactics by a stepped-up canvassing campaign and leaflets refuting Farber's charges and their support, especially the support of young Jewish students, could blunt the charges about Abzug's pro-Egypt sympathies.

More money was eventually raised, but the students did not appear in great numbers. In the final two weeks of the campaign, when the 180,000 college students in New York were released from their classes, the Abzug campaign had a total of between 50 and 75 students who could be said to have done work on at least a semiregular basis. They were not all New

301

York City college students. Some came from places as far away as Northwestern University; and some were high school students. While the volunteers who did the most work for Farber were mostly middle-aged women who found companionship in his radio shows, the majority of Abzug's volunteer workers were women who had been attracted to her by her affiliations with the Women's Strike for Peace, and the women's liberation movement.

Abzug finally beat Farber, 47,128 to 38,438. Given the overwhelming Democratic registration, the margin was far slimmer than anticipated. Some of the causes for the relatively narrow victory, like the apathy born of the notion that she would win in a walk, were not of her own making. But she worked under other handicaps which were of her own making. Her domineering personality lost her votes, while the whiplash of her tongue lost her the student volunteer workers she might have otherwise had. Despite her natural appeal to liberals and radicals, her failure to draw any significant electioneering support from the colleges suggests that there may be limits to how far even an authentic radical can go in giving personal, non-ideological offense to even a radicalized or politicized student generation—like the one in New York City—and yet have their active support in elections.

17
Lowenstein:
A Loser-Winner

The outcome of a contest does not carry its full meaning on its face. It must be viewed in the context of its opportunities and constraints, the resources a candidate commands, and whether or not he exploits them and makes the most of his opportunities and overcomes some of the constraints. The question of context is particularly important in the case of Allard K. Lowenstein, the Democrat-Liberal of New York, whose name had practically become synonymous with the McCarthy campaign, and who spearheaded many of the campaigns backed by youth. In seeking re-election to a seat in the House of Representatives,* he was conspicuously supported by a sizeable army of young volunteers, yet went down to defeat. But defeat was not the disaster for him that his opponents sought.

At 41, Lowenstein in 1970 was a campus hero with a following of many thousands of students. As a former president of the National Student Association, Lowenstein was first in the line of those prominently associated with the N.S.A. who emerged in the 1960's as leaders of various reform or change-minded national movements. He had been a special assistant

* Stephen Schlesinger monitored the 1970 contest in New York's fifth congressional district. He placed at my disposal the core of the raw material he assembled bearing on that contest.

to former Senator Frank Graham, president of the University of North Carolina; and he was an architect of the Mississippi Freedom Democratic Party and the author of *Brutal Mandate,* in which he described the repression he had witnessed in Southwest Africa. But he was best known for his work as organizer of the Coalition for a Democratic Alternative, which became the Dump Johnson Movement, and then provided the initial organized impetus behind McCarthy's 1968 campaign. As a delegate to the Chicago Democratic Convention from New York, he had been a leader in the fight for the minority plank on Vietnam.

A member of the Democratic party who proved to be more of a gadfly to it, Lowenstein has been at least a step ahead of the party's established liberals in most of the great issues and controversies they faced in the 1960's. Yet his compulsion to action and the hurtling intensity with which he buzzed and jumped from one organization to the next, led critics to say that he was a self-seeker.

In 1968, Lowenstein won the Democratic nomination for Congress in the fifth congressional district in New York's Nassau County. His drive, his eloquence, his embattled air, and his sense of urgency drew to his candidacy an extraordinarily large following from all age groups, but especially from the young. On a weekly basis, there was a regular turnout of almost 400 student workers in the last month of his 1968 campaign, and more than 1,500 student workers for the windup days. In addition to these young people drawn from remote areas as well as New York, adults regularly manned many of his storefront campaign headquarters. But the help of the young was an important element in his upset victory in 1968, where he tallied 99,193 votes to the 96,407 of his Republican opponent, a margin of 2,666. With that same upset victory, he also became a prime target for a Republican-Conservative counterattack.

The counterattack began in 1969 when the New York State

Legislature, under Republican control and with Republican Governor Nelson Rockefeller in a support role, gerrymandered the fifth congressional district to solidify the Republican strength in the area. In the redistricting, five towns that had gone for Lowenstein in 1968 were sliced off, and some 25,000–30,000 voters, oriented toward conservatism, and mainly situated in a middle-class area called Massapequa were added on. In its new boundaries the district contained approximately 180,000 voters, with a combined Republican-Conservative registration of 105,000 and a Democratic registration of around 75,000. It is a suburban district, dotted with small wooden frame houses and gardens—clean and controlled. It is predominantly white, Catholic, middle-class, and small town in outlook—unlikely soil for Lowenstein to flourish.

In 1970, the Republican candidate who challenged Lowenstein's bid for re-election was 39-year-old Norman Lent. Prior to his endorsement by the Conservative party, Lent had not shown strong conservative leanings. A graduate of Cornell Law School and a veteran of two years service in the Korean War, he had subsequently been elected to the New York State Legislature as a senator. His record there was mixed, but on balance, it would be fair to have classified him among moderate Republicans of the Rockefeller stripe.

In 1966 Lent sponsored a bill preventing drug users, including those smoking pot, from obtaining marriage licenses without a doctor's certificate stating that they were cured of addiction; the bill brought Lent a harvest of publicity, but it died in committee when serious questions were raised about its constitutionality. He introduced and obtained the enactment of a bill that banned mandatory busing of school children, which was declared unconstitutional in 1970 by the New York State Supreme Court. On the other hand, in January 1970, he introduced a bill to ban in New York, by 1975, new cars with internal combustion engines. He also voted to establish the Department of Environmental Conservation. As chairman of the Joint Legislative Committee on Public Health, he supported the state medicaid program and his own prepayment health plan. He supported an abortion reform bill, which, more than anything else, certified his "liberalism."

In 1970, however, Lent's generally moderate demeanor turned out to be a velvet glove sheathing a mailed fist. From the moment he received the Conservative as well as the Republican endorsement for the congressional race, he moved hard to the right and went on the offensive in a campaign that was designed, after the fashion of Agnew's jeremiads, to rough up the atmosphere. His paramount intention, as far as he had any, was to show up Lowenstein as an enemy agent. Perhaps to his own surprise, Lent almost over-reached himself and helped turn what was considered a walkover for him into a surprisingly close contest.

Lowenstein's 1970 campaign headquarters was in Freeport, Long Island, along a side street where two-story wooden buildings enclose stores on the first floor. His office interior on the second floor of one of these stores resembled a schoolhouse, with large rooms filled with chairs, blackboards, and desks. The furnishings were ramshackle, the place lacked heating, and smelled of decay. But it was a thriving command center presided over by Paul Offner, a lanky six-footer, with a sad, furrowed face, and a quiet, soft-spoken voice who was Lowenstein's campaign manager.

Offner, who had come to know Lowenstein through the National Student Association, had been pulled by him into the civil rights movement and into the Dump Johnson drive. He had also been involved in Lowenstein's 1968 congressional bid as campaign coordinator for several towns in the district. Patience was among the virtues Offner brought to the campaign. He was one of the few individuals who could deal with Lowenstein's chaotic life—as when the candidate suddenly disappeared for a day, or changed his schedule for the tenth time en route to a meeting, or berated his staff for something he never told them, or held an impromtu party for hundreds of friends at an hour's notice. Offner picked up the pieces and tactfully put a cooling hand to the heated forehead of staff or backers who had been jarred by the latest turn in Lowenstein's humor. All this was to the good, but Offner's patience had a negative consequence as well. Because he seldom pulled in the reign on the bit—or perhaps because he knew the futility of trying to do so—Lowenstein ran away with his own campaign. As the candidate that was his right; yet because Lowenstein assumed control over even the trivial details of scheduling, speeches and strategy—instead of laying out a broad plan of what he wanted done while others filled in the details—he wasted time that could have better been spent in meeting the new voter in his gerrymandered district. The result was an occasionally inspired campaign that often ran along in a ragged, zig-zag fashion.

Young people who volunteered to work for Lowenstein were warmly welcomed—straights, hippies, military, college students, or high school students. Only those who were carefully groomed, however, were used "out on the street." Those who were not, were assigned work in the campaign offices. If the latter were upset by the assignment, they were gently told that it would be a waste of time for them to canvass; they would rile the conservative voters of the district by their long hair and dungarees. Some of the youngsters would then voluntarily spruce up. Conversely, some of Lowenstein's young workers often complained about the confused state of the campaign. "This," said a young volunteer from Bryn Mawr, "is the most depressing election I've ever worked in. There is no organization, no plan, no money, no movement. I mean, I really dig Al, but he's a terrible guy to work for." Much the same sort of reaction could be heard in any campaign headquarters, and in

Lowenstein's case, the young people seemed to enjoy complaining about him. Doing so equalized the distance between them, reduced everything to the plane of family intimacy, and gave the young volunteers a sense of being part of the inner circle of makers and shakers. Yet the campaign did in fact have a scatter-pattern appearance beyond the standard confusion of any campaign.

This was not by any means the same as saying that it was fuzzy-minded. Lowenstein, who was looked upon as the epitome of the New Politics, saw clearly the need for a stroke of political generalship in the best Old Politics tradition. The root of the matter involved Massapequa—the area that had been added onto his district in the course of Republican gerrymandering.

Aside from the fact that he was not known to the people of the area as a man who could do something for them in the Congress, he was known as someone who was not "one of their own." He was Jewish, and they were predominantly Catholic.

So, as any experienced and wise ethnic politician would do, during the summer months when student volunteers for Lowenstein were home on vacation from Notre Dame, he put them at the forefront of an imaginative "service canvass" concentrated in Massapequa with its bloc of make-or-break votes. The object of the canvass was not to solicit votes directly, but to show the new voters in the district the kinds of services that Lowenstein as a congressman wanted to provide them. It was also designed to bring their specific discontents to light so that he might try to provide answers to them. In addition to the Notre Dame students, the canvass made prominent use of many local high school students who attended either Massapequa or Berner High School. Virtually all voters in the Massapequa area were covered by the "service canvass" during the months of June, July, and August.

It became obvious in the fall, however, that there was a

marked difference between Lowenstein's 1970 campaign and the contest in 1968. In contrast to 1968, when his workers in storefronts and on the streets were an abundant mixture of adults and college students, in 1970 most of the active workers were high school students. "The average age of the volunteers," observed Offner at one point, "has dropped 15 years since 1968." Lowenstein attracted the high school crowd because in the previous two years, he made a point of speaking at all the high school graduation exercises in the district, bringing with him celebrities like Charles Evers and Bill Bradley, the basketball star.

Compared to other congressional contests elsewhere or to congressional elections generally, college students came forward in extraordinary numbers as volunteer workers on Lowenstein's behalf. But compared with 1968, there was none of the rip-tide flow of them or the urgency, or novelty of the earlier occasion. A number came to the campaign from around the country as a result of Lowenstein's complex, nationwide web of relationships. When he pulled on one strand, the young people at the end pulled their own friends in with them to participate in the campaign.

The greatest spur to the Lowenstein campaign dated from the hour when his Republican-Conservative adversary, Lent, proceeded to lash at Lowenstein as a man who "echoes the voice of Hanoi," who was "the chief apologist for the Black Panthers," the "darling of the new left," a "neoisolationist," a "supporter of the smut peddlers and dope pushers," and a "coddler of the leaders of violent confrontation."

The leading local daily newspapers could not stomach these charges. *The Long Island Press,* for example, described Lent's campaign editorially as a "shocking display of falsehood and innuendo." *Newsday* called it "cheap demagoguery," which "echoes the political paranoia of the early '50's." In a front page interview with *The Long Island Press,* Donald Rumsfield,

309

director of the Office of Economic Opportunity, a former Republican representative from Illinois, and a cabinet-level adviser to Nixon, went out of his way to repudiate Lent's line of attack. "Lowenstein," he said, "is certainly a man who is loyal to this country in all ways. . . . He has set an example for others to follow. They see they can effect change by remaining part of the system."

The claim that Lowenstein was "coddling the leaders of violent confrontation" proved to be particularly embarrassing for Lent. He was promptly and persistently asked to reconcile that charge with Lowenstein's long record of opposition to violence. Moreover, the fact that Lowenstein had no sympathy with the politics of violent confrontation was dramatically underlined when he spoke to the students at the State University at Stony Brook, and members of the local SDS set about to disrupt the meeting. The next day, newspaper headlines read: "Lowenstein Defies Pelting by Screaming State University Mob." It was not part of the conscious intention of the SDS to stir a sympathy wave for Lowenstein. The SDS had simply set about in its robot-like way to try to make it clear to the students of Stony Brook that Lowenstein was "just another fink liberal." But the effect was to win Lowenstein public support.

Lowenstein, meanwhile, met the charge of disloyalty to the country by accepting every opportunity to speak in the halls of the American Legion or in the halls of the Veterans of Foreign Wars. Nor would he concede the symbol of the American flag to the right. Wherever he went, he handed out flag pins bearing his name. Then again, as a seal of approval on his respectability, he brought together in one advertisement a list of very respectable people who had endorsed him. They ranged from Senators Edmund Muskie and Gaylord Nelson to former New York City Police Commissioners Vincent Broderick and Francis Adams—and "thousands of Republicans and independents." He also made much of the fact that Lent had not accepted his challenge to a debate, and had refused to indicate how he would vote with respect to certain key issues. Lowenstein, for his part, left nothing in doubt. In the midst of the campaign, he returned to Washington to vote against President Nixon's anticrime bill.

In parts of the district where no storefronts were available, Lowenstein offices were set up in trailers. The student-leader in charge handed the volunteer workers maps of the neighborhood and instructions on what to say to voters, and where to go at the end of the day for food and lodging. Lowenstein apparently had no fears about using many out of state students to canvass even in conservative areas. The numbers used, based on samples taken at different points in the campaign, appear in Table 3:

TABLE 3

| COLLEGE | WEEKEND OF | | | |
	OCT. 10	OCT. 17	OCT. 24	OCT. 31
Notre Dame (50 during the summer months)				40
University of Michigan				57
University of Pennsylvania			40	40
Oberlin			25	25
Yale	40–60	40–60	40–60	85
Smith	30–40	30–40	30–40	65
Cornell (P)			100	100
Brown (P)			40–50	40–50
Princeton (P)			30–40	30–40
Hofstra	20	20	20	50
Columbia	5–10	5–10	5–10	5–10
New York University	5–10	5–10	5–10	5–10
Syracuse	5–10	5–10	5–10	5–10
Stony Brook	5–10	5–10	5–10	5–10
Nassau Community	5–10	5–10	5–10	5–10
			Approximately 600 on Final Weekend	

P = Princeton Plan Students

311

The coordinator of volunteers for Lowenstein was Matt Werner, 22, a June 1970, graduate of Cornell. Despite his youth, Werner had extensive campaign experience. In 1966, he had been a storefront coordinator in Lester Wolff's successful campaign for Congress; in 1968, he had worked in the McCarthy campaign and then shifted over to the Lowenstein race; the next year he worked for John Lindsay in the New York mayoralty contest.

Werner observed that in 1968, student recruitment was merely a clerical job, since Lowenstein was then an exciting new star on the political horizon. Young people put in 16 hours straight without complaint. But by 1970, the novelty had worn off, and there was a visible decrease in the urgency of the campaign. "Some kids," said Werner, "felt that Al couldn't lose; others that he couldn't win in the gerrymandered district. Either way, what difference did it make? The students who came out to help did so from a sense of duty, not from any deep seated visceral commitment."

Werner was sharply critical of the Princeton Plan and the Movement for the New Congress. By forcing students into the last two weeks of the race, said he, the Princeton Plan worked against candidates like Lowenstein, in that it persuaded students to do nothing until those last 14 days. He observed that in 1968, Cornell, for example, sent a steady stream of students into the Lowenstein campaign for a sustained period of two months; in 1970, very few arrived until the last 14 days. As for the Movement for the New Congress, Werner maintained that:

it contributed less to any campaign and puffed itself up more than any other organization helping out in 1970. Student recruitment depended not on whether one college was more apathetic than another, but on whether one student recruiter was more energetic than the next. . . . It was a critical error for the MNC to insist that all campus recruiting be placed under its umbrella. The umbrella plan of MNC hampered recruiting. It diverted resources from campaigning, funneled them into intraorganizational squabbles, and wasted money on peripheral activities of self-promotion and media. MNC convened general meetings on a campus for political work in general, not for a specific candidate. This made more abstract and vague the notion of working in a specific race.

The 600 students who turned out for Lowenstein in the last weekend, though half the total at the same point in his 1968 race, had no small impact on the voting constituency. Lowenstein and his strategists discovered that they gained votes wherever a substantial number of students canvassed in the new parts of the district. In Massapequa, for example, his student canvassers helped him crack open many closed areas and substantially reduce Lent's vote. Lowenstein strategists also discovered that the maximum effectiveness of canvassing is attained when it is tried for the first time in a new area. The second time, like any form of advertising, diminishing returns set in. In retrospect, it was felt that with the exception of the new area of Massapequa, it would have been better for Lowenstein to have concentrated his efforts on grass roots activity—literature drops, rallies, sound trucks, and mailings—and, most especially, radio-TV.

In the Lent camp, meanwhile, headquarters often seemed bare of students. Some high school students were drawn to his campaign, as well as some students from Adelphi, Hofstra, and C. W. Post colleges. These three colleges were among the student citadels of Buckley strength, with whose candidacy Lent maintained a close personal liaison. Caroline Lanford, Lent's coordinator of volunteers, revealed after the campaign that though Lent had reached 23 towns in the district with high schools, and though he had a small group of students working for him in each school, the total of student workers never numbered more than 100 in the aggregate. She said:

It was the cool thing to work for Lowenstein. He had us beat with the kids. Many students even broke with their parents to work for him. So we considered ourselves fortunate to get the turnout we did. In the end, the students we got generally reflected the political feelings of their parents.

Since the Conservative party had endorsed Lent, the Buckley campaign for the Senate and the Lent campaign for the House drew on each other's resources in an interplay that was to prove critical to Lent's victory. There was also an exceptional out-pouring of adults who worked specifically for Lent. They participated in literature drops, phone canvassing and meetings, and carried the Massapequa area for Lent by 8,000 votes; but, the majority in Massapequa would have been far larger if the Lowenstein student workers had not themselves worked over this new area. In the end, these same 8,000 votes turned out to be the margin by which Lent beat Lowenstein on election day, the total count standing at 94,000 to 86,000.

In the postmortem, facts and figures supported a conclusion reached by James Wechsler, editor of the editorial page of *The New York Post*. It was that "the outcome of the contest was an astonishing moral victory" for Lowenstein. He had accomplished the no small feat of looking like "a reasonable crusader" in a time of "confusion and uncertainties." He ran ten percent ahead of Arthur Goldberg, the Democratic candidate for Governor, in the same district. He ran even with Buckley in many parts of the district, and he had to contend with "the most scurrilous Agnewism any candidate encountered anywhere." Lowenstein, in a word, turned out to be far stronger with the voters than the Lent people thought. They believed he would be vulnerable to attacks because of his stand on Vietnam and because of his liberal views on crime control. Lent's assaults on these two fronts no doubt took its toll, but Lowenstein managed to blunt much of the thrust by visibly moving to the center, by surrounding himself with the symbols of patriotism and respectability, and by an investment of considerable money in advertising and promotion.

What he could not overcome was the fact of Buckley's senatorial candidacy and the physical restructuring of the district. In Lowenstein's 1968 upset victory over the Republican-Conservative nominee Mason Hampton, the latter received an insignificant number of votes on the Conservative line. In 1970, however, many conservative voters in the district, attracted by Buckley's Catholicism and individualist politics, cast their ballots on the Conservative line for Buckley and continued to pull the same lever all the way across to Lent's name. He received about 28,000 votes on the Conservative line. These were really bullet votes for Buckley, with spin-off benefits for Lent. As for the effect of redistricting, Lowenstein's vote on the Democratic line exceeded Lent's on the Republican line by 5,000. But the new gerrymander brought in the conservative votes that went to Buckley, and from there to Lent. As one observer said, "The outcome demonstrated that by redrawing district lines, almost anyone can be retired temporarily from public office."

Student involvement was of slight direct importance to the Lent strategy; indirectly, however, he used Lowenstein's student support as evidence of his radicalism. In Lowenstein's case, it was different. Student involvement clearly aided him in the areas where they canvassed; but in a congressional district which seemed to incarnate Middle America—and in a contest which appeared to be a classic struggle between a strong liberal and a strong conservative and their two opposing value systems —student participation could not make up the difference between defeat and victory for Lowenstein. Students clearly did lessen the margin of his defeat which was no small achievement, considering how many obstacles the Republican-dominated New York State Legislature put in Lowenstein's path in order to redistrict him out of Congress.

18
Hoff and the Peculiar State Vermonters Are In

O N the face of things, the 1970 contest that shaped up in Vermont had a dialectical neatness in which the terms of opposition were clearly visible to the naked eye.* Senator Winston Prouty, 64—a Republican in a state where Republican dominance had been as much a fixed feature of the local scene as the Green Mountains, the white wooden houses, and the local libraries which still bear the name of Atheneums—was the incumbent. The challenger, Philip Hoff, 46, was the first Democrat elected governor of the state since the pre-Civil War era. As governor for three terms (1963–1969), Hoff had stimulated the industrial growth of the state in an effort to make Vermont more a part of a modern United States.

Prouty had a taciturn political style; Hoff, an animal magnetism ceaselessly on the move and ceaselessly affirming its presence. Prouty was a moderate hawk on the Vietnam war; Hoff a

* I am greatly indebted to Professor Richard Warner of the University of Vermont who monitored the 1970 U. S. Senatorial contest in Vermont. I am also indebted to Philip Hess of the University of Chicago who reviewed this chapter in draft form and made important contributions to it.

moderate dove. Prouty was indifferent to any standing outside the state; Hoff gave the impression of being a man who looked upon Vermont as a stepping stone. Yet what seemed at first a clearcut contest, in actuality, was far from clear. The contest resembled a monologue by Francis Colburn—a former University of Vermont art professor who became a folk humorist—entitled, "Vermonters and the peculiar state we are in."

The peculiarity that came as the greatest jolt to Hoff's corps of student workers was the discovery that Vermont is the one state in the union where the ordinary nonvoter tends to be a Republican. By the diligence of their own efforts in voter-contacts, they had brought out the Republican nonvoter against Hoff. They learned on election day that nothing fails like success.

So it was also in the case of Hoff personally. When he became governor of Vermont in 1963 in a surprise victory, the state was one of the most rural in the Union with, as the saying went, "more cows than people." Personal per capita income was low, and there was not a single urban center large enough to be classified statistically as a "metropolitan district." Hoff was primarily responsible for attracting industry, enabling his domain to become a net importer of population with per capita personal income increasing faster during his administration than in any other state. The ratio between cows and people shifted in favor of people.

If Vermont was a place where a booster mentality was dominant, then Hoff's leadership in spurring economic growth and bringing the state to the main stream of American life should have found Vermont parents naming their newborn children after him. But many adult Vermonters did not like industrialization and tended to mistrust outsiders. Moreover, a not inconsiderable number of "sun-tanners"—non-native-born Vermont residents—had found in Vermont a wintry but emotionally comforting rural haven where they could escape from urban reality. They had no desire to have their haven broken into by too much progress.

To such Vermonters in 1970, Hoff was not regarded as a political charmer. Prouty, a physically plain, shy man who hardly ever visited Vermont and who seldom declared himself for or against any issue (his political ads on TV were cast, typically, against a background of cello music) had a peculiar appeal to voters.

The 1970 Senate race in Vermont was not, at bottom, a contest between an incumbent and a challenger. It was a referendum on Hoff and his governorship—a referendum on whether Vermont wanted to continue to break out of its rural past or to remain in it as long as it could.

Isolationist-minded Vermonters are not always consistent in their outlook. It is part of the "peculiar state they are in" that isolationism in Vermont resembles the parochial regionalism of southerners. It is an isolationism in favor of all things local and against all things national; but not against the international. Concerning issues in the world arena, many Vermonters, in common with many southerners, are internationalists. They were the first citizens to approve American membership in the United Nations. They were proud that a "local boy"—Senator Warren Austin—was the first man to serve as the American representative at the United Nations; they were proud of Senator George Aiken, the ranking Republican on the Foreign Relations Committee.

As members of a "peculiar state" Vermonters are inward looking on domestic matters yet cannot be considered reactionaries. A Vermont politician can be "liberal," provided he is not identified as a "spender." It is even possible for a politician to be a "spender," provided he demonstrates that he recognizes "the value of the dollar" in his private life. They trusted Senator George Aiken's liberalism and "spending," since Aiken was a wealthy farmer. They elected and re-elected to the Senate

Ralph Flanders, one of the rare men in American public life who in the depths of the Great Depression embraced the policies of deficit spending referred to as Keynesian economics. He brought those policies to bear not only on his work as a founding member of the Committee on Economic Development, but as a senator. Yet he also was a manufacturer of tools as well as a banker.

In 1970, Prouty's records on specific social, economic, and environmental issues differed more in degree than in kind from Hoff's postures. Prouty was not known as a liberal; Hoff was. Prouty had no liberal organizations backing him in the campaign; Hoff did. Prouty was the owner of woolen mills and was used "to meeting a payroll"; Hoff was a lawyer, and in Vermont eyes, "never met a payroll" but "collected fees." So his liberalism was suspect and his "spending" seemed "profligate." In reality, when Hoff was Governor, his recommended budgets to the legislature were balanced every year, and the budget remained balanced in every fiscal year of his governorship but the last two. In fiscal 1968, there was a paper deficit; in fiscal 1969, there was a 7 million dollar deficit, the result of actions by the Republican-controlled legislature.

Historically, Vermont was the first state in the Union to outlaw slavery. And today, Vermont contains only 1,000 black people. Yet, in 1970 Joe Jamele of the *Rutland Herald* provided evidence that "the only difference between Vermont and Mississippi is the Mason-Dixon line."

Specifically, in March 1968, when the Kerner-Lindsay report updated Plato's "two cities" concept into "two societies," Hoff (one of the few nonstudents in Vermont who read the report) was concerned that Vermont make an appropriate "response." He and his advisers—principally Benjamin M. Collins, the Governor's Secretary for Civil and Military Affairs—got in touch with Mayor Lindsay and devised the Vermont-New York Project. This project brought together black and Puerto Rican youth from New York City and white Vermont youngsters, and they participated in educational, recreational, and artistic activities together during the summer of 1968 at several locations in Vermont. While state funds were not spent on the project in 1968 or 1969, after which it was discontinued, the impression became widespread in Vermont that Hoff had diverted state moneys to the project and that he was importing blacks to compete for jobs with white Vermonters.

This erroneous impression hampered Hoff's efforts to capitalize on the unemployment issue. Hoff's student canvassers were told: "If Phil Hoff is so concerned about jobs, why did he bring all those niggers up here to take ours?"

At a Republican dinner in Barre on October 3, Al Capp, the cartoonist, accused Hoff of bringing "rapists and thieves" to Vermont. Hoff student canvassers were to discover that voters cited the Vermont-New York Project more than any other issue in the campaign. Another issue, also first publicly raised at the Barre dinner, was even more controversial and damaging to Hoff. Walter "Peanuts" Kennedy, their Republican Majority Leader and now Speaker of the Vermont House, injected the issue of Hoff's "drinking problem" into the campaign by declaring that the Republicans present at the Barre dinner had seen "Phil Hoff plastered all over this state." The pun was to be the most memorable of the campaign, and the most effective as well because of Hoff's response to it.

The Vermont-New York Project was connected with the issue of "priorities" in the minds of many voters. Hoff recognized that in Vermont, as elsewhere, Vietnam had "outlived the issue of the war." For a time he tried to promote the broader issue of national priorities and the need to shift spending funds to domestic programs. Working for the Council of State Governments with Urban America and the Urban Coalition, he was an articulate and well-informed adherent of reallocating the national budget. Since the reallocation usually suggested by advocates involved massive aid for the cities and their ghettoes, the prospect of such a shift in federal spending had no great appeal in a state without large cities. And while Vermont was not heavily dependent on defense contracts, General Electric, the largest employer in the city of Burlington, locus of the Democratic base, was—and is—primarily engaged in weapons production.

This hard fact ties in with Vermont attitudes toward gun control. Generally speaking, the popularity of gun control in America varies inversely with the time elapsed since the last assassination of a prominent national leader. In a hunter's paradise like Vermont—a once independent republic where sturdy yeomen defended their land against New York, New Hampshire, and the British—gun control was suspect. When Hoff endorsed limited gun-control legislation after the King and Robert Kennedy assassinations, he was in step with the national mood, but well out in front of his Vermont constituency. He was not forgiven, even when he publicly announced—after his gun control position had been distorted by his opposition—that he had modified his stand. Even worse, some of Hoff's young volunteers resented his shift.

The bias of many Vermonters in favor of parochial concerns was evident within the Democratic party. Since the Civil War, the Democratic party in Vermont has been a cozy little clique of "boys" who do not try harder because they are comfortable being second best. Based mainly in Burlington and Winooski, they had no ambition to expand. In Chittenden County they were regularly elected to local office—mayoralities, judgeships, and seats in the state legislature. Whether a Democratic or Republican administration reigned in Washington, federal patronage in Chittenden was dispensed to and through local Democrats. It was all part of a "live and let live" arrangement with Vermont Republicans.

Hoff's achievement of three gubernatorial victories in a row

—based on an *ad hoc* coalition of dissident Democrats, independents, and liberal Republicans—was a source of concern to Chittenden's regular Democrats. They had hoped, in a Walter Mitty dream, that the first Democratic governor of modern Vermont would be one of their own, such as J. William "Billy" O'Brien of Winooski, probate judge of Chittenden County. Alarmed and resentful when they faced a contest for the probate judgeship which carried a ten year term and which they considered their own, they were convinced that Hoff was bent on purging Chittenden's Democratic party and making himself the head of a new statewide organization.

Hoff may have hoped that he could build up the Democratic organization. But the composition of the coalition that elected him also inhibited him from establishing himself as the head of the statewide party. The independents and liberal Republicans who supported him would have turned against him if he had concentrated on building Democratic support. Hoff's alternative, as indicated by his actions during his final year as governor, was directed toward identifying himself as a force in the national Democratic party, but his attempt, which involved many journeys outside the state, was featured and not always favorably in the Vermont press, especially by *The Burlington Press,* the state's largest newspaper.

Hoff endorsed Robert Kennedy in 1968, and after Kennedy's assassination he supported McCarthy; yet, at the convention in Chicago, his vote was cast for McGovern. His dovish stance was resented by the Democrats in Chittenden, who were acutely aware that the military provided jobs in Burlington and Winooski. They reacted by helping to undermine his race against Prouty. Democrats such as State Senator Fiore Bove—a restauranteur who had opposed Hoff in the primary—and John J. "Jumping Jack" O'Brien, publicly announced their opposition or nonsupport of Hoff's campaign, while Judge "Billy" O'Brien endorsed the Vermont Democratic ticket without any specific

322

mention of Hoff. John Burns, former mayor of Burlington and a typical Chittenden Democrat, attacked Hoff for his support of students, observing that "I don't get along with those barefoot, long-haired, misled college students and hippies. And Hoff has his share of that kind working for him, too."

Hoff was careful to avoid controversial young people. He disassociated himself from student radical action by describing as "stupid," a sit-in before the Federal Building in Burlington. He refused to open his doors to thousands of students who indicated their eagerness to work for him as volunteers from areas in and outside Vermont. Hoff eventually picked a group of young staff aides who painstakingly screened potential student campaigners. Those who were unfit, either in dress or in speech, were not enlisted. But some 2,000 students worked in some way and at some point in his campaign. In fact, Hoff stated that some 500 students "were the campaign" in the September primary. These students comprised both his staff and his field force. Most of these 500 were students from Vermont colleges, but a good number came from out of the state, and elaborate nettings of camouflage had been employed to conceal their out-of-state residence.

During the spring and summer months preceding the September primary, the students in the Hoff campaign were kept organizationally separate from the rest of the Hoff staff. Pat Dunne, a University of Washington law student, was named director of the Division of Youth. Officially, Dunne reported to Professor Kenneth Olson, Hoff's field director, but he had frequent access directly to the candidate. Two other law students, Vermonters William Sorrell, soon to enroll in Cornell Law School, and Joe Sensenbrenner from Pennsylvania, reported to Dunne. Sorrell was responsible for the counties of northern Vermont; Sensenbrenner for the south.

Under Sorrell, there were nine county coordinators, most of whom were Vermonters. Some 20 students, many of them out-of-staters, formed a core group under Sensenbrenner. The student organization worked closely with mostly young, professional, field men—all established local Democrats—assigned to a particular town or county. Their average age was around 28 or 30.

Students also participated at Hoff headquarters in Burlington. Three of them in particular—Richard Sachs, a Vermont graduate student in history, Philip Hess of the University of Chicago, and Chris Lyman of the Harvard Law School—performed critically important functions in connection with the news media.

Other students worked on special projects in fund-raising and voter registration. After the primary, these students were integrated into the regular campaign organization. A party regular was assigned as coordinator to each county, and most coordinators had student assistants. On paper, it looked fine. In practice, it was something else.

Hoff, in the words of Hess:

really loved young people, and to an astonishing degree, solicited their advice, listened carefully to what they had to say, and often acted on their advice. Yet in time, a mutual disenchantment set in. The harder they pressed him to take a stand on issues, the more resistance they met. Hoff became aware that he faced a revolt and had several meetings with the students in an attempt to calm them down. He never put a flag in his lapel, but his switch on gun control led some of his student workers to feel that "he was not so great" after all.

Aside from the estrangement between the candidate and his young supporters, clashes were frequent among the party coordinators in each county, their student assistants, and the student force in the field. Although students in the field were supposed to report to a student coordinator, they often kept the information to themselves because they did not like the party coordinator; conversely, the instructions of a party coordinator designed for the students in the field were often aborted by the student coordinators. Meanwhile, these "old pols" who were part of Hoff's organization, tended to be "labor skates," and many of the students viewed them with the hostility they adopted toward all hard-hats. Where the "old pols" in the rural countryside were farmers, the student reaction, if anything, was worse. Out-of-state students who worked with them came away from the experience muttering that they "would never again return to this chipmunk state."

In a campaign where divine intervention alone may have been required for Hoff to win, his case was worsened by a series of mischances. The first was his own reaction to the charge that he had a "drinking problem." Previously, few people in Vermont had been aware of the existence of the problem or of his mastery of it. But Hoff became irate after it was aired, and on impulse over a weekend, made a full disclosure of the fact that he had once had more than an ordinary taste for liquor but had since licked it. If confession is good for the soul, it proved otherwise among Vermont voters; they now learned first-hand of Hoff's former drinking habits and transformed the matter into a major campaign issue.

From that time on, Hoff went off on a tangent and tried to win the election by harping on the theme of Prouty's absentee-ism from his work in the Senate. Some of his young staff felt this was as much of a pseudoissue as Hoff's former drinking habits, but their attempts to persuade him got nowhere. In fact, they boomeranged. Prouty answered in kind by taking note of Hoff's absenteeism from the state in pursuit of his national ambitions.

The worse byproduct of Hoff's repetitive charges about Prouty's absenteeism was its effect on Senator Aiken. At the outset of the race, Aiken had taken a neutral stance, but the absenteeism charge was an attack on the Senate club, where an attack on one is frequently regarded as an attack on all. Hoff's attack moved Aiken, the Jove of Vermont politics, to declare Prouty innocent of the charges hurled against him, citing figures to show that while he may have been absent from the floor of the Senate, he was present and at work on other matters related to his duties as a senator. Hoff replied that Aiken's figures were "hogwash"—a reply that only served to cement Aiken's support of Prouty.

There was still another mischance after President Nixon's visit to the Air National Guard hangar at the Burlington airport on Saturday, October 17. A few pro-Prouty students made welcoming signs and helped many adult Young Republicans and the Prouty campaign staff prepare for the president's visit. Headlines on the occasion were made, however, by student protesters, most of whom had not participated at all in the electoral politics of 1970. In a pale precursor of the San Jose incident, the shower of rocks they allegedly hurled at the president —mentioned in later campaign speeches—was imaginary. The rocks involved amounted to a small piece of gravel which came nowhere near hitting the president. But, although there was no shower of rocks, there was a torrent of obscenity, and the citizenry of Vermont was outraged.

All this came on top of an earlier row within the Hoff camp between the Burlington members of the regular Democratic organization (who had been working for Hoff) and the leaders of his student volunteers. Many of the student leaders had worked in the 1968 McCarthy campaign and felt it was imperative to conduct a state-wide canvass where every voter would be reached. The regulars argued that such a tactic would "only stir things up." The students won the argument, and followed through on it.

Hoff canvassers—most of whom were students—succeeded in contacting every voter. Voter contact, for most of the students, was their most important learning experience. For some of them, it was a kind of sensitivity training in which they learned, for the first time, that in politics, two plus two doesn't always make four. The more voters the students contacted, the larger the voter turnout on election day, and the election day turnout by Vermont standards was extraordinary. Since the habitual nonvoters the students helped bring to the polls tended to be Republicans rather than Democrats, Hoff's student volunteers, by their exertion, increased Prouty's victory margin, in both absolute and percentage terms. The final results were Prouty, 89,000 votes, or 59 percent, and Hoff 61,000, or 40 percent.

But in retrospect, it was not a mistake to make external use of students in the Hoff campaign. The mistake was to conduct a long, expensive campaign which seemed to be based on the incorrect assumption that Hoff had an identification problem in Vermont. All Prouty had to do was to keep mum and watch Hoff defeat himself. Hoff was "too much of a good thing" for Vermont as governor, and the student campaigners—in their zeal to turn in a social science textbook performance of how to conduct a thorough canvass—may have been too much of a good thing for Hoff.

19
Rawlings and Populism in the Old Dominion

THE 1970 senatorial contest in Virginia developed into a three-way struggle between Senator Harry F. Byrd, Jr., running as an independent, George Rawlings, the regular Democratic candidate, and Ray L. Garland, the regular Republican.* The outcome is of special interest because it demonstrated how far the Nixon administration was prepared to go in pursuit of its Southern Strategy—cheerfully knifing Republican Garland in the back to support Byrd—and because Rawlings, a liberal, sought to win the election through a populist appeal to the Wallace vote at the same time that he openly welcomed student support.

The Byrd machine in Virginia, founded in the late 1920's by Harry F. Byrd, Sr., is the only present political organization whose longevity exceeds that of the Chicago Democrats. Until recent years, it alone decided who would climb up the state's

* Ken Bode, director of the Center for Political Reform in Washington, D. C., monitored the 1970 U. S. Senatorial Contest in Virginia. Aside from the indispensable assistance he rendered in the preparation of this chapter, he was of immense help to me at many other points in the writing of this book.

Rawlings and Populism in the Old Dominion

political ladder. What is more, it determined who would get ahead and who would be held back in the fields of law, education, banking, and the ministry in Virginia. Understandably, the knowledge of its power seeped down like a noxious miasma into Virginia's colleges and universities. Every student knew that unless he were prepared to assault the machine frontally and be rewarded by a beating for his valor, his course of action was predetermined. He had to be careful not to say or do anything that would damage his standing with the machine when he sought its endorsement for his career. The only alternative was to shake the dust of Virginia off his feet and start somewhere else.

The Byrd machine was dominated by the personal leadership and will of Senator Harry F. Byrd, Sr.; by regularly returning him to the Senate, it helped him accumulate enough seniority to become the chairman of the tax-writing Senate Finance Committee—with all that the office implied by way of national power. By regularly returning his handpicked choices to the House, it enabled them to accumulate enough seniority to become chairmen of committees controlling the work of the House. Within Virginia itself, the machine directly controlled the governorship, the state judiciary, the leadership and control of the state Democratic majority of the State Senate, the leadership and control of the state Democratic party, both seats in the U.S. Senate, the Virginia delegation in the U.S. House of Representatives, the major educational offices of the state, the major county boards and mayoralities, and so on. It would promote no one who stood outside the machine, and it would permit no one to progress from state politics to the stage of national politics who did not conform to the catechism of ideological orthodoxy laid down by Senator Byrd.

Its record was generally free of blemish in matters related to "dollar" honesty. It was hard to recall when a figure conspicuously associated with the Byrd organization had ever been

329

caught in the kinds of thievery that characterized northern urban machines. Honesty, however, and corruption have connotations wider than the dollars and cents boundaries set by auditors and accountants. The Byrd machine both depended on and supported a fundamental corruption of the democratic process. By its system of poll taxes, literacy tests for voting, and the gerrymandering of voting districts, it effectively disenfranchised tens of thousands of poor whites and blacks in Virginia so that a comparatively small circle of whites was counted on to ratify the decisions the Byrd machine made for them.

While presiding over a political system that disenfranchised the poor, Senator Byrd corrupted the phrase "Jeffersonian Democracy," to mean low taxes for the people who could best afford to bear the burden of taxes. All the other code words in his public declamations about state's rights, balanced budgets (regardless of economic conditions), no debts, no deficits, no borrowing (regardless of urgent needs), were simply extensions of his stand with respect to tax policy.

He was far from backward, of course, in getting porkbarrel funds from the federal government to pay for projects of special concern to his supporters in Virginia. But his version of Jeffersonian Democracy meant that the state government refused to do—either on its own or with federal help—what it could have done to deal with an increasingly chronic backwardness in schools, health facilities, housing, roads, and other public services. Some of the native-born gentry of Virginia, bearers of ancient and honored family names, now and again tried, without success, to awaken Virginians to the costs of their fealty to the Byrd machine. Others of the same class found Byrd's Jeffersonian Democracy to their liking. So did many wealthy northerners who were drawn to Virginia because of its ante-bellum structure. They established themselves in the state as "gentlemen farmers," became ardent supporters of the Byrd machine and ardently embraced his "philosophy" of government.

Rawlings and Populism in the Old Dominion

In the early 1950's, Senator Byrd's rule of the Democratic party in the state—and of its associated cog, the Republican party—came close to being shaken by a revolt from within. Younger state legislators grew restive under the political yoke they wore and wanted their voices heard in decision making. Then, the Supreme Court rendered its decision in favor of school desegregation. Senator Byrd's use of this decision served, among other things, to force the restive young legislators back into line, for Byrd was the source of the "Southern Manifesto" calling for "massive resistance" to the Supreme Court's decision—a call which released and legitimized racist passions in Virginia and other southern states. Within Virginia these passions overrode all other considerations as the Byrd machine united in opposition to the mixing of the races in public schools. In the name of massive resistance to desegregation, it initiated a series of measures that had the effect of closing many public schools and nearly wrecking the Virginia school system.

In 1958 Senator Byrd announced that he meant to retire from the Senate. But when it became clear that if he retired the Democratic state machine he had built might be destroyed by the long suppressed factional dissensions inside, he made an about face, and instead of retiring remained in the Senate for almost eight years more. The machine, though, did not run as smoothly as before. There was, for example, the successful rebellion of J. Lindsay Almond Jr., who had come up through the ranks of the Byrd organization. Elected governor in 1959, by the end of one year he broke with his patron over the issue of massive resistance to integration. Backed by enfranchised and restive white Virginians who did not want to see their children lose still more months of schooling, Governor Almond replaced the state's commitment to "massive resistance" with a "freedom of choice" plan of his own.

In 1964, Senator Byrd was re-elected to the Senate for his

sixth term, and the next year his organization elected yet another in its long string of Democratic governors—Mills F. Godwin, Jr. But before Godwin could be sworn in, Virginia's outgoing Governor Albertis S. Harrison, another product of the Byrd machine, received a letter from the Senator, that announced his resignation, for reasons of health. Harrison promptly appointed Harry Flood Byrd, Jr., to succeed his father in the Senate, where he would serve on an interim basis until 1966 when an election could be held for the remaining four years of the term. Harrison's endorsement of the younger Byrd's credentials proclaimed that he was "steeped in the political philosophy of his conservative father."

In the closing weeks of the Democratic senatorial primary of 1966, the elder Byrd died of a malignant tumor. His son was a near casualty in the Democratic primary. He defeated his rival, former State Senator Armistead L. Boothe, by the narrow margin of 8,200 votes out of the 435,000 that were cast.

One of the ingredients in the survival of the machine—namely, strong leadership—was eliminated when the senior Byrd died. There was no other single political figure to take his place. But other changes as well weakened the machine. The Supreme Court decisions of the 1950's and 1960's enfranchising the southern Negro meant that the Byrd dynasty could no longer depend for its survival on the absence of black votes. By the same token, the outlawing of the poll tax in federal elections in 1964 and in all elections two years later, meant that the machine could no longer depend for its survival on an arrangement which kept many people—white and black—from the ballot box. The outlawing of the poll tax brought into the political process thousands of new Virginia voters, and thus altered the balance of voting power. Negro voter registration alone doubled from about 125,000 to 250,000 in a four-year period, and the black vote seldom favored the organization.

The change that had overtaken Virginia's Republican party

also had a significant role. After 1948, the Democratic party's mass base began to erode as conservative Democrats started to move to the Republican side in presidential and, in some cases, congressional elections. Moreover, Virginia entered a stage of rapid industrial growth in the last half of the 1960's— a development that brought in many new residents. In contrast to the gentry-minded migrants from the North who accepted the Byrd machine, thousands of young executives brought in by industrialization were not in sympathy with the machine and its interlocked Republican cogs. Top executives, who formerly approved of the Byrd philosophy of government and looked favorably on Virginia because its "stability" induced "confidence," began to change when their ablest employees, or those they wanted to hire, turned against Virginia's social, educational, and cultural wasteland. Some of the change-minded newcomers linked up with the battle-scarred anti-Byrd Democrats, but many were associated with those Republicans who had long wanted the party to become independent of the machine.

Republican strength in Virginia emerged in the 1968 elections, which produced, for the first time in memory, more Republicans than Democrats in the Virginia delegation to the House. The following year, Linwood Holton, supported by a coalition of liberals, moderates, and conservatives, was elected the first Republican governor in Virginia since the Reconstruction era.

As often happens in American party politics, developments in the Republican party in Virginia were reflected in the Democratic party. In 1969, an energetic coalition of moderate and liberal Democrats supported State Senator Henry Howell in the Democratic gubernatorial primary. He ran against former Ambassador William Battle, a conservative Democrat with only tangential connections to the Byrd organization. The first round was inconclusive, and in the subsequent run-off, Howell lost by a hairline margin to Battle, who was defeated by Holton in the general election. Yet the strength shown by the combined moderate-liberal Democrats warranted the belief that the power of the Byrd machine was waning. A sizeable number of young people and students from Virginia's otherwise torpid colleges were conspicuously identified with Howell's candidacy, and if there were the makings of an antistudent backlash, it should have been clearly visible. But there was none.

Against this background Senator Byrd on March 17, 1970, declined to sign a Democratic loyalty oath, claiming that it would unequivocally commit him to support the 1972 presidential nominee of the Democratic party. Consequently, he said, he would not enter the Democratic senatorial primary but would seek re-election to the Senate as an independent. His supporters insisted that the Senator's decision to carve out an independent course was prompted only by the loyalty oath provision, which was part of a general package of party reforms in Virginia, but modifications made in the oath after Byrd refused to sign it could have provided him with a pretext for returning to the Democratic fold.

The Senator's adversaries insisted that Byrd had a different motive for taking an independent course. In 1970, all the signs indicated that Byrd might lose in a Democratic contest for the party's senatorial nomination. Anti-Byrd Democrats cited reports that Byrd had engaged the Oliver Quayle polling organization to conduct a preprimary sample of opinion among Virginia Democrats, and decided against running when the results showed the continued strength of the Howell forces. According to most of the Virginia press, Byrd did not feel that he was deserting the old Democratic organization because there was virtually no organization left to desert. It was more likely that when Byrd was weighing the pros and cons prior to making his decision, the decisive factor was the prospect that if he left the Democratic party—however temporarily—he would take with him whatever remained of the old Byrd organization.

Rawlings and Populism in the Old Dominion

Virginia Republicans, unlike Virginia Democrats, make their major party nominations under a convention system instead of a primary. In times past, their conventions frequently served the Byrd dynasty. As the state convention was due to meet in the early summer of 1970, the key question was whether it would follow the lead of Governor Holton and his group of anti-Byrd Republicans, and nominate a Republican to oppose Byrd and a Democrat, or follow Representative Joel T. Broyhill of the tenth congressional district, and directly endorse Byrd's candidacy or, alternatively, would indirectly promote his cause by neither nominating a candidate of its own nor endorsing Byrd.

Although Broyhill was known in northern Virginia as "Mr. Republican," his notion of adjourning without nominating a Republican for senator was in keeping with his political position as a long-time ally of the Byrd dynasty. He represented the older generation of Republican politicians, but he also spoke for others. Prior to the GOP nominating convention in Virginia, for example, the president of the undergraduate division of the University of Virginia Young Republicans sought to swing the State Young Republicans behind Broyhill. Several presidents of Young Republican Clubs on other campuses, along with the officers of the state-wide organizations, followed suit. More significantly, Broyhill's position was shared by President Nixon, by Attorney General John Mitchell, by White House political operatives, by the Republican National Committee, and by Senator John Tower of Texas, the finance chairman of the Senate Republican Campaign Committee. In their view, the objectives of the administration's Southern Strategy could best be served if the Virginia Republican party worked for Byrd's election.

Convention delegates who, if left to themselves, might have favored the Broyhill course, flared with resentment against "outside interference" when Harry Dent of the White House staff invaded the convention floor to press the case on behalf of Byrd. They were open to arguments in support of the proposition that Virginia Republicans should nominate a senatorial candidate of their own, which was publicly and effectively spelled out by Governor Holton. He pointed out that Virginia Republicans, in their own self-interest, must at long last carve out a place in Virginia independent of the Byrd organization.

When the "no action" resolution was brought before the convention, the vote of 634 to 419 against it gave Holton and the Virginia Republicans he represented a clear-cut public victory. When the convention next turned to the nomination of a senatorial candidate, the outcome was predictable. Ten days before, Ray L. Garland, a 36-year-old bachelor from Roanoke, teacher of civics and history, and member of the Virginia House of Delegates, entered the race at the urging of the anti-Byrd Republicans. Since the latter just proved that they had the votes to control the convention, Garland was nominated.

In making Garland their senatorial candidate, the reform Republicans hoped that their nominee could either generate or benefit from the upswing of a youth frontlash movement. Garland had boyish features and a youthful manner; yet he turned out to be an accomplished speaker. The *Washington Post* observed:

His words are articulate, the phrasing forceful, and it is all delivered staccato style in a solid baritone voice. The performance leaves an unmistakable impression of a stern lecture, a style Garland may have picked up during his ten years as a part-time history teacher.

Garland carried his brisk style into face-to-face meetings with small groups of people during the campaign. He remained the least well-known of the senatorial candidates, but people who had been initially inclined to dismiss him as a nonentity finally accorded him considerable respect. Garland's troubles were due not to any antiyouth backlash, but to the lack of support from the national leaders of the Republican party and from the Republican youth of Virginia.

The Democratic candidate was George Rawlings, a 48-year-old lawyer from Fredericksburg—one of the most rural and conservative sections of the state. Fredericksburg itself has been described as a place where "there are more Lee shrines than bookstores, more Stonewall Jackson memorials than Volkswagons." Yet in this unpromising habitat, Rawlings made a spectacular debut in electoral politics; he took on the Byrd machine in a 1962 contest for a seat in Virginia's House of Delegates, won, then was twice re-elected before being defeated in 1969 by a conservative, Byrd supporting Republican.

In his years as an elected official, Rawlings had become prominently identified as one of the leaders of the moderate bloc in the legislature, and a force in the liberal wing of the Democratic party. An early opponent of the policy of "massive resistance" to the Supreme Court's school desegregation decision, he also opposed the poll tax, literacy tests, and legislative apportionment schemes designed to ensure the election of Byrd-controlled whites. His position took courage in the Old Dominion, but Rawlings also laid the groundwork for "the new populism" which was to be a hallmark of his 1970 campaign.

Rawlings earned the bitter enmity of the Byrd machine in an event that made nationwide headlines in 1966, when he challenged and beat "Judge" Howard W. Smith in the fight for the Democratic nomination for the U. S. House of Representatives in Virginia's eighth congressional district. Smith had long held that seat—often without opposition—and through the seniority system, rose to become the chairman of the House Rules Committee. A Dixiecrat with a despotic nature, Smith used his post to bury progressive measures related to civil rights, labor, health, education, and welfare. But Rawlings's victory retired him from public life. In 1970, prior to Byrd's announcement that he was running as an independent, Rawlings was the only declared candidate for the Democratic senatorial nomination. Immediately after Byrd's announcement, two other Democrats entered the race. One was Clive DuVal, a noted conservationist and lawyer who was a member of the liberal bloc in the Virginia House of Delegates; the other was Milton Colvin, a political science professor at Washington and Lee College. With only 130,000 Democrats participating in the party primary, Rawlings defeated DuVal—his major rival—by a scant 700 votes. Colvin ran a poor third, but his 12,000 votes confronted Rawlings and DuVal with a run-off primary until DuVal decided to accept an offer to become Rawlings' financial chairman for the general election.

Despite his efforts, funds for Rawlings were hard to come by. The anti-Byrd Democrats, after waging two gubernatorial primary contests in 1969, were suffering from physical and financial exhaustion. Their slender reserves were further depleted in the three-man senatorial primary, so they were in no position to come forward with the money required to help Rawlings offset Byrd's well-financed campaign.

Rawlings' campaigning also jarred Virginia's moderate and conservative voters. In an attempt to "make news" in order to gain exposure, he exaggerated his style—in dress, in speaking, on issues—and damaged his appeal. After the senatorial primary, for example, *The Richmond Times-Dispatch,* commonly regarded as the state's leading newspaper, termed Rawlings "one of the most radical Democrats who ever came down the Virginia political pike." Its sister newspaper, *The Richmond News-Leader,* called him, "Screaming George Rawlings" and added, "to merely listen to him is to be exasperated."

While the press was rendering these judgments, professional observers of Virginia's voting behavior noted Rawlings' hairline margin of victory, the overall low voter turnout in the Democratic party, and—more strikingly—low voter turnout in the traditional areas of Byrd strength. They concluded that con-

Rawlings and Populism in the Old Dominion

servative voters were holding back until November, which indicated either a strong base for Byrd's independent candidacy, or a good chance for Garland—provided he had strong Republican support.

Rawlings did not accept this interpretation. He based his chances of success on waging a populist campaign. In this respect, he was like Senator Gore and a number of other Democratic candidates in 1970; but he differed from the "sidelash populists" in that young people, from the very beginning, were virtually everywhere and at the center of everything done in his campaign. If they were a source of embarrassment in some respects, the fact is that Rawlings could not have mounted any kind of effort without them.

The populist bent of Rawlings' campaign was based on an analysis made by his 33-year-old campaign manager, George Wallace Grayson—a professor of political science at Mary Washington College. Grayson argued that Rawlings could win if he held the rock-bottom, baseline minimum Democratic strength that Humphrey polled in 1968, and added to it the lower middle-class white defections from the Wallace voters of 1968. The reasoning in support of this thesis went along these lines: In a three-way race, the Democratic nominee needed only 37–39 percent of the vote to win. In 1968, with everything going against the Democrats, Humphrey received 32.5 percent of the ballots cast in Virginia. Rawlings could be expected to beat that rock-bottom base. But in order to win, Rawlings would have to get some 15–20 percent more votes, and the best potential source was the Wallace voters. Rawlings, it was calculated, needed only 30,000 of these votes—or less than ten percent of the total 1968 Wallace vote—to win a victory above the bedrock Democratic vote.

Grayson recommended a five-point program for attracting Wallace voters. First, he must stress his loyalty to the Democratic party (of Roosevelt, Truman, Kennedy). Second, he

339

should identify himself with traditional Democratic programs, such as Social Security and Medicare. Third, he should continue to hammer away at populist economic issues (unemployment, inflated medical costs, high interest rates). Fourth, he should use a hard-hitting approach in bringing these issues to the public's attention (except, of course, to middle-class and intellectual audiences). Lastly, Rawlings should employ special tools, such as ads on country music stations to reach blue-collar, low-income whites. Grayson observed that Henry Howell lost his populist-style campaign for the Democratic gubernatorial nomination in 1969 only because he "didn't have the money for media." Analyzing the Howell campaign county by county, Grayson observed: "Where the media stopped, he lost."

Grayson based the Rawlings strategy on a low aggregate voter turnout in the election.

We've targeted our voters, [he said] as the traditional Democrats, the laborers, blue-collar workers, lower-middle class whites, and the black voters. What we're going to do is pull those voters, and if the turnout is low enough and we pull our people well enough, we can win. We're going to have the best hauling and calling operation in the state of Virginia this year.

One priority of the Rawlings campaign was a voter registration drive specifically aimed at blacks. Carleton Terry, then 23 years old, a political science major at Antioch College who had some political experience, was named "minority coordinator." He was in the hottest of all the hot seats in the campaign because the black vote was critical to Rawlings. The black vote has become steadily more important in the politics of the Old Dominion even though the black proportion of the population is both diminishing and shifting. The blacks account for about 20 percent of Virginia's population, but between 1960–1967 their proportion of the state's population fell by 5.3 percent. The white population increased by 16 percent, and the black by only 8 percent. Meanwhile, blacks are leaving the rural areas of Virginia, especially in the central and southern parts (notably Wise and Tazewell counties). They also are leaving certain cities—especially Suffolk and Norfolk—and are congregating in northern Virginia around the District of Columbia. Blacks, in short, are "moving to the suburbs." But there remains a heavy concentration of blacks in the eastern, Tidewater portion of the state.

Terry had responsibility for registering the black voters and dealing with the 250,000 blacks who were already registered. Yet he encountered great difficulty in getting young blacks to help the registration drive. He explained:

Black students will participate much less than white. At the moment they're not going into electoral politics. They're not interested in it, and have no particular commitment to the Democratic party. They are less interested in making it than was true of the students who preceded them in the black colleges. They want to be relevant to the black community, and they don't see electoral politics as being an avenue to that end.

On the same ground, Terry urged Rawlings to stress Nixon's Southern Strategy more in talking to black audiences, and to present both Byrd and Garland as being sympathetic to and representative of that strategy. "I kept telling George," he said, "to play down the fact that he's a Democrat. It doesn't make any difference to the blacks that he's talking to."

Terry was particularly plagued by the shortage of funds. He made use of local grassroots organizations like the Petersburg Voter Education League and the Chesapeake Voter Education Association. The NAACP also had a voter registration drive in Virginia—but it was not coordinated with the Rawlings effort. Impartial observers who were familiar with the hard realities, recognized that Terry's budget of $10,000 for both the voter registration and vote drive was far short of what was needed. One observer explained:

341

When black workers take a day off to man the precincts and polls, they have to be paid. Also, when they use their cars, they've got to get gas money. Of course, not all of the money is for precinct workers. Some of the money gets lost in the black organizations. Everyone knows that, and nobody cares. These groups are vital to us, and you've got to keep them going. Election time is when they get things cranked up. Carleton Terry simply didn't have the funds.

Rawlings combined positive rhetoric for the "little guy" with very strong negative rhetoric about controls on the "big guys"—usually the corporations, utilities, and monopolies. Howell bumper strips and buttons with their populist emphases cropped up during the Rawlings campaign, but Rawlings' anti-Byrd campaign was characterized by a predominantly negative impetus. Wherever practical, as in his brochures, which inveighed against oil depletion allowances, high interest rates, and consumer frauds, he sought to link all of them to Senator Byrd personally, claiming that "Harry Byrd, Jr., is their best friend in Washington."

Rawlings' methods of bringing his views to the attention of Virginia voters illustrate both his personal style and his financing. Rawlings, of course, was no different from any other Democratic candidates in that he lacked the funds for extensive television campaigning. In Rawlings' specific case, he recognized he could never compete with the Byrd TV blitz that was expected. So to get exposure he could not afford to buy, he encouraged the young members of his staff—most of whom were veterans of the peace movement and knowledgeable in the arts of "guerilla theatre"—to manipulate or manage the news by having him deliver his statements in ways and at places that would attract coverage by newspapers and by the radio-TV stations.

To dramatize his theme of "Get Virginia out of the Byrd Cage," for example, Rawlings called a press conference at the Norfolk City Zoo. While guinea fowl squeaked, and ducks quacked, the candidate stood by the peacock cage and delivered his message. Flanking him, for added carnival effect, was a camper truck with campaign slogans on both sides and a loud speaker that blared music, anti-Byrd exhortations, and the nerve-shattering squawks of jungle parrots.

The "guerilla theatre" tactics succeeded in gaining for Rawlings considerable cost-free publicity, but there was a serious question whether Rawlings did not pay a price for it. Neutral observers reasoned that Rawlings was already burdened by his largely unwarranted image as a kind of Jerry Rubin let loose amidst dignified Virginians. His reputation both blinded Virginians to the reality of his moral courage and made them deaf to his arguments. He may have repelled many Virginians who, after four decades of Byrd rule, had come to believe that the mark of a great statesman was a crabbed, unsmiling hard-eyed dryness. Any backlash he suffered on this account was a personalized affair. It was an anti-Rawlings, not an antistudent backlash.

In going down to defeat the main factor was his inability to bring to the polls anything that remotely resembled the full black vote that was indispensable to his prospects. Rawlings was endorsed by the Richmond-based Crusade for Voters, the major black organization in the state, and nominally endorsed by most of the other black political groups in the state. It was conceded afterward that Rawlings won 90 percent of the black vote that did turn out, but only 40–45 percent of the registered black vote actually turned out—a disappointment disastrous to his cause.

Garland's campaign was dogged by difficulties of a different order. He and his strategists tried to take the middle ground between Byrd on the right and Rawlings on the left, declaring that the "great issue in the last third of this century is how we protect and preserve our institutions from the extremists on the left and on the right who would subvert those institutions and substitute a nostrum peculiar to their own ideology." Yet all the while that Garland was trying to pre-empt the middle, he and his advisers recognized that Byrd was clearly the man they would have to beat. Whenever Garland had occasion to mention either of his opponents by name, it was the incumbent Senator Byrd, whom he described as "a system wrecker"; as "one who has often put himself above and outside the democratic process." Garland recalled that "in the 1950's when the law didn't suit the senior Byrd, he became an architect of massive resistance to the law. It apparently mattered little to him that the public school system where our young people learn about democratic processes could have been destroyed." And, he said, when the two-party system didn't suit Byrd, he put himself "above and outside it" by fostering a multiparty system that could be "something of a catastrophe" to responsible party government.

Garland, like Rawlings, was armed with some political arithmetic which pointed the way to a possible victory. "There are about 100,000 moderate Democrats," he said, "who will have difficulty stomaching either Mr. Byrd or Mr. Rawlings. We have high and I believe realistic expectations of sizeable support from this group. In fact, I believe they will hold the key to this election." Garland's expectations were reinforced by a study of the make-up and voting habits of the Virginia electorate, indicating that it was within the range of possibility for Garland to win.* The study drew the following profile of Virginia voters:

> *Hard-core Republicans*—32 percent. A hard-core Republican was defined as anyone who voted for both GOP senatorial candidates in 1966. Presumably, the study said, all hard-core Republicans would vote for Garland.

---

* The study was initiated by Senator Hugh Scott of Pennsylvania, the Senate Republican Minority Leader whose unusually large interest in the Virginia election was all the more striking when viewed alongside the Nixon administration's official hands-off posture and unofficial support for Byrd.

Rawlings and Populism in the Old Dominion

Hard-core liberal Democrats—32 percent. A hard-core liberal Democrat was defined as anyone who voted for Humphrey in 1968. The study said that virtually all hard-core liberal Democrats may begin the campaign leaning toward Rawlings.

Liberal Democrats—6 percent. Those who voted for Byrd's Republican opponent in 1966.

Nixoncrats—11 percent. Moderate Democrats who voted for Nixon in 1968.

Wallaceites—24 percent. Described by the study as a mix of populism and racism.

The profile of voters, according to the study, pointed to "two swing groups . . . which can add to the minimum Republican total in a three-way race in 1970." These were identified as the "Nixoncrats" and liberal Democrats.

These conclusions were not self-executing. Men and money were both needed to effect them. In the case of manpower, most Republican students in Virginia's universities and colleges belonged to the Young Republican clubs, which had endorsed the Broyhill "no action" proposal prior to the state Republican nominating convention. They refused to support Garland. The majority of the young who participated in the fall campaign took one of two courses. Those who worked in the open confined themselves to the campaigns of Republican candidates known to be pro-Byrd men within the Republican party; others, who also wished to maintain their credentials as Republicans, assumed that Byrd would remain the ultimate source of power in Virginia and worked covertly for Byrd, often with the tacit approval of local party committees.

As for funds, Garland like Rawlings, ran a frugal campaign. His attempts to get help from the national party were rebuffed. The Nixon administration's preference for Byrd became progressively more obvious. After being turned down by the Republican National Committee, Garland approached Senator John Tower, finance chairman for the Republican Senatorial

Campaign Committee, which dispensed substantial funds in 1970 to administration favorites; Tower was indifferent to Garland's plight. Senator Byrd was conspicuously photographed standing at the side of President Nixon when a new welfare measure became law, and later Attorney General Mitchell appeared at a fund-raising gathering for Byrd.

In the late summer, Garland projected a barebones campaign with an estimated budget of $125,000. (About the same time, Rawlings's spending projections were about $250,000, and Byrd's were being conservatively estimated at $600,000.) The budget forced Garland to scrap his plans to hire a full-time press secretary, and opt to "serve as his own press secretary." In addition, his television work was handled by a local crew in Roanoke with advice from a professional from Philadelphia who was brought in for only two days of production and editing. The candidate also acted as his own time-buyer. Instead of zeroing in on the supposedly more effective but notoriously expensive spots, prefilmed and packaged distinctly to the candidate's advantage, Garland was forced to move to five-minute programs. One five-minute spot featured an appeal for funds, another a capsule biographical background of the candidate.

One particular episode in the course of the campaign epitomized Garland's handicaps. Republican Senators Robert Packwood, 38, of Oregon, and Marlow Cook, 44, of Kentucky, were elected for the first time in 1968, and both are relatively independent. Cook led the unsuccessful Senate fight for confirmation of President Nixon's nomination of Judge Clement F. Haynesworth to the Supreme Court, but the next year voted against confirmation of Judge G. Harold Carswell; Packwood voted against both Haynesworth and Carswell. Garland needed support from men like Packwood and Cook to offset constant rumors—and evidence—that the national party favored Byrd. They came to Virginia and generated publicity for Garland.

The consequences, however, were not pleasant. Garland was

Rawlings and Populism in the Old Dominion

forced to renounce Packwood's support when he found himself running on the Oregonian's record—or was accused of doing so by Senator Byrd. Byrd cited Packwood's voting record in the Senate, and observed that Packwood had described Garland as "his kind of man." Byrd then asked rhetorically: "What kind of man is that? The kind of man who would vote against both of President Nixon's efforts to put a southerner on the Supreme Court of the country, against antibusing legislation, against the District of Columbia Crime Bill, and against freedom of choice legislation for our schools." Garland responded by repeating what he felt he had to say in the peculiar circumstance of the 1970 campaign; he would have voted for both court nominees and for all three of the legislative propositions that Byrd said Packwood voted against. These remarks did not endear him to the liberal "swing groups" whose vote he needed to "augment the minimum Republican total" in a three way race.

The results on election day were 505,055 or 53.3 percent for Byrd, 294,212 or 31.1 percent for Rawlings, with Garland in third place with 145,292 or 15.4 percent. Like Rawlings, Garland did not suffer antistudent or antiyouth backlash. As a relative unknown contending against the best known political name in the state, and as a victim of the Nixon administration's determination to sacrifice a fellow Republican to the interests of the Southern Strategy, the obstacles to victory proved insuperable. He was hurt, of course, by the ambiguous political game played by university-based Young Republicans who saw in Byrd a better means of promoting their careers, but it is doubtful that support from them would have helped. The battle waged by Garland and Rawlings, with the help of youth, could not overcome the Byrd forces of Virginian conservatives, young and old.

20

The Fate and
Freedom of
Albert Gore

I N the spring of 1970 few incumbent Senators facing re-election were as besieged by students and other young people as Senator Albert Gore.* Gore was then in the grip of the sidelash theory and did not want to be identified with the young. He planned to wage his campaign in the traditional fashion that had kept him in office continuously for 39 years, but when he awoke to the fact that the human base underlying the old ways had decayed and that he was in desperate need of young volunteer workers, it was too late. He could not retrieve the source of support he had rejected. Conceivably, he might have overcome the odds against him with the support of the young; without it, he went down to defeat.

* Thomas Bevier of the *Memphis Commercial Appeal* not only contributed valuable material of his own to this chapter, but called my attention to a critically important study of the Gore campaign made by Professor David F. Price of Yale University. Professor Price, on his part, in a generous gesture of collegiality, allowed me to make free use of his study while it was still in manuscript form, though it has since been published in *Soundings,* spring 1971. The full text of his study will reward any reader, since it is shot through with political implications that go far beyond the 1970 Senatorial contest in Tennessee.

348

The Fate and Freedom of Albert Gore

Gore's successive victories in his contests for elective office had proved a powerful sedative, making it difficult for him to adjust to changing times and changing electioneering techniques. His Senate campaigns were conducted as a "talking around" operation with friends and neighbors, with his staff consisting chiefly of his wife, Pauline, their son and daughter, Gore's long-time administrative assistant, William Allen, and his organization—a circle of old friends and notables thought to be influential in their local communities. He did not possess anything remotely resembling a precinct apparatus for door-to-door canvassing. The very nature of the opposition he faced in his successful initial bids for the Senate Democratic nomination, and then for the Senate itself, obscured from his view the possible need for such apparatus.

In 1952, for example, the first time he won the Senate, he did not have to run very hard to win. His adversary was Senator Kenneth McKeller, a gift to America from the Memphis Democratic political machine run by E. H. "Boss" Crump. Rising by the seniority route of squatter sovereignty to a position of tyrannical power in the Senate, McKeller had gained a distinction of sorts through his high-handed outrages against public decency. In 1952, however, he was 83 years old and too feeble to campaign effectively; he was toppled by "young" Gore who then went on to win the Senate seat.

Six years later, Gore was again fortunate in the Democratic primary when his challenger turned out to be Prentice Cooper. Cooper had served three terms as a Democratic governor of Tennessee, largely because of the support he received from "Boss" Crump and his Memphis machine. But he had been out of public life for a decade—since 1948—when he had been recalled under clouded circumstances as ambassador to Peru. In 1958, he vacillated between seeking another term as governor or running against Gore. When he finally made a late entry into the Senate Democratic primary there was no Crump to tell him what to do. The Boss had died in 1954; Gore won the nomination by 122,000 votes, and Republican opposition in the fall was again an exercise in tokenism.

After 1958, Tennessee's political climate caught up with the economic and social changes that had been underway in the state. Rapid urbanization, stemming from rapid industrialization, had changed the once sleepy cities of Nashville, Knoxville, and Chattanooga, and a number of smaller towns into throbbing industrial and commercial centers surrounded by residential suburbs. Memphis passed St. Louis in population and contained one-fifth of all Tennessee voters.

With the exception of the cotton plains, Tennessee was no longer a place where the typical farmer was lost in rural isolation. He was likely to be a marginal farmer who, because he could not compete in the marketplace with the produce of the fertile Midwest, became a factory worker during the day, moonlighted a small tobacco crop on the side. Along with the marginal farmers, Tennessee had many old people, and Gore's populism—whose tap-roots went back to pre-TVA days when Tennessee was among the most ragged states in the Union— along with his consistent support for better roads, better medical facilities, better schools, increases in Social Security allowances, and "tax relief" for the "little man," still drew a favorable response from all such people. Gore's trouble was with the new class of Tennessee suburbanites.

For the most part, the mothers and fathers of the new suburbanites had been impoverished southern Democrats. Their upward bound sons and daughters—generally in the 30 to 45 age group—moved to the suburbs and became conservative Republicans. Urbanization and industrialization had converted them into a new class of property owners, businessmen, bankers, engineers, corporate managers, and operators of the satellite service functions that go with the emergence of large-scale corporate enterprises. Their children were, in the main, too young to

350

be either in college or eligible for the draft, so they had little sympathy for, or understanding of college students. They had no sense of what lay behind the campus turmoil, and why young men resisted the draft. They were repelled by any signs of deviant behavior among young people and looked suspiciously at Senator Gore because he did not join them in denouncing all the young "trouble-makers."

A more focused cause for change in the Tennessee political climate was the post-1958 increase in racial tensions. In pre-Civil War years, Tennessee's geography had made the eastern part of the state "free soil," the western part "slave soil," and the middle an uncertain mixture. In the Civil War itself, the same geographical lineup divided the Unionists—Republicans or Democrats—and the Secessionists. Afterwards, the impoverished country of eastern Tennessee around Chattanooga remained a Republican stronghold whose so called "patched pants" Republicans were moderates on race relations. Middle Tennessee around Nashville remained strongly Democratic and served to balance the Republican eastern district while it accepted a moderate approach to race relations. Although western Tennessee—around Memphis—also remained strongly Democratic, the northern Mississippi influence and insistence on racial segregation was deeply rooted.

After 1954, Tennessee experienced a sharp rise in racial tensions growing out of school desegregation decisions, the wave of black student sit-ins, and the outcropping of other local black groups who were bent on exchanging their many unredressed grievances for full civil rights. In the 1960 presidential election, local hostility to John F. Kennedy's expressions of sympathy for the civil rights movement, coupled with the hostility of Protestant fundamentalists in eastern Tennessee to his Catholicism, helped keep the state in the Republican column where it had been in the presidential elections of 1952 and 1956. But the major state offices, senatorial seats, and most of the Tennessee delegation in the House remained Democratic. The 1960 results encouraged Tennessee Republicans to enlarge their mass base and to marshal their strength for state as well as presidential elections. Accordingly, they stepped up their activity in middle and western Tennessee and won over many disaffected Democrats.

Their efforts showed up in the 1964 elections. Tennessee voters gave Lyndon Johnson a solid majority over Barry Goldwater, but Gore, who ran against Dan Kykendall—a Republican barely known even in his own hometown of Memphis—won only 53.6 percent of the vote. A further sign of gathering trouble loomed in 1966, when Tennessee's second seat in the Senate was won by Senator Everett Dirksen's son-in-law, a young Republican named Howard Baker. Then came the 1968 presidential election. Richard Nixon, as the Republican candidate, won the state with 38 percent of the popular vote. The runner-up was George Wallace with 34 percent of the vote. Humphrey ran third with only 28 percent.

Gore was fully aware of the implications of the 1968 presidential vote. To his credit, he did not play it safe in his encounters with the Nixon administration. On the contrary, he voted against the authorization for the antiballistic missile; and he helped organize the Senate bloc that defeated the confirmation of Nixon's nomination to the Supreme Court of two southerners —Clement F. Haynsworth, Jr., and G. Harold Carswell. This latter action was a real defiance, especially when invidious contrasts would be drawn in Tennessee between Gore's rejection of two conservative southerners and his early expressions of support for Justice Abe Fortas.

For their part, the political field marshals of the Nixon administration regarded Gore as politically vulnerable. What is more, the Tennessee contest in 1970 seemed an ideal setting for the Republican Southern Strategy. The Republican candidate could appeal to the martial tradition and patriotism of Tennes-

352

see by portraying Gore as a man whose criticism of the American role in Vietnam gave aid and comfort to the nation's enemies; he could denounce Gore's stand in favor of hand-gun controls as an act designed to deny Tennessee hunters their manhood. The Republican candidate also could criticize Gore as a "traitor to the South" because of his Senate votes against Haynsworth and Carswell; and he could appeal to the new possessing class in Tennessee by portraying Gore as a man who, as a high ranking member of the Senate Finance Committee, advocated "populist" tax policies and welfare measures which would use the earnings of hardworking people to support the profligate and the shiftless.

The Nixon administration's choice of a Republican candidate in the 1970 race against Gore fell on Representative William Emerson Brock II of Chattanooga. Brock, then 31, was the grandson of the founder of the Brock candy company. Active in Republican politics for years, he was president of the National Federation of Young Republicans when he was elected to the House of Representatives in 1962 from the third congressional district of southeast Tennessee—the first Republican to be elected to the House from that district since 1924. He was reputed to be an efficient organizer, and his subsequent election victories laid to rest the theory that his first triumph was a fluke and enhanced his reputation for efficiency. Most important, he was an early Nixon supporter.

When Brock became the candidate, it was decided to engage Trevleaven Associates, the same advertising agency that merchandised the Nixon candidacy in 1968, to promote him. His name soon became increasingly familiar across Tennessee in advance of the party primaries held in August 1970. Visually, Brock was a picture book conservative: his hair was combed harshly back, not a wayward strand out of place; his suits were generally dark and funereal; and his speaking voice was a near monotone. While detractors found him dour, claiming that a rose would wilt the moment it was placed in his hands, his admirers claimed that he affected an austere manner to mask his innate shyness.

Brock was a hawk on the Vietnam War, and in domestic matters, his voting record as a member of the House was distinguished only by its negativism. A phrase on his 1970 campaign billboard read: BILL BROCK BELIEVES. Yet a list of 50 major votes in the House revealed that he had voted 'no' with such automated consistency that Lloyd Armour, the associated editor of *The Nashville Tennessean,* concluded that Brock had:

voted against the farmer, the miner, the veteran, the laboring men and women in industry, the aged, the sick, the cities, the poor and for that matter, every taxpayer. [Further, Armour commented, Brock had been] against public works, against the University of Tennessee, against the Appalachian Regional Commission, against greater safety for state airways, against the Transportation Act, against the Clean Air Act, against the Elementary and Secondary Education Act extension, against an extension of the Hill-Burton Act to provide hospital aid and new clinics.

Brock was a formidable opponent, partly because the administration was backing him to the hilt to defeat Gore. The White House, speaking through Vice President Agnew, let it be known that Gore was "the number one target marked by the Republicans for defeat in 1970." But if Gore knew that he must "run scared," against his Republican adversary, he failed to muster the expertise required for a modern campaign. As a loner rather than an organization man "running scared" meant coming back to Tennessee from Washington every weekend only to do those things that Gore personally—and his family—could do. In particular, it meant personal calls by the senator to local television newscasters and newspaper editors at a time when news was generally slow and when the interviews he gave on the issues of the day could be broadcast on Sunday night or on Monday morning.

Belatedly and reluctantly, he acceded to the advice of friends and senate colleagues and engaged Charles Guggenheim of Washington as a source of professional help with television advertising. Just as belatedly and reluctantly, he yielded to the pleas of his family and hired a press aide—Tom Gilliam, a 23-year-old reporter from *The Nashville Tennessean*. But there was no systematic organization of a Gore campaign at any time prior to the August primaries.

Gore, in a sense, was trapped by his own personality. On the campaign trail, as on the Senate floor, he confided in and depended entirely on his family—especially his wife. He disliked long-range planning—let alone being managed or manipulated by someone else. His political style was part of a broader complex of things that included unquestioned integrity, moral bravery, a stubborn tenacity, and many of the marks of the self-made man. Although these qualities had an unmistakeable personal and political appeal, they needed to be projected, and the task was too formidable to have been done by him and his family. Yet he continued to campaign as he had in the past.

Although Gore had spent many years in Washington diligently attending to the general needs of his native state and the specific needs of its citizens, he had come to a point in political life where the highly personal, individualized problems of constituent services, patronage, and political fence-mending bored him. It bored him to the extent that he never effectively replaced the one staff member who maintained his personal contacts in Tennessee's 95 counties before the 1964 campaign. Between 1964 and 1970, those contacts were handled in only a hit-or-miss way. In 1970 Senator Gore kept William Allen in Washington until one month before the August primary in Tennessee, at which time the senator's old friends in the Tennessee counties had not been lined up, nor had most of the county campaign managers been appointed. During the primary contest itself, the state finance chairman for the Gore campaign was on a vacation in Europe.

Since the late 1960's, Senator Gore's stand against the Vietnam War had made him a hero to tens of thousands of young people around the country. So following the Cambodian invasion and Kent State, swarms of students from Tennessee and from other states volunteered to work in Gore's forthcoming campaign. Gore's own son observed that, at the time of Cambodia and Kent State, "The people on my father's staff were frightened to death of the students. Student offers of help made in person and those that came pouring in by mail, were politely but firmly turned down."

The students were told that they were often a liability to campaigns; if they wished to work they could do so quietly and individually in their home counties. They also were told that the campaign was not yet underway but that when, and if, their help was needed they would be called. At the end of the campaign Gore changed, but his campaign never entirely escaped the costly burden of the springtime antistudent reputation it gained in student circles.

The truth is, that no one near the heart of the Gore campaign had stopped to think about how students might be used, if at all, in relationship to existing organizations; nor to the kind of large-scale voter contact work that struck most outside analysts as being of central importance. The last thing Gore personally thought about was the kind of direct mail campaign and systematic precinct and ward work which had become a standard component of senatorial campaigns, and which Brock was to use extensively and successfully.

In late May, among the other letters received by the Gore office in Washington, one was from David F. Price, 30, an assistant professor of political science at Yale who had been reared in Erwin, Tennessee. Price volunteered to come back to Tennessee and to work on the Gore campaign for part of the summer. The Gore office in Washington was still in the tight grip of a negative attitude toward any kind of volunteers, and the reply to Price, while polite, was not overly encouraging. A month later, Senator Gore was prodded by his son and daughter to make some concessions to the overwhelming student interest in his campaign. They decided on limiting the effort to young people who were natives of Tennessee or who attended Tennessee schools. This effort called for a student coordinator—if only to control the students and to keep them from getting out of hand.

In late June, Price was invited to come from New Haven to Nashville with no precise job description of his assigned role as student coordinator and with no idea of the rudimentary state of the campaign. Price later reported:

Once I got there, it became apparent that the real problem was not in getting campus groups recruited and formed, but in organizing the whole campaign. I didn't have the slightest interest in the traditional youth organizations—which are good ways of keeping the kids out of the way. Senator Gore was in no position where he could afford to do that.

Price began cautiously to design some sort of program where students might be used in neighborhood contacts. He went after the relatively straight students and laid down the law about how they were to act and work. "Everybody," he revealed, "was afraid they would cause a negative reaction. They didn't. The prophecies of doom just didn't materialize."

It was also late June when William Allen finally left Gore's Washington office and came to Nashville in order to organize the counties for the campaign. The job entailed selecting campaign managers in each locality and setting them to work, lining up old friends, finding replacements where the old stand-bys "just couldn't go along with Albert any more."

The demands on Allen were enormous, [Price has written in *Soundings*], for he . . . bore the brunt of the campaign's tardiness in attending to everything from fund-raising to the renting of office space, and he was necessarily preoccupied with the mending of per-

357

sonal and organizational ties that too often had fallen into serious disrepair. He did not have time, as he often complained, "to think." His natural instinct was to run an "insiders" campaign; the notion of large-scale media, mail, or voter-contact work was unfamiliar and unsettling to him. Pressed for time and made doubly unsure of the new ideas by virtue of the fact that it was mainly untested newcomers who were advocating them, Allen and others close to the senator adopted a cautious posture, acknowledging that "some new things" indeed would have to be done but attempting to run a tight ship in the meantime.

The "newcomers" included James F. Schaeffer, a Memphis attorney who, to everyone's surprise (and sometimes consternation), was beginning to demonstrate that he did not regard his position as campaign manager as a figurehead postion; Dale Ledbetter, a Memphis native, Washington lawyer, and Schaeffer protege; and two workers trained under the New Democratic Coalition auspices whom on faith I invited to join us. We reinforced one another in our conviction that interest-group mailings and large scale voter-contact work in the high-Democratic areas should include—canvassing-registration drives, and election-day follow-up. These were of crucial importance and large numbers of volunteers, far from being a burden, were actually essential to the enterprise. With Schaeffer's encouragement, and sometimes using him for protective cover, we were able to work up standardized kits for canvassing on foot or by telephone, to develop handouts directed at lower-income voters, to put volunteer coordinators to work on pilot projects in various cities, and to lay the groundwork for a fall mailing to every educator in the state.

The extensive help Gore needed was underscored by the results of the Democratic primary, where his challenger, Hudley Crockett, Democratic Governor Bufford Ellington's press secretary, was underfinanced and relatively unknown. Gore had previously been quoted as saying that if he didn't win the primary by more than 10,000 votes he would be a "dead duck" in the general election. "That was a typographical error," Schaeffer said later. "The figure he used was 100,000. The newspapers dropped a zero." Gore won the primary by only 31,000 out of 508,500 votes, and many observers felt if the campaign had gone on for another two weeks, Crockett would have defeated Gore. An analysis of the primary results revealed that only 56 percent of the people who had voted in 1968 voted in either the Democratic or Republican primary in 1970, and those not voting tended to be Democrats and / or Gore supporters.

After the Democratic primary, Senator Gore and his intimate advisers were forced to come to terms with the fact that they could no longer depend solely on old friends in the counties. His only chance for victory depended on holding together the combination of voters who had supported him in the past, which meant that the "new people" in his headquarters had to avoid doing or saying anything that might alienate Gore's old basis of support.

Because of the help Gore eventually received from many young people as the campaign wore on, his campaign staff came to regret the haste with which students had first been turned away, and their persistence in staying away because they felt unwelcome. Time and again, for example, the new people would clear the hurdles of planning and organization only to find that their design for an urban canvass had to be drastically scaled down simply because there were not enough volunteers available to carry it out. A few student volunteers might suffice to pass out handbills at a football game, but foot-slogging through the neighborhoods and housing projects, following specific instructions, and keeping meticulous records, called for battalions of volunteers.

Despite his initial brush-off, Gore came to respect the young volunteers who worked for him. His wife, on the other hand, continued to hanker for how things used to be done. As a veteran of many election battles and as Gore's closest confidante, she regarded his young workers as trespassers. In turn, the young volunteers thought her overbearing, and flashed a warning sign to each other when she was nearby: PAULINE IS WATCHING YOU.

Even so, Gore ultimately and openly acknowledged that students were important to him; Brock continued to appeal to antistudent sentiment as part of his overall southern strategy. Brock also promoted a "don't kick the South" sort of regionalism; he avoided overt racism but ignored the black electorate; he praised President Nixon and damned the "ultraliberals" who were responsible for a litany of evils. He declared:

Our colleges are infested with drug peddlers. Our courts are disrupted. Buildings are bombed and schools threatened. Our law officers are threatened, beaten and murdered. Pornography pollutes our mailboxes. Criminal syndicates infiltrate legitimate business. Rapists, robbers, and burglars make our streets and homes unsafe.

This litany did not stand alone. Brock insisted that all of them were directly spawned and encouraged by Gore's "ultraliberalism," by his stand against the Vietnamese War, by his opposition to the Supreme Court nominations of Haynsworth and Carswell, and by his alleged support for gun controls.

Brock proved the right candidate for a highly organized campaign, which was carried out by Kenneth Dietz, a partner in Trevleaven's agency. Everything for him had to be in its place, and the place for youth was far to the right and at the bottom of an organizational chart where a box read: "Young Volunteers for Brock—John Stamps." Stamps, 29, a printing company salesman from Nashville, served as state Chairman of Young Voters for Brock (YVB). At one point during the campaign when Dietz discussed the role of youth in the Brock organization, he claimed to have YVB organizations in 90 of the 95 counties and on all 37 college campuses in Tennessee. "The young people," he said, "set up their own programs and supervise them." In practice this meant that any time Brock went into a county there would be a contingent of Brockettes— young girls in red, white and blue outfits with short skirts— waiting for him. It also meant that young people provided a "blitz force" by passing out literature in the precincts. "Most of

360

our students," Dietz observed, "are from white and middle- or upper middle-class families. We've created a contrast to those working for Gore. But we've told our people not to shy away from long hair, though we don't have any way-out types."

Despite systematic organization, the number of young people who worked for Brock is as difficult to estimate as the number in Gore's camp. Dietz claimed that 3,500 to 4,000 worked for Brock, although he conceded that only a small part of the total was continuously active. After the election, Brock, in a rare lapse into a nonconservative hyperbole, claimed that around 30,000 young people between the ages of 18 and 28 worked for him. Whatever the correct figure, it is doubtful that the Brock-ettes had anything more than a marginal bearing on the results of election day.

But the young people in the Gore campaign got a badly needed shot in the arm when Vice President Agnew visited Memphis in late September on a political mission for the Brock candidacy. Although Gore had not been invited to the welcoming party at the Memphis airport, he showed up just the same, and smilingly voiced three words of greeting: "Welcome to Tennessee." Gore's beau geste toward a man primed to attack him was a piece of theatrics; because it was out of the ordinary, it set off ripples of excitement, delighting Gore's volunteers and boosting their morale. They were further spurred to work harder for him by Agnew's extravagant praise of Brock and demagogic attack on Gore:

There have been complaints, that Bill Brock has invited his friends into Tennessee to address the people here. Well, let me say that Bill Brock is not ashamed of the president and the vice president of the United States. They are his friends and he has welcomed them to his home state of Tennessee.

But when the incumbent senator [Gore] comes home, you do not see him bringing down to Memphis his radical-liberal friends he hobnobs with up in Manhattan and Georgetown, because these friends would not sit very well with the people of Tennessee.

The vice president also linked Gore with Senator George S. McGovern, whose party reform activities had raised the hackles of southern Democrats. Agnew described McGovern as "one of the acknowledged leaders of this left-wing Senate cabal . . . going about the country raising money for a select group of radical-liberal friends," while Gore was "the leading beneficiary" of that money-raising effort, having received $60,000 from the McGovern group for his Tennessee campaign. Agnew then pulled out all the stops on the Southern Strategy. He associated Gore with the Senate's refusal to confirm the Supreme Court nominations of Clement F. Haynsworth and G. Harold Carswell, appealing simultaneously to concealed racism and overt regionalism:

That crowd in the Senate which talks so much about ending discrimination committed an act of discrimination against the South: they went over to the Supreme Court and nailed a shingle to the door, no Southerners need apply.

The vice president's visit to Memphis earned an estimated $125,000, after expenses, for the campaigns of Tennessee Republicans, but it also helped Gore.

President Nixon also spoke for Brock in Tennessee, but it is doubtful that his visit made much difference. He had nothing to say against Gore that Brock had not already been saying for months, and the influx of support from Washington did not go down well with many voters, especially since Brock had accused Gore of relying on outside support.

Gore, hewing to a populist line, had relatively little to say about Vietnam. But while Brock construed the Wallace vote to be mainly an anti-Humphrey vote and tried to make it appear that Gore was another Humphrey, Gore appealed to the Wallace vote with an economic pitch. On the campaign trail he regularly listed 50 economic issues which he had voted for, and which Brock had voted against. He also cited unemployment figures, calling attention to plants in Tennessee that were closing or laying off workers because of a "Nixon-inspired recession." Although the audience being appealed to—the old farmer-labor-populist coalition—had been shrinking in size over the preceding two decades and was divided within, it was still sizeable and not at all moribund. The life left in his old sources of support was aroused by reminders of past benefits, and enabled him to make astonishing gains in the last weeks of the campaign.

The economic attack shook Brock, who came under fire from some of his fellow Republicans for dwelling so long on his own hawkishness. Rattled by doubts, he began to run scared in so desperate a way as to accuse Gore of being against prayers in the schools. Both men had agreed not too many hours before that they were for voluntary prayers in the schools, and Gore, a southern Baptist, had supported in principle a constitutional amendment to allow for voluntary prayers proposed by Tennessee's Republican Senator Howard Baker. Brock was evidently afraid that Gore was gaining on him.

Brock had the accidental good fortune of having as his gubernatorial running mate—Dr. Winfield Dunn, a Memphis dentist and son of a former Mississippi congressman. Dunn, a 1960 convert from the Democratic to the Republican party, had spent the years immediately following in building the Republican party in Memphis. He was not well known outside that city, but when he suddenly emerged as the surprise victor in a three-cornered race for the Republican gubernatorial nomination, his pairing with Brock amounted to a coalition of the western and eastern wings of Tennessee Republicans. In eastern Tennessee Brock could count on being the residuary legatee of votes cast primarily for Dunn in western Tennessee.

In Gore's case, the Democratic gubernatorial candidate, John Jay Hooker, could not bring him additional sources of political strength. Although Hooker boasted a close identity with the late Robert Kennedy, he also received unfavorable publicity when the *Wall Street Journal* focused on several of his firms that were in deep financial trouble. One of his firms, Whale Inc., filed for bankruptcy protection almost coincidentally with the start of the 1970 fall campaign, and in a second, originally known as Minnie Pearl's Chicken Systems Inc., there were accusations that insiders made killings by selling its stock at peak price while public investors lost heavily when the price took a nose dive.

At the outset, it was assumed that Brock would run well in the traditional Republican stronghold of eastern Tennessee and that Gore would make a strong showing on his home grounds in middle Tennessee. If so, the election would be decided in western Tennessee—or more particularly in the city of Memphis, where one-fifth of the state's vote was concentrated. Yet it was precisely in Memphis that Gore's political troubles were most acute, because the city was the center of racially-oriented Wallace voters. In Memphis and elsewhere, Gore concentrated on pocket-book issues in the hope of winning back Democrats who had voted for Wallace.

The work done by a small group of youthful volunteers helped to prevent a total shambles in Memphis. Led by Knox Walkup, a Harvard Law student and the son of a Memphis Presbyterian minister, the volunteers conducted an experimental summertime canvass in selected Memphis precincts, which resulted in a collection of data that was used by volunteer precinct workers organized to function on a broader basis in the fall election. On election night, the crowd gathered in principal Gore headquarters around the state was comprised mainly of youthful workers—the very people Gore had once feared and rejected. Those in Gore's Memphis headquarters shared the conventional wisdom that Gore would come into Shelby County —meaning Memphis—nearly even with Brock. If so, their own earlier efforts in the face of massive obstacles in Memphis would go far toward determining the final result.

The Fate and Freedom of Albert Gore

A little after nine o'clock that evening, it was obvious that Gore had lost. The final vote was 562,645 for Brock and 518,858 for Gore. There were no recriminations against Gore and he was not tarnished by defeat. If anything, his light shone even brighter in the eyes of his young workers. He augmented their respect for his character, for his public record, and for what he was able to achieve in a contest where he faced overwhelming odds—some, of course, of his own making.

As a study of the election returns later showed, the young people in Gore's Memphis headquarters on election night were right in expecting that he would come to Shelby County nearly even with Brock—Brock's majority in eastern Tennessee was almost offset by Gore's majority in middle Tennessee. Gore lost the election in conservative western Tennessee or, more precisely, in Memphis. While he won back much of the Wallace vote in the area, he did not win enough of it.

As in other electoral contests, it is impossible to gauge the precise effects that youth had on the fortunes of the senatorial rivals in Tennessee, but rough approximations can be made. In the case of the Brock candidacy, for example, the efforts of the Young Voters for Brock probably made no difference one way or another. Gore's state campaign manager estimated that youthful workers meant 25,000 more votes for him, or roughly four percent of the total.

This estimate of four percent corresponded with the conclusions in a study made by Michael Lupfer, an associate professor of psychology at Memphis State University, of the 1970 senatorial voting patterns in the make-or-break Shelby County. In an attempt to gauge the impact of youth on the Gore campaign in that county, Lupfer used the factors of past voting records, racial composition, median property values and union membership to identify two sets of precincts with similar profiles and variables (though young people worked in only one of the two sets). By comparing the election day returns of the two, Lupfer concluded that there was a four percent increase in the vote for Gore in the precincts worked by young people. So if an army of Gore workers had been available to work at least all the key urban precincts in Tennessee, instead of only a fraction of them, the results might have been different.

Of course, an army of youthful workers for Gore might have provoked an antistudent backlash. Still, it seems clear that without his student workers, Gore would have suffered a larger defeat. The young volunteers for Gore enlisted in his campaign because of his stand on the Vietnam War, his liberalism on the race issue, and his opposition to Haynsworth and Carswell. To many county managers, ideological affinities played a role of secondary importance to personal and political ties. But the young workers—as well as educators, men, and women—were notable for their preoccupation with the issues at stake. This preoccupation did not make them strident or doctrinaire in their approach to the less committed, but they had an air of grim determination that enabled them to withstand the absence of personal recognition and to put up with many annoyances without complaints. Price is worth quoting again:

It was often said during the course of the campaign, both in praise and in blame but usually in exaggerated terms, that Senator Gore's "principled" stand had brought him political difficulty on the one hand and national recognition and "Eastern money" on the other. What was less frequently recognized, even by the senator himself, was the extent which his most faithful workers were considerably farther leftward on the spectrum than he and had been drawn into the campaign precisely because they admired the courage and tenacity of these stands—and his continuing refusal to play up to "law and order" and antistudent sentiments.

PART III
Conclusions

21
Apathy: Shadow
and Substance

I

Apathy, as bleak as a tombstone summary of a life, became the term favored above all others by political analysts to describe the 1970 campaign role of students and other young people. Was this term accurate? Did apathy stand as one with the objective realities of the matter? The answer is an ambiguous yes and no.*

It is yes when judgment is based on the superficial observation that student electoral participation fell far short of the springtime predictions that students were poised to recruit a vast army of campaign workers in the fall. The answer is no when it is recognized that the springtime predictions were pitched to such unreasonably high expectations that the failure of students to realize them resulted in an exaggerated impression of apathy on the part of the young. The answer is also no if the 1970 level of student electoral participation is compared either with the performance of students in previous congressional campaigns or with the extent to which the electorate

---

* Professor Arthur Naftalin of the University of Minnesota—the former Mayor of Minneapolis—was the source of many shafts of light that were followed in the writing of this chapter.

as a whole participates in electoral politics beyond the act of voting.

It is as difficult to measure apathy or torpor in political campaigning as it is to measure commitment or enthusiasm. But some statistical findings are available, in the form of opinion surveys, that were taken after the 1970 elections. They focused exclusively on students rather than youth as a whole. The ease with which a student sample can be identified partially explains that focus. In addition, because students were leaders in the formation of organizations pledged to elect a new Congress, and because they possess both energy and flexible schedules which enables them to participate more readily in electoral politics than any other group, the form and force of their apathy or enthusiasm invites a close-up view.

Some sense of the extent of student apathy—or conversely, the extent of student electoral participation—can be gained by distinguishing between appearance, and the substance of reality in the student electoral picture. To this end, it is best to advert to a review of two related phenomena: the nature of the 1970 springtime perceptions which contributed to the inflated predictions about student electoral participation in the congressional campaign; and the structural reasons—apart from any factors of apathy—why those predictions could not possibly be fulfilled.

II

As previously noted, the overblown predictions made in the spring of 1970 about an imminent mass uprising of student campaign workers, were rooted in a number of illusions. Perhaps the most glaring were the distorted impressions gained from the student springtime strike. To be sure, the strike in the wake of the Cambodian invasion and the killings of students at Kent State and Jackson State was the most concentrated single protest demonstration of students in American history. It was not, despite the well publicized views of some observers at the time, a universal strike. Although the number of institutions comprising the structure of higher learning in the United States depends on how a college or university is defined, the 400 colleges and universities which were shut down by the strike represented, at best, only 25 percent of the total. The remaining 75 percent adhered to their regular academic routine.

It was also widely assumed that the student strike in the spring of 1970 reflected the passionate depth of student opposition to the Cambodian invasion and to the Vietnam War generally. The proliferation of antiwar groups on almost every campus, coupled with the spring Harris poll projection of two million students who intended to work for peace candidates in the fall, linked students and antiwar sentiment in the public mind. But even though the Harris poll and other opinion surveys revealed that a majority of students had come to oppose the Vietnam War, the precise relationship between opposition to the war and student opinion could not be determined. The polls, for example, did not reveal whether student opposition to the war had intensified, nor did they indicate whether there was a uniformity of student opinion about the war and how the American involvement in the war might be ended. There also is some question whether student opposition to the Cambodian invasion, in particular, and to the Vietnam War in general, caused the contagion of strikes that infected campuses in 1970.

The survey material prepared for this study by Professors Jack Dennis and Austin Ranney of the University of Wisconsin deals with these aspects of student sentiment. Since their work will frequently be cited in the concluding chapters, it should be explained that the Dennis-Ranney survey consisted of a questionnaire sent to a probability sample of students in 70 colleges located in 20 states where the Movement for a New Congress (MNC) was active. Some of these colleges had adopted the Princeton Plan for "released time" so that students could take part in the 1970 election. Others were non-Princeton Plan colleges which carried on academic business as usual, although sometimes with informal encouragement of student campaign activity. The questionnaire was mailed to the sample immediately after the November election, and the findings to be used here are based on completed questionnaires that were returned by 750 Princeton Plan and 1,650 non-Princeton Plan students representing 50 colleges in all.

The Dennis-Ranney survey was originally structured to get at the differences—if any—between Princeton Plan and non-Princeton Plan student responses to the questionnaire. Their data have been reworked for this study. Unless otherwise indicated, however, the responses that follow are expressed as aggregates. That is, they are the results reached when the replies received from the Princeton Plan and non-Princeton Plan students are combined and averaged, making for an overall impression of student activity and attitudes. The results reached in this way are not accurately representative of national student body opinion because they are weighted by an over representation of Princeton Plan respondents, who are known to comprise a "liberally" biased sample of the student population. Yet precisely because of this "liberal" bias, the picture which emerges when Princeton Plan and non-Princeton Plan student responses are combined and averaged, is all the more interesting because of the "conservative" political accent that crops up here and there.

From a demographic standpoint, the two groups of students were reasonably well matched by sex and race; approximately 60 percent of all the respondents were male and 92 percent were white, although they differed in other points of detail. The Princeton Plan students generally had higher grade averages.

Apathy: Shadow and Substance

Sixty percent of the Princeton Plan students covered by the survey had fathers who had attended or graduated college while less than 50 percent of non-Princeton Plan parents had better than a high school education. Slightly more of the Princeton Plan than of the non-Princeton Plan students were in the social sciences, humanities and physical sciences; slightly more of the non-Princeton Plan students were in agriculture and medicine.

In addition, the Princeton Plan colleges were mainly well endowed private schools. In contrast to the diversified non-Princeton Plan group, Princeton Plan students were more highly selected, had been more active politically in such event politics as antiwar demonstrations, and generally came from wealthier families. Fewer among them had to work at summertime or schoolterm jobs in order to help pay for their education. Accordingly, they were better placed to devote their time to campaigning, or could more readily dip into their own pockets to meet the transportation and living expenses incurred in connection with off-campus electioneering efforts.

The Dennis-Ranney survey reveals that student reaction to the Vietnam War in 1970 was not all of one piece. On the contrary, it is clear that students did not comprise an immense body of Siamese twins tied at the head to the same outlook. Rather, they had swirling and particularized reactions.

For example, although 55 percent of the respondents said yes and 45 percent said no when they were asked if they took part in the student peace movement of 1969–1970, it did not follow that those who answered affirmatively were involved in great commotions. Over 20 percent of those students who admitted to participation in the activities of the peace movement took no part in mass demonstrations, strikes, or boycotts; instead, they were involved in "rap" sessions with other students and faculty members. While some 12 percent of the respondents indicated that they spent 65 days or more on peace activities, the single block of time which stood out among the replies was a one-to-five day participation, perhaps reflecting a one-shot participation in protest, demonstration, or strike. The respondents, moreover, displayed no euphoria when they were asked to rate the effectiveness of the student peace movement in the three years between 1967–1970. According to the survey, only 5.5 percent thought the movement was "very effective;" roughly the same number thought it was "counterproductive;" a little more than 30 percent thought it was "not very effective;" while 50 percent felt it was "moderately effective."

When respondents were asked to identify the national problems that concerned them most, 49.1 percent—just under half of the total—named the "war, Vietnam, defense, draft." The remaining 50.9 percent spread their choices over a range that covered everything from ecology to drugs, unemployment to civil rights, and aid to education to excessive government spending. Moreover, when respondents were asked what should be done about the war in Vietnam, at one extreme 29.6 percent —almost one third—favored the "immediate removal of all our armed forces from Vietnam," and less than one-twentieth —only 3.8 percent—favored "using all military force necessary to win the war as soon as possible." In between these positions, two formulas for "gradualism"—"the removal of all our armed forces from Vietnam by the end of 1971," or "the removal of our armed forces gradually as the South Vietnamese are able to replace them"—were favored respectively by 32.1 percent and 25 percent. Thus the "dove" responses—i.e. those calling for immediate withdrawal or a "fixed date" withdrawal—added up to 61.7 percent, while the hard-core "hawk" element amounted to 31.8 percent of the respondents residing on campuses six months after the Cambodian intervention and the rash of student strikes.

The figures just cited do not by themselves dispute that anti-war sentiment was the main cause of the student strike in the spring of 1970. But they hint that the event was triggered by something more than the Cambodian invasion specifically and the Vietnam War generally; and that hint has been underlined by a Chicago-based survey team tangentially connected with the National Opinion Research Center at the University of Chicago. Its findings indicate that the springtime strike was provoked mainly by student reactions to the killings at Kent State and Jackson State, not by the Cambodian invasion.

But the widely held assumption that Cambodia precipitated the student strike was coupled with two further views shared by many springtime observers. They tended to assume that Vietnam would be the issue in the fall election, and that nothing would intervene between the spring and the fall either to defuse Vietnam as a cause for explosive controversy, or to displace it with other issues of pressing concern to students.

In their view, it therefore followed that there would be a close accord between the number of student strikers and the number who would participate in the congressional campaign.

By the fall of 1970, however, events moved in directions opposite to the springtime exercise in divining the future. American troops had been largely withdrawn from Cambodia; American combat forces in Vietnam proper continued to be reduced in number; and "hawk" and "dove" candidates alike were uncertain about the actual state of American opinion toward the Vietnamese conflict, with the result that many of them found silence to be the better part of political valor.

By native instinct, or on the cautionary counsel of the polling organizations they employed, candidates chose not to make Vietnam an issue on which to stand or fall at the polls. Instead, economic and social issues emerged as the significant issues of public controversy which led some students—who joined the springtime strike because of their opposition to the Cambodian invasion—to drop out of the electoral campaign feeling stripped of their cause or candidates to whom they could attach themselves. In their disenchantment, they refused to participate in the 1970 campaigns, and took the position that if the war were not given priority, then no other issues merited their commitment.

Admittedly, students who took this view and opted out of electoral participation were in a minority. They had struck in protest against the killings at Kent State and Jackson State. The months that intervened between the spring and the fall had much the same sort of dulling effect on their psyche that the passage of time tends to have on a family that once felt sharply the death of a close relation. Students tended to forget the sharp poignancy of what they felt when the killings occurred. As their memories grew dim, many students who took to the streets in the spring of 1970 appeared to lack a motive to stay in the streets for fall electioneering.

Over and above all other considerations, the inflated predictions in the spring of 1970 about the extent of student electoral participation in the fall, drew much of their quality from a number of inflated—and equally false—perceptions. The first was that student organizations that had been effective in mobilizing support for antiwar protests were tantamount to a national network that could readily be adapted to the purposes of a congressional campaign. It was true that many young people across the nation had come to know each other through the antiwar movement, but this development did not mean that an institutionalized network was at hand. The network, such as it was, was not institutionalized. On the contrary, it was an informal and inchoate set of groupings, subject to recurrent internal schism.

In connection with the false analogies drawn to the McCarthy campaign, a point previously made bears repetition. McCarthy's loose-jointed and almost anarchic campaign structure was a reflection of his own distinctive outlook, personality, and estimate of the tactical means at his disposal to gain the

376

ends he had in view. It was uniquely suited to the temper of the young people who rallied to his cause and the times in which they exerted their effort. In 1968, his young supporters could, and did, subject themselves for a while to a considerable measure of self-discipline—certainly at the staff level. Yet, if McCarthy had been a strong-willed, administrative type of candidate who adhered to a detailed battle plan worked out by a self-assured, professional staff, young people might well have been constricted in their scope for action.

Since none of these things were true, many young people in 1970—especially those who had only heard about the legends of the McCarthy campaign and had not lived through its realities—wrongly concluded that a loose organization was symptomatic of a "new politics" and that the way to get things done was with a mass of young volunteers. They were not aware that the major contribution young people made to the McCarthy candidacy, particularly in New Hampshire and often despite the candidate himself, involved the thorough organization and systematic application of all the techniques of the "old politics" over a protracted period of time.

III

Enough has been said about the false perceptions in the spring of 1970 which contributed to the distorted predictions about student electoral participation in the fall congressional campaign. More remains to be said about the structural reasons why the predictions could not be fulfilled.

Take first the mechanics of the Movement for a New Congress (MNC). The leaders of the MNC—based at Princeton—were not so naive as to believe that good intentions alone would attain the objectives they had in mind. They knew that good intentions, divorced from an effective mobilization and organization of student manpower, amounted to mere wishful thinking. Yet their own organization was of necessity contrived in haste, and the bugs in the communication lines running from the headquarters in Princeton to regional centers around the country interfered with swift and coherent communication, which was the critical factor in their plan to mobilize large numbers of students for electioneering purposes. This weakness was not the fault of the national leaders in Princeton headquarters. Even in long established government agencies, or in national corporations manned by experienced people with command of ample funds and the latest in communication technology, failures are frequent in the flow of information from headquarters to agents in the field, or, for that matter, from one office cubicle to the next. Breakdowns were inevitable in an organization like MNC which was born overnight, lived from hand-to-mouth (yet stayed in the black), and was staffed by student volunteers who worked for "glory," for "recognition," for "the fun of it," for "experience," for strongly held political convictions—who worked, that is, for everything except money. Breakdowns did occur, and adversely affected the battle plan MNC hoped to pursue.

The first phase in the order of battle was to recruit student workers for the primaries, followed by an intensive canvassing of voters in the fall. The second phase was to conduct a crash program of last-minute canvass effort for candidates who appeared to be on the brink of success as election day drew near. The third phase was to provide a "Kelly-girl" type of electioneering service where students could be concentrated in pinpointed areas in need of supplementary canvassing or other emergency assistance.

The first two phases were soon derailed: the overburdened MNC headquarters failed to get complete profiles on the candidates and races falling within their jurisdiction to the regional centers. These formal regional control points located mid-way between Princeton and each campus ultimately were scrapped when it became clear that the best way to rally student workers was to place them in direct touch with a candidate. Local MNC chapters became conveyor belts carrying students to the head-quarters of locally endorsed candidates. In the end, there was only minimal liaison between the regions and Princeton. Repre-sentatives from Princeton, however, still sent out bulletins to the local chapters, kept in touch with them by telephone, and sometimes made on-the-spot visits. Eventually, however, MNC's campaign effort amounted to helter-skelter *ad hoc* ar-rangements made by local chapters.

When the regional centers were still part of the MNC scheme of things, regional student coordinators often faltered in the face of tasks that had to be discharged in a race against the ab-solute of time itself. They were either in no position to mobi-lize the student volunteers who came forward at the height of the May-June campus strikes, or they did not think it neces-sary to recruit student volunteers. The experience at the Uni-versity of Chicago, where the local MNC office housed its Mid-west regional coordinators, deserves mention since it was representative. David Affelder of Washington, D. C., a founder of the University of Chicago's satirical Students for Violent Nonaction and later the president of student government on the Midway, described what took place.

The heads of MNC Midwest were the victims of mistaken expecta-tions following the Kent State events. They were sure that students would come to them and offer their services. The organizers sat around, ran a few ads, put up some posters, and tried to stuff some leaflets into the hands of busy people. They failed to realize the need for personal contact to recruit. Many people, if directly asked would have said yes. A good number of those who did say yes ini-tially, would in fact have worked if they were quickly put to work. But the collected names got stale while MNC waited for the candi-date data from Princeton, and people found other things to do.

MNC, the largest campaign organization on campus attracted only one percent of the student body, though as late as October 23, a *Maroon* survey [the student newspaper] indicated that 12 percent of the students questioned were planning on working in the elections. MNC leaders failed to hit the streets and the telephones in an effort to round up the workers they so badly needed.*

At various schools, many seniors who had taken part in the spring strike were graduated in improvised commencement exercises. Afterwards, they either went to work or entered the graduate schools of other institutions. Many undergraduates due to return to campus took advantage of the strike to start their vacations early. Many more could not afford to spend the summer doing volunteer work in primary contests; they needed paying summer jobs to help meet the bills for their schooling. It was as late as mid-September or early October when students returned to campus for the fall term. There were the usual annual turnovers of student leaders, the usual drop-outs of students who decided not to go ahead with their schooling, and the usual tran fer students who either did not find a place in local political activities, or were overloaded by the pressures of adjustment to their new environment.

These factors made for widespread student noninvolvement in the fall election, but noninvolvement derived from these factors did not always imply apathetic indifference. Moreover, there was a range of local contests with few if any opportunities for students to participate in a congressional campaign even if they had wanted to do so. In some cases, for example, the race by Representative Pete McCloskey of California, the incumbent favored by students ran for re-election without opposition. In other cases—Representative Don Frazier of Minneapolis is one example—many students would have welcomed a chance to work, but the candidate was adequately supported by the regular organization he had formed and had little need—or

* In a letter to me—November 20, 1970.

desire—for student volunteers. In still other cases—as in the re-election of Representative Abner Mikva of Chicago—students would have come out in great numbers, as they had done in previous campaigns, if the race had been in doubt; but Mikva's re-election—prior to the 1971 redistricting which has forced him to establish a new political base of operations—seemed assured, so relatively few students were required to assist his return to Congress.

All of this is not meant to imply that students and young people were activist rather than apathetic in 1970. It implies only that what appeared to be a clear-cut case of apathy on the surface, was often much more confused and complicated when subsurface realities were taken into account.

The Dennis-Ranney survey provides confirmation on this point. When the student respondents, for example, were asked to indicate "the degree of attention they paid to the 1970 election," only 13.1 percent answered "practically none," 54 percent answered "some," and 32.1 percent answered "a great deal." In addition, 14.2 percent indicated that they "gave money, paid membership dues, or bought tickets to help a candidate or party;" 35.6 percent "attended one or more political meetings, rallies, or dinners directly related to the 1970 election," and 64.1 percent "tried to convince someone to vote for one of the candidates or party slates." It is fair to suggest that if the same questions were put to a sample of the national electorate, the affirmative responses would be lower than those in the student sample. Conventional political wisdom, which is based primarily on public opinion data, maintains that only three percent of the general public take active part in political campaigning and that the financing of campaigns depends on the generosity of less than 12 percent. If these proportions are accurate, then students were far less apathetic than the population on a whole.

But exactly how many students actively participated in organized campaigning for any candidate or party? To arrive at the answer by an indirect route, it is worth noting that the Dennis-Ranney survey revealed that giving time off to students for campaigning in 1970 made relatively little difference in the degree of their involvement in the electioneering process. Among Princeton Plan respondents, 14.8 percent reported that they had campaigned in some form, as against 10.7 percent for non-Princeton Plan students. The results here roughly correspond with the findings of studies made by other sources. Ithiel de Sola Pool of M. I. T., who surveyed campaign activity at the Princeton Plan institutions, for example, reported a 15 percent rate of student campaigning. Jack Gilead of Queens College reported a 17 percent rate of student campaigning there, while the *Gallup Opinion Index* in its issue of February 1971, placed the campaign participation rate of college students nationally at 14 percent.*

Given a student population of seven million, an active participation of 14 percent means 980,000 students—an impressive number by any standard. The more conservative estimate of 12 percent, which is the combined Dennis-Ranney figure, means there were 840,000 student campaigners. These figures dramatically contradict the *Congressional Quarterly* estimate of 75,000 students who worked for peace candidates in 1970. Part of the staggering differences between the claims of student respondents to opinion pollsters and the estimates of professional observers could be based on the so-called "lie" factor in polling —i.e. the tendency of respondees to answer a question more

* The salient exception to this cluster around 15 percent was at Princeton University. According to William Murphy, 24 percent of the students in a sample taken at Princeton claimed to have engaged in some form of campaign activity. The ten point difference between Princeton and the average of other Princeton Plan colleges may be due to the fact that Princeton was both the fount of the pre-election recess philosophy and the national headquarters of MNC, of which Murphy was one of the national co-directors.

according to what they conceive is the expected answer than the truth, and the difficulty professional observers face in quantifying their naked-eye judgments. Nevertheless, even if no single figure can be considered as wholly accurate, any figure between 400,000 and 900,000 suggests that the politicization of youth over the 1960's had a considerable effect on the electoral energies that went into campaign 1970.

When students were asked in the Dennis-Ranney survey if they had actively campaigned for a candidate or a party in the 1968 presidential contest, 15 percent of the respondents answered yes. In 1970, the combined response was 12 percent. The reported participation of Princeton Plan students remained constant at 14.8 percent for both 1968 and 1970, but that of non-Princeton Plan students dropped from 15.3 to 10.7 percent. Congressional elections, of course, generally attract less interest than presidential elections, but if the percentage of campaign involvements on the part of Princeton Plan students can be ascribed to the recess, and if the drop of 4.6 by non-Princeton Plan students can be ascribed to the lack of a recess, was the difference worth the considerable dislocation of the academic year that accompanied the recess? To ask the question is not to prejudice any conclusions that might be reached about whether the recess enabled some students to work more effectively to influence the outcome of some key races for the Congress, thereby making a selective and even significant contribution to the nature of congressional representation. It is to ask if giving students an academic recess for political work at the expense of academic disarray was offset by the benefits accruing to the electoral process as a whole.

Forms of electoral participation, of course, varied from individual to individual. Some students worked only for candidates at the national level; some worked only for those at state and local levels; and some worked for candidates at all levels. So, too, some students worked only in primary campaigns; some

383

worked only in the general election; and some worked in both the primary and general election. Then again, in segments of time ranging anywhere from one to five hours to uncounted hours, some students were out on the street contacting voters personally; some manned telephone banks for voter contacts; some arranged meetings, or helped staff a headquarters, and some did liaison work with supporting campaign organizations such as the MNC. Others drove sound trucks, or watched at the polls, or transported voters to the polls, or baby-sat so that voters would be free to get to the polls. Significantly, 93 percent of the students responding to the Dennis-Ranney survey said they spent no time writing speeches, while only 2.3 percent reported that they spent six or more hours doing research work on behalf of a candidate.

IV

It is clear that the conventional picture of student apathy in the 1970 elections calls for substantial modification. But it is still worth pondering why many more students failed to participate in organized campaigning in 1970 and, beyond what has already been said, whether it is possible to pinpoint the causes for what can be called authentic—rather than assumed—apathy on the part of students.

In answer to these questions, it is important to note that most of the major primary contests were over by the time the student strike in the spring of 1970 gave currency to the proposition that students would electioneer on behalf of congressional candidates of their choice. As the primary results in many places presented students with equally unattractive rival party candidates, or with those whose shades of difference could not excite students to exert themselves on behalf of Candidate

Apathy: Shadow and Substance

Tweedledum as against Candidate Tweedledee, a genuine apathy did develop in many areas.

There also was considerable apathy traceable to the defeatism spread by news reports about the first major infusion of students in a contest where they tried to help a peace candidate win party nomination. The early June Democratic primary in New Jersey was held—directly under the concentrated eye of the news media—in the immediate wake of the student strike and the overnight formation of an organization like MNC. The student backed insurgent candidate Lew Kaden, a former aide to Robert Kennedy, received only 34 percent of the vote in his primary fight for the Democratic congressional nomination against incumbent Representative Edward Patten in a Middlesex County district.

While student-aided candidates later won a number of critical Democratic primaries held around the country for House and Senate nominations, these successes somehow failed to offset the psychological effects of the defeat of Kaden. As a virtually unknown candidate running against an entrenched and popular congressman, he never had a chance to win. But the odds against him were seldom taken into account in the construction reporters placed on the results of the primary contest. Instead, in the summer months, they continued to harp on Kaden's race and to ascribe his loss to an antistudent backlash. The conclusion, through constant reiteration, passed as a maxim in many quarters—including student quarters.

The defeatism traceable to some such cause, along with other causes for student apathy is apparent in the findings of the Dennis-Ranney survey. When respondents who did not actively participate in 1970 political campaigning were asked to state the reasons why not, seven percent replied that they thought their help "might do more harm than good"; 16.8 percent replied that there was "no qualified candidate for whom they could work"; 3.4 percent replied that they "didn't believe in the system"; 2.1 percent replied that there were "better, more effective things to do like organizing against the war"; 3.4 percent replied that "they were not old enough to vote"; 5 percent replied that they "did not know enough about politics"; and 5 percent replied that they were away "from their home state," or were out of the country. But the single leading reason given for nonparticipation was represented by 31.9 percent of the respondents who were genuinely apathetic in declaring that they "lacked the time and were too busy."

22
The Faces of Backlash

I

Different tests of public opinion extending from the 1968 presidential election to the spring of 1970 provided evidence, seemingly convincing, that the public was coiled for a massive backlash against students and other young people. The signs which appeared to confirm this view have been noted in part throughout these pages, but there were other signs. A 1968 Michigan Survey Research Center study, for example, reported that a majority of Americans not only approved of the way the Chicago police dealt with young protesters on the site of the Democratic Convention, but thought that the press, in reporting the event, showed bias against the police. The same study underlined two more points: that among voters who thought that the Chicago police used too little force against young protesters, many deserted the presidential candidacy of Hubert Humphrey in November 1968; and that there was a strong correlation between antistudent attitudes in the electorate and the votes cast for George Wallace.

Successive Gallup polls released between late May and early June 1970, placed "campus unrest" first on the list of specific

387

national problems; so much so, that 82 percent of the people polled who were 21 and older opposed the student strike in May–June of that year. Another indication of backlash appeared in the failure of the referendums to lower the voting age to 18 in a number of states; in Missouri, the mere attempt to stage such a referendum obtained only one-fifth of the required 100,000 signatures necessary to place the proposal on the ballot. Then there was the Harris poll of September 12, 1970, which asked a sample of voters whether students should be "let off to campaign." In response, 63 percent of the sample opposed the idea, while only 23 percent favored it. The results were repeated in a Gallup poll for October 1 which had asked a sample of voters: "Would you like to have one of the students come to talk to you about his views, or not." Among the respondents, 62 percent said no, and 38 percent said yes. These figures seemed to be natural confirmation of a view put forward by Senator Ralph Smith of Illinois in an attack on his opponent Adlai Stevenson III: "The issue that's of greatest concern to most people is the possibility of violence on our campuses this fall."

These publicized findings help explain why even some candidates for re-election in 1970 who were strongly favored by students initially sought to avoid being publicly identified with them. Senator Edward M. Kennedy, whose re-election was never in doubt, despite the shadow of the controversial tragedy on the Chappaquiddick bridge the summer before, surprised many of his young supporters when he spoke about the "hijackers of the university," whom he said, "must be deterred and repudiated. Any person who hands them aid and comfort, any person who grants them sympathy and support, must share the burden of guilt." [1] Such strong language from a champion of many youth causes, including the lowering of the voting age, the draft lottery, and a rapid end to the Vietnam War, revealed that in 1970 liberal candidates turned from sympathetic explanations of the causes of the frustration of youth to hard-line attacks on campus unrest.

But if the electorate was poised for an antiyouth backlash, then the 1970 "law and order" electioneering strategy of the Nixon administration and its like-minded supporters among congressional candidates should have led to a cavalcade of thundering victories at the polls. Its strategy was based on the assumption that the "social issue" was of supreme concern to a decisive majority of the American electorate. The majority, it surmised, would respond to a polemical call on election day for a punitive expedition against "permissiveness" in the treatment of youth, against the "effete snobs" who taught and coddled students, against the "radical-liberal" candidates supported by students, and against the "Eastern Establishment"—the ultimate evil which subsumed all the other evils gathered beneath the canopy phrase, "the social issue."

The administration's "law and order" strategy, although applied throughout the nation, differed in detail from one place to the next. In the Middle West and Far West, it had the brute force of a full-back plunge into the line. In the South, the strategy was shiftier, in keeping with the administration's Southern Strategy which was composed of a slight tinge of racism and overt appeals for regional separation. In the Northeast it was a component in an antidove, ethnic-oriented, anti-intellectual onslaught. Yet whatever form it took, the "law and order" strategy did not provoke the anticipated backlash in 1970.

But the fact that the backlash fell far short of expectations in 1970, did not mean that it was negligible. It had some effect, although the overall election results and the specific cases cited in these pages present no clear or consistent picture of its influence. Some candidates who were ardent devotees of the polemics of law and order won; others, equally committed to stimulating the backlash, lost; but whether candidates lost or won frequently depended on factors other than this highly charged emotional issue. It is always difficult to assess with precision the influence of any single issue—particularly one that plays on emotions in a national election. It has been made more difficult in 1970 by the fanciful suppositions that attained the aura of truth.

Nevertheless it is possible to gain some approximation of what really happened by examining the campaign and its outcome in its differing contexts. The 1970 elections, like any national election, has a historical context which must be considered. The historical pattern shows that in most off-year elections the party in control of the White House loses seats in Congress. The average off-year loss in this century has been four Senate and 35 House seats. Since the Republicans in 1970 gained one Senate seat while losing a net of nine in the House, the Nixon administration felt justified in claiming a victory.

The Democrats, for their part, could point to their own impressive strength in retaining control of Congress though they had lost the presidency two years earlier. They could also observe that President Nixon and Vice President Agnew engaged in more extensive campaigning for congressional candidates than any of their predecessors. Apart from campaigning on television, Nixon appeared at one or more rallies for 38 Republican candidates for governor and U. S. Senator, and also appeared on behalf of 236 individual candidates for the House. Agnew was even more active, campaigning for 262 candidates for the House, Senate, and governorships—some of whom Nixon had campaigned for and whom he had not. In terms of personal appearances, the president's scorecard was disappointing—only six of 17 gubernatorial candidates he favored were victorious, only eight of 21 senatorial candidates, and only 114 of 236 House candidates. Similarly, Agnew's personal favorites won 124 races but lost 148. In contrast, the Democrats won 53 percent of the nationwide vote and picked up 11 gubernatorial seats while winning control of both legislative houses in 24 states.[2]

On the basis of these results, it appears obvious that the "law and order" strategy failed to attain the great end it had in view. The reason is that the "economic issue" surfaced in the 1970 campaign as a strong if not an over-riding competitor to the "social issue." In many cases, however, the administration's monopoly on the "law and order" gambit was broken by liberal Democratic candidates who had previously been captive to the fear that if they spoke "law and order" they would be associated with racism. In 1970, on the advice of polling organizations, they decided to unshackle themselves from that fear, and to embrace the cause because blacks as well as whites felt the need for law and of order in their communities.

II

Given the results, it is appropriate to inquire to what extent voter hostility toward students involved in campus disorders, protest marches, and violence, was convertible into voter hostility toward youth *as* youth. Similarly, to what extent was voter hostility toward youth *as* youth convertible into voter hostility toward any candidate for whom students and other young people worked openly as canvassers? These questions were central to a survey made after the 1970 elections by Professor Henry Bienen and William T. Murphy, Jr. for use in this book.

In the two weeks following the 1970 elections, Bienen and Murphy directed a team of interviewers who conducted telephone surveys in the following seven congressional districts: Maryland's fourth (Paul Sarbanes); New Jersey's fourth (Frank Thompson) and ninth (Henry Helstoski); New York's twenty-seventh (John Dow); Massachusetts' third (Robert Drinan);

391

Wisconsin's first (Les Aspin); and Michigan's sixth (Charles Chamberlain). Of these men, the first six were victorious peace candidates; in the Michigan district, John Cihon, a peace candidate, lost to Chamberlain. Respondents were chosen from a random sample of voters who lived in precincts that had been worked exclusively by students, and a total of 2,190 usable interviews were obtained.

The restricted nature of the Bienen-Murphy survey—and the "lie factor" present in any postelection survey which asks respondents how and why they voted—necessarily qualifies its findings. The special character of the district contests covered by the survey, limits the extent to which the findings can be said to apply to other election contests. Yet the worth of the Bienen-Murphy survey lies precisely in the modest claim it sustains—namely, that 1970 voter attitudes toward students and student attitudes toward voters, were far more mixed and complex than the simplicities of the hour and the commentaries of political pundits suggested.

The sample was first asked whether they were canvassed prior to the election, and if so, by whom. Only one-third of the respondents who said they had been canvassed would positively identify the person who contacted them as a student. Almost an equal number of respondents could not remember the canvasser, and close to 20 percent thought the student who did so was simply a party worker. Most of the male student workers in the districts surveyed had dressed in coats and ties when they were out ringing voter doorbells, though quite a few were dressed more casually, and many had long hair, beards or mustaches. In any case, it appeared that two-thirds of the voters were so unconcerned over the age or profession of canvassers they confronted that they could not positively say that the persons who contacted them during a canvass were students.

Another attitudinal question posed in the Bienen-Murphy survey asked whether it was "a good idea or not such a good idea for college students to support one of the candidates and to work on their own time to help him win?" In all seven districts, an overwhelming proportion of the respondents replied in the affirmative. Eight out of every ten approved, while less than one in ten disapproved. These findings contrast with responses to the Harris poll in September 1970 in which 73 percent of a national sample did not think students should be "let off to campaign." The contrasting responses say as much about loaded wording of survey questions as they do about unfulfilled backlash threats.

Since all seven candidates ran on strong antiwar platforms and had large numbers of students working for them, another Bienen-Murphy question was designed to determine the relationship between voters' positions on the Vietnam War and their feeling about student electoral activism. The respondents indicated a weak correlation between these two matters, while the differences that showed up were predictable. Those with "dovish" views were most in favor of students working; those with "hawkish" views most opposed; and those with a "qualified" position on the Vietnam issue ranged in between. The attitude of the doves is understandable, but a notable feature of the responses was that even among the hawks, only about one in ten voiced disapproval of student campaign participation.

Since students worked only for Democratic candidates in the seven contests, some conclusions can be drawn about their acceptance by voters with differing political attachments. In all seven of the districts, the "Independent Democrats," not the voters who strongly identified themselves with the Democratic party, were most favorable to student campaign workers. In their own speculations, Bienen and Murphy observed that in the three districts—those of Thompson, Drinan and Dow— where over 90 percent of the independent Democrats thought such involvement was a good idea, large university communities existed. Most of the student electioneering effort—and the postelection telephone surveys in the three districts in question—were in and around these communities. It is plain that while many of the avowedly most liberal voters in such communities think of themselves as independents, they generally support Democratic candidates. They are not a "know nothing" type of independent. They may be "weak party identifiers," but they are well informed, issue-oriented, and make up a small but politically sophisticated segment of the population. In university communities, then, it was not surprising that this kind of independent voter would strongly favor student participation.

Another question put to the sample was designed to get at the reasons for approving or disapproving student involvement in the congressional election. Of the voters who disapproved, it is enough to cite the three leading reasons they gave, ranked according to the percentage of the total sample they represented: "Students should be studying in school"—1.6 percent; "Students don't have enough experience and neither know the candidates nor the problems"—1.3 percent; "Students are not legally old enough to participate"—0.8 percent. Of the voters who approved, it is again enough to cite the main reasons they gave, ranked according to the percentage of the total sample they represented. "Everyone should get involved; it's the democratic way"—25.7 percent; "Students have a right to work for the candidate of their choice"—15.2 percent; "They are more aware and knowledgeable than the average citizen"—12.8 percent; "They are future voters and leaders and bring new blood to politics"—12.3 percent; "They will get good experience in learning practical politics"—9.1 percent; and "It will keep them in the system"—5.7 percent. Interestingly, voters who were either doves, or strongly identified with the Democratic party, were inclined to cite the factor of new blood and future leadership, while hawks and voters over 50 were inclined to cite the value of getting a lesson in practical politics.

The most important of all the questions asked was also the

one whose responses may not have accorded with reality. Voters were asked to state what effect they felt student workers had on how they voted. Subject to a great number of imponderables, Table 4 presents the findings of the survey as they bore on that question. It indicates that of the seven candidates in the different districts, Drinan received the largest marginal gain from student workers—29.4 percent. At the same time, students working for him also produced the largest negative effect in all seven districts—3.8 percent. An explanatory note by the survey authors helps to resolve the apparent anomaly:

Drinan had used students extensively in his insurgent [Democratic] primary victory over Phillip Philbin, an incumbent Congressman for 28 consecutive years. The close, bitter primary resulted in a great deal of bad blood between various Democratic factions. The situation was further exacerbated by Philbin's decision to run again in the November election as an Independent. Quite a few Democrats, mainly Philbin adherents, were negatively affected by the student intervention on Drinan's behalf. Students had helped defeat their candidate in the primary and were working against him again. On the other hand, Drinan supporters were highly receptive to the young people whose volunteer labor had greatly contributed to their candidate's success.

Overall, student campaigning was a positive force in the seven contests, with almost 26 percent of all respondents claiming that the campaign efforts of students had "some effect in making me vote for their man," while a mere 2.4 percent replied that such activities had caused them to cast their vote against the student-backed candidate. It is safe to conclude, as Bienen and Murphy did, that an antiyouth backlash was not a factor in the seven congressional districts covered by the survey. A significant number of voters did not identify the canvassers who contacted them as students; negative attitudes toward campus dissent, drugs, and student life style were not translated into negative feelings about students working in elections. On the contrary, there were positive identifications toward the stu-

TABLE 4
Effect of Student Canvassers on Voters, by District

	THOMPSON	HELSTOSKI	DRINAN	CIHON	SARBANES	DOW	ASPIN	ALL DISTRICTS
No Effect	60.6%	62.4%	43.4%	62.0%	46.3%	49.0%	59.8%	51.8%
Negative Effect	1.1	0.6	3.8	3.0	1.1	1.0	0.5	2.4
Positive Effect	18.1	11.9	29.4	12.0	21.1	22.4	6.8	25.9
Other	9.6	13.4	16.6	12.0	10.5	14.3	17.7	10.9
No Answer	10.6	11.2	6.8	11.0	21.1	14.3	15.7	11.1
N =	(473)	(159)	(474)	(382)	(227)	(225)	(221)	(2161)

dents. Voters did not translate negative feelings about campus dissent into the act of voting against student-backed candidates.

By and large, the electorate surveyed in the seven districts showed itself able to distinguish among young people and their different activities. There was no contradiction in being against campus dissent and not being against students in the electoral process. "If the starting place"—Bienen and Murphy observed and this study reaffirms—"had been an analysis of what is legitimate and what is illegitimate political activity in the minds of large numbers of people, positive reactions to students in politics might well have been predicted from attitudes held concerning the value of participating in the electoral process."

The evidence, then, argues that the backlash strategy did not create a real backlash. With the division between the White House and Congress and the emergence of economic problems, the appeal for law and order and against student power in 1970 did not wash with the American public. The outcome of the election does not mean that voters were for campus dissent, drugs, violence, and other ills, real and imaginary, associated with youth. But it did suggest that there was no automatic association between them, and the voting public overall did not react negatively to those candidates who attracted and made use of young people in their campaigns. If anything, the 1970 results demonstrated that Americans behaved in a traditional manner, accepting if not encouraging youth who gave their time and energy to candidates of their choice.

III

An inquiry into the assumptions made about a backlash would be incomplete if it dealt solely with alleged voter hostility to students. The question that remains to be examined concerns

397

student attitudes. There were many predictions that student campaigners, exposed to voters and to the electoral process, would emerge from the experience in an embittered and alienated mood. In fact, the prediction that if students were granted "released time" in order to participate in the congressional campaign, their disenchantment with the whole order of American politics would be "revisited on the campus," was frequently cited by some institutions as the reason they rejected the Princeton Plan.

As it turned out, there was a grain of prescience in these predictions. Some sense of the matter comes into view when the responses to a group of questions posed in the Dennis-Ranney survey, along with the responses elicited from student campaigners who were interviewed in person, are held in a single vision. The students who took part in the campaigns were asked whether they felt their campaigning had been a valuable personal experience. Thirty-nine percent strongly agreed; 45 percent agreed; three percent disagreed; a little over one percent disagreed strongly; and ten percent would neither agree nor disagree. Positive responses also prevailed when the students were asked whether "the candidate and his organization made good use of the student volunteers in his campaign." Forty percent agreed with the statement; 33 percent strongly agreed; approximately 15 percent were ambiguous in their response; and only a little more than 11 percent disagreed to any extent.

Some significant differences between the Princeton Plan campaigners and those from non-Princeton Plan campuses arose in response to the statement that "My efforts made a significant contribution to my candidate's doing as well as he did." About five percent of both groups strongly agreed, and approximately ten percent of both groups strongly disagreed. The ambiguous "agree/disagree" response came from 25.9 percent of Princeton Plan students and 34.6 percent of the non-Princeton Plan students. But the disparity between the Princeton Plan students

—of whom only 19.4 percent agreed and 37 percent disagreed that they had made a useful contribution where they campaigned, and the non-Princeton Plan students—of whom 19.8 percent disagreed and 26.7 percent agreed, can be explained to some extent. The Princeton Plan students worked mainly during the last two weeks of the campaign, so their experience was apparently frustrating. Moreover, the expectations of the Princeton Plan youth were probably exaggerated from the beginning, which made for later disappointment.

When the survey asked the respondents who actively campaigned how "they felt about voters after the 1970 election as compared to how they felt before 1970," the gravitational center was expressed by the 48.7 percent who said they felt "about the same." In other words, there was no change either for the better or for the worse in the attitudes of approximately half of student campaigners. Of the remaining half, the 20 percent who said they felt "somewhat more favorable," were almost exactly offset by the 19 percent who said they felt "somewhat less favorable." The net change for the worse—such as it was—amounted to the difference between the two percent who said they felt "a lot more favorable," and the 7.8 percent who said they felt a "lot less favorable."

The respondents were also asked how they felt about "electoral politics in America after the 1970 election as compared to how they felt before 1970." Again, there was a gravitational center of 55.8 percent who said they felt "about the same," which meant that for the majority of young campaigners there was no change either for the better or for the worse as a result of their campaign experience. But, in contrast to the gradation in responses about the American voter, the responses about American electoral politics showed a pronounced turn for the worse. A minuscule 0.3 percent, which was statistically meaningless, felt a "lot more favorable"; only 6.2 percent said they were "somewhat more favorable," but 25.7 percent said they felt "somewhat less favorable"; and 9.8 percent said they were a "lot less favorable." Over one-third—35.5 percent—of the young campaigners whose energies and ideals were put to the test in the 1970 elections came away disillusioned with the political process.

In 1970, many students who became door-to-door canvassers for candidates for the first time engaged in political conversations with Americans who had their own interests, values, and priorities. Student canvassers learned that everyone in the world did not think as they did. Some who made this discovery collapsed or slunk back to their campus cloisters, muttering that they would never again expose themselves "to the people." Others, fewer in number, felt better educated for their encounters and more alive to the infinite variety of individual interests and views which make the wheels revolve in a democracy.

The experience of James Scheurmann is similar to that of many others. Scheurmann, an 18-year-old Pittsburgh youth whose father is a district Republican leader, went to a Catholic secondary school. While still in school he spent his free time doing volunteer work related to the poverty program in Appalachia, and after enrolling at the University of Chicago in the fall of 1970, he brought with him a strong commitment to social justice as well as strong antiwar feelings which he soon made manifest. In this militant spirit he volunteered to work in Representative Abner Mikva's campaign for re-election to Congress, and because of his own Pittsburgh background, was assigned to canvass for Mikva in the steel-worker section of the district. As Scheurmann relates, the experience was instructive:

I volunteered to canvass for Mikva in the fall of 1970 because he was a liberal in domestic matters and anti-Vietnam War in foreign matters. I was all primed, if necessary, to explain his stand on the Vietnam War to the people whose doorbells I rang. But no questions were asked on the point. That puzzled me, until the regular Democratic precinct captain explained the lay of the land to me.

The Faces of Backlash

There are a lot of old people in the area. Their most immediate concern was not the war. It was that the U. S. Post Office, as part of its plan to reduce the pick-up stops for mail trucks, had removed a number of mail boxes in the area that had been there for years. The old people who depended for their contacts with the outside world on "the letter" now had to walk at least eight blocks instead of maybe two to mail a letter. This was hard on them when the weather was bad. The regular Democratic precinct captain, who was right on top of the situation, had been in contact with Mikva about it, and Mikva in Washington was after the Post Office Department to restore some of the removed mail boxes.

At first, I couldn't understand how people could be deeply concerned about a mail box when there was the war in Vietnam to worry about. On second thought, though, I realized that the mail box had as immediate an importance to the old people in the district as Vietnam had to me. I had my eyes opened to a broader view of politics than the one I originally brought to my work as a volunteer—that trying to help out in something as undramatic and pedestrian as a mail box is a necessary and proper concern of politics—good politics.*

His views, in modified form, were echoed by a young volunteer worker for Gary Hart in California. When the election was over, and he was asked what effect the Hart campaign had on him, he replied:

I don't think I'm quite as idealistic as I was. When you are a student but not participating in door-to-door canvassing in electoral politics, it is easy to be in the radical bag and to think that the revolution is coming and that it's only a matter of time before the people rise up. But then you go out and you walk a precinct, and you find out that the revolution just is not happening anywhere. It isn't that you find a minority of people talking about revolution and self-determination. You don't find anybody talking that way.

To a liberal, the Vietnam War was the issue. To Joe American, student unrest and drugs were the issues. But I would say that only ten percent of the people talked about national and international is-

* Interview between James Scheurmann and myself on November 18, 1970.

sues or problems. People were interested in local issues. In Simi Valley, we ran into one housing tract where the only thing the people wanted to know was whether Gary Hart would help them get a sewer system. All the other tracts in the area had got their sewers except this one. That is all the people in that one tract wanted to talk about, sewers.*

The surprising elements of a student backlash against other students appeared in connection with the answers forthcoming when the Dennis-Ranney sample was asked: "How did the respondents feel after the 1970 elections about college students who could have but didn't participate in the campaign, compared to how they felt about these students prior to 1970?" While 63.3 percent of the respondents answered "about the same," 22.5 percent answered "somewhat less favorable," and 7.2 percent answered "a lot less favorable." Only 3.5 percent answered "somewhat more favorable" and 1.5 percent answered "a lot more favorable."

The students who were most conspicuous in their failure to participate in the 1970 campaign were the minority of radical activists who pronounced their hostility to electoral politics and offered in its place a politics of "revolutionary action." Yet the high theoretical excuses they gave for their antielectoral politics struck many other students after the 1970 congressional contest as a windy rigamarole in justification for a "cop-out." They lost, at least for the time being, the moral authority which once legitimized their hold on the psyches of their fellow students. The postelection student backlash against the would-be student revolutionaries places the latter among the biggest losers in the 1970 election, along with political parties which alienated over 30 percent of those students who worked in the campaigns and impressed only seven percent favorably. The remaining 60 percent did not change their generally unfavorable view of the parties as a result of their experience.

* This statement was taken from the notes provided the author by Mrs. Steven Roberts.

So while the backlash in practice did not conform to theory, for the students, it did have some perverse effects. But neither the surveys nor analyses of specific electoral contests provide much in the way of insight to the most important and difficult question, the future of youth participation in politics.

NOTES

1. *New York Times,* October 14, 1970.
2. *U. S. News and World Report,* November 16, 1970.

23
Coda

I

As a coda to this analysis of youth in electoral politics, we must look at the events in the distant and immediate past and try to draw from them—if only in sketchy form—some notion of the future shape of American politics. To restate the task, we must examine closely the young Americans who were "socialized" or "politicized" in the decade of the 1960's, and render some sort of account about the ways in which their collective experiences will affect American politics over the 1970's.

This foray is quite different from the problem facing the historian or the biographer, who deals with a period or a life that is concluded. The biographer can define the significance of his subject by looking backwards and surveying an activity from the end to the beginning. Viewing things in perspective, he can assert that some acts were wise and some foolish; that some led to misery and remorse; and some to achievements that purified (in the popular mind) the squalid means used. Similarly, the historian can make judgments based on a perspective of time that enables a sober weighing of the evidence, free from the hurly-burly of present events, and the inflamed passions of partisan personalities.

To some extent, interpretations and judgments can be made, if only hesitantly, concerning the young Americans who were socialized or politicized in the previous decade. But unlike the

404

founding, the nation has fallen prey to spasmodic bouts of violence. The Revolution itself, the Whiskey Rebellion, the great Civil War, the extermination of the Indians, the many bloody confrontations between labor and management, and the growing militancy of blacks—all testify that a resort to force is part of American life. [1]

Yet most of the violent eruptions that are so much a part of American history concerned specific aspects of the nation's economic and social order, or were protests against particular institutions. Even in the greatest and bloodiest of conflicts, the southern Secessionists incorporated within their own framework of government most of the institutional features of the Union against which they rebelled. [2] But in the 1960's, especially after 1964, mass protests or violence were not confined to a specific set of grievances. Everything in sight appeared to come under attack: the institutional structure of the government as a whole; the structure of the colleges; the structure of family life; the structure of the economy; the relationship between the races; the relationship between the sexes; the legitimacy of authority in the churches; the claims of science and technology; and all other aspects of the nation's internal life, as well as all aspects of the nation's role in the world.

It was a time when militant young people saw themselves as the avante garde of an irrepressible revolution that would overthrow what they variously called the "system," the "power structure," the "establishment," or the "military-industrial complex." The militants included student rebels in the universities, blacks in the ghettoes, the young who favored the freaking out style of the Yippies, draft resisters, even enlisted men and officers in the armed forces and members of religious orders. [3] Despite their differences in other respects, they all questioned the legitimacy of the American government and the authority of American institutions—public and private.

The "revolutionary" posture of the young militants—their

406

period piece of a historian or the concluded life dealt with by a biographer, the political life of those who participated in political events in the 1960's is not over and laid out for requiem. It is a living force whose consequences will be unfolding in the 1970's and beyond.

In the following years, some of these young people may infuse into the body of American politics the views and values that were shaped for them by the urgency of events, and retained their shape after the events cooled. Others may infuse into that body successive revisions of what their past experiences meant to them. Still others may conclude that successive events which once seemed as disconnected as two boulders on opposite shores of the Atlantic, comprised the bridge over which the past reached the present.

Yet if the mobility of youth and its future complicates what is to be ventured here, we can at least begin by asking if the experiences of socialized or politicized young Americans in the last decade unfold along the lines of "youth movements" or "youth revolts" in other countries in modern times, or whether they are something unique to America itself?

It has often been said that America is a "young country" with a "cult of youth." Yet American scholarship prior to the 1960's produced only a slim body of analytical literature focused expressly on the sociology, culture, and politics of youth. In the absence of a more ample and solid body of studies that could anchor the subject to American soil, American scholars who began to write extensively about American youth after the onset of the 1960's, tended to look to "youth movements" or "revolts" in other countries to seek parallels and comparisons.

The quest for parallels drew its motive force from the belief that nothing that was known about the American past could serve to cushion the impact of the tumult associated with American youth in the 1960's—especially in the stormy years from 1964 to 1970. This belief is debatable, for ever since its inflamed rhetorical advocacy of "revolution" and their predictions about the "inevitability" of it—had none of the depth or resource of the works of John Locke, Thomas Jefferson, John Adams, Thomas Paine, Henry Thoreau, Karl Marx, Lenin, or Mahatma Ghandi. They advanced little original political theory. When they were not an eclectic amalgam of fragments from the works of the revolutionary immortals, garnished over by shreds of Mao, Guevera, Fanon, and Marcuse, they had the ephemeral quality of handbills printed in haste on an afternoon to announce a meeting scheduled an hour later. Yet they had a frightening effect on some observers who confused their cries for rebellion with a planned revolution, assumed all who preached for revolution had the same violent revolution in mind, and feared that the revolution being called for was near at hand.

In the absence of anything in the American past that could help explain this state of affairs, many thoughtful observers of youth—scholars like Walter Laqueur, Seymour Lipset, Bruno Bettelheim,[4] and the contributors to a special youth issue published by *Daedalus* in the spring of 1968—looked beyond the United States for insight into what was occurring within its borders. Some found it in the general psychology of youth, viewed without reference to any specific historical context; others in the history of Europe from the early nineteenth century to the eve of World War I; still others in the post-World War II history of nations comprising the "Third World." Certainly, young people played a role in toppling governments in Japan, Argentina, Venezuela, South Korea, South Vietnam, Indonesia, and Turkey; student strikes in 1968 alone paralyzed universities in nations as far apart geographically and culturally as France, Mexico, West Germany, Japan, Czechoslovakia, Italy, and Brazil. A United Nations Report, which examined these events and projected the consequences into the 1980's when the 12–25 age group might total one billion persons, noted that "youth of the world will begin to predominate in world affairs." It went on:

World opinion is going to become increasingly the opinion of the world's youth and the generational conflict will assume proportions not previously imagined. Young people in all walks of life, are prepared to march, to demonstrate, and to riot if necessary in support of views which may not be those of the electorate nor of the majority; nor yet of the government.[5]

As this commentary about the future role of youth in the world was being written, some observers were scanning Europe's past for parallels to the American situation in the 1960's. They came upon striking symmetries between the current American scene and youth movements—both cultural and political—in Europe, where the cults of youth and youthful eruptions have had a long and checkered history. For instance, the social phenomenon of drug taking, which was rationalized as a means of gaining heightened sensibilities, became a prominent feature of the decadent phase of the Romantic movement in the nineteenth century—especially in England and France where many of the celebrated literary figures including Coleridge, Hazlitt, and Baudelaire participated. The modern "happening" began in 1910 with the youthful Italian Futurist movement, which held public meetings in Trieste, Parma, Milan, and other Italian cities, reciting poems, reading manifestos, showing ultramodern paintings, and calling for the prohibition in politics of all people over 30. The Russian revolutionaries in the Czarist era were young, and many both preached and practiced violence. The youth of *Neue Schar* in post-World War I Germany have been described by Laqueur as "long-haired, sandaled, and unwashed. They castigated urban civilization, read Indian philosophy, practiced free love, dreamed, sang to the music of the guitar, and attended lectures on the 'Revolution of the soul.' "[6] They distributed asters and chrysanthemums at their meetings and read Hesse, Spengler, Tagore, Lenin, and Zen Buddhism. In Germany, too, at Goettinger University, the phrase "student power" was coined in 1920.

Most movements had avowed political aims, usually revolutionary in the sense that they challenged the existing order. Those who espoused the cause of young Germany, young Italy, young Hungary or young Poland, inspired their own national version of the familiar saying that "he who is not a radical at twenty does not have a heart; he who is still one at forty does not have a head." Yet the "radicalism" of Europe's political youth movements was not all of one piece. Some were of the extreme Left; others of the extreme Right; some which began at one extreme ended at the other. Some occurred in social contexts where traditional, agrarian based cultures were breaking down; where values congenial to industrialization were becoming influential; and where young people bent on participating in the emergent industrial structure, clashed with established elites representing the agricultural past.

Other youth movements resisted the march of industrialism and defended traditional society against the threats and insecurities of change. Some clamored for constitutionalism; others raised the black flag of anarchy; and many manned nationalist barricades. Youth was a significant force in many political movements in Europe, but the qualities most admired in youth —idealism, a passion for justice and fraternity, a will for self-sacrifice—were not confined to movements that were "wholesome," "progressive," or "constructive." They were also present in movements that were decadent, reactionary, and destructive. Italian youth flocked into the Fascist movement led by Mussolini, and young Germans were prominent in the early Nazi movement. Both movements attracted thugs and hooligans, but they also appealed to young idealists committed to justice and fraternity, believing in building a more equitable society and willing to undertake sacrifices for their countries. As

409

it turned out, they left a trail of bleached bones, including their own, in whatever direction they marched. But the march itself began with a call for a great national revival to be led by the regenerating power of youth.

Superficially, at least, the role of revolutionary American youth in the 1960's bore a resemblance, polemically and tactically, with the German experience between the wars. But if the youth movement in the United States had something in common with youth movements in Germany and elsewhere, the parallels were seriously misleading in fundamental respects. They obscured what was distinctive about the American situation, as it arose in a specifically American context. They obscured the origins of the American youth movement, which sprang from the politics of hope and legality; they also obscured the fact that while some American young people were converted from a politics of hope to the politics of confrontation, the numbers involved were always very small, and dwindled—rather than expanded—as time passed. The American experience, in short, had different roots and has followed a different course than the German pattern.

II

The American youth movement appears more evolutionary than revolutionary. To be sure, some young people have either driven themselves, or were somehow driven, to acts of lunacy. Yet, except for the random "bang" triggered from time to time by urban guerillas, most of the clamor that once characterized young revolutionaries has been reduced—at least temporarily —to the hum of the sea in a sea-shell. There are now fewer calls to battle against the institutional structures of the American state and society. There are even fewer responses, perhaps because the structure possessed more adaptability and strength than its detractors considered possible.

Yet, before any reference to the young revolutionaries is placed in perspective, it is essential to assess the mixture of things they injected into the body of American politics. On the negative side, the young revolutionaries cheapened and corrupted language in their rhetorical flights. For example, "repression" and "slavery," have been corrupted to cover cases where a college freshman, bored with a required course, declares himself a slave on a plane with the blacks on the Mississippi plantations before the Civil War. "Genocide" now covers the availability of contraceptive pills in ghettoes where mothers have ten or more children whom they cannot support. "Nazi" has been employed indiscriminately against police, judges, and other public officials, while "free" has been applied to those who knowingly defy the law.

This debasement of the integrity of words, which leads in turn to the debasement of the body of American speech and communications in general, is not so easily ejected as waste material. Many young people who had no revolutionary intentions have been affected by this corruption of language. As a result, their perceptions are consequently distorted and the realities they mean to convey are frequently misunderstood or misinterpreted.

On the positive side, the attack of the young revolutionaries on what they regarded as the wrongs of American society riveted the attention of other young people—and the media—on many human inequities which pervaded our national life. They helped shake up the unwarranted complacency that had infected most Americans. Even in the very act of breaking laws, they spurred a new and widespread interest in the nature of law itself.

Law, as taught before the 1960's, consisted of a series of "how to do it" courses in contracts, torts, trusts and wills, taxation, corporations, criminal law, real and personal property, and so on. Little attention was given to the inner life of the law, its sources of its legitimacy; its limits and capabilities; its relationship, if any, to justice; to the uses or nonuses of law as an instrument of social change; and to the logic or illogic of law. Now, perennial but neglected questions about law are being asked by more young people than ever before in modern American history.[7] They have become the source of a revival of a spacious view of law, which is likely to be imprinted on the future politics of law-making. Similar questions are being asked of the academic disciplines of economics, history, political science, and sociology. The openness of young minds to new ideas and new scholarly approaches also holds promise for the future.

But the future is not all bright. The impact of the Vietnam War on the young, revolutionary or evolutionary, remains clouded. There is some doubt concerning just what role the protests against the war—which sounded loudest on various campuses of the nation—played in shaping presidential decisions. But there is little question that they served as an effective "lobby" for the special interests of students, since only three percent of the total U. S. combat force in Vietnam was made up of men drafted from the nation's colleges.

The campus protests against the war have had other consequences. They appear to have intensified the current crisis of legitimacy which has gripped the American military establishment; and they have spurred the movement toward an all-volunteer, professional army. While a crisis of legitimacy and an all-volunteer professional army may be as mismatched as a wedding between a cat and a dog, this is something which youth has failed to appreciate. In the absence of a "presence" within the army of a cadre of college trained civilians in uniform, there is a chance of losing a significant deterrent on adventurism by the professional army itself, or by the policy makers who are allegedly in command of the army. Conceivably, students in the next decade may be around to protest against the students before them who were instrumental in the creation of an all volunteer professional army.

III

The key impact of the youth movement, though, is likely to be political. A number of trends that were set in motion in the 1960's became discernible in the 1970 election campaign and seem certain to continue into the future. First, the rising generation appears to have outstripped its parent generation in its allegiance to more "liberal" programmatic politics. Second, the young seem increasingly indifferent to the claims of party loyalties, and increasingly responsive to both issues and individuals. Third, while the young are inclined in the direction of "liberal" programmatic policies, they seem strongly inclined—despite all the revolutionary brouhaha of the latter half of the 1960's—to remain committed to established legal procedures and existing institutions as the means of attaining and applying those policies. Fourth, if they are denied the "liberal" policies they favor, and if they are denied leaders who can articulate the issues with conviction and integrity, those who grew up in the 1960's are unlikely to attempt a fresh assault on the existing political system. But there is a possibility that a high proportion of the rising generation—which is large in absolute numbers as a result of the past World War II baby boom—will contract out of electoral politics, retreating either into apolitical pursuits or into nonelectoral forms of political expression.

The Dennis-Ranney survey material provides some supporting evidence for these suppositions. When the respondents were asked to give their political party identification, just 1.9 percent answered "strong Republican," and only 5 percent answered "strong Democrat." The 13.8 percent that identified as "independent Republican," added to the 32.1 percent calling themselves "independent Democrat," and the 29.6 percent of nonparty "independents" make up to just over three-quarters —75.5 percent of the total. These figures reinforce the national trends as reported in the Gallup and Harris polls cited earlier.

While the Dennis-Ranney survey material dealt only with students, its findings conform to those made by a spot check survey conducted for this study by the Oliver Quayle polling organization in order to determine the differences between all voters and those under 26 years of age—including those between 18 and 20. To avoid distortions or exaggerations that could result from the charged political atmosphere on the Atlantic and Pacific coasts, the Quayle organization limited its survey work to Minnesota and Virginia at the end of summer of 1970, before the general campaigns had shifted into high gear. In Virginia, personal interviews were conducted with 455 resident voters plus 87 young adults. The sample was drawn on a modified probability basis with proper representation of differing counties and cities. In Minnesota, the respective figures were 460 plus 76. Typical interviews lasted an hour, were conducted in the home, and included both closed-end queries (in which the respondent chooses from among multiple choices offered him) and open-ended questions (in which the respondent answers in his own words).

The statistics have both short- and long-term significance. On President Nixon's job performance rating (excellent, pretty good, etc.), 53 percent of the Minnesota voters interviewed gave him a favorable rating, while only 38 percent of young adults did the same. There were approximately 30 percent less pro-Nixon young people than Minnesota voters in general. In Virginia, voters in general gave President Nixon a 51 percent favorable job rating against 43 percent for young adults. When it came to an expression of opinion on Vice President Agnew's job performance, 45 percent of all Minnesota voters held favorable opinions, as against only 20 percent of young adults; in Virginia the results among all voters were 46 percent pro-Agnew, compared to 37 percent among young adults.

Asked about Vietnam, dovish attitudes—"We should get out of Vietnam now or at least within 18 months no matter what" —were embraced by 41 percent of all voters and 48 percent of young adults in Minnesota; in Virginia, the figure was 35 percent of all voters and 44 percent of young adults.

On the race question, which was checked only in Virginia, 45 percent of all voters felt the United States had gone far enough in assistance to blacks, but only 38 percent of the young adults shared this view. In this respect they were 20 percent less "conservative" than voters in general. The opinion that the United States had not gone far enough in helping the blacks was held by 32 percent of all voters and by 47 percent of young adults, which made them 46 percent more "liberal." The blacks in the sample, incidentally, represented 17 percent of the respondents.

Whether these results confirm the theory that young adults do not vote in a bloc, youth is a political force to contend with simply because it is so large. An impressive number of young voters, for example, cast their ballots in 1968 for George Wallace rather than for Nixon or Humphrey. Nationwide, survey estimates tend to place around 20 percent of American youth —not just students—at the conservative, if not the reactionary, end of the political spectrum. The middle view is held by 45 percent, while 28 percent identify within the liberal-to-radical left ideological range. Yet of immediate interest is the fact that in the surveyed states of Minnesota and Virginia, "liberal" attitudes on the Vietnam War, the Nixon administration, and race relations were expressed by between 20 and 30 percent more young adults than voters in general. If this situation carries over into the nation as a whole, it has even greater significance. The data, when coupled with demographic trends and the lowering of the voting age, mean that young adults might provide a liberal candidate in 1972 with a critical margin of votes—*if* they vote. In 40 states, the number of eligible new voters exceeds the plurality by which the 1968 presidential candidate carried the state. If the rest of the voters divide as they did in 1968—and this is a very big "if"—the youth vote could then give the liberal candidate a victory margin of 1.5 million. Or to put the case differently, if 50 percent of the age group between 18 and 25 voted Democratic by a two to one margin, nine states that were lost to Humphrey in 1968—including California, New Jersey, Ohio, and Illinois—would end in the Democratic electoral vote column.

The big "if" in this projection arises from the apparent growing indifference of youth to the claims of party loyalties, and their increasing responsiveness to "the issues and the man." The Dennis-Ranney survey material on students, pointed in that direction. It is confirmed for youth as a whole by the pattern of registration among first-time voters. It appears that while two-thirds of the first-time voters choosing a political party at registration time choose the Democratic party, most young voters are registering as independents.

There was a time when it was fair to say that the "independent" often turned out to be an indifferent or indolent voter. But this is no longer the case, and independence may become ever more pronounced in the immediate future. If party structures are unyielding and make no room for new blood, if party hierarchs arrange things among themselves without providing a forum where proposals for action can be freely discussed, and if the only ability shown by those who are put forward as party candidates is their availability, then a concerned rising generation of voters may well declare its own independence from the

416

congealed mess. This gesture may perhaps be the first step toward forming a third force which, although incapable of becoming a majority unaided, will influence the major parties and compel them to rethink their performance and practices.

Whether this participation will continue, and to what effect, will depend in good measure on whether young whites and young blacks can bridge the difference in the gravitational center of their political interests. In the specific case of the "urban crisis," for example, young blacks tend to see the crisis in terms of poverty, unemployment, and slum living. Young whites tend to see the crisis in terms of ecological conditions, transportation, and cultural resources. One side cannot muster any great enthusiasm for the principle interests of the other, with the result that each goes its own political way. If both concerted their strength toward shared objectives, the politics of the mass could result in mutual gains more substantial than incremental nibbles.

IV

A final word. Conversations with many young leaders of the rising generation indicate that they have learned by direct electoral experience that they must proceed as best they can to bridge the gap between the Old Politics and whatever the New Politics may turn out to be.

That gap is scarcely new in America. It dates back to colonial New England when the town hall meeting (really a church meeting converted to secular political purpose) was the official forum where decisions were reached on the merits of "issues" and the integrity of principles. But the taverns, frequented by people living in the town or coming in from the countryside to escape from loneliness, became "natural" electioneering centers. At the same time, the militia muster in which young people were prominent became a "natural" instrument of electoral politics. A man's rank as a militia officer often determined his place in the local hierarchy of elected officialdom. There followed the confrontation between the "unofficial" forum for electoral politics hinged to the tavern, and the militia muster, and "official" forum, hinged to the town meeting.

One statement of the clash in colonial New England is a polemical blast from the 26-year old John Adams soon after he became a "freeholder" and the town surveyor of Braintree. As a reformist in politics, he promptly launched a crusade against the town's taverns. There were twelve of these, but he appears to have been mainly concerned about the two that were owned respectively by militia Captains Eben Thayer and Dick Bracket. His blast reads in part: [8]

[Here in the taverns,] the time, the money, the health and the modesty of most that are young and of many old, are wasted; here diseases, vicious habits, bastards, and legislators, are frequently begotten. [In the evening] you will find the house full of people drinking drams, flip, toddy, carousing, swearing, but especially plotting with the landlord to get him, at the next town meeting, an election either for selectman or representative. Thus the multiplicity of these houses allures the poor country people who are tired with labor and hanker after company, to waste their time and money, contract habits of intemperance and idleness, and by degrees to lose the natural dignity and freedom of English minds, and confer those offices, which belong by nature and the spirit of all government to probity and honesty, on the meanest, the weakest, and worst of characters.

As Catherine Drinker Bowen continues the story:

He went downtown, applied to the Court of Sessions, procured a committee of inquiry. After infinite labor he actually succeeded in wiping out the greater number of licensed taverns. It was an astonishing victory; such a thing had never happened in the whole of Suffolk County. Walking downtown, expecting congratulations,

418

John was staggered at the "ill will" that met him on Braintree streets. He went home very thoughtful. . . . "This is multiplying and propagating enemies fast. I shall have the ill will of the whole town. . . . This will not do."

In no time at all the licenses, by some means or other, were renewed, the houses reinstated to the last and lowest den. John saw them filled with thirsty citizens and felt not only depressed but silly. [His father commented] "A township is not to be pushed and shoved like a private person. Reform in politics comes slowly, slowly. For years I have said it. . . . You have not chosen to hear me." [9]

That was how the young John Adams learned the lesson that the young James Scheurmann and others learned through participation in electoral politics in 1970. But the conflict between the Old Politics and the New Politics was not dead during the intervening 200 years. It appeared, for example, at the end of the nineteenth century, in the rise of the Progressive movement. The typical Progressive leader was young, well educated, of middle- or upper middle-class background, relatively secure financially, and in contemporary terms, an issue-oriented amateur politican. He wanted all issues to be settled on the basis of principle. If the arena in which he acted was the city and the question at hand a limited one, his tendency was to endow the issue with generality—either by making it a national issue, or finding in it wider implications. He saw each battle as a "crisis," each victory as a triumph, and each loss as a defeat for the cause. The ethic of the amateur, being in essence a reform ethic, became the basis for his involvement in civic reform and assaults on the machine. He wished to moralize public life, to rationalize power with law, and he insisted that correct goals would be served only if they were set, and the implementing officials selected by correct procedures.

In *The Amateur Democrat,*[10] Professor James Q. Wilson distinguishes this type of politician from the "professional politician," who "is preoccupied with the outcome of politics in terms of winning or losing. Politics, to him, consists of concrete questions and specific persons who must be dealt with in a manner that will 'keep everybody happy,' and minimize the possibility of defeat at the next election." The professional politician rarely broods about his function in society, the larger significance of the issues with which he deals, or the consistency of his procedures with some well-worked out theory of democracy. As Wilson puts it, "He sees the good of society as the by-product of efforts that are aimed, not at producing the good society, but at gaining power and place for one's self and one's party."

The political ethic of the followers of the professional politician places constraints on him entirely different from those placed on the amateur. The latter, in a position of leadership, is constantly "constrained by the need to demonstrate to his followers that he is more concerned with issues and candidates than with personal success or organizational maintenance." The professional is not expected to take positions on the controversial and abstract problems of public policy, or help club members devise organizational procedures which will give them control over his behavior. "He is expected to win elections, and by winning them, provide a stream of inducements which the followers will require as a condition of their contributing time, effort, and money."

As "amateur" politicians, young Progressive spokesmen in the years immediately prior to World War I were concerned with such substantive goals as the regulation of industry and railroads, antitrust action, minimum wage and hour laws. But the central preoccupation of the membership—whether they rallied around Robert La Follette, Theodore Roosevelt or Woodrow Wilson—was a concern for procedural or formal changes in political institutions. In their view, the cardinal problem of democracy was to improve the quality of leadership. Bad leaders must be displaced by good ones. Executives must have more power, not less. Good and powerful executives would weaken or destroy the political bosses by rendering them unnecessary for operating the government and by making it unprofitable for businessmen to bribe the bosses to do their bidding.

To achieve these objectives, the young Progressives sought to expose wrong-doing in high places, to kick the rascals out of municipal government, to end the "spoils system," and to establish a strong civil service in its place. Since party loyalties in the South and in the North had been fixed by the Civil War so that competition between the parties had become virtually meaningless in many states, the young Progressives called for the direct primary to permit a contest within the dominant party, and to force professional politicians in the one party states to be responsive to "issues."

In 1912 the Republicans split when the young Progressives followed Theodore Roosevelt into the hastily mobilized Bull Moose party. Some of these young "amateurs," like Alf Landon of Kansas, afterwards returned to the Republican party and, with the support of the "professionals," rose to high places in its hierarchical structure. Others, like young Harold Ickes of Illinois, and Henry Wallace of Iowa, never found their way back and wandered around as politically displaced persons for two decades, until they ended up as Democrats and Cabinet members in Franklin D. Roosevelt's New Deal. In the person of F. D. R., they could see a synthesis of "amateur" and "professional"—of Old and New Politics.

There is, to repeat, a clearly marked tendency among the rising generation of young people to achieve that kind of synthesis in electoral politics. In the 1970 campaigns, young volunteer workers learned firsthand that a politics of issues with no organization of the precincts to back it up is a mirage, while a politics of organization with nothing to promote except the turn of its own wheels goes nowhere. The resolve is present to unite issues and organization in a single political body.

If so, long after the 1970 congressional elections are forgotten, their most important consequences will not have been the specific electoral victories or defeats, but the injection into the bloodstream of American politics of the young men and women who, during the 1968 and 1970 congressional campaigns, had the courage to open their eyes to American politics, the magnanimity to learn the lessons it taught, and the will to apply these lessons in a democratic context.

NOTES

1. Richard F. Rubenstein, *Rebels in Eden: Mass Political Violence in the United States* (Boston: Little, Brown, 1970).

2. F. Merton Coulter, *The Confederate States of America, 1861–1865* (Louisiana: Louisiana State University Press, 1947).

3. Noam Chomsky, et al, *Trials of the Resistance* (New York: A New York Review Book, distributed by Random House, 1970); Philip Berrigan, *Prison Journals of a Priest Revolutionary* (New York: Holt, Rinehart and Winston, 1970); Willard Gaylin, *In the Service of Their Country: War Resisters in Prison* (New York: Viking, 1970); Jerry Rubin, *Do It* (New York: Simon & Schuster, 1970); David Harris, *Goliath* (New York: Richard W. Baron, 1970); Lee Lockwood, *Conversation with Eldridge Cleaver* (New York: McGraw-Hill, 1970).

4. Bruno Bettleheim, "Violence: A Neglected Mode of Behavior," in *Violence in the Streets,* Shalom Endleman, ed. (Chicago: Quadrange, 1968); Seymour Lipset, "Student Opposition in the United States," *Government and Opposition* 1(1966): 351–374; Seymour Lipset, "University Students and Politics in Underdeveloped Countries," *Comparative Education Review* 10(1966): 132–162; Seymour Lipset, *Student Politics* (New York: Basic Books, 1967).

5. *New York Times,* February 16, 1968.

6. Walter Laqueur, "Reflections on the Youth Movement," *Commentary* 47(June 1969): 36–37.

7. Bruce Wasserstein and Mark J. Green, eds., *With Justice for Some: An Indictment of the Law by Young Advocates* (Boston: Beacon Press, 1971); Stephen Gillers, *Getting Justice: The Rights of People* (New York: Basic Books, 1971); Jack D. Douglas, ed., *Crime and Justice in American Society* (New York: Bobbs-Merrill, 1971); Robert Paul

Wolff, ed., *The Rule of the Law* (New York: Simon & Schuster, 1971); Leonard Downie Jr., *Justice Denied: The Case for Reform of the Courts* (New York: Praeger, 1971).

8. Page Smith, *John Adams,* Vol. 1 (New York: Doubleday, 1962), p. 59.

9. Catherine Drinker Bowen, *John Adams and the American Revolution* (New York: Grosset & Dunlap, 1950).

10. James Q. Wilson, *The Amateur Democrat* (Chicago: University of Chicago Press, 1968), pp. 1–31.

Index

425

Index

Index

Index

Index

430

Index

Index

433

Index

Index